A FINITE THINKING

Cultural Memory
in
the
Present

Mieke Bal and Hent de Vries, Editors

A FINITE THINKING

Jean-Luc Nancy

Edited by Simon Sparks

STANFORD UNIVERSITY PRESS

STANFORD, CALIFORNIA

2003

The essays "A Finite Thinking," "The Unsacrificeable,"
"The Sublime Offering," "Shattered Love," and "Elliptical Sense"
originally appeared in French in 1990 in the volume entitled
Une Pensée finie © 1990 Editions Galilée. All other essays were
added by the author and the editor when they configured this
volume for English publication; © 1983, 1993, 1997, 2003
Editions Galilée.

Cet ouvrage, publié dans le cadre d'un programme d'aide à la publication,
bénéficie du soutien du Ministère des Affaires étrangères et du Service
Culturel de l'Ambassade de France aux Etats-Unis. [This work, published
as part of a program of aid for publication, received support from the
French Ministry of Foreign Affairs and the Cultural Services of the
French Embassy in the United States.]

Stanford University Press
Stanford, California

Printed in the United States of America
on acid-free, archival-quality paper.

Library of Congress Cataloging-in-Publication Data

Nancy, Jean-Luc.
   A finite thinking / Jean-Luc Nancy ; edited by Simon Sparks.
      p.   cm. — (Cultural memory in the present)
   Includes bibliographical references.
   ISBN 0-8047-3900-5 (alk. paper)—
   ISBN 0-8047-3901-3 (pbk. : alk. paper)
      1. Thought and thinking—Philosophy.   2. Sense (Philosophy)
3. Finite, The.   I. Sparks, Simon, 1970–   II. Title.   III. Series.
B2430.N363F56 2003
194—DC21

                                                    2003002090

Original Printing 2003

Last figure below indicates year of this printing:
12   11   10   09   08   07   06   05   04   03

Typeset by Tim Roberts in 11/13.5 Adobe Garamond

Contents

VI. WORLD

CODA

PART ONE

THINKING

A Finite Thinking

Does existence have a sense?—this question required several centuries even to
be understood completely and in all its profundity.
—Friedrich Nietzsche, *The Gay Science*[1]

Because philosophy opens out onto the whole of man and onto what is
highest in him, finitude must appear in philosophy in a completely radical
way.
—Martin Heidegger, *Kant and the Problem of Metaphysics*[2]

Sense [sens] is already the least shared thing in the world. But the
question of sense is already what we share, without any possibility of its being held in reserve or avoided. So, the question of sense, then, or perhaps
we should say: rather more and rather less than a question, a concern,
maybe, a task, a chance.[3]

Of course, by "sense" I mean sense in the singular, sense taken absolutely: the sense of life, of Man, of the world, of history, the sense of existence; the sense of the existence that is or that makes sense, the existence
without which sense would not exist; equally, the sense that exists or produces existing, without which there would be no sense.

∼

Thinking is never concerned with anything else. If there *is* anything
like thinking, it's only because there's sense, and if there's anything like
sense it's only in the sense that sense is always given and gives itself as
something to be thought. But as well as thinking there's also intelligence
or, worse, intellectuality: each of these are more than capable of devoting
themselves to the job in hand as if, in the first instance and exclusively, it
were *not* a matter of sense. This cowardice, or this laziness, is pretty common. Perhaps from the very moment that there is discourse—and there's

always "discourse" (always a discourse of sense, never a silent *ecstasis*, even though it's at the limit of words, their very limit)—it's unavoidable in every effort or inclination to think. Yet it seems that this fin de siècle has more or less its own form of cowardice and intellectual irresponsibility, carrying on precisely as if it did not remind us, if only by virtue of its symbolic value (but also because of other circumstances, other politics, technologies, aesthetics), with a certain brusqueness, of the question of sense, its chance or its concern. Won't the century that has just come to an end have been a century of innumerable destructions of sense, innumerable deviations, derelictions, weaknesses—in short, the century of its ultimate *end*?

Ultimately, are we going to think the end? Intellectual cowardice reacts badly to the word "end"—the "end" of philosophy, the "end" of art, the "end" of history . . . , and so on—as if it feared being deprived of the facts and certainties without which it would find itself forced to engage with what it wants to avoid, namely, the extremity, the radicality of thinking. And this is precisely what is at issue, precisely what *has* to be at issue: unreservedly thinking this polymorphous and proliferating end of sense, because only here can we have any chance of thinking the provenance of sense and of thinking how sense comes to us anew.

∼

The title "a finite thinking" puts three very simple things into play: on the one hand, it denotes that there is, for us, a thinking that's finished, a mode of thinking that has been lost with the destruction of sense, that is, with the completion and buckling of the West's resources of signification and meaning (God, History, Man, Subject, Sense itself . . .). And yet, in its accomplishment and withdrawal, like a crashing wave whose ebb leaves behind the lines of a new high-tide mark, this thinking leaves us with a new configuration (its own, then its own undoing of itself at its own limit). Equally, it suggests that a thinking equal to the significance of the end has come our way, if I can put it in this way, a thinking that has first of all to measure itself against the fact that "sense" *could* have ended and that it *could* be a question of sense's essential finitude—something that would, in turn, demand an essential finitude of thinking. In fact, and this is the third thing raised by the title, whatever the content or the sense of what I am calling "finitude" (and this collection of essays is concerned with nothing else, even though it's a long way from being a treatise on the subject), we can at least be sure that any attempt to think such an "object" is going to have to marry its form or condition, while also being a finite thinking: a thinking that, without renouncing truth or universality, without renouncing *sense*, is only ever able to think to the extent that it also touches on its own limit and its own singularity. How are we to think everything—sense as a whole, even though it's not as if we could *not* do so, sense being indivisible—in *a* thinking, within the limit of one trifling study? And how are we to think the fact that this limit *is* the limit of *the whole* of sense?

I've no direct answer to this, so let me simply affirm a necessity: "the working out of the innermost essence of finitude must itself always be fundamentally finite."[4]

~

What is sense? What is the "sense" of the word "sense" and what is the reality of this thing "sense"? What is the concept? What is the referent? What immediately springs to mind is that the concept and the referent must be one and the same here, since it's as a concept (or, if you like, as an idea or a thought) that this "thing" exists. Sense is the concept of the concept. We can analyze this concept as signification, understanding, meaning, and so forth.[5] But what is implied, articulated, and exploited in all these analyses is that the concept in question, across its entire extension and the whole of its meaning, can't simply be the concept (or the sense) *of* something that would stay put, set within an exterior reality, without any intrinsic relation to its concept (at least in the way in which we tend to understand the relation of a stone or a force to its concept). The concept of sense implies that sense is being grasped or is grasping itself *as* sense. This mode, this gesture of grasping or grasping itself as sense, is what produces sense, the sense of all sense: like a concept that would itself have the stony quality of the stone or the force of force, its concept and its referent are indissociable. (And it's this that's the absolute of sense at the very horizon of every metaphysics of Knowledge and of the Word, of Philosophy and Poetry.) Sense is only what it is in itself, if it is, indeed, "to itself."

The same goes for the other sense of the word "sense," for its sensible sense: to sense is necessarily to sense that there is something like sensation. Sensing senses nothing if it doesn't sense itself sensing, just as understanding understands nothing if it doesn't understand itself understanding. The "other" sense of the word sense is only "other" in terms of this sameness.[6]

All of which leads to a chiasmus: what senses in sense is the fact that it includes what it senses, and what produces sense in sense is the fact that it senses itself producing sense. Of course, we can always object that in this way we have merely pushed back ad infinitum the question of the sense of sense, or that, in this oxymoronic game, where nothing tells us what it might mean "to sense sense" or "to understand sensing," we have even lost any possibility of posing it.

It's doubtless no coincidence that this double aporia refers us back to the most powerful distinction that philosophy has to offer: that between the sensible and the intelligible. Moreover, we could easily show that there is no philosophy, no poetry, which hasn't claimed, in one way or another, to have overcome, dissolved, or rendered dialectical this double aporia. This is always going to be the most extreme point of metaphysics I mentioned a moment ago. The task that follows philosophy, our task, is the same, altered only—but altered in truly unlimited fashion—by the end of sense.[7]

∼

The entire work of an epoch—that of philosophy going deeper into its own end, deconstructing its own sense—has already taught us about another deployment of the same aporia (*not its "solution," but rather the thought of the absence of solution as the very site of sense*), a deployment that we can try to state as follows.

Sense depends on relating to itself as to another or to some other. To have sense, or to make sense, to be sensed, is to be to oneself insofar as the other affects this ipseity in such a way that this affection is neither reduced to nor retained in the *ipse* itself. On the contrary, if the affection of sense is reabsorbed, sense itself also disappears. The same can be said of the stone (at least according to our representations of it), as it can of the great monoliths, monuments and monograms of philosophy: God or Being, Nature or History, Concept or Intuition. "The end of philosophy" means laying out this reabsorption of sense—what it *also* means, however, is the question of the part of sense that resists, reinitiates it, and opens it once again.

Sense is the openness of a relation *to* itself: what initiates it, what engages it, what maintains it *to* itself, in and by the difference of its relation. (Here, "self" denotes as much the "oneself" of sense, if we can speak in these sorts of terms, as any constitution of the "self," understood as "identity," as "subjectivity," as "propriety," etc.) The *to* of the to itself, along with all the values that we can give it (desire, recognition, specularity, appropriation, incorporation, etc.), is first and foremost the fissure, the gap, the spacing of an opening. Again: "Significance [*Bedeutsamkeit*: the propriety of having or producing sense] is that on the basis of which the world is disclosed as such."[8]

But "openness" has today become a somewhat jaded motif, the evocation of the easy generosity of a right-thinking, fashionable discourse (in which "alterity," "difference," etc. also figure): a moral propriety, then, rather than an ontological one. Now, it is *being* that should be at issue here. What would sense be or what would make sense, at least in the sense of the sense of being . . . , what *could there be*, what *could be*, if there were no sense (of being)?[9]

The openness of the to-the-self needs to be thought alongside this ontological radicality, therefore (whatever becomes of the "sense" of "ontology"). Basically, this is what defines, for our time, what is essential in the work of thinking.

~

To say that being *is* open isn't to say that it's first this or that and then, over and above this, marked or distinguished by openness. Being *is* open—and this is what I'm trying to establish in terms of the being of sense or in terms of being -to -the self—only *in* this openness as such; it is itself the open. In the same way, the self that is to-itself by and in alterity doesn't possess this "other" as a correlate or as the term of a relation that would happen to "relate" to itself. Thought rigorously, it is not a matter of "other" or of "relation." Rather, it is a matter of a diaresis or a dissection of the "self" that precedes not only via every relation to the other but also via every identity of the self. In this diaresis, the other *is* already the same, but this "being" isn't confusion, still less a fusion; no, it is the being-other of the self as neither "self" nor "other," nor as some founding or original relation between them. It is less than and more than an origin; it is the to-itself as the appropriation of what cannot be appropriated in its *to*-being—of its sense.

The self that lies at the origin of this being, appropriating its own end (such is, or appears to be, the Hegelian and philosophical Self in general, even if it somehow manages to dilute this appropriation, whether in a "regulative idea," or in every form of relativism, or in an "enigma of ends," or in an "incessant pursuit of the question," in short, in a scattering of thought)—this self would be senseless [*insensé*], somewhat in the manner of a game whose rules specify that the winner be given in advance. This is the insanity on which philosophy touches at its end (schematism/absolute knowledge/death of God). And it is precisely this touch that produces the thought of the end, in every sense of the term.

There is sense only once this being -to itself no longer belongs to it-self, no longer comes back to itself. Only once it *is* this not -coming -back -to itself: this restless refusal to come back to itself in such a way that it does not simply "remain" outside, either in the sense of a lack or in the sense of a surplus, but as itself the *to* of being to itself, the open of its open-ness. Sense is the to-itself whose *to* determines the *self* to the point of pos-sibly being the transformation of the "self," the disinterestedness of the "self," its very forgetting as well as the interweaving, in it, that it properly *is*, of a "you," a "we," and even of the "it" of the world.

~

A simple, hard, and difficult thought, then. One that appears to run counter to all thinking. Yet one, too, that thinking knows—understands and senses—in the same way that it thinks what lies within itself. A thought that appears to be in permanent rebellion as much against any possibility of discourse, judgment, or signification as against intuition, evo-cation, or incantation. Yet one, too, that is only present by way of those discourses or words that it violates—whose violence it *is*. This is why we call this thought "writing," that is, the inscription of this violence and of the fact that, through it, all sense is *excribed* [excrit], ceaselessly refuses to come back to itself, and that all thinking is the finite thinking of these in-finite excesses.

A thought that is devoted to the thinking of a single sense, then, since it's clear that there cannot be several senses, hierarchies, situations, or conditions more or less "full" or more or less worthy of sense. (We'll come back to the notion of evil, the self-suppression of sense.) What is essential to *this* sense, however, always assuming that there is an "essence," absolute sense in its absoluteness and its singularity, is that it neither grasps nor presents its unity or its oneness. This "single" sense has neither unity nor oneness: it is (the) "single" sense (of "a single" being) because it is sense *each time*. It's not sense "in general," therefore, nor is it sense once and for all. If it were, it would be completed, reabsorbed, and senselessly insane. Infinite and insane.

Finitude designates the "essential" multiplicity and the "essential" nonreabsorption of sense or of being. In other words, if it is as existence and *only* as existence that being comes into play, it designates the *without-essence* of existing: "When being is posited as infinite, it is precisely then that it is *determined*. If it is posited as finite, it is then that its absence of ground is affirmed."[10] Here I transcribe groundlessness (*Abgründlichkeit*) as "sense." Groundlessness isn't a lack on the part of being that needs to be undergone, justified, originated. Rather, it is being's reference to nothing, either to substance or to subject, not even to "being," unless it be *to* a being-to, to itself, to the world as the openness, the throw or the being-thrown of *existence*.

More rigorously still: being isn't Being; it's neither substantive nor substance. "Being" is only being, the verb—at least insofar as we can desubstantialize the verb itself, destabilize grammar. And not the intransitive verb that language gives us, but the intransitive verb "be-ing," which doesn't actually exist:[11] "being a being," in the same way that we talk about "doing or founding or eating a being," but in such a way that it transmits no quality or property, in such a way that it transmits *itself* alone, transmitting *to* the being in question nothing other than this *to* of transmission, the being-to of sense, giving existence being as sense. Not, however, in the sense of the "meaning" or the "sense of being" as a content of signification, but in the sense of the being-sense of being. Not, therefore, "giving" it per se, being merely the *to*—the presentation, tension, direction, abandonment—of an offering that, with a single stroke, without any ground whatsoever, makes a being "indebted" to or puts it in excess of its own existence, having *to* be (existence, the self), having to appropriate itself as the inappropriable character of the groundlessness that would have been its being, both more and less than an origin.

"Finitude" doesn't mean that the totality of sense isn't given and that we must defer (or abandon) the appropriation to the point of infinity, but that *all* sense resides in the nonappropriation of "being," whose existence (or whose existing) is appropriation itself.

What makes sense for a being isn't the appropriation of a Sense that would produce senseless existence like a monolith of being. On the contrary, it is, on each occasion and from each birth to each death, the appropriation (*to* itself) of *there being no sense* to this senseless sense. This is, for example, what a thought of death means when, rather than thinking that death gives sense, it thinks that sense makes sense because death suspends its appropriation and appropriates the inappropriable character of being-to, which is itself no longer *to* anything else. Let me put it another way: what carries the whole weight of thinking, in an expression like *zum Tode sein*, being-toward- (or to-) death,[12] isn't death but the *toward* or the *to*, "death" merely indicating that this *toward* or this *to* is maintained, as a structure of being, "up to the end"—which is always the absence of any "end," of any extremity at which the infinite circle of an insane appropriation might be completed. Being-to "ends up" being-to, something that's neither a circle nor a tautology, still less an appeal to any morbid heroism and, less still, an invitation to turn death into the mark of a mission or a service. It is appropriated death that is senseless. Sense is existence that is always being born and always dying (being born *is* dying). All of which doesn't take anything away from the hardness of death, from anxiety before it. Nothing that I have said brings either consolation or compensation. Rather, it simply indicates that, in finitude, there is no question of an "end," whether as a goal or as an accomplishment, and that it's merely a question of the suspension of sense, in-finite, each time replayed, re-opened, exposed with a novelty so radical that it immediately fails.

~

The new, as the very event of sense, eludes itself. I can never say: "Look, here, thus, the sense of my existence." By saying it, testing it out, even, I'm already steering sense in the direction of an accomplishment. Yet the very thing that eludes it, or the eluding that sense itself *is*, is something that we have always already understood. Essentially, a finite thinking of finitude is a thinking of the fact that we, as beings, from the moment that we exist, have *already* "understood" the finitude of being. An ontology of finite being describes nothing less than "what all of us, as men, always and already understand."[13]

"Understand" doesn't mean grasping a determinate concept but entering into (already being within) the very dimension of "understanding," that is, relating to some particular *sense*. It means *being born* to the element of sense in the singular mode of its presence. Being born properly means coming to a presence whose present has already escaped, is already missing from the "coming *to.*" But it is still a matter of coming. And, in this coming, of "understanding," of having already "understood" the coming-presence or the presence-to of existence. Of being that comes into the world; of being that comes into sense. And being, too, that comes to sense [*au sentir*] *as* sense [comme *au sentir*]. I can't say any more here than what I've already said regarding the aporetic nexus of the sense of "sense." Other than that, it doubles the "already" of Heidegger's "already understood." We have already understood because we have already sensed; we have already sensed because we have understood. Or, rather, we have already come *into* sense because we are already in the world; we are in the world because we are in sense. One opens the other—this is all that is "understood."

Sense is existence in this ontological priority, whence it is reached and whence it fails, whence it reaches its failing point. How can we turn away from this hard, striking, obscure point? Birth has already turned us toward it. But how can we simply open our eyes? Death has already closed them. To obey this double constraint—the very *absolute* of existence—is to enter into a finite thinking.

～

Or, rather, it is to enter into the finite character of *all* thinking because, in truth, no one is unaware of this point, which lies at the heart of all philosophy, however "metaphysical" it may be. Not a single thinker has thought, if they have thought anything at all, without thinking this. All that remains for us is to think this *finite* character as such and without infinitizing it. This task is as finite as any other. Equally, it's certain. Yet this doesn't mean that we have some knowledge of its accomplishment. Everyone asks: "What should we think?" (at least they will, so long as they don't prefer the injunction: "Don't think too much!"). Well, what we have to think is this: that thought is never given, neither at the beginning nor at the end. From which it follows that it is never "giveable" as such. There's not an "ounce" of sense that could be either received or transmitted: the finitude of thinking is indissociable from the singularity of "understanding" what is, each time, a singular existence. (All of which isn't to say that there's nothing that we might think "in common," as it were. I will come back to this.)

～

Existence is the sense of being. Not, however, according to a relation to "being" in general (as if *there were* such a thing . . .), but in such a way that it concerns each time a (finite) singularity of being. Here "singularity" isn't simply understood as the singularity of an individual (not simply as Heidegger's "in each case mine"), but as the singularity of punctuations, of encounters and events that are as much individual as they are preindividual or common, at every level of community. "In" "me" sense is multiple, even if, here or there, this multiplicity can also comprise a sense that is "my own": "outside" "me," sense lies in the multiplicity of moments, states, or inflexions of community (but equally, then, in what is always a singular "we"). In any event, the singularity of the sense of being means that being's production of sense is not the being-self of an essence. Essence is of the order of having: an assembly of qualities. By contrast, existence is itself its own essence, which is to say that it is without essence. It is, by itself, the relation to the fact of its being as sense. This relation is one of lack and of need: "The privilege of existing shelters in it the necessity [and the distress: *die Not*] of having to need the understanding of being." Existence does not have what it always already and constantly has. Why? Precisely because it is not a matter of having. To exist means: to lack sense.

On the other hand, what *is* in the mode of essence—if anything can *be* such[14]—no longer has any sense. It is simply senseless. Equally, lacking sense, or to be lacking through sense, isn't the same as lacking a fullness, a lack that would bear all the marks, the traces, the premises of what it actually lacks. On the contrary, to lack sense, to be in the distress or the necessity (*Not*) of sense *is* exactly that, namely, sense. From which it follows that to lack sense is, properly speaking, to lack *nothing*.

We've certainly not managed to shake off the fascination with lack (abyss, nonplace, mourning, absence, etc.) which, while clearly necessary for the recent history of thinking, no less clearly runs the risk of a dialectic-nihilistic confusion. And yet, it's not as if "to lack nothing" (to be *in* sense) is the full, satisfied condition of an essence. The negative theology of all that could hardly be more obvious. To lack nothing, despite everything that's lacking: this is what it means to exist.

In an entirely different register, Heidegger speaks of "being charged with a responsibility [*Überantwortung*] toward beings" and "toward oneself as a being." This means having to respond to the fact that there are beings and that I "myself" am. Hence, "understanding" of being is "the essence of finitude." Finitude resides in the fact that existence "understands" that "being" does not rest on the foundation of an essence but uniquely *responds to* and *from* the there is of "being." In other words, it is a matter of *responding to* and *from* oneself as the existing of an existence. *Finitude is the responsibility of sense*, and is so absolutely. Nothing else.

And so I would also want to add: finitude is the *sharing* of sense. That is, sense takes place on every occasion of existence alone, on every singular occasion of its response-responsibility; but this also means that sense is the lot, the share of existence, and that this share is divided between all the singularities of existence. (From which it follows that there is no sense that could engage merely one being; from the outset, community is, as such, the engagement of sense. Not of *a* collective sense, but of the sharing of finitude.)

~

Another name for this is "freedom." Understood thus, freedom is not a sense conferred on existence (like the senseless sense of the self-constitution of a subject or freedom as an essence). Rather, it is the very *fact* of existence as open to existing itself. This fact *is* sense.[15] Indeed, it is the only fact that makes sense by itself. And this is why, amongst the thinkers who have come before us and who, at the point at which one epoch touches on another, have still expressly attempted to think "sense," not one has failed to demand that freedom be seen not so much as the means to but as the very *being* or truth of sense. Such is the case, most visibly, with Marx and Heidegger (as Sartre clearly saw). So, too, Rimbaud, albeit in an entirely different way.[16]

These thoughts produced the rupture of the century, measuring up to the "death of God" because they show, or at least suspect, that what is at stake here is sense, all sense—and that it's not "freedom" that is sense (the discourse of the Enlightenment, of Kant and Hegel), but sense that is freedom, *as finite sense* or as the infinite absenting of the appropriation of sense. "Freedom" (if we need still to hold onto this word) is the act of the distress or the necessity (*Not*) of sense.

But, whether in sum or in part, these thoughts are over. They thought to close off the loop of first and last signification: man's self-production, the heroism of the abyss and of destiny, or the mastery of consciousness, definitively unhappy though it may be.[17] Doing so, they denied the finitude that they had seen on their horizons. Put differently, they ended up exploiting the "death of God," reconstituting or refounding an infinitely appropriated or appropriable sense, up to and including its negativity. But the "death of God"—as this history has taught us—cannot, by definition, be exploited. We note it, and think *after* it. That's all.

This is why the century was broken apart, split, opened on the "question" of sense. On the one hand, we have the final deployment of the senseless, simultaneously monstrous and exhausted. On the other, we have the weakened, distraught, or maudlin thought of the little -or -no sense (the absurd game of the tatters of "humanism"). Finally, we have the imperious necessity of the themes of the condition of possibility for sense in general: forms, procedures, fields of validity, forces, the interplay of everything that produces or seems to produce effects of sense—logics, languages, systems, codes (everything that used to be called "formalism," even though its only concern was with finding new approaches to the question or the task of sense).

This history has today provided us with the motif of sense placed under the need to think its finitude, not to fill it or to pacify it, and certainly not to do so through the insidious movement of a negative theology or ontology, in which the senseless ends up closing off sense itself. So not this, then, but to think anew and with all rigor the inaccessibility of sense as the very means of accessing sense, an accession that takes place *not* as something inaccessible but as an in-accession to itself, to the suspense, the *end*, the limit at which it simultaneously undoes and concludes itself without ever mediating between the two.[18] A finite thinking is one that *rests* on this im-mediation.

If our concern here ought to be with "freedom," this isn't, let me say again, because it's something like "freedom" that "fulfills" sense (and certainly not in the sense that human freedoms calmly play in the empty space of divine necessity). No, it is because "freedom" might just be the word, albeit provisional and uncertain, for what exposes this lack of sense and exposes, too, sense as an essential lack. Hence, the *sense* of "freedom" is nothing other than the very finitude of sense.

∼

Our history has often been presented as the process of a collapse or a destruction of sense in the planned savagery of a civilization at its limit, a civilization that has itself become the civilization of the extermination of the sense not merely of "civilization" as a whole but of sense itself.

This distress or this disarray, which, until this moment, nothing has alleviated, still pertains to sense. Indeed, in the West's own terms, it is perhaps the greatest distress and the greatest necessity of sense—so long as we can actually take such a measure and so long as the representation of an incommensurable distress, inscribed behind the great events and the triumphs, is not necessary for each epoch—as if the West had given itself this law or program.

We might now be able to say that this distress and necessity, as *ours*, as the distress and necessity of our present history—of this "time" of our being born to sense—must be understood as the distress and necessity of finite sense. In this regard, it doesn't really matter whether we call ourselves "moderns" or "postmoderns." We're neither before nor after a Sense that would have been nonfinite. Rather, we find ourselves at the inflection of an *end* whose very finitude is the opening, the possible—the only—welcome extended to another future, to another demand for sense, one that not even the thinking of "finite sense" will be able to think through, even after having delivered it.

A finite thinking is one that, on each occasion, thinks the fact that it is unable to think what comes to it. Of course, it isn't a matter of refusing to see ahead or to plan. Rather, a finite thinking is one that is always surprised by its own freedom and by its own history, the finite history that produces events and sense across what is represented as the infinity of a senseless process.[19] And this is also why, in our own time, it's pointless to seek to appropriate our origins: we are neither Greek, nor Jewish, nor Roman, nor Christian, nor a settled combination of any of these—words whose sense, in any case, is never simply given. We are neither the "accomplishment" nor the "overcoming" of "metaphysics," neither process nor errancy. But we do exist and we "understand" that this existence (ourselves) is not the senselessness of a reabsorbed and annulled signification. In distress and necessity we "understand" that this "we," here, now, is still and once more responsible for a singular sense.

Now, our distress manifests itself under four different headings: extermination, expropriation, simulation, technicization. Every discourse that deplores our time draws on these four motifs. (Are there any discourses on our time that do other than deplore it? Distress itself has become an object of intellectual consumption, from refined little nostalgias to punk nihilism. Which shows us, as if we needed to be shown, that the truth of distress lies elsewhere.)

~

Extermination: in camps, by force of arms, by labor, by hunger or misery, by racial, national, and tribal hatred, and by ideological rage. Just reading the daily newspaper becomes an exercise in endurance and accountancy. The extermination of persons, of peoples, of cultures, of the South by the North, of ghettos and shanty towns by immense conurbations, of one part of the South by another, of one identity by another, deportations and drugs of every kind. "To exterminate" means "to finish with" ("final solution"), and here that means to abolish the very access to the *end*, to liquidate sense. In the history of humanity, there's nothing new about crime, or about massive destruction. But here is a kind of general and polymorphous manhunt, articulated in an enormous economic and technological network, as if sense, or existence, were ready to *finish themselves off*, in order to do away with the *end* that was proper to them.

The question of evil has always been posed—and "resolved"—against a horizon of sense that ended up (without ever really ending) by converting or transforming its negativity.[20] There were two possible models for this conversion (crudely, we could call them the ancient and the modern, even though their actual manifestations were far more complex than this). First, there is the model of *misfortune*, of unhappy fate or tragic *dystychia*. Evil in this sense is given or destined [*envoyé*] to existence and to freedom as such. It comes from the gods or from destiny and it *confirms* existence in its opening to or as sense, regardless of whether this entails the destruction of life. This is why evil is borne, recognized, lamented, and overcome by the community. Terror and pity are responses to the curse or malediction.

Then, second, there is the model of *sickness*. It confirms the normativity of the norm in the very act of rupturing it. Evil in this sense is an accident (and, in principle, can always be mended) and belongs to a lesser order of existence, if one that's not actually null and void. Ultimately, in the classical universe, evil does not exist at all, except as a surface appearance, and death is by right absorbed or resolved (by the progress of knowledge, as in Descartes, or in universal exchange, as in Leibniz).

The evil of extermination is quite another thing: it is evildoing (or *wickedness).*[21] It does not come from outside and it is not something less than being; rather, existence is unleashed against itself. Here, evil affirms itself and affirms its (metaphysical, political, or technological) right. It seems—and this is a new thought—that existence can grasp its own being as the essence and hence as the destruction of existence and, moreover, as the senseless insanity that closes off the aspect of existence that opens onto to the need for sense. Extermination doesn't just exterminate *en masse* or totally; it exterminates "distress" itself. After all, the two go hand in hand: the immensity of the murder bringing about the negation of the singularity of each instance of "distress" and each "necessity" of sense; it is the negation of the "eachness" of sense, of being-toward-self.

So from now on, we have to stay with the following implacable, perhaps even revolting, thought: finitude is so radical that it is *equally* the opening of this possibility in which sense self-destructs. Finitude is sense as it absents itself, up to the point where, for a single, decisive moment, *insanity* is indistinguishable from the sense that is lacking. (No doubt we ought also to ask: has this ultimately taken place? If it has, wouldn't *everything* already have been destroyed? But then our question would have to be: hasn't everything already been destroyed? And if it is not, if being-toward-sense *resists*, and resists *absolutely* (and if it didn't, who would be left to have the "sense" of "evil"?), it resists at that very *real* point where insanity becomes indiscernible from the sense that is lacking.)

To discern within this indiscernible: that is what freedom ultimately boils down to. To discern senselessness without the help of Sense,[22] not with nothing to hand, to be sure, but with that part of (the being of) existence that we already have in our grasp. To be deprived of rules, without being deprived of truth.

It is in this sense alone, then, that an *ethics* is possible. What this means is that we can't fall back on an ethics of "misfortune" or an ethics of "sickness," whose use can, for us, only ever be analogical and provisional. It has to be a matter of an ethics of evil as wickedness. This doesn't require the norm or value of some "good" or other; the access of existence to its real sense is not a "value" that we could promise to the infinity of a good will. Precisely because this access can never be appropriated as a "good," but because it is the *being* of existence, it is and has to be presented in existence as existence. Here, "having-to-be" is the form taken by "being," since this being is *to*-be. But "duty" doesn't point to the infinite realization of a "kingdom of ends." Instead, it obligates freedom; or, more accurately, it is freedom that binds and obligates itself, punctually, immediately, without delay, as its own *end*, in both senses of the word. Freedom obligates itself *insofar as it does not appropriate its sense for itself* and, too, insofar as it open to the senseless. We might say, then, that being (the being of existence) *is* duty; but duty indicates the finitude of being, its missing sense.

We're not proposing a morality, but a tendency to conserve and to augment the access of existence to its own inappropriable and groundless sense.[23] An ethics is not only possible, but certain to emerge, carried along by what we already know about being. This doesn't mean that all practical decisions can be considered, negotiated, and taken swiftly and simply. Rather, it means that if the call for an ethics is today a constant testimony to our distress, distress already knows what ethics amounts to: the restoration of existence *to* existence. Clearly a "humanism" isn't going to be enough here, since it would obscure the very need for this restoration. (And does it need to be said that every human life has an absolute and immediate right to what, in a civilization such as ours is supposed to be, is called "living"?)

~

Expropriation: there is a big difference, actually an opposition, between treating the inappropriability of sense as what is most proper to finitude and expropriating from beings their conditions of existence. In other words, thinking about the lack of sense does not entail abandoning the critique of what, following Marx, used to be called "alienation." Nor, moreover, is it a question of regarding the material, economic, and social condition of men as a negligible happenstance, external to the domain in which a thought of finite sense would operate.

The "material" condition of existence is, on the contrary, each time what makes up the "each time." A place, a body, flesh, a gesture, a job, a line of force, an ache, ease or misery, having time or into time: these define the finite *each time* of any access to finite sense. They don't "determine" it in the sense of a causal instance; rather, they *are* it—and even when the entire dualistic arrangement of our vocabulary and our discourse (even when it tries to be "monistic") tends to obscure it, a thinking of finite sense is essentially a "material" thinking about the "materiality" of the access to sense. Because sense is finite, there is no reaching outside of this world. Because there is no "outside," it can't be reached.

The "philosopher" who talks about "sense" is, along with his thought, nothing other than a material singularity (a packet of "sense," a place, a time, a point in history, a play of forces), who cannot, after all, guarantee that we are any nearer to the "sense" that is in question. The thinking of finitude is itself a *finite* thinking because it has no means of access to *what it thinks, not even through thinking that it has no such access.* There is no privileged "speculative" or "spiritual" order in the experience of sense. Yet existence alone, insofar as it *is, hic et nunc,* is this experience. And the latter, always and each time, is an absolute "privilege," which, as such, misidentifies itself *qua* "privilege" and *qua* "absolute." There's nothing to say about when or how such an existence *exists.* ("To write"—and I will come back to this—is to say this not-saying.)

But there still has to be something or some "one" who can exist. Some being must be, *hic et nunc.* Existing is a here and now of being, it is *to be* a here -and now of being. There are conditions in which this is not possible—and even if existence, undoubtedly, always and without end, *resists,* even though it resists to the very end and beyond, and even though we can never simply say "this life has no meaning," there are still circumstances in which beings are not only abandoned, but in which they are, as it were, stripped of the conditions of existence. When this happens, beings are the pure instrument or object of a production, of a history, process, or system, always deported in advance from the here and now, always and only in the elsewhere and in the afterward of hunger, fear, and survival, or of wages, savings, and accumulation.

All the same, not being expropriated by the *hic et nunc* doesn't mean that we appropriate it for ourselves. There's no symmetry. *Hic et nunc* means merely to exist; it is finite existing "itself." Granted, we can never say that "this life" or "this moment of life" "makes no sense." But precisely because we can't decide with respect to sense, we can't decide—we can least of all decide—that all conditions are the same. Yes, every existence is *in* sense; but no one can consequently decide that the condition of possibility for certain existences is and has to be a *sacrifice* of life (of all forms of "life"). Since the here-and-now *is* finitude, the inappropriability of sense, every appropriation of the "here" by an "elsewhere," and of the "now" by an "afterward" (or by a "beforehand") is and does *evil.*

How are we to decide what makes a "here and now" possible and to decide what does not "alienate"? Nothing and no one can decide this. Each time, however, a here and now, an *existing,* must be able to decide *to be,* and to be open *to* sense. Each time, being has to be *allowed* to be, delivered and abandoned to its finitude.

Is this any different from the reputedly "normal" conditions for the exercise of basic freedoms, which presuppose life itself and a few other guarantees? In a sense, it is not—today, at least, and for us. But it must be so in that this "leaving," this "abandonment," is presented to beings as their very finitude. That is to say, the gesture doesn't refer to a horizon of "visions of the world" and of "man," one in which an essence and a sense would already be decided and within which would be exercised the "free choice" of a "subject," actually *already* "alienated" by this horizon. On the one hand, there are basic conditions (on which civilization wreaks constant havoc) whose empirical basis is also the "transcendental" of the here and now of existence. On the other, there is this: in letting the finite being be, *finitude* as such must be indicated.

This demands an altogether different thinking of "alienation" or "expropriation" (or indeed of "exploitation"). Altogether different, yet just as uncompromising as that of Marx when faced with the "primitive accumulation" of capital.

"Alienation" has often been represented as the dispossession of an original authenticity which ought to be preserved or restored. The critique of this notion of an original propriety, an authentic plenitude or reserve, contributed, in large part, to the disappearance of alienation as a figure for the loss or theft of man's original and ownmost self-production. In fact, existence is not self-productive, even if it isn't the product of something else. This is also what *finitude* means. Nevertheless, it remains the case, as we have seen, that beings can have their condition or conditions of existence expropriated: their strength, labor, body, senses, and perhaps even the space-time of their singularity. Equally, it's true that this is still happening and is part of extermination as we've just described it, and that "capital" or the "global market" only endures and prospers by a massive expropriation of this sort (and today, above all, of the South by the North, even though we know that this isn't the only expropriation of its kind). It isn't a question, therefore, of giving up the struggle, but of determining in what name we carry it on, in what name we desire the continued existence of beings. Up until now, the struggle has been guided by the regulative idea of the (original and final) self-production of man and, at the same time, by a general and generic concept of this "man." Undoubtedly the conditions of struggle are going to change if that struggle must now be thought with reference to finitude and its singularities. Access to finite sense does not presuppose auto-production and its reproduction, it "desupposes" it. It deposes the reign of process and the linking of *time* to the logic of process and procedure: that is, a linear, continuous time, without *space* (of time), and always *pressed up* against its own "after." (The Heideggerian time of "ecstasis" is also undoubtedly too *pressed* or *hurried*.) But access implies, on the contrary, the opening up of time, its spacing, the de-coupling of productive operations: the finite here -and now. And it implies that the latter be grasped in forms other than those subordinated to process, such as "empty time," "recovery time," and also "leisure time" (where "leisure," and that includes "culture," means inanity with respect to sense). It implies, in other words, the space-time of the here and now: concrete finitude.[24]

Birth and death *space*, definitively, a singular time. All access to sense, to what is "finite" in sense, spaces the time of general reproduction. Access produces nothing, and is not producible. But it takes place—if it is possible to say such a thing—as the inappropriable singular materiality of a here -and now. Let us say this: as enjoyment—if the notion of enjoyment is not that of appropriation, but of a sense (in all the senses) which, here and now, does not come back to itself.

∼

Simulation: the truth of '68, which the opinion makers stubbornly try to twist or obscure,[25] is twofold (provided one looks for it beyond the developmental crisis of a slightly backward society). On the one hand, it involves the emergence of new and previously unheard of forms of social struggle that do not conform to the syndicalist-political model. This is not the place to discuss these. On the other hand, '68 unleashed the critique of the society of the "spectacle" (this was the word used by the Situationist International), of seeming or simulation. From the Marxist heritage of a critique of social and cultural appearances emerged a general denunciation of a reality represented as entirely given over to the simulation of its true nature, and of social, political, and, ultimately, human reality.[26]

This critique was made—and achieved posterity—under the sign, once again, of "alienation" (again, this was the word used by the SI). General simulation alienates life by tying it to the reproduction of the functions of the "market-spectacular society" and prevents it from tapping into the creativity it harbors, blocking the desire to create which constitutes the real man. There is no point in repeating the critique of the duality of alienation and original authenticity which this account presupposes. No doubt the "life," "creativity," and "imagination" invoked here belong to a metaphysics which is still that of auto-production or the subject, of the generic subject-man. The great theme of simulation, which still proliferates today, is not free of Platonism.

All the same, the *soixante-huitarde* version of the critique of appearance, more Nietzschean than Marxist, was an "artistic" one. (In fact, that tendency is not entirely absent in Marx). This version subtly altered the themes or schemes of a critique of inauthentic appearance (especially when care was taken, the artistic model notwithstanding, not to fall back into aestheticism). This discrepancy can be formulated as follows: "creation" is not production, not so much because it operates on the basis of nothing, but because it operates *for* nothing, for no purpose other than to leave the "creator" surpassed, surprised, ravished by his or her own creation. Finally, however, it is still a question—in a sense, more than ever a question—of a *subject* acceding, infinitely, to his own sense. And that is why the model has remained, up to now, essentially linguistic, verbal, and poetic.

How, then, should a thinking of finite sense handle the theme, so insistent and insidious, of simulation? Here all theologico-aesthetic schemes give way: essentially (for which read: existentially), existence *lacks* a sense, in the form of a God or a work, and belongs to this lack.

The more or less confused suggestiveness of "authenticity" prevented us, in '68, from coming to grips with this lack. However (and this is why it is crucial to recall what *emerged* in '68), the critique of the "spectacle" undoubtedly revolved, albeit obscurely, around something like this: no form, image, or game, no "spectacle" even, is worth much if the *sense* of *existence* is not implied in it in some way, is not touched by it. Everything else is consumption of "cultural goods." And the critique of production is worthless if it does not include the critique of what could pass itself off as the production of sense itself. Which means (if the interpretation of an intellectual movement may be pushed farther than that movement was able to think) that what is at stake is *not the representation of a presence* but access to existence, which is not presence, access as exiguous, fugitive, and excessive, and also as *lacking*, as it could possibly be. Thus, without a doubt, the critique of general simulation is mistaken about itself: it is not a question of simulated or simulating (and dissimulating) representations, but rather a matter of what does not pertain to representation at all.

Today, in a certain way, "simulation" just proliferates. Moreover, it has spread out to such an extent that it presents and takes pleasure in itself at the same time as it undoes itself, ultimately spinning in a void—rather like a television set that no one is watching. Thus any critique which seeks to destroy simulation and accede to the authentic, the real, or "life" is blunted, because the simulacrum can no longer mask anything. The "simulacrum," most often understood as a sort of "image," merely presents its enigmatic nudity as image. Art, for example, has long drawn the rigorous consequences—often in impoverished fashion, it is true—of the end of art as the representation of the absolute, the Idea, or Truth.[27] But in this way it opens up the question of what "art" could mean.

It is thus the realm of representation in its entirety which spins in the void once the presupposition of complete presence and of a closed circle of sense is exhausted. This presupposition is still lodged, if only in a negative form, in the modern and postmodern tradition of a "presentation of the unpresentable"—if, in the final analysis, the "unpresentable" can only be conceived of as infinite. Whether this infinite is "good" or "bad," monumental or fragmented, surrealist or Situationist, expressed in great art or in a great life, it is always the indication of a secret nonpresence.

Now, if all there is is the finite—if the *there is* [il y a] is finite—then everything is presented in it, but in a finite presentation which is neither representation nor the presentation of something unpresentable. The *nothing* that existing *lacks*, this zero of sense which makes sense (but which is not a secret), comes to presence—and in art, or in what we should now call by another name, this is what we are dealing with. Which implies that any problematic of representation (of all seemings and all signs also) turns on an axis so fine that we can barely make it out. The issue of "simulation" changes completely if *mimesis*[28] becomes the concept, not of any representation, but of a presentation of *that which does not have to be presented,* of what could not be completed, neither Nature nor Idea, which is to say, finitude itself, insofar as it is a coming *to* presence without presence (and with secrecy).

Thus it is no longer a question of (re)presentation: neither presentation for a subject, nor the reproduction of an initial presence. The banishing of this double concept also supplants all simulation. (This does not mean that there is truth in every image and in every spectacle. Rather, it means that "truth" is no longer sought for in the regime of representation.) It is a question of what *coming* or *birth to presence* means. To exist: the coming to presence of absent sense, sense coming to its absence, to the absent-ing of all presence and any present. It is a question, furthermore, of a *mimesis* that one could try calling mimesis of *appresentation*, on condition that one hears in the prefix the sense of spacing, of distance." "Presenta-tion" *as* the spacing of sense.

~

Technicization: "Technology" is without a doubt one of the most ill-formed concepts in current discourse (which only leads to more chatter about it). Already, the unqualified use of the term obscures the fact that there is no technology that is not technology *of* some determinate opera-tion or other (be it chimney-sweeping or the recording of the images cap-tured by a space telescope). The vague idea of a general technology, a sort of vast machinic or combinatorial apparatus embracing technolog*ies,* has gotten about. Undoubtedly, the interdependences, interfaces, and interac-tions between technologies never cease to multiply. Nevertheless, transport technology remains transport technology, fertilization technology remains fertilization technology. One would be hard pressed to identify the ab-solute nexus of all technologies. The representation, in comics or in the cinema, of a single, gigantic, universal computer presupposes the resolu-tion, in this computer, of the question of *what* technology (taken ab-solutely) is the technology *of.* But if one wishes to ask this question, the re-sponse is there, and was available before the computer and the giant puppet show of universal robotization. Technology "as such" is nothing other than the "technique" of compensating for the nonimmanence of ex-istence in the given. Its operation is the existing of that which *is* not pure immanence. It begins with the first tool, for it would not be as easy as one imagines to demarcate it clearly and distinctly from all animal, if not in-deed vegetable, "technologies." The "nexus" of technologies is existing it-self. Insofar as its being *is* not, but is the opening of its finitude, existing is technological through and through. Existence is not itself the technology of anything else, nor is technology "as such" the technology *of* existence: it is the "essential" technicity of existence insofar as *technology* has no essence and stands in for being.

"Technology"—understood this time as the "essential" technicity that is *also* the irreducible multiplicity *of* technologies—compensates for the absence of *nothing;* it fills in for and supplements *nothing.* Or again:

technology compensates for a nonimmanence, that is to say, for an absence of what is represented as a "natural" order of things, in which means are given along with ends, and vice versa. It is, in this sense, transcendence over "nature." But nature represented as pure immanence would be that which does not pertain to sense, and which does not *exist*.[29] In which case, technology transcends—nothing. Or else "nature" designates an exteriority of places, moments, and forces: technology is the putting into play of this exteriority as existence, a "transcendence" not opposed to the "immanence" of the world. Technology doesn't reform a Nature or a Being in some Grand Artifice. Rather, it is the "artifice" (and the "art") of the fact that there is no nature. (Law, for example, is also a technology or technique.) So much so, in fact, that it ultimately designates that there is neither immanence nor transcendence. And this is also why there is no technology "as such," merely a multiplicity of technologies.

"Technology" is a fetish-word that covers over our lack of understanding of finitude and our terror at the precipitate and unbridled character of our "mastery," which no longer knows either end or completion. Undoubtedly our incomprehension demands a new sort of thinking, and our terror is not baseless. But we will gain nothing from exorcising a purely verbal demon, one that is a false concept. It is quite remarkable that Heidegger's theses on "technology" have become the most "popular" part of his thought. This happened for two reasons. First, the most important contribution of this thinking appears to lie in a denunciation of the "ruthless conquest," total and leveling, of the earth, for the sake of autonomized aims deprived of any existential guarding of being. Insofar as Heidegger put forth this discourse (and he did), he was less original there than almost anywhere else in his work. (With a symmetry that is not accidental, the same could be said of some aspects of his treatment of poetry.) The denunciation of "technology" is the most banal, and the most vain, gesture of the "technological" age. But, second and more remarkable still, we almost always forget how Heidegger (in a smaller number of texts, it is true) tried to formulate at least the demand that "technology" itself be understood as the "sending of being," as being sending itself as its ultimate message: which means, as existence and sense themselves. Thus dispatch or sending is the finite sense of being as the *final* sending (outward) of the West. To "inhabit" technology, or to "welcome" it, would be nothing other than inhabiting and welcoming the finitude of sense.

I don't want to take Heidegger's thinking any further than this, any more than I want to claim to have "solved" the "question of technology." I want simply to situate it, in the knowledge, as I have already said, that our incomprehension and terror are not groundless. This is also to say that finitude is limitless, and that humanity can destroy itself in the implosion of its technicity.

It is entirely legitimate to say that the current movement of technicization is accelerating and proliferating, and that in it technologies are constantly multiplying and transforming themselves, weaving a network that is ever more dense. How, though, can we avoid asking whether technicization—the development of technologies—may not actually be a law that was laid down with the very first technology or, more exactly, whether growth and proliferation, to the point of panic, may not actually belong, rightfully or in essence, to a gesture of compensation—with no prospect of that which is compensated (an immanence) ever coming *to being*? It is no accident that the comforting dreams of a return to a "degree zero of development" were quickly extinguished by their own insignificance. Today, we know that a well-thought-out ecologism determines new technological advances.

By contrast, we could quite legitimately point to the role played by technologies in extermination, expropriation, and simulation. But there's no sense in imputing these to "technology," as if it were some sort of diabolical entity, because no such entity exists.[30] Moreover, there is no point in adopting a moral discourse about the "evil uses" to which technologies are put. Nor is it a question of employing technology "beneficently" in the name of some pre-existing "good." Rather, it is a matter of getting at the *sense* of "technology" as the *sense* of existence.

What manifests itself as irresistible global technicization is accused of having no other end than itself. (I'm leaving aside the ends of the market and of expropriation.) What if this "end," which can no longer be represented as the reign of robots, or even of computers (but only, at the limit, as total implosion), what if this end, which *is* in effect only in an indefinite technicization, *also* exposes its finite sense? What if it also exposes us (in hardship and trouble) to the finitude of sense? The "reign of technology" disassembles and disorients the infinite sealing off of a Sense. In the same way, undoubtedly, as it disconcerts and displaces, endlessly, the completion of a "work," in such a way that technicization could, in all rigor, be called "un-worked," or without work [*dès-œuvrée*].[31]

Instead of returning nostalgically to pious images (or essences) of the artisan and life in the fields (an old refrain, as old as our history), this would be a matter of thinking the following: that all technology, over and above the technology that it is, and in being the technology that it is, contains an implicit knowledge of sense as finitude, and of the sense of finitude. Nothing, perhaps, better bears this out than the questions, demands, and undecidabilities which subtend the decisions that have to be taken, each day, by the technicians of biological, ecological, energetic, and urban manipulation.

~

Each one of these tasks requires a finite thinking.

Not a thinking of relativity, which implies the Absolute, but a thinking of *absolute finitude*: absolutely detached from all infinite and senseless completion or achievement.

Not a thinking of limitation, which implies the unlimitedness of a beyond, but a thinking of the limit as that on which, infinitely finite, existence arises, and to which it is exposed.

Not a thinking of the abyss and of nothingness, but a thinking of the un-grounding of being: of this "being," the only one, whose *existence* exhausts all its substance and all its possibility.

A thinking of the absence of sense as the only token of the presence of the existent. This presence is not essence, but—*epekeina tēs ousias*—birth to presence: birth and death to the infinite presentation of the fact that there is no ultimate sense, only a finite sense, finite senses, a multiplication of singular bursts of sense resting on no unity or substance. And the fact, too, that there is no established sense, no establishment, institution or foundation of sense, only a coming, and comings-to-be of sense.

This thinking demands a new "transcendental aesthetic": that of space-time in the finite here and now, which is never *present*, without, however, being time pressed up against its continuum or its esctasis. Finitude: the "a priori" irreducibility of spacing. Equally, though, this thinking demands the material transcendental aesthetic of the disparity and dislocation of our senses, our five senses, whose organic and rational unity cannot be deduced or grounded.[32] The division of the five senses, which one could say is emblematic of finitude, inscribes or exscribes the division of finite sense.

As for the "transcendental analytic," it should present the disparity and dislocation of the five senses and the sixth, that of the concept. A schematism which does not return to the homogeneous. A "hidden art" for which no secret is any longer to be awaited.

No doubt, an "art" (a "technique") is always the clear consciousness (if it is a "consciousness") of the splitting and sharing of sense and the senses, of their absolute difference and of the very sense of what it displays. However, a finite thinking cannot be an aestheticizing thinking, nor aesthetic in the sense in which every thought of the beautiful, and even of the sublime, has insisted, up until now, on extending to infinity (imprisonment, revelation, or secret) the arc of finitude.

A finite thinking follows this outline: only to retrace it. A finite thinking does not add to existence the seal or confirmation of its sense. It simply takes up the challenge of that which "we understand already and without end": the being that we are. Thinking, here, is coextensive with existing, and consists in thinking this thought: that being-for-itself does not turn back on itself. This doesn't mean that it would be enough to "exist" (to be there, in the most banal sense of the term) in order to think, or that thinking (in the banal sense of forming representations) is sufficient for existing. It means, rather, that the fact of existence cannot be its own truth, which is to be the fact of a *sense*—and that the concept and the signification of sense cannot be *its* own truth, which is to be the sense of this *fact*. It means that existence must be thought, and thought existence, in order that it is—in order, simply, to *be*.

We bump up against an empty circularity here, in which the meaning of each of these words evaporates. In truth, though, meaning or signification is being exhausted here. Here, words are no longer just words, language is no longer just language. It *touches* its limit, and displays it. There is no longer "sense" as the meeting-point of all these meanings. In the same way, there is no concept as the auto-conception of the concept, nor as the presentation of a "thing in itself." And man is not the auto-production of his essence. But *sense* is the sharing and splitting of language thanks to which language does not complete itself (nor initiate itself): the difference between languages, double articulation, the differ*a*nce of sense, the sharing of voices, writing, its exscription.

Yet here we discover that thought, which is language, *is*, however, *not* language. Not because it is "something else" (something fuller, more present), but because language itself, in "essence," is not what it is, does not confer the sense that it endlessly promises. A finite thinking inhabits, writes (in) the finitude that language *is*, which it displays or exposes. We could say, then, that a finite thinking makes itself *adequate* to the existence it thinks. *But this adequation is itself finite*, and it is there that access to the missing sense, or its inappropriation, obtains.

How can and must this thought, given over as it is to what is not-sense [*remise au pas-de-sens*] as its ownmost object, be written? This is what it does not and cannot know, and what it must invent for itself each time a single invention alone is possible, all discourse being suspended.

Very quickly, we are threatened by the unbearable preposterousness of "doctrine." The more we repeat "finite thinking," the more we risk conjuring up the specter of a "system." Or, more simply, the pitiful shadow of the "answer to all questions." But it's precisely "answers to all questions" that have saturated us and worn us out. No, "finitude" isn't a new response or a new question. It is, as I've already said, a responsibility before the not-sense that affects all sense, before what has to be and has to constitute *our sense*. A responsibility of thinking taken to the limit of all our meanings and, consequently, *also*, as I have continually been trying to show here, the meaning of "finitude." There is no sense of the words "end" and "finite" that would allow us to think that whose *index*, held out at the very limit of our history, bears the name "finitude"—or the name *the absolute of existence*. There can be no doctrine or system here. Only rigor.

It's no accident that contemporary philosophy—especially in its French singularity—has done its thinking with a formidable mobilization of language and writing (often called "rhetoric" or "affectation" by those who are oblivious to the epoch and don't feel the heaviness and difficulty of thinking). Once again, as happens with every great rupture of sense, philosophy no longer writes in the same way. Nor does poetry. Perhaps "philosophy" or "poetry" will no longer be written as such. These illimitable words carry the entire weight of a question of sense, and most of all carry the proposition that a "question" of finite sense isn't a question that could be articulated in terms of sense, even as we can't disarticulate it in terms of some non-sense. Hence, it's not even a question. Not "What is finite sense?" but simply, "The finitude of being suspends the sense of *that which is* sense." How do we write that?

Rimbaud: *How to act, O stolen heart?*

There is real disappointment here, and suffering: and this is why thinking is hard. But the disappointment comes from waiting and from expectation, and there's waiting and expectation because there is, *already*, sense. This isn't a promise that might or might not be kept. Nothing is promised to existence. Hence disappointment itself is sense.

This is what has to be thought, therefore. And it is not absurd. It makes or constitutes existence (as well as community, history, and freedom). But thinking it through brings thought to an end: only a finite thinking can take the measure of this extremity. The part of finite sense that is left over is only vestigial and fragmentary. There is nothing to record and take down; that's what sense is; that's all, end of story. We've always already said too much, thought too much. Yet we've never said enough, because each time it starts all over again. And what is this "each time" of existence? A "here and now"? What is a birth, or a death, a singular coming to presence? How many times does this take place in a life? In a history? And how many times in a community? And what is the "one" in a community? The event of sense, insofar as it is lacking, is neither the continuity of a substance nor the discrete rarity of an exception. It is *being*, the thinking of which is the ontological ethics of this "neither . . . nor," held in strict abeyance, unsublated, above the abyss.

Here, thinking burrows back to its source. It *knows* this source, its very being, as what is, in itself, neither thought, unthought, nor unthinkable, but the finite *sense* of existing. Thinking burrows back to its source and so, as thought, opens it and drains once again as it both gathers *and* scatters it. Thought has to think itself as what loses itself in thinking—necessarily, if the sense that it thinks is the sense of innumerable finitudes and appropriations of nothing.

We might be tempted to write: "If a finite thinking never sees the light of day, if it doesn't find its voice in writing, then we will have failed to think our own times." As if, in such an injunction, we knew and anticipated an essence of finite thinking, with its form, if not its norm. But no, a finite thinking is already working, or un-working, already prior *and* already posterior to what we can say about it, here or elsewhere. It's written *here*, but before and after this "here," finishing it off already, and not yet. Already for yesterday and tomorrow making and carrying sense away—a thinking that can no longer impose itself, nor even propose itself, but that must, with all its resources, *expose itself* to what is finite about sense. Multiple and each time singular—what is a "time" or "occasion" of thinking? what is *a* thought?—hard, entrenched, as material as this line of ink, but still fugitive, a finite thinking. Just *one*.

Translated by Edward Bullard,
Jonathan Derbyshire, and Simon Sparks

2

Concealed Thinking

Perhaps more than ever—assuming such a formula can be allowed—
we have become aware of how the eternal return of the same dead ends and
the same distress (to give just a few one-word examples: "values," "right,"
"war," injustice") lays bare and accentuates not just our exposure to the impossible but also the manner in which this exposure measures us; that is to
say, gives us our measure as human beings, a properly uncompleteable
measure and one that can contain no conciliatory horizon.

Here, I want to engage Sartre and Bataille, knowing as I do that both
of them already knew about this exposure. They knew about it because of
having lived through an era not just of crisis but of contraction and con-
vulsion. An era of revulsion. An era of nausea and exasperation, which we
still remember (and of which they are a part), though it is a painful memory because it's not just the memory of a past, but one that reaches toward
the future like a voiceless souvenir of Western history, at least a memorial
of how, staggered and broken, history comes down to us; a memory, then,
whose unbearable insistence follows us. We say that we are in crisis or in
distress, but it was in Bataille's and Sartre's time that the boil was first
lanced: the terrifying insufficiency of all the various assurances of knowing,
believing, and thinking, and the necessity of confronting the lasting failure
of accomplishment [*un inachèvement durable*], the impossibility of ending,
and even the responsibility of not ending.

Both Sartre and Bataille realized this, but not in the same way.

∼

What they realized ultimately lies beyond what is evoked by words like "properly unachievable." Such words need to be heard literally. What is properly unachievable doesn't hold its achievement at arm's length, like a regulative idea, like an ideal receding into the heavens of Ideas or values, nor does it hold out for its achievement like an inexhaustible act of mourning. What is *properly* unachievable has a failure of achievement as a dimension of its propriety or as its very propriety, absolutely and unconditionally. In short, it is not even a question of a failure of achievement, therefore; it is a matter *not* of a negative nor a privative propriety but, but somewhat clumsily, of the proper fullness of the proper. (Still, this clumsiness is itself the condition of the designation, not because of some linguistic defect but because language always says too much, always says more than it says and says that it does so, hounding itself to the infinite extremity of its saying.)

Ultimately, everything is going to turn on this point: whether or not to bring language—and hence thinking—into the ambit of this extremity.

~

No doubt it is this extremity, more than anything else, that separates Sartre and Bataille. And on this point Sartre commits (in a way that is entirely understandable and that Bataille himself makes possible) a mistake that draws a definitive line, not between the two men or between two different "conceptions" (and we could, if we wanted, compare the way in which each wants to escape the whole idea of "conception"), but between two incompatible experiences or relations to experience, experiences that perhaps always divide up, between all of us, the apprehension of the world today: that is, the apprehension of a vertiginous dissociation of experience itself.

If it's true that there has, for us today, been a noticeable shift in the language and style of philosophy—if it's true that there's been a shift, for some of us at least and in certain aspects, away from the needy and formal servility that characterizes the work of knowing and of thinking, not enslaved in a cowardly sort of way, but ultimately still enslaved to the horizons of science and sense—then we owe this to Bataille more than to anyone else, to something that he not opposes to, but conceals from Sartre. And that also means from philosophy. Of course, Sartre isn't just the "philosopher" in all this, and Bataille knew better than simply to bid

farewell to philosophy in a way that would ultimately be of little consequence to it. All the same, the contrast between them can certainly be
played out as the division between two different ways of relating to the exercise of thinking, which also means, as the division between two different
relations to Heidegger, between two proximities to and two distances from
the thinker who suggested that the experience of our time be termed "the
end of philosophy and the task of thinking." In the details of what I am
going to sketch out here, we can see a division in or a tearing of the figure
of Heidegger.

~

Granted, Sartre is almost always concerned with an extreme limit of
thinking that no work or project of signification is going to be able to appropriate, since this extremity can't be *given* but is itself merely a gift responding to the gift of a being whose "existence is a lost generosity by dint
of its being for no one."[1] Still, in an almost paradoxical manner, Sartre
fails to recognize—particularly in Bataille's thinking—and fails to take responsibility for a necessary, insistent motif that had already been ad-
vanced and intensified through the very different ways of thinking proposed by Kierkegaard and Marx, Nietzsche and Heidegger, before
reaching its peak in Bataille: the motif *not* of a philosophical use, however
necessary that may be, but of an address *to* such a use, an address that, on
the basis of itself, carries an intimation of the extremity without which it
cannot think or without which it thinks precisely nothing, an extremity
that puts into play the very thinking that philosophy is in the business of
setting up.

What is at stake, then, is what stops thinking from being a thinking
of crisis or distress without being itself a thinking that is *in* crisis or *in* distress; that is, without being a thinking that is not put into play as such, the
necessary condition if thinking is to protect itself as much from sufficiency
as from renunciation—and, consequently, the condition for thinking's being able to take place on the level of what we share with Sartre and Bataille
as the modern tradition of the liberation of humanity.

What is at stake is that which, without renouncing either critique or
the search for "positive propositions," as we say, can no longer be satisfied
with its propositions without indicating the excess that has to overflow and
consume them, going beyond any sense that they might have had so as to

give them a sense of the necessary effort and audacity of thinking itself. For all that, however, this thinking does not sink into the pathos of skepticism or of heroism; rather, it envisages directly the primitive and final fact of a thinking secured by nothing outside its own freedom (neither "God" nor "total man," nothing, then, if we can say that . . .); there is no thinking, no articulation of sense, that doesn't have something of the uncompleteable about it, that doesn't exceed sense, like an intimation, a binding, implacable obligation, logical as much as ethical, to conceal itself as thinking in the very act of thinking "in order," if you'll allow me to risk the phrase, to be thinking ("in order to make sense" and "in order to free itself"—and if I'm talking about "risk," it's simply in order to avoid the risk of introducing any hint of a finality).

~

Bataille wants to consider thinking in terms of this intimation alone. Sartre, by contrast, continues to believe that although the extremity (which he certainly wants to acknowledge) can't be relinquished, it can, by concealing and withholding itself ever more emphatically, give rise to a discourse that is virtually infinite and capable of inspecting, not the limit, but the movement of this displacement. With a single gesture, he situates himself on the side of history and language, these being represented as the two faces of a single work of infinite or indefinite pursuit, a work that seeks to master the sense and liberation of a humanity, yes, defined by this very freedom, but defined according to an ambiguity in which the continuity of the movement in some way effaces the shattering of interruption that marks the extremity of an active infinite. And it is precisely because of this reserve that we must oppose Sartre to Bataille. But let me pause for a moment in the face of what holds them closely together: what's crucial here isn't the awarding of a victory (always a pretty questionable move in the order of thinking), but better understanding a stake that is essentially our own.

In a certain way, it is Bataille as much as Sartre who wants to see humanity defined by its liberation—a humanity for the sake of this alone. Both think only of the possibility of articulating the experience of a world divested of origin or end (regardless of whether it's the divine or the human name for this end), and thus of a world experienced *as* this divestiture; taken as experience, however, this is no less the *praxis* of a sense and of a truth—even, if you prefer, the *praxis* of subjects of sense and of truth.

In the wake of the same era and the same difficulty inherent in Marxism thought as *final* liberation, both Sartre and Bataille are after what has become necessary—what has become necessity itself—ever since truth showed itself to reside neither in the heavens nor in the morrow, namely, to affirm truth here and now, to be capable of a truth *of* the here and now, of *us*, therefore, in our world. In Sartre's own words, it is a matter of thinking the fact that "truth is action, my free act. Truth is not *true* if it is not lived and done."[2]

∽

I should immediately add: by using Sartre's own words to illustrate the point, I have already compromised, ruined, even, the proximity that I wanted to indicate between Sartre's and Bataille's aims or concerns. Indeed, this really does need to be said, since, in the final analysis, it's perhaps always going to be words (vocabulary, style, and tone) that measure the most clear-cut differences between thoughts concerned with the same objects in the same era.

Still, it's not as if I'm rushing headlong into this necessary indication. Once again, we need to stop a moment under the axiom of the proximity or the sharing, however approximate it may be, of a single preoccupation—a proximity without which, moreover, the confrontation wouldn't have been quite so heated, and perhaps wouldn't have taken place at all.

As such, I want to maintain this proximity between Sartre and Bataille, a proximity whose limit, whose dissolution, even, I want to show simply in order to penetrate further, as it were, into the concealed intimacy that is also, once again, our own. Let us say, then, shifting terms somewhat, that both Sartre and Bataille (and they're not alone in this) are anxious [*dans l'angoisse*], experiencing the cessation of a sense that is neither a lack nor a loss but the point at which truth arises as this very cessation.

∽

All we need to do, therefore, is consider the following question: Precisely what truth is it that arises here? Sartre says: It is an act, a lived experience [*un vécu*] and a doing. "Lived experience" is a fairly murky category, and one that appeals, moreover, to a somewhat dubious, sentimental depth. But we don't need to dwell on this. Rather, we need to address the fact that, so far as truth is concerned, Bataille doesn't disavow the term "lived experience." (I'm not about to follow the texts, even though one could; here, I'm not really interested in philology.) What he means by this, though, is the "lived experience" of a cessation of what goes under the name "lived experience"—we might be tempted to say: a "deadening of experience" [*un mouru*], if this didn't introduce a tonality that is undeniably false and if, moreover, the "deadening of experience" weren't precisely the concept of an insurmountable contradiction.

So let us say the same thing in a slightly different way. It is a matter of "not-knowing" and so of nothing less than the entire modern experience of thinking. Indeed, since Kant, a not-knowing lies at the very heart of thinking. And already in Kant, as in Hegel and Heidegger and so also in Sartre and Bataille, the site of not-knowing is called "freedom." Sartre envisages not-knowing literally (and this, too, could be shown in the texts). Yet he also says the following, a remark cited by Bataille in his response to Sartre: "Bataille refuses to see that not-knowing is immanent to thinking. A thinking that thinks that it does not know is still a thinking."[3]

Bataille doesn't challenge Sartre on this point. But the question here is one of knowing (or of not-knowing . . .) how to think a thinking that is *still* a thinking even when its content is not-knowing.

Perhaps there's nothing more important than thinking this "still thinking," if it is true that we are, even more immediately than either Sartre or Bataille realized, at an extremity where the movement of knowing meticulously traces the contour of not-knowing.

Hence, when we say that the thinking of not-knowing is *still* a thinking, we can also and before anything else understand by this a sustained identity of thinking, of its subject (and this is what Sartre actually emphasizes). In fact, though, we do so only at the cost of seeing not-knowing itself as an object, one that is identical to knowing: its negative identity, its lack or its impossibility. Now this is precisely what needs to be called into question: if not-knowing is the negative side of knowing, it marks a limit or a powerlessness beyond which the position of knowing still remains *de jure* possible (future knowing or divine knowing, for example). If a final knowing is possible, the totality of being will ultimately need to be gathered somewhere as the appropriated knowledge of some subject (albeit being itself). Hence, somewhere, a truth subsists, at least virtually, and a final ground for things is established.

Now, this is not what Bataille means when he speaks about non-knowing. For him, "not-knowing" designates, on the contrary, knowing that there is no knowing beyond our knowing, that "knowing" designates merely the knowledge of an object (essentially, then, we are still swimming in Kant's vast wake), and that the totality of being cannot be addressed by a knowing. To know all this, that is, to *not-know*, understood this time in its verbal rather than in its substantive sense, isn't to postpone final knowing until a later date or to a higher register, but to enter into the obscurity and the opacity of what is no longer a matter of knowing in any way, shape, or form. The thinking conceived thus is "still a thinking," then, but in a sense hitherto unknown. It introduces a change in level and a rupture in thinking itself: it is thinking concealing itself from itself (and "conceal" is a word that continually appears in Bataille).

Concealed thinking is no more annihilated thinking (unconscious, asleep, dead thinking) than it is maintained, self-identical thinking. It is thinking that conceals itself from the anticipations and the demands of knowing (in the modes of intuition or the concept, of representation or calculation), while still remaining *thinking*: that is to say, an act that, before anything else, is present to itself ("everything of which I am aware as happening within myself," says Descartes—and hence sensation or feeling as much as knowing or willing). The thinking of not-knowing is thus a thinking that has nothing that it might think as an appropriable content, merely self-presence without content. (In a sense, we could show how it is Descartes's *cogito* that is being taken to its limit by Kant and Hegel. Bataille knew this and showed as much. As I have said, though, I'm not concerned here with the texts. Rather, it is the movement of a thinking that demands our attention.)

∼

The fact that thinking has no content doesn't mean that it is empty. Or, if it does, the emptiness in question is a substantial emptiness: not a pit or an abyss into which thinking slides, but the *night*, as Bataille likes to put it, the night into which we advance and sink by *seeing* obscurity, itself the privation of sight [*vue*].

If thinking is generally represented as sight, what is involved here is its representation as the sight of nothing rather than a nothingness of sight. It is the sight of nothing, at any rate, of no object or content. Its sight is nothing other than its penetration into the night. But what it sees as the night into which it penetrates is also itself: seeing nothing, and seeing that it sees nothing, it sees the faculty or the power of seeing reduced to itself. Not, however, in the sense that it would be turned back on itself; the night stands before it and presents it with sight that doesn't see anything but merely sees. Neither self-presence in itself nor self-objectification, but concealed sight, sight subtracted but not suppressed, abducted, stolen, or destroyed, diversified and presented as such. There's nothing to be seen, and so neither sight itself nor a contortion of the subject in the object, but the power of seeing stretched to its limit, stimulated by being concealed from sight.

"To be concealed" is to take by surprise, unexpectedly. Thinking won't have anticipated what is concealed, what conceals itself from thinking but, in doing so, also conceals thinking from itself. Knowing doesn't anticipate not-knowing. Yet if knowing holds rigorously to what moves it—to its ultimate ground, to truth and the sense or meaning of being—then it steps outside itself and into not-knowing.

What concealed thinking thinks—what it thinks, what it sees, and what it touches upon surreptitiously, what not-knowing not-knows, in other words—isn't something in the night that might be divined from its contours, its breath, its rustling. Rather, it is the night itself, the condition and the element of invisibility. Night thus gives itself as the truth of a thing that is no longer the object of a knowing but the thing restored to its ultimate ground or to its sovereign sense.

This sense is the concealment of sense. That is to say, it makes sense by concealing itself. In concealing itself, and in concealing itself alone, it carries the thing to the nocturnal incandescence of its absolute presence, of its emergence and its ground or foundation: the *thing itself,* the thing that is no longer taken up in the return to an "other thing" (through difference and proximity, through the relation of cause and effect, principle and end, and so on). And it's thus that language makes sense: it relates all meanings to one another, right up to the nonsignifying point of the flight of sense from all these senses that refer back and forth between themselves. We make sense, we give it and we even think it. But what is the sense of this power of sense, a power that isn't simply "in" us or "outside" us, a power that is perhaps in us only insofar as it is outside us?

The sense of sense is one of self-concealment. In the night, then, as in anxiety and in the solitude and horror that accompany it, but equally in the strange communication of laughter, it's not the chaotic din of an absurdity that is triumphant. Rather, it is sense itself or *the truth of sense*, sense freed up in its naked power: sense sensing, therefore, a remark that is far, far removed from anything like a play on words but, quite the contrary, involves the very play of sense, that which opens it and puts it into play: its body. It senses. It senses, not in the sense that it appropriates a signification for itself, but in the sense that it senses itself concealing itself. It *touches* on its extremity as the eye touches on the night in which it is lost. Self-possession shows itself to be outside of itself.

This sense, we could say, is mad. Bataille himself claims that "freedom is mad."[4] This madness, however, is not the absence of reason, any more than it is some sort of "excess of reason." Rather, it is a reason that doesn't give up, that doesn't give in, since it carries on trying to give reasons. It knows, then—that is, it un-knows and it senses, sensing nothing—that what gives reasons, what gives grounds, is the concealment of reason.

But what does this concealment involve?

To conceal, *dérober*, to dis-guise, if you like, is also to disrobe. And yet this is but one aspect of the term, since "robe" and "disrobe" have the same origin (as English "rob" or German *rauben* suggest, the robe would, in the first instance, be a garment seized by a thief). We all know Bataille's phrase "I think in the same way that a woman undresses," and there are plenty of texts that deal with what is thus laid bare. A thinking that conceals itself, therefore, is also one that undresses itself, that disrobes, exposing itself, more specifically, as a naked woman: as truth.

To be naked is, first and foremost, to be undressed, to be without any covering that could present or signify a state or a function. It is to reveal everything but, at the same time, to show that there is nothing more to see. It is to show that there's nothing beyond nakedness except still more nakedness. Hence, I cannot see nakedness except by placing it at a distance from the object, by situating it in terms of the (medical, anthropomorphic . . .) object. I see nakedness only by entering into it, or by letting it enter into me.

What this means is that nakedness can only be opened or, rather, that it is itself an opening. And this, in turn, means that nakedness touches on the other. There is no solitary nakedness. If I am naked and alone, I am already an other to myself, an other with myself. By its very essence, a nakedness touches on another nakedness: it wants to touch, no longer to see, to enter into the night of nakedness. It touches it and opens it by opening itself to it. And yet, essentially obscure and devoid of all foundation, all it opens is its closure; it leads onto the night. But it still leads; it still opens.

Nakedness discloses the fact that "truth takes place only in passing from one to another"[5] (and Bataille offers a little clarification of the point: "it begins with conversations, shared laughter, friendship, eroticism"). Night or nakedness, insofar as they give nothing to be seen, give this: the fact that sense only gives itself by passing from one to another. In this passage, sense is concealed from the "one" as much as it is from "the other." As such, it is devoid of any sense of appropriation. Likewise, and this is actually the same thing, language is what it is only between us. There is no private language. And yet, *between* us, there is nothing, certainly nothing upon which we might confer a signification without the immediate threat of suffocation (whether the signification is that of the mystical body, communal race, etc., or the mutual surveillance of all too clear-sighted looks, the "hell of other people" as Sartre has it, and between the contrasting figures of himself and Bataille lies the formidable modern worry over the "between-us" that conceals itself).

~

In short, what we need to do is to give some sense to this between-us; this, however, can only be the sense of the passage from one to the other. Hence, the sense of passage is the sense in which signification is confused with directional sense, and directional sense heads in all directions at once. The between-us is, very precisely, the place of the sense of sense, passage in every sense of the term: transmission *and* transgression, the step from one *to* the other *as well as* the step from the other beyond the one. This is why, moreover, the between-us, whenever it takes place, is always the between of nakednesses. This doesn't mean that only nakedness allows us to be between us; rather, it means that when we are between us—when this happens—we are naked.

Denuded, we are immediately concealed, since there is nothing that could render us visible, knowable, identifiable. Here, we are more likely to be identified with the movement that conceals us, a movement that is as worthy of the name "love" as it is of "death," "tears," or "laughter," "language," and "thinking." When, as the saying goes, I am "truly" thinking, all I can actually do is reach out into the night, toward an other that I do not see, offering the nakedness of a thinking that knows that it is concealed: unaccomplishing, unable to stop, unable to communicate anything but still communicating this: the fact that thinking no longer responds to anything, despite its being the very movement of responding (of giving accounts, of giving grounds or reasons). When I read Bataille or Hegel, Descartes or Rimbaud, I'm always reading the fact that they're not responding to me in any way whatsoever, that each one of them provides me with a sense, a ground, or a reason for no more than an unstable and tenable instant (so long as I don't look to fix it in an imaginary response, in a doctrinal lesson, in a belief). Essentially, each of them hands over to me [*me passe le relais*] or, as we say, passes me the baton [*le témoin*] of sense. And it is here, in this passage alone, that there is such a thing as sense.

Equally, though, the passage is a concealment, since it maintains its sense only in this incessant passing into the other—in me outside of me to the other. But this is the truth of sense. To seize is to seize a chance. Chance is a nakedness,[6] "it waits for us to undress it."[7] This has the sense of seizure and surprise, but it also has the sense of an anxious, feverish anticipation that has to know that it cannot simultaneously wait *and* desire, since seizing has to come as a surprise if it is to surprise chance. This agitation, this anxiety, is the agitation and anxiety of thinking in the night that conceals it.

What is at stake here, however, is nothing more than this: chance signifies that the passage doesn't obey an external necessity. It is the effect neither of a transcendental law nor of the willing of a principle or an end nor of the totalization, however tendentious it may be, of a history. Rather, it is the absence of such a necessity that turns away from knowing. Not-knowing is the not-knowing of the freedom of sense—that is to say, of the necessity of chance.

～

Concealed thinking thinks the fact that there is no reason for us to be here, the fact that there is no reason why the world is here, the fact that there is no reason why we are in the world—indeed, this is what "being in the world" means. To think this nothing is to think naked thinking: a thinking that appeals to its passage to the other alone, without intention, beyond all intention, for nothing, nothing except our being between us, nothing except our being in the world—and this "except" is itself devoid of intention, of project, of end. Both Sartre and Bataille experienced the

necessity of undoing the hegemonic ties of finality without ever withdrawing thinking from the urgency of communication or community, without
ever withdrawing it from a difficult and perilous generosity. (This is what
each of them, in quite different ways, failed to find in Heidegger or Freud,
hoping to find it instead in an overhauled version of Marxism.) Finality
concerns a supposed knowing; generosity exposes to not-knowing.

~

Hence, concealed thinking only thinks what conceals it from itself.
As such, it is "still thinking." Like all thinking (apperception), it grasps itself, but not in the intentional act constitutive of an object or a project; indeed, it grasps itself in the relinquishment of any object or project, of any
intention and so, too, of any consciousness. It grasps itself as something
that is relinquished; it grasps what is left for thinking when there's nothing
left to think. It sees itself naked, exposed, deprived not only of its objects
and their operations, but of any form of self-certainty, the certainty of its
own disappearance, a *cogito* whose *cogitatio* this disappearance *is*, a silent
implosion as well as a pit of anguish or a jerk of laughter. A *cogito* ex-cogi-
tated, thought outside itself.

The division of a thinking outside thinking is a constant and constitutive movement in the modern experience of thinking. It begins with
Kant, for whom the entire operation consists precisely in detaching thinking from knowing. Thinking beyond knowing, intellectual intuition beyond sensible intuition, reason beyond understanding, faith beyond reason, the transformation of the world beyond its interpretation, art beyond
science, thinking beyond philosophy, "originary thinking" beyond thinking itself . . . ,[8] madness, silence, not-knowing, these are a few of the links
in a peculiar and powerful chain: the modern history (although perhaps
not quite so modern, extending as it does right back to the *noesis noe-
seos* . . .) of a necessary overcoming of the thinking of knowledge and
recognition, the history of an overcoming and subversion of philosophy
and theoretical postulation—an overcoming and a subversion that arise
from within philosophy itself.

On this account, though, Sartre, who insists that non-knowing is *still*
a thinking, actually confirms a continuity in this overcoming and subversion. He still holds to the irrefutable and necessary right of "accounting
for." Bataille, however, represents neither a renunciation nor a prophecy,

but the same insistence followed right to the end: to the point of accounting for an extremity that can no longer be accounted for. Yes, it is still a
thinking; but it is one that confronts the excess of this "still."

The point of such an excess—the point of the leap, of the throw, of
shock, surprise, the point of thinking's passage to *still* thinking, the crossing over from the "still" in the sense of "in the same way" to a "still" in the
sense of a "moreover," to the still other or the still further—is the point of
concealment, the extremity at which we can think along the lines of concealment, thinking having already passed into the other, having already
been absorbed by this other sense that gives it the other, but that also works
to finish off—or to begin completely anew—every conceivable sense of
the other, in excess of sense, the "*flip* side of all thinking."[9]

In the intimacy of this excess, thinking turns back on itself, which
also means that it exposes itself to its absolute outside: the twisting and
tearing that define thinking itself, the double *still* of thinking. This thinking loses itself and still thinks this loss, yet it still loses this thinking in such
a way that it no longer exists either as a thinking of loss (a philosophy of
non-sense, of grinding doubt, of nostalgia or cruel irony) or as a loss of
thinking (delirium, orgiastic delight, the paralysis of consciousness). It
doesn't exist at all, either positively or negatively, and yet it insists in the
night as an "illumination."[10] All this, though, is only the night's illumination of itself.

∼

Of course, the motif of nocturnal illumination brings us dangerously
close to a sort of mysticism; this needs to be pointed out, since it is the central term in the dispute between Sartre and Bataille, the term that will be
central to Sartre's contempt for Bataille's way of thinking. (Once again, I
don't want to go back over the texts. What strikes me as rather more important is to address the question of whether or not Sartre's vehemence at
the time indicates a troubling proximity that might warrant consideration.
Moreover, Sartre the man, if not Sartre the theoretician, is clearly more
anxious, less confident—even less tragic—than Bataille the man and the
thinker.)

The night's "illumination" doesn't produce a vision; in a sense, nothing happens. And yet the illumination stressed by mystics is played out
around an excess of vision [*une sur-vision*], an exquisite excess of sensibil-

ity, one that is unsustainable, yes, but also ecstatic, and that is also to say: transported, carried away, uplifted. Bataille always ends up understanding the mystical as a way of getting a result, getting there by virtue (and/or by the calculation) of a method, a desired approach. Yet thinking can only be concealed insofar as it doesn't wish for what doesn't await it, insofar as it doesn't calculate its arrival time, even simply in order to abandon it.

This happens by not happening [*cette venue vient comme ne venant pas*]. It is "what doesn't happen,"[11] identical in this regard to being, simply and as a whole. It runs alongside being and the event of being, but resembles it only by way of a concealed resemblance. It is, moreover, the concealment of all resemblance and thus of all identification. The arrival can in no way offer its own concealment as the event of being, which, in fact, lies outside or on the other side of the point at which it conceals itself. There's no vision here, then—merely the disappearance of vision. It's not a matter of seeing, therefore, but of *looking*, of the eye opening onto the impenetrable night. Here, there is only the imperceptible exhaustion of thinking, sliding outside itself, a slippage, therefore, the minute and decisive slippage between what is *still* a matter of vision and what is still a look, still blind. If we're going to think what is brought into play here, we're going to have to elaborate the intimate difference, minute but also absolute, between vision and look.

No doubt we will have to be attentive to this slippage if we are going to give it its chance. Yet the only thinking that is able to think it is one that has made the initial resolve to surrender to it but that has in no way renounced the demand of thinking, of thinking rigorously. And yet the system of this rigor does not construct itself in terms of means and end, instruments and productions, principles and consequences. It can't, since here means and ends, method and knowing, are confused: the not-knowing in which thinking slides outside itself—in itself outside itself—is identical to the exact coincidence of thinking and its flip side. Put differently: of thinking and the thing that is being thought. Put differently again: not-knowing is identical to truth.

As has already been said, this truth lies in the other. It takes place as communication to the other from out of an opening of sense that doesn't refer back to me and of which I see simply the nocturnal void. I enter into death or I enter into the other, it's all the same. I enter at the point at which I cannot enter as the subject of my intention and its objects (neither theoretical intentionality nor practical will), and so I look without seeing [*j'en-*

tre en regardant sans voir]. The "subject," if there is one, is a subject of this look, not of a representation, concept, signification, or figuration.

If the *end* is thus beyond both object and subject, beyond circumscribed and signified sense, this doesn't mean that it lies in a supra-signifying beyond to which I would end up being initiated (mysticism always involves initiation). It's a matter here not of signification but of what, right up against signification, slips alongside it, next to it, prying itself from it through a minute difference: its communication. (And for Sartre, as for Bataille, truth is its communication to the other.[12]) Communication isn't the movement of significations; rather, it brings such significations into contact with the openings of sense. Without this contact, signification wouldn't signify. Yet whatever happens to the significations being exchanged (whether they are transformed, lost, misunderstood, well translated), with this contact it is the very possibility of sense that is illuminated—and its fire is a nocturnal one. Sense in the other is for me both the truth and the night of sense. Birth and death, love and hate, signal nothing other than this.

I cannot speak—and that also means that I cannot think—without this "sense in the other" already resonating "in me," without its night already standing against my eyes. "To pass from one to the other" isn't just one more operation for thinking; it is thinking *itself* insofar as it conceals itself in the truth of sense.

Such are the stakes of the cracked nudity that haunts Bataille's work—not in the manner of an aroused voyeurism but in the sense of the night of a clear eroticism. Beneath the removed or raised garment, and so no longer beneath, strictly speaking, but exposed, nudity is what conceals and what conceals itself: leading into the space that the intimacy of the other *is*, not only for me but for itself as well. Leading, then, not into a mystical union in which a knowledge of one in and through the other might be reconstituted, but into the renewed concealment of not-knowing that, rather than uniting us, divides us: an infinite agitation of sense. Concealed thinking is identical to communication, and this identity is itself the night of not-knowing.

∽

If concealed thinking is neither mystical nor philosophical, therefore, if it is accomplished neither as ecstasy nor as knowing, if it is essentially *concealed*—thereby, and thereby alone, being the thinking that it is—and if this is the thinking that our thinking ought to be, if this, truly, is the thinking that our thinking already is and has been since the period denoted by the names "Sartre" and "Bataille," then how is this thinking to be addressed?

How, indeed, can we address that which, so far as we are concerned, can be neither religion nor science nor philosophy and that we need more than ever now that we have done with religion, science, and philosophy, now that we have passed beyond this configuration, now that we know all this—without ever knowing what it is that we are becoming, if not a humanity whose sense is naked and exposed?

Both Sartre and Bataille laid bare and exposed the sense of this sense. Furthermore, their confrontation gives it its sense: this incomplete (and doubtless incompleteable) confrontation between someone who is still attempting to discern a history (a thinking) and someone who is already looking into the night (into the other side of thinking), each one of whom knows in some obscure way—knowing through a concealed knowing—that they are thinking *the same thing.* Here, though, "the same thing" doesn't indicate an identical object; rather, it indicates the "sameness" that is so problematic for our identity, for us, for we members of a humanity laid bare and exposed, we members of a concealed humanity . . .

In short, it would be a matter of thinking how we can grasp—without ever capturing or reducing to something that has been caught—the chance of being in the world and the chance, too, of our exchanging signs there, this chance that is almost impalpable and, more often than not, painful to the touch. The signs that we exchange are unending; they do not refer to a shared signification—whether that of science, religion, or philosophy. And yet this concealment is our being in common. In the same way, Sartre and Bataille, by failing to understand one another, understand one another rather well, perhaps too well to avoid colliding with one another, and represent accordingly a type of shared exhaustion of the assurances of signification. In a way, we have all been and still are "Sartre and Bataille," so long as concealed thinking hasn't yet become our way of thinking.

Sartre speaks of a "perpetually active understanding [that] is none other than existence itself," describing this understanding, in order to distinguish it from "knowing," as "the dimension of *rational not-knowing* at the heart of knowing."[13] We will always be able to ask whether, in this text from 1960, Sartre doesn't actually risk a belated and furtive homage to

Bataille (who would die two years later), perhaps even more than homage, a sign of community. However this may be, what is important here isn't his intention per se, nor is it, as elsewhere, his attempt to correct "non-knowing" with something more "rational" (a correction or modulation that Bataille doesn't simply repudiate). No, what is important here is that, obliquely and from a distance, as it were, Sartre approaches the necessity of thinking concealed thinking: the sense of this naked absence of sense that we ultimately *know* and share *as* our very nudity, humbly get gladly, in the everyday or in what is truly exceptional.

From this point on, it falls to us to approach from a new perspective that which is neither science nor religion nor philosophy—that which, far from providing a sense that might be exchanged, is itself the sense of the exchange (the exchange itself as sense, even) of our existence in common. "In a sense" this is what we call *praxis*, that is, action that transforms its agent rather than its object or its matter. Far from being the mastery of a means with a view to an end, *praxis* is the endless transformation of the subject of sense in itself: a sense that is nothing other than its communication—and, by the same token, its concealment. The concealment of thinking is its *praxis*: thinking that undoes its objects in order to become the thinking that it is: *we*, with one another and with the world.

Translated by James Gilbert-Walsh

PART TWO

EXISTING

3

The Unsacrificeable

Pamphile says that, having learnt geometry from the Egyptians, Thales was the first to inscribe a right-angled triangle, whereupon he sacrificed an ox.
—Diogenes Laertius[1]

I

It is, no doubt, reasonable enough to attribute the practice of sacrifice to Lascaux Man at the very latest. Thus we need to address about two hundred centuries of sacrifice, then the millions of sacrificial rites already carried out in our own century, at the edge of the West or in some of its most secret recesses.

Any such account would need to conjure up the spectacle of innumerable altars or consecrated places, the fumes rising from them, the blood flowing over them, the wine or waters spilt upon them, the fruits, breads, offerings of every conceivable sort laid upon them. Equally, this spectacle would need to allow us to gauge the peculiar absence of sacrifice in us, for us. Either its absence or its ambiguous and indistinct presence. Wherever there are still altars, priests tell us that it's no longer a matter of the same sort of sacrifice. I will come back to this, since it goes to the very heart of the matter. More often than not, however, there are neither altars nor priests. As a result, all those things for which sacrifice is prescribed—participation, communion, community—or, rather, those things for which we *imagine* it was prescribed, are no longer preserved, at least not in the same way. Every time nihilism declares that "there is no more community," it also announces that there is no more sacrifice. Is it possible to take up this expression in a way that wouldn't be nihilistic? That is the question that I want to address in this essay.

All of humanity, or near enough to make no difference, has practiced something that we might call "sacrifice." But the West rests on another foundation, one in which sacrifice is exceeded, surmounted, sublimated, or sublated in a singular way. (Is this the same as saying that it is itself sacrificed? I will come back to that.) We would need to evoke another representation here: the image of the past ten centuries, during which sacrifice, first at the edge then at the heart of Western foundations, is shaken loose, sublated, transfigured, or withdrawn. This happens with the prophets of Israel, with Zoroaster, Confucius, the Buddha, and, finally, with philosophy and in Christianity. Unless we ought to say that it completes itself *as* philosophy and *as* Christianity or, if you prefer, as onto-theology. Nothing, perhaps, marks out the West more distinctly (albeit obscurely) than this dialectical assumption or subsumption of sacrifice. Bearing in mind the limits of history proper, it should be said that the Indo-European period immediately presents sacrifice in a weakened, displaced, if not diluted form. Everything happens as if the West began where sacrifice ends. It is certainly not enough, as Bataille, for example, pointed out on numerous occasions, to say that an evolution is taking place, driven by a growing horror of immolation and the search for "less harrowing religious attitudes."[2] Instead of grasping the reasons for this (apparent) "humanization" of sacrifice (which is easily confused with the very origin of the West), we need to grasp what is at stake deep within it.

This is what my epigraph is meant to indicate. The little story about Thales takes us back to the time of a strange amalgam, when science was celebrated by sacrifice, a time when, as we know, or as we *think* we know, the origin of geometry stood precisely within the dissolution of this amalgam. (In analogous fashion, Hegel, with a mixture of interested curiosity and disapproval, tells us that Xenophon, at the head of his army, allowed his military choices to be dictated by the daily sacrifice.)[3] Today, other sciences take sacrifice as their object; finally, however, all they tell us is that this object is ill constructed and artificial, "a category of bygone thinking." They might even go so far as to say: "In our system, sacrifice exists at most as little more than an empty vessel, nothing but a strategic position in which distrust or fascination, the refusal of the other, is set in place."[4] We can no longer understand Thales' gesture; we do not even know whether, or how, he himself understood it—and yet it seems that we are still increasingly attracted, if not fascinated to the point of hallucination, by this very gesture.

(All the same, something else needs to be added here: confronted with non-Western practices of sacrifice, the inappropriate character of our idea of sacrifice is doubtless not entirely distinct from many other sorts of impropriety, indeed, from impropriety in general. In a sense, we don't really know what "eating," "kissing," or "commanding" mean outside of the West, and so we don't really know anything that we haven't already told ourselves. Now in the case of sacrifice (as in other things), it so happens that the very *word* we use is of our own making. This Christian/Latin word says something that no other word can say. It does not translate: rather, it inaugurates a meaning. In the final analysis, "sacrifice"—in all possible senses of the word—is a Western development. We can doubtless brush this argument aside by saying that ultimately the same goes for everything. In the case of the word "sacrifice," however (although perhaps this isn't unique to it), what's notable is that the new word simultaneously claims to recover the meanings of other, earlier words *and* to establish a new meaning that might abolish or sublimate those earlier terms. There would be an obscure sacrifice of words within the word "sacrifice." Undoubtedly, the entire lexicon of the "sacred" takes part in this sacrifice. But I can't dwell on this question here.)

II

Bataille's thinking cannot but haunt contemporary reflection on sacrifice. I will discuss this thinking later. For the moment, I want to draw out three distinctive traits that give his thinking its exemplary character.

1. This thinking doesn't come about purely by chance or through the whim of an individual but is firmly tied, on the one hand, to an entire sociological, ethnological, and anthropological context, and, on the other, to a philosophical, theological, and psychoanalytic one. One way of confirming this would be to refer, for example, to Georges Gusdorf's book *L'Expérience humaine du sacrifice*, published in 1948 after having been "written in captivity."[5] His perspective is entirely different from that of Bataille, whom he nevertheless cites (and whom he knew personally). Yet beyond the symptomatic case of these two authors, the network of references, the importance conferred upon the object, and the tendency toward the idea of a necessary "surpassing" of sacrifice all testify to the contemporaneous concerns of a much wider community. There is something like a critical, or

crucial point of contemporary thought in the question of sacrifice. We will perhaps find out later what causes it, and in what way it concerns us.

2. Bataille's thinking, as we know, displays more than a particular interest in sacrifice: it is obsessed and fascinated by it. For Bataille, "the lure of sacrifice" is a response to the fact that "from childhood onward, we await this derangement of the order that stifles us . . . the negation of this limit of death, which fascinates like light."[6] With sacrifice, it's a matter of nothing less than "being the same as the magnificence of the Universe."[7] Thus Bataille could write: "The question of sacrifice should be called *the last question.*"[8] We also know that Bataille didn't just want to *think* sacrifice; he wanted to think *according to* sacrifice. and he actually wanted sacrifice itself. At the very least, he never stopped presenting his own thought as a necessary sacrifice of thought. With the same movement, the motif of sacrifice in Bataille involves the sacrificial gesture itself, the establishment of community or communication, art in its ability to communicate and, finally, thought itself.

3. Yet we also know that a steady displacement, a lengthy diversion, led Bataille to denounce the comedy of sacrifice and, eventually, to abandon the idea of making it his goal. But this abandonment, doubtless always fragile and ambiguous, never ends.

The questions that I want to ask here, without restricting myself solely to Bataille, originate in his experience of thinking and what it exemplifies for us.

What is it about the fascination with sacrifice? Where does it come from? To what does it commit us? To what is it committed? What is it that actually constitutes our relation to sacrifice? Is not the whole of the West, in a sense, determined there? And, as a result, doesn't this relation tie us to the closure of the West? Isn't it about time that we acknowledged the end of real sacrifice and the closure of its fantasy? Isn't it time that we concerned ourselves with a participation and a communication that would no longer owe anything to sacrifice? One that would no longer be a product (I am thinking here of René Girard, and an entire contemporary Christian movement) of the revelation of a nonsacrificial religion, which can only ever trap us in the revolving door of this very revelation?

III

What is the nature of the West's initial relation to sacrifice? More precisely, upon what kind of relation to the sacrifices of the rest of humanity (or the representations of these sacrifices) does the West map out, so to speak, its own "sacrifice" (perhaps, if it needs repeating, the only one that genuinely answers to the name "sacrifice")?

Socrates and Christ show it to be a decisive and founding relation. In both cases, it is a matter of a simultaneously distanced and repetitive relation. Both figures (the double figure of onto-theology) quite deliberately and decisively distance themselves from sacrifice *and* point toward its metamorphosis or transgression. Above all, therefore, it is a matter of a mimesis: early sacrifice is, up to a certain point, reproduced in its form or schema, but reproduced in such a way as to uncover within it a completely new content, a truth previously buried or unrecognized, if not perverted. In the same way, *early* sacrifice is represented as having constituted only a previous imitation, a crude image of what *transfigured* sacrifice will henceforth bring about. Basically, though, there is perhaps precisely nothing that we can say about "early sacrifice" except that all representations of it are constructed on the basis of transfigured sacrifice. Yet this new sacrifice doesn't derive from its brutish prototypes by way of a simple transmission or natural generation: the gesture of a "mimetic rupture" is necessary to inaugurate it.

(Let me ask in passing, without wanting to hold up our inquiry, whether there is, in a general sense, any "rupture" that would not be "mimetic." Isn't this principle applicable to the dominant interpretations of what we call, amongst other names, "the killing of the father" or "revolution"? To what extent might these interpretations be dependent upon the gesture made in relation to sacrifice? That is, upon a gesture in which sacrifice has to be sacrificed—immolated, abandoned—so that we might finally dedicate (or sacrifice) ourselves to the revealed truth of sacrifice? A sacrifice to sacrifice through the sacrifice of sacrifice, therefore. Of course, in any such formulation the value of the word is continually and dialectically displaced. Finally, though, this displacement perhaps accounts for the dissolution of every value associated with the word and so, if the term still means anything, of the thing itself. I shall come back to this.)

The mimetic rupture of Western sacrifice (or, if you prefer, *to* Western sacrifice . . .) suggests a *new* sacrifice, one distinguished by a number of characteristics. This doesn't simply mean that all trace of these characteristics is absent from early sacrifices—as far as it is possible to track down the truth of these "early" sacrifices (this is the whole problem, of course).

Four characteristics, though, are clearly required and presented by the onto-theology of sacrifice:

1. It is a self-sacrifice. Both Socrates and Christ are condemned by an iniquitous condemnation that neither the victims nor the executioners portray as a sacrifice. Yet the final outcome of this condemnation is still represented as a sacrifice sought, intended, and demanded by the victims' entire being, by their life and thought and message. It is the sacrifice *of the subject*, in the fullest sense of the word and fullest duality of the genitive.

The *Phaedo* suggests nothing other than the reappropriation of the situation by the subject Socrates: he is in prison, he is going to die there; all earthly life is designated as a prison, one from which he plans to free himself through death. *Philosophy* appears thus not simply as *knowledge* of this liberation, but as its genuine *operation*: "Those who have purified themselves sufficiently by philosophy live thereafter altogether without bodies," and so forth.[9] A few moments after having uttered these words, Socrates will drain the hemlock without hesitation, asking of the gods "that my removal from this world to the next may be prosperous."[10]

In the case of Christ, the Pauline doctrine of *kenosis* is familiar enough: the gesture by which Christ, "being in the form of God . . . humbled himself,"[11] becoming man even unto death. God, lord and master over the death of all creatures, inflicts this death upon himself, returning to himself and his glory the life and love that he has lavished upon creation.

In both cases, the event of sacrifice proper (if we can still speak in such terms), the actual putting to death, merely punctuates and lays open the process and the truth of a life that is itself sacrificial through and through. With the West, it is no longer a matter of life sustained by sacrifices nor even, in keeping with a very Christian expression, a matter of a "life of sacrifice." Rather. it is a matter of a life that, in and for itself, is nothing other than sacrifice. Augustine writes: "When the Apostle exhorts us to make our bodies a living, holy host, suitable for God . . . we ourselves are this entire sacrifice of which he speaks."[12] The life of the subject—what Hegel calls the life of Spirit—is the life that lives by sacrificing itself. In a different vein, Nietzsche, too—who elsewhere distrusts the morality of sacrifice—testifies to this sort of life:

"To give one's life for something"—great effect. But people give their lives for many things: emotions need to be satisfied, individually and all together. . . . How many have sacrificed their lives—or even worse, their health!—for a pretty woman! When one has the temperament, one instinctively chooses what is dangerous: the adventure of speculation, for example, if one is a philosopher; or one of immorality, if one is virtuous. . . . *We are always sacrificing.*[13]

2. This sacrifice is unique, and it is consummated for all. More precisely still, within it all are gathered, offered, and consecrated. Let me cite Paul again: "And every priest standeth daily, oftentimes ministering and offering the same sacrifices, which can never take away sins. But this man, after he had offered one sacrifice for sins . . . , by one offering he hath perfected forever them that are sanctified."[14] Or Augustine: "The whole city of the redeemed, the entire assembly of saints, is offered to God by the supreme pontiff in one universal sacrifice. In the form of a servant, he offers up himself for us through his passion, so that we became the body of such a noble leader."[15]

The uniqueness of sacrifice is thus transferred—or dialecticized—from a position of exemplary uniqueness, whose value lies in its exemplarity (this is, above all, Socrates' sacrifice, and we might also ask, Isn't sacrifice, in a general sense, the example of examples?), to the uniqueness of the life and of the substance in which—or to which—every singularity is sacrificed. At the end of this process, of course, we find Hegel: "The substance of the State is the power by which the particular independence of individuals and their absorption in the external existence of possession and in natural life are experienced as nothing; the power which promotes the preservation of universal substance by the sacrifice—at work within the inner disposition that this power implies—of his natural and particular existence."[16]

In a way, Socrates' disciple furnishes the moment of exteriority in this dialectic: Plato's *Laws* establishes the prohibition of private sanctuaries and sacrifices increasingly performed, anywhere and at any time, by "women in general" and anxious people.[17] As Plato makes clear, moreover, if the impious *do* offer such private sacrifices, the whole city will suffer as a result. So there is a communication, or contagion, of sacrificial effects, and it is the role of state sacrifice to ensure the smooth running of the city. Long after Plato, and long after Hegel himself (not that I would want to suggest any straightforward affiliation), Jünger describes thus the experience of "total" war: " *The vast sum of consented sacrifices forms an entire holocaust that unites us all*"—a phrase cited by Bataille as a salute to "mysticism."[18] Western sacrifice upholds the secret of a participation or communication devoid of limit.

3. This sacrifice is inseparable from the fact that it is the revealed truth of every sacrifice, or of sacrifice in general. It is not simply unique, therefore, but, by virtue of its uniqueness, elevated to the principle or the essence of sacrifice.

Remarkably enough, the *Phaedo* is framed by two references to what I have called "early" sacrifice. At the start of the dialogue we learn that, after the judgment, Socrates' death had to be deferred because executions were forbidden during the annual voyage to Delos that celebrated Theseus's victory over the Minotaur, that is, until the end of the sacrifice to which the Athenians were honor bound. At the end of the dialogue, on the other hand, Socrates, already half-paralyzed by the poison, utters his final, dying words: "Crito, we ought to offer a cock to Asclepius. See to it, and don't forget."[19] Any interpretation here—and this is precisely what the text intends—is doomed to a pointed ambiguity: *either* Socrates, who recovers the health of the soul by sacrificing his body, is giving thanks to the god of healing, *or* he is bequeathing, with a degree of remoteness and perhaps with some irony, a sacrifice that is empty when compared to the one that the philosophical purification is at that very moment performing within him. Either way, the truth of sacrifice is brought to light in terms of its mimesis: early sacrifice is an external and, by itself, futile figure of this truth in which the subject sacrifices itself, in spirit, to spirit. Through spirit, it is to *truth itself* that true sacrifice is offered up, in truth and as truth that it is accomplished. In the central section of the dialogue, dedicated to the truth of the immortality of the soul, Socrates warns: "As for you, if you will take my advice, you will think very little of Socrates, and much more of the truth."[20]

After Paul, Augustine, and the entire tradition, Pascal writes: "Circumcision of the heart, true fast, true sacrifice, true temple: the prophets showed that all this must be spiritual. Not the flesh that perishes, but the flesh that does not perish."[21]

4. Hence the truth of sacrifice *sublates*, along with "the flesh that perishes," the sacrificial moment of sacrifice itself. And this is precisely why Western sacrifice is basically an overcoming of sacrifice, its dialectical and infinite overcoming. Western sacrifice is already infinite in that it is self-sacrifice, universal sacrifice, and reveals the spiritual truth of all sacrifice. Equally, though, it is—indeed, *has* to be—infinite because it absorbs the finite moment of sacrifice itself and because, logically, it has to sacrifice itself as sacrifice in order to attain its truth.

This is how we need to understand the shift from the Catholic Eucharist, consummated in the finite character of sensible beings, to the inner cult of reformed spirit. And how we need to understand its speculative truth:

The negation of the finite can only take place in a finite way; with this we come to what is generally called sacrifice. The immediate context of sacrifice is the surrender of an immediate finitude, in the sense of my testifying that this finitude ought not to be my own and that I do not want to keep it as such. Here, negativity cannot manifest itself through an inner process, because feeling does not yet have the necessary depth. . . . Rather, the subject . . . is only to surrender an immediate possession and natural existence. In this sense, sacrifice is no longer found in a spiritual religion, and what is there called sacrifice can only be so in a figurative sense.[22]

IV

Mimesis, then: spiritual sacrifice will be sacrifice only in a figurative sense. In truth, it is "the reconciliation of the absolute essence with itself."[23] Mimesis, *but* repetition: sacrifice is overcome *in the name of a higher, truer mode of sacrificial logic alone.* Indeed, the reconciliation of essence demands nothing less than its passage through absolute negativity and through death. It is through this negativity—and even *as* this negativity—that essence can communicate with itself. "Sacrifice" means: the appropriation of the Self in its own negativity; and if this sacrificial gesture has been abandoned to the finite world, it is simply in order to draw out all the more clearly the infinite sacrificial structure of this appropriation of the Subject. With this, the external *mimesis* of early sacrifice becomes the inner and true *mimesis* of genuine sacrifice. Bataille writes, for example: "In a certain sense, sacrifice is a free activity. A kind of mimeticism. Man takes up the rhythm of the Universe."[24]

We might call this mimesis "transappropriation"—an appropriation, through the transgression of the finite, of the infinite truth of this very finitude. In a sense, there is no longer any sacrifice: instead, there is process. In another sense, this process only matters because of the moment of the negative, in which the finite has to be negated, and this moment remains, in spite of everything, a transgression of the law, the law of self-presence. This transgression occurs in pain, in horror, even. For Hegel, for example, it is the somber, bloody, yet ineluctable face of history. Yet this is how Spirit completes its infinite self-presence and the law becomes restored and glorified.

Nietzsche, too, sometimes sees history in terms of the necessity of sacrificing entire generations so as "to strengthen and raise higher the general feeling of human power through this sacrifice—in which we and our neighbor are included."[25] Such a sacrifice is opposed to one performed by "the good" who, says Zarathustra, "crucify the one who writes new values on new law-tables, and sacrifice the future to themselves."[26] And yet it opposes it only by remaining sacrifice, just as Dionysus opposes the Crucified; it is the power of dismemberment against the dismemberment of power. All this presupposes the Maenads, the orgiastic, a point of infinite dismemberment and pain.

Such is the consequence of mimetic rupture: sacrifice is the sublation of its finite functions and its exteriority, yet a fascinated gaze is still fixed on the *cruel* moment of sacrifice as such. We have already seen that the very Hegel who abandons religious sacrifice also reclaims for the state the full value of warlike sacrifice. (And what does Marx say of the proletariat? Those who "possess a character of universality because of that universality of their sufferings.")[27] Although sublating sacrifice, the West *constitutes* a fascination with and for the cruel moment of its economy. And does so, perhaps, in parallel with the extension and exhibition of suffering in the world of modern war and modern technology—at least up to a certain point, to which we will return. The "flesh that does not perish" remains the torn flesh of a beautiful body, and the secret of this horror continues to cast an obscure light over the central point of sublation, over the heart of the dialectic: *in truth*, in spite of Hegel, it is this secret that makes this heart beat; or, more seriously, it is the dialectical gesture itself that inaugurates this secret. Western spiritualization/dialecticization invented the secret of an infinite efficacy of transgression and its cruelty. After Hegel and Nietzsche there is an eye fixed upon this secret, with the feeling of a clear, necessary, and unbearable consciousness—the eye of Bataille, for instance.

But what does this eye actually see? It sees its own sacrifice. It sees that it can only see because of an unbearable, intolerable vision—that of sacrificial cruelty—or it sees that it sees nothing.

Indeed, if it is always going to be a question of the ancient sacrifice that lies at the heart of modern sacrifice, we need to acknowledge that the mimetic rupture has made us lose sight of the ancient truth of this sacrifice. Or, as I have already suggested, the rupture is set up by the representation of the "loss" of a "sacrificial truth"—and by the fascination for the "truth" of the moment of cruelty, the only so-called truth preserved from those ancient rites. As is the case at other decisive points in our Western discourse, the representation of a loss of truth—here, the truth of sacrificial rites—leads directly to the representation of a truth of loss: here, the truth of the victim, the sacrifice itself.

Nonetheless, this truth of loss, of sacrificial destruction, isn't always presented so clearly. It can be difficult to resolve the diversity of ancient rites into a unity. Just as specialists today tell us that "sacrifice" is an artificial notion, so it's not certain whether the spiritualizing consciousness of sacrifice has always been entirely clear about its own resumption of thoroughly heterogeneous sacrificial functions. It would be useful here to follow the complicated (and doubtless barely unified) destiny of functions such as the remission of sins, the preservation of grace, and the acquisition of glory in the history of theology, to limit ourselves to just the three functions that Thomas Aquinas identifies in sacrifice (and the same undoubtedly holds for the three different modes of sacrifice: the martyr, austerity, the works of justice and the cult).[28] In reality, one thing is clear: the interiorization, the spiritualization, and the dialecticization of sacrifice (or sacrifices . . .).

Yet this clarity is itself somewhat obscure. What spiritualization brought to light as "early" sacrifice is, in fact, a pure economy of exchange between man and the divine powers. Everything can be reduced to the following formulation from Brahminic ritual (or at least to our meager understanding of it): "Here is the butter, where are the offerings?"[29] The condemnation of the "economism" of sacrifice runs through Plato as it does through Christianity, Hegel, Bataille, and Girard. As such, the Western sublation assigns a unity to the ancient rites (one of exchange) in order to refuse it: it demands the "spiritual" unity wherein sacrifice should go beyond itself, while remaining true sacrifice.

This first—simplistic and mercantile—version of sacrificial economy is hotly disputed. The *do ut des* is seen as inadequate to explain sacrifice. Yet even when it is depicted as a means of access to the cohesion of the various parts or forces of the Universe, or as an expulsion of menace from communal rivalry, it is still a matter of a general economics. In fact, economism forms the general framework of representation in which the West takes over *a priori* all early sacrifice, with the intention of proceeding to a general "sublation" of this economism. Spiritualization has undoubtedly rendered us incapable from the outset of understanding the proper significance and context of early sacrifice. We have absolutely no idea what the one who says to his gods "Here is the butter, where are the offerings?" is really saying because we know nothing about the community in which he lived with his gods or about the community of sacrifice that existed between them. We also know nothing about the cohesion and communication between the various parts of the Universe. Similarly, we do not know what mimesis actually *is* in this context, which is a way of answering another accusation leveled at early sacrifice—that it is only a simulacrum, since it doesn't result in self-sacrifice. At most, we might follow Lévy-Bruhl's guess that mimesis is *methexis*, participation (which, moreover, refers the question of mimesis back to the question of economy). But we have no idea what "participation" means—except to say that, for us, it means a confusion of identity and a communion whose secret lies precisely in sacrifice. Hence we go round in circles. Yet one thing, and one thing alone, *is* clear: what we represent as the bonds or communication of sacrifice stems from what we have already invested in this idea. And this all boils down to the word "communion." What we would need to say, then, is this: we know precisely nothing about a noncommunal mimesis/*methexis*; what we do know, though, is that communion implies a sacrificial negativity, one that thus "sublates" what it is that we know precisely nothing about . . . (in broadly similar fashion, Freud had no idea what "identification" meant, and in equally similar fashion, we would need to ask whether Girard knew what was meant by the contagion of mimetic violence).[30]

The denunciation of economism and simulation runs through every dialecticization of sacrifice, Bataille's included. This denunciation, already confused, actually denounces itself. In fact, and this is undoubtedly what we need to acknowledge in Bataille's work, the fascination with sacrifice doesn't prevent us from locating within its dialectic (or in its spiritualization) a generalized "economism" and "mimeticism." Sacrifice as self-sacrifice, universal sacrifice, the truth and sublation of sacrifice, is the very institution of the absolute economy of absolute subjectivity, which can only really mime the passage through negativity, in which, symmetrically, it can only reappropriate or transappropriate itself infinitely. The law of dialectic is always a mimetic law: if negativity was indeed the negation that it properly ought to be, transappropriation would be unable to break through it. Transgression is thus always mimetic. As is, as a result, communication or the participation that is the fruit of transgression.

Ultimately, everything happens as if the spiritualization or dialecticization of sacrifice could proceed only by way of a tremendous act of self-denial. It denies itself under the figure of an "early" sacrifice, one that it claims to know but actually constructs for its own ends and itself ratifies in the form of an infinite process of negativity, which it passes off under the "sacred" or "sacralizing" label "sacrifice." In this way, however, the sacrificial destruction that it makes such a show of abandoning to "early" sacrifice is installed at the heart of the process. At its center, this double operation simultaneously combines, in an onerous ambiguity, the infinite efficacy of dialectical negativity and the bloody heart of sacrifice.

To broach this denial or this manipulation is to touch on this simultaneity; it is to be obliged to wonder whether dialectical negativity washes away the blood, or whether blood must, on the contrary, inevitably hemorrhage from it. In order to prevent the dialectical process from remaining a comedy, Bataille wants the blood to flow. He wants to weigh up the horribly lacerated corpse and the gaze—distraught or ecstatic?—of a tortured young Chinese. But in so doing, Bataille brings to completion the logic of the sublation of sacrifice, a logic that would tear sacrifice away from its repetitive and mimetic character *because of its inability to know what repetition and mimesis* (or *methexis*), and hence sacrifice, *really are.*[31] Even this logic, which is presented simultaneously as the rupture *and* as the mimetic repetition of sacrifice, would, in this very movement, be the sublation and truth of sacrifice. Hence we would have to assume that the tortured man sublates, in ecstasy, the horror that tears him apart. But how are we to assume this if the eye that watches, and not the eye that is here being watched, does not know what it sees, nor even if it sees? How are we to assume this without the subject of this gaze having already appropriated the dialectic of the distraught and the ecstatic? How are we to assume it, then, without letting fascination form itself into the dialectical mastery and knowledge of sacrifice?

This is why, in the final analysis, this perhaps inevitable fascination cannot be tolerated. This isn't a matter of sensitivity or squeamishness. Rather, it is perhaps a matter of knowing what *sensibility* means or, more accurately, of knowing whether sensibility can have good grounds for wanting to be sublimated in sovereign fashion into what devastates it. It is a matter of knowing whether horror should simply be left, so to speak, as horror, something that suggests that transgressive appropriation (that of the death of the subject and of the subject of death) is no more than an inept delusion.

Bataille concludes somewhat abruptly: "It is time to acknowledge that nostalgia for the sacred necessarily comes to nothing, it is misleading: what the contemporary world is lacking is the offer of temptation.—Or it lacks the offer of temptations so heinous that they are useful only in so far as they deceive those whom they tempt."[32] The ambiguity is not entirely assuaged in these lines, whose syntax works to keep it alive: on the one hand, the contemporary world "is lacking" truly sacred "temptations," given immediately and without recourse to nostalgia; on the other hand, however, this world is *itself* "lacking," this time in the sense that it is at fault, its temptations illusory. The fact remains, therefore, that sacrifice, or something about sacrifice, is always lacking.

Out of all of this, I want to hold onto the following yawning ambiguity: if the inanity of sacrifice is recognized by the West, itself the inventor of this very sacrifice, it is perhaps only ever recognized in terms of the idea of a sacrifice *of* this sacrifice. In this way, however, the dialectic continually renews itself. Bataille knew this, and utterly despaired in the face of such knowledge.

V

Bataille knew that sacrifice is irredeemably and comprehensively lacking. He knew that it is lacking as the practice of a vanished world. He knew that it is also lacking insofar as there is no comprehensible continuity between that world and our own (in other words, he knew that there is basically no convincing reason for the disappearance of ancient rites, any more than there is for the appearance of the West). Thirdly, he knew that it is lacking insofar as it seemed to him that, for us, the sacrificial demand was simultaneously upheld and impossible to satisfy. At its limit, therefore, Bataille's thinking is perhaps less a thinking of sacrifice than a thinking ruthlessly drawn or torn by the impossibility of renouncing sacrifice. On the one hand, indeed, spiritual sacrifice renews the comedy that he exposes in its supposed history; on the other, the noncomedy of bloody horror is intolerable to the *spirit* of Western sacrifice . . .

Here, too, Bataille will have gone only so far, finding in literature, or in art in general, an answer to this lack. (Contemporaneously, Heidegger was speaking, apropos the idea of art, of the putting [in]to [the] work of truth, naming "essential sacrifice" as one of the ways in which this putting [in]to [the] work happens within art; yet in the same essay, he found it necessary to include "offerings and sacrifice" in the heart of beings open to the clearing of being.[33] Here, though, I can't deal any further with these suggestions.)

A link between sacrifice and art, and no doubt literature in particular, unarguably runs throughout—or doubles—the Western process of the spiritualization of sacrifice. Book 5 of Augustine's *Confessions*, for example, begins: "Accept the sacrifice of my confessions, presented by the hand of my tongue, which you formed and exhorted to confess your name"—and, in so doing, paves the way for everything in our literature that concerns "confession." But is there finally any real distinction between "confession," literature, and art in general? Isn't the transgressive presentation of a subject, who thereby appropriates himself and allows himself to be appropriated, a dominant theme of art? The Kantian sublime unfolds in a "sacrifice" of the imagination that "sinks back into itself but consequently comes to feel a liking that amounts to an emotion."[34] The entire program of poetry is given in this note by Novalis to *Heinrich von Ofterdingen*: "Dissolution of a poet in his song—he shall be sacrificed among savage peoples."[35] And, moving quickly over this in order to come back to Bataille, who writes: "Poetry . . . is . . . the sacrifice in which words are the victims. . . . We cannot . . . do without the efficacious relations that words introduce between men and things. But we tear them from these relations in a delirium."[36]

More precisely, art supplements, takes over, or sublates the impasse of sacrifice. This impasse stems from the following alternative: "If the subject is not truly destroyed, everything remains in ambiguity. And if it is destroyed, the ambiguity is resolved, but resolved in the void where everything is eliminated."[37] The alternative, then, is that between simulacrum and nothingness, which is also to say that between the representation of early sacrifice and the postulation of self-sacrifice. "But," Bataille continues, "it is precisely this double impasse that results in the meaning of the moment of art, which offers man an uninterrupted rapture by throwing us upon the path of a total extinction, and leaving us temporarily suspended there."[38] This "uninterrupted rapture" is still a dialectical formula. There is rapture to the extent that art keeps us "suspended" on the verge of extinction—a way of recognizing a new form of simulacrum. But it is "uninterrupted" because it brings with it the intense restlessness of emotion that approaches extinction. This emotion is not strictly one proper to art: it is possible only in the approach to the bloody heart of extinction. Bataille writes a little further on:

"The endless festivity of works of art is there to tell us that a triumph . . . is promised to whomever leaps into the uncertainty of the instant. This is why we cannot be too interested in those moments of mass intoxication that shoot through the opacity of the world with apparently cruel flashes of lightning, in which seduction is bound up with massacre, torture, and horror."[39]

Art itself displaces the gaze once again: the "appearance" of cruelty is in fact singularly ambiguous. Simultaneously restricted to simulacra *and* holding for this cruelty alone, this horror that it brings to light and that only means something (if we still have to speak in these terms), only has any force, if it is not simulated. The article is entitled "Art, an Exercise in Cruelty." Whatever turns it takes and however short it may be, its concern is the actual *exercise* of actual cruelty, at least in terms of its emotion. And yet artistic mimesis, as mimesis and, paradoxically, *despite* its avowedly mimetic character, ought to open the way to a genuine *mathexis*, to a genuine participation in what is revealed by the horror of the emotion. Art is worthwhile, then, only if it still refers to the sacrifice that it supplements. It can only sacrifice sacrifice by continuing to sacrifice it to sacrifice. (Schelling, by contrast, writes that "pure suffering can never be an object of art.")[40]

Bataille sees the difficulty and immediately changes direction. Speaking of the sacrificial events evoked throughout the text, he writes: "This is in no way an apology for horrific events. It is not a call for their return."[41] And yet he cannot but shift position once again and slip a restriction into his refusal (and not, in this context, a denial): "But . . . in the moment of rapture, these moments . . . bear within themselves the whole truth of the emotion."[42] And further on: "The movement [of art] effortlessly places it on a par with the worst and, reciprocally, the depiction of horror reveals within it an opening to everything possible."[43] In this reciprocity—how could we miss it?—something about mimesis is annulled or, rather, mimesis reveals (and Bataille does indeed speak in terms of revelation . . .) an actual *methexis*. Through a still quite real transgression, art communes with horror, with the pleasure of a momentary appropriation of death.

As such, art either falls well short of what is asked of it: it still just—and only—mimes the spilling of blood, or it answers it all too well, suggesting the real emotion of real horror.

By dismissing the wearisome horror and pale glamor of spilt blood, by replacing it with a rapturous horror, albeit one "on a par with the worst," what we see is that, on the one hand, we no longer have any means of access to actual sacrifice but that, on the other, thought itself is still modeled on the logic of and the desire for an infinite "transappropriation." For Bataille, however (and perhaps, perhaps even undoubtedly, for the entire Western tradition), the only question is that of an inaccessible accession to a moment of disappropriation. But sacrificial thought does not stop appropriating or transappropriating this means of access. From the moment that it is placed under the sign of sacrifice, the very chasm of horror, its "opening to everything possible," is appropriated. And this because the sign of sacrifice is the sign of the repetitive and mimetic possibility of a means of access to the obscure place from which repetition and mimesis are supposed to derive. But what if there were no such place and, as a result, nothing sacrificeable?

Equally, we could say: it is by appropriating death that sacrifice conceals itself from the truth of the moment of dispropriation. For Bataille himself, what is finally at stake in sacrifice is not death: "The awakening of sensibility, the passage from the sphere of intelligible (and useful) objects to excessive intensity is the destruction of the object as such. Of course, this is not what we usually mean by death . . . ; it is, in a sense, quite the opposite: in the eyes of the butcher a horse is already dead (meat, an object)."[44] On this reckoning, it is easier to grasp the substitution of art for sacrifice. But this could only ever be at the cost of a genuine suppression of sacrifice. In fact, in this very passage Bataille inserts one of his most severe condemnations of sacrifice: "This is not what we usually mean by death (and *sacrifice is fundamentally misguided*)." As long as the sacrificial moment is maintained within art, with its emotion "on a par with the worst," such misguided zeal cannot be absent. Put differently, it should not be a matter of sacrifice and the horror of death, whether on a real or a depicted altar, leading onto itself alone and not into a "sovereign moment." Once again, if "sovereignty is NOTHING,"[45] as Bataille tired himself out saying, is there anything that could be sacrificed for it?

VI

Before putting this question to the test in more detail, I want to follow Bataille one step further. I want to follow his reflections on the Nazi camps through the most developed of his texts on this subject (about which, however, he wrote very little), "Reflections on the Executioner and the Victim," a text that deals with David Rousset's *The Days of Our Death*.[46]

This text makes no mention of the word "sacrifice." What it does do, however, is present the components of a sacrificial logic. First of all, the camps display the very thing that is at stake in sacrifice: "In a universe of suffering, of baseness and stench, we still have the *luxury* [*le* loisir] of measuring the abyss, its absence of limits and this truth that obsesses and fascinates." Yet in order to know the "depths of horror," we "must pay the price." This price, if I understand Bataille correctly, is double: it consists, first, in the conditions necessary for "a senseless experience" and thus in the very existence of the camps; second, it consists in a will that agrees to face this horror as a human possibility. This will has to be that of the victim. (Bataille finds it in the "exaltation" and "humor" present in Rousset.) To refuse it would be "a negation of humanity hardly less degrading than that of the executioner." If it isn't a matter of self-sacrifice, it at least appeals, in spite of everything, to the position of a subject. Undoubtedly, as Bataille goes on to say, "horror is evidently not truth: it is only an infinite possibility, having no limit other than death." Yet the "fascinated" approach to truth supposes that, "in some way," "abjection and pain reveal themselves fully to man." Such a possibility was given by the camps. We can see this most clearly in "the depths of horror" that "lie in the resolve of those who demand it." This resolve on the part of the executioners is a resolve that seeks "to ruin the refuge that, in the founding of civilized order, reason itself *is*." (We should recall that, for Bataille, the Jews at Auschwitz were "the incarnation of reason.") And yet civilized reason is only ever a "refuge," limited and fragile. The "rage of the torturer" that rises up against it comes from humanity alone, and not even from a special brand of humanity ("parties or races which, we might suppose, are in no way human"). No, this possibility is "*ours*." For reason to know this possibility as such is for reason to be capable of "calling itself unreservedly into question," something that secures no definitive victory, merely the higher human possibility of "*awakening*": "But what would awakening be if it shed light only upon a world of abstract possibilities? If it did not first awake to the possibility of Auschwitz, to a possibility of stench and of irreparable fury"? Within the realization of this possibility comes, then, a necessity.

For Bataille, this necessity clearly derives from the fact of the camps' existence and from the will to face up, without any moral refuge, to what they have shown. This isn't situated as an *a priori* demand. Not for a moment do I want to suggest the slightest complicity, however unconscious, on Bataille's part. No, I believe simply that we need to consider the following: the logic being pursued here is the dark reverse of a clear logic of sacrifice (so long as we can isolate such a "clarity" . . .). This logic states: only extreme horror keeps reason awake. The logic of sacrifice says: the only awakening is an awakening to horror, in which the instant of truth shines through. The two statements are a long way from being conflated. But the latter can always harbor the truth of the former. If Bataille does *not* draw the same conclusion and if the camps remain for him *beyond* sacrifice (this, at least, is what he *says*), then isn't this because the horror of sacrifice falls silently outside any sacrificial *sense*, outside any possibility of sense? Bataille can't bring himself to say this and, despite everything, preserves the possibility, broached at the very end of the text, of seeing "poetry" as a form of "awakening" (although we know now to what sacrificial return "poetry" is destined, however much it may be "on a par with the worst").

Here, sacrifice would silently fall headlong into an antithesis that is also its culmination: a revelation of horror with no accompanying means of access, no appropriation, save that of this infinite or indefinite revelation itself.

A sacrificial interpretation of the camps is thus undoubtedly possible, even necessary, but only if we're prepared to invert it into its antithesis (from Holocaust into Shoah). Such a sacrifice leads nowhere, provides no means of access. In a sense, though, it could be called a model of self-sacrifice, since the victim of the camps, reason itself, is *also* on the side of the executioner, as the analysis of the state-controlled and engineered mechanics of extermination has constantly emphasized. Bataille writes elsewhere: "The unleashing of passions that was rife in Buchenwald or Auschwitz was an unleashing governed by reason."[47] And it wouldn't be surprising were a certain rationality to culminate in self-sacrifice, if self-sacrifice—which we can now, to be sure, equate with Western sacrifice as a whole—accounts for a certain process of Reason. As Heidegger might have put it: reason appropriates the abyss of its own subjecthood.

At the same time, however, and without contradiction, the camps represent an absence of sacrifice. They bring into play an unexpected tension between sacrifice and the absence of sacrifice. And it is fairly significant that the description of the privileges of the Aryan race in *Mein Kampf* culminates in the possession of an absolute sense of sacrifice: "The Aryan does not attain his full greatness through his spiritual properties in themselves, but attains it insofar as he is ready to put all his capacities at the service of the community. In him the instinct of preservation has reached its noblest form, for he voluntarily subordinates his own self to the collective and, when it is required, he will even sacrifice it."[48] Or again: "Posterity forgets those men who only served their own interests, and celebrates those heroes who renounced their own happiness."[49] Thus the Aryan is basically one who sacrifices himself for the community, for the race; that is, one who gives his blood for the greater Aryan Blood. He is thus not merely one who sacrifices himself but is, in essence, sacrifice *itself, sacrifice as such.* Of course, there's nothing to be sacrificed here; he has only to eliminate what is not himself, what is not living sacrifice.

Immediately after this description of the Aryan race comes the description of another race, one dominated by the instinct of preservation: "In the Jewish people, the will to sacrifice does not go beyond the pure and simple instinct of individual preservation."[50] So there is a double reason why the Jew is not sacrificed, and why he ought not to be sacrificed: on the one hand, nothing from him should be appropriated, the only requirement being the defensive and hygenic one of ridding oneself of his vermin; on the other, sacrifice is fully present, invested and completed with the Aryan race as such. It is the Aryan who, by exterminating the Jew, sacrifices himself to a severe duty.

We had the moral right, we had the duty towards our people to annihilate this people who wanted to annihilate us. . . . We can say that we have fulfilled the most difficult duty out of love for our people. . . . You have to know what it is like to see one hundred bodies side by side, or even five hundred or one thousand. To have kept control and, at the same time . . . to have remained decent, that is what has hardened us. This is a glorious page of our history, never written and never to be written.[51]

This was how Himmler presented this sacrifice of duty to his Gruppenführer in 1943: the sacrifice that not only defies human strength but even sacrifices any memorial to the glorious sacrifice that it is. In this way, Himmler simultaneously declares that, on the side of the victims, it is a matter of what is intolerable, while on the side of the executioners, it is a matter of the most silent, inner sacrifice.

True, Himmler doesn't use the word "sacrifice." Indeed, that would honor the victims far too much, would allow them to claim too great a part in this account of the executioners' glory, something that must be refused them. At precisely this point, it seems to me, sacrifice itself disappears. Moreover, it's not as if the camps can be described in terms of rites (or, if they can, that is only by way of certain misdirected, perverted aspects of such rites). Bataille notes that "the rite has the virtue of fixing 'sensory attention' on the burning moment of passage: for sensibility, either what is already is no longer, or what is no longer is more than what was. This is the cost by which the victim escapes debasement, by which the victim is deified."[52] Without rites, all that's left is debasement.

Hence it is the S.S. man or the Aryan who draws or absorbs into himself the power and fruit of the sacrifice, of its secret; he is already, in his very being, the sacrificial secret itself. Confronted by him, we are left with naked horror alone, a parody of immolation and of fumes rising toward the sky, a parody that no longer has even the right to this name. With sacrifice even the possibility of examining the simulacrum vanishes. The Aryan presents devastation, night and fog: yet *Nacht und Nebel* is just as easily the disastrous secret of his own appropriation, of the regeneration of his Blood. This is no longer Western sacrifice, but the eclipse of it [*c'est ne plus le sacrifice occidental, c'est l'occident du sacrifice*]. A second rupture takes place, and this time it is the rupture of sacrifice itself. Or, rather, it is its brutal interruption: in place of immolation there is no more immolation.

In 1945, while in exile, Hermann Broch published *The Death of Virgil*. In the part entitled "Fire—Descent," in which Virgil undergoes the temptation to sacrifice the *Aeneid*, Broch offers a picture of this decline of sacrifice. It is no longer an art fascinated by horror, but an art that knows it must now wrench itself from fascination:

On every side the cities of the globe were burning in a landscape devoid of scenery, their walls crumbled, their flag-stones cracked and burst asunder, the fumes of decay on the fields reeking of blood; and the godless-godseeking lust of sacrifice raged everywhere, sham-oblation after sham-oblation was heaped up in a frenzy of sacrifice, men mad with sacrifice raged all about, slaying the next in turn in order to shift their trance onto him, razing their neighbour's house and setting it in flames in order to lure the god into their own; they stormed about in evil vehemence and evil rejoicing—immolation, slaughter, brand, demolition.[53]

VII

" . . . immolation, slaughter . . . " We can no longer distinguish between them. Immolation has itself been put to death. "Godless," "sham"
sacrifice has forfeited all right and all dignity. Transgression transappropri-
ates nothing. Or, rather, appropriating nothing more than the this: the victim as cadaver, the expanse of the mass grave, and the other (for whom the
name of "executioner" is hardly fitting) as a pure instrument in the mass
production of the mass grave. As such, the decomposition of sacrifice not
only proves to be entirely possible thanks to technological means, but also
declares itself an exemplary, hideously exemplary, figure of technology.[54]

This doesn't necessarily involve a condemnation of that "technology." Quite the opposite. What is *hideously* exemplary here (that is, if I can
put it this way, hideous in exemplary fashion) is that "technology" is presented as the operation of a kind of sacrifice, or of the last secret of sacrifice, even though sacrifice decomposed within it. Rather, then, the question that needs to be raised is this: Shouldn't the age of technology be
understood as the age of the end of sacrifice? Shouldn't it be understood as
the age of the end of transappropriation? Or, to put it another way, as the
age of a completely different mode of appropriation: no longer the mode
of sacrificial transappropriation, but that of what Heidegger himself tried
to think as *Ereignis*? Stretching this interpretation somewhat, and without
being able to analyze or justify it here, I will say that "technology" *is Ereignis*, that is, the appropriating event of finite existence as such. In a sense,
then, rather than appealing to an "essence" of technology, wouldn't it be
more appropriate to think about technology itself in a way that, by turning every possible mode of appropriation back on itself and on its own
"one dimensionality" (if, for a moment, I might venture this term in a
nonreductive sense), it opens up once more the question of finite existence
as such and the question of its equally finite appropriation. (Here, though,
we would need to engage with Heidegger in a very intense way.)[55] Granted,
the technology of the camps is one of technology's possibilities, but it is its
sacrificial possibility. Inversely, the immolation that took place in the
camps is certainly one of the possibilities of sacrifice, but it is its technological possibility, one that contradicts sacrifice. Why? Because the Aryan
is sacrifice, and, rather than using technology for sacrifice, he uses it to exterminate the nonsacrificial. This is why the camps present not just horror,
but a lie. They are a sham—a fact borne out, moreover, by the coded vo-

cabulary of their administration, beginning with the expression "final so-lution." (Heidegger, it seems, had no idea about this particular lie. On the contrary, his references to technology, to the "sending" of being, to "danger,"[56] seem to make his subsequent shameful silence about the camps almost inevitable: a silence, perhaps, about a "sacrifice" that—like Bataille?—he believed should be thought, without ever daring to name it as such.)

Sacrificial transappropriation is the appropriation of the Subject who penetrates into negativity, who keeps himself there, enduring his own dis-memberment, and who returns sovereign. (Indeed, this negativity might still be playing the same, subtle role when Bataille calls it "unemployable negativity.") Fascination with sacrifice expresses the desire for this transfig-uration. Perhaps this is what Lacan means when, talking about the camps, he says that "sacrifice signifies that we try to find evidence of the presence of the desire of this Other, whom I have called the *obscure God*, in the ob-ject of our desires."[57] An obscure other desire consecrates my own desire as *its*, thus constituting me as the absolute propriety of the Self and its limit-less self-presence. This demands sacrifice, the production of the object as reject, even if the object is the subject proper—which actually transappro-priates it.

If sovereignty is nothing, though, if "the obscure God" is nothing more than the very obscurity of desire faced with its own truth, if existence simply aligns itself with its own finitude, then we need to think it at a dis-tance from sacrifice.

On the one hand, we need to acknowledge once and for all what has been at stake since the beginning of the Western sublation of sacrifice: we know precisely nothing about early sacrifice. We need to admit that what we think of as a mercantile exchange ("Here is the butter . . .") gave support and meaning to countless individual and collective existences; equally, we need to admit that we have no way of knowing what underlay this gesture (all we can do is guess, very vaguely, that this exchange itself went beyond exchange, and that *mimesis* and *methexis* here have nothing to do with what our representations of them actually show; perhaps the simulacrum here doesn't actually simulate; perhaps participation here doesn't actually achieve anything in the way of communion). Still, we know that it's absolutely im-possible for us to say, "Here are lives, where are the others?"

From this it follows that we need to concede once and for all that the economy of Western sacrifice is finished, that it ends in the decomposition of the sacrificial operation itself, this bloody transgression that overcame and infinitely appropriated the "moment of the finite."

On the other hand, though, finitude isn't a "moment" in a process or an economy. Finite existence doesn't have to give rise to its meaning with a burst that destroys its finitude. It's not just that it *doesn't* have to do it but, in a sense, it simply *can't* do it; thought rigorously and in accordance with its *Ereignis*, "finitude" means that existence can't be sacrificed.

It can't be sacrificed because it's already, not sacrificed, but offered to the world. There is some resemblance between the two, of course; so much so, perhaps, that we'd hardly notice the difference. Yet nothing is more different.

We might say: existence, in essence, is sacrificed. This would be to repeat one form of the basic expression of Western sacrifice. To it, though, we'd have to add another form, the *pinnacle* of our morals, which necessarily follows from it: existence, in its essence, is sacrifice.

To say that existence is offered is, it's true, to employ a word from the vocabulary of sacrifice (if we were speaking in German, it would actually be the same word: *Opfer*, *Aufopferung*). But this is simply in order to try to underline the fact that if we have to say that existence is sacrificed, it is sacrificed *by* no one and *to* nothing. "Existence is offered" means the finitude of existence. Finitude isn't a negativity cut out of being and, through this incision, offering a means of access to the restored integrity of being or sovereignty. Finitude expresses what Bataille means when he says that sovereignty is NOTHING. Finitude corresponds simply to the matrix-formula of the thought of existence, the thought of the finitude of being or even the thought of the sense of being as finitude of sense. And this formula? "The 'essence' of Dasein lies in its existence."[58] "Dasein" is a being, a being that exists [*l'existant*]. If its essence (in quotation marks) lies in its existence, this is because a being that exists has no essence. It cannot be referred back to the transappropriation of an essence. Rather, it is offered or presented to the existence that it is.

A being that exists exposes the being of its essence devoid of all essence and, as a consequence, devoid of all "being": the being that *is* not.[59] This negativity, however, doesn't operate dialectically so as to allow this being to be or, finally, to allow it to be a transappropriated Self. On the contrary, this negation confirms "inappropriation" as its most appropriate mode of appropriation, as, in fact, the only mode of all appropriation. Equally, the negative mode of this utterance—"being is not"—doesn't bring a negation into play, but an ontological affirmation. This is what *Ereignis* means (and, in a different context, it is also what "freedom" means[60]).

A being that exists happens. It takes place. And this happening or this taking place is merely a being-thrown into the world. In this throw it is offered. And yet, it is not offered by anyone or to anyone. Nor is it self-sacrificed, since nothing, no being, no subject, precedes its being-thrown. In fact, *it isn't even offered or sacrificed to a Nothingness, to a Nothing or to an Other, in whose abyss it could still impossibly enjoy its own impossibility of being.* And it's on precisely this point that Bataille and Heidegger need to be relentlessly corrected. Corrected: that is to say, led even further away from the slightest drift to sacrifice. This drift toward or through sacrifice is always connected to the fascination with an ecstasy turned toward an absolute Other or toward an absolute Outside, into which the subject is emptied the better to be restored. In this way, the subject is promised, through some mimesis and through some "sublation" of *mimesis, methexis* with the Outside or the Other . . . Western sacrifice corresponds to an obsessive fear of the "Outside" of finitude, however obscure and groundless this "outside" may be. "Fascination" already indicates something of this obscure desire to commune with this outside.

Western sacrifice seems to reveal the secret of *mimesis* as the secret of an infinite, trans-appropriating *methexis* (the Subject's participation in its own subjectivity, so to speak). *This is the appropriation of an Outside that, by being appropriated, abolishes the very idea of a "methexis," and of a "mimesis."* Ultimately, no secret is actually revealed. Or, rather, all that's revealed is the fact that there is nothing *but* this secret: the infinite sacrificial secret.

Yet the exact opposite of this revelation without revelation, an opposition that lies at the very limit of the disintegration of sacrifice, might be that there is no "outside." The event of existence, the fact that there is, means that there is *nothing else*. There is no "obscure God." There is no obscurity that could be God. In this sense, since there is no longer any clear divine epiphany, what "technology" presents to us might well simply be, if I can put it this way, clarity without God. This clarity, though, is the clarity of an open space in which an open eye can no longer be fascinated. Fascination is already proof that something has been granted to obscurity and to its bloody heart. And yet there is nothing that can be granted, nothing but "nothing." "Nothing" isn't an abyss open onto an outside. "Nothing" affirms finitude and this "nothing" immediately leads existence back to itself and to nothing else. It de-subjectifies it, removing from it any possibility of its being appropriated by anything other than its own event, its advent. This sense of existence, its sense proper, is unsacrificeable.

In a way, it's true, there is no horizon; that is, there is no limit to transgress. In another way, though, horizon is all there is. On the horizon something is constantly rising and setting. And yet this is neither the rise nor the fall, the orient nor the occident of sacrifice. It is, so to speak, "horizonality" itself. Or, rather, finitude. Or, better still, it is the fact that sense needs to be made of the infinite absence of appropriable sense. Again, "technology" might well constitute just such a horizon (so long as "technology" is understood as the regime of finitude and its "unworking"). That is, and there's no getting away from it, the closure of an immanence. This immanence, however, would neither lose nor lack transcendence. In other words, it would not be sacrifice in any sense of the word. What we used to call "transcendence" would signify instead that appropriation *is immanent.* Such "immanence," however, is not a vague coagulation; it is nothing more than its own horizon. The horizon holds existence at a distance from itself, in the separation or the "between" that constitutes it: *between* life and death . . . We don't enter into this between, which is also the stage of *mimesis* and *methexis.* Not because it would be an abyss, an altar, or an impenetrable heart, but because it is nothing other than the limit of finitude. And this limit, if we're not going to confuse it with a "finiteness," Hegelian, for example, is a limit that leaps over nothing. Existence alone leaps, leaping over itself.

Is it simply a matter of shaking ourselves out of a mediocre and limited life? The suspicion that such is the case can only have come from a mediocre and limited life. And it's this very life that can suddenly be carried away, fascinated by sacrifice. It's not a matter of denying misery or death. Still less is it a matter, were this possible, of throwing ourselves into something for the sake of some transappropriation. No, it is a matter of a misery that no longer sacrifices and that we no longer sacrifice. This misery, though, is certainly a real one, perhaps the most real of all. It does not rule out joy (or pleasure), nor is it the dialectical or sublimating threshold that leads to it. There is no threshold, any more than there is any sublime or bloody gesture for crossing it.

After all, Western sacrifice has almost always known—and has almost always been prepared to say—that it was sacrificing to nothing. This is why it has always tended to say that true sacrifice was sacrifice no longer.

In the future, though, it will fall to us to say that there is no "true" sacrifice, that real existence is unsacrificeable, that the truth of existence is to *be* unsacrificeable.

Existence isn't to be sacrificed, and can't be sacrificed. It can only be destroyed or shared. This is the unsacrificeable and finite existence that is offered up to be shared: *methexis* is henceforth offered as the sharing out of the very thing that it shares: both the limit of finitude *and* respect for the unsacrificeable. The effacement of sacrifice, the effacement of communion, the effacement of the West: this doesn't mean that the West could be reduced to what came before it, or that Western sacrifice could be reduced to the rites that it was supposed to have spiritualized. Rather, it means that we are on the verge of another community, another *methexis*, one in which the *mimesis* of sharing would efface the sacrificial mimicry of an appropriation of the Other.[61]

Translated by Richard Stamp and Simon Sparks

The Indestructible

Destruction has become a fact of culture or of civilization. It has become not only, as is always the case, an action perpetrated, and not only a grand-scale operation, systematic in its object and methods (the genocides, the camps, the Armenian catastrophe, the Jewish Shoah, Hiroshima and Nagasaki, the Stalinist deportation, the shelling, napalm, defoliation, and oil fires that characterize modern warfare, the gassing of the Kurds, and so on—a litany that's both unbearable and entirely necessary), but also a "value" or the distorted reflection of a value, the index, even, of a duty, a task, or a destiny. Perhaps this history is itself in the process of touching upon its limit; at the very least, though, we'd need to say that destruction has ended up becoming just such an index, if not *the* index, of our culture. From cathedrals to skyscrapers, construction had been one of our great motifs—the builder's grand gesture of power and domination. Yet all construction rests upon ruins or provides shelter from the powers of ruination. "Reconstruction," a postwar motif, wasn't the renewal of something prior but simply, as the term indicates, a testimony to the onslaught of destruction. The latter began long ago; it has henceforth left a definitive mark upon the movement of the West, leaving us anxiously awaiting a motif that would oppose destruction while avoiding any return to either construction or reconstruction.

Until recently, *destroy*[1] was the name of a mode, a genre, an ethical and aesthetic demand. If the word is no longer much in fashion, the thing itself still haunts our manner of existence and thinking. It is important, however, to recall how a comparable demand, though made in a different tone, could be heard as early as 1909, when Marinetti wrote, in the "Futurist Manifesto": "We will glorify war—the world's only hygiene—militarism, patriotism, the destructive gesture of the freedom-bringers, beautiful ideas worth dying for, and scorn for women. . . . We will destroy the museums, libraries, academies of every kind."[2]

We would need to go back to the ambivalence of the romanticism of *ruins*, or back to Nietzsche ("We must be destroyers!"), to Mallarmé ("Destruction was my Beatrice"), to move from these to Freud's *Destruktionstrieb* or to the Nietzschean echoes in Benjamin's "destructive character." It goes without saying, perhaps, that these figures are all quite different—if not actually opposed. Yet the fact remains that a major theme of necessary or desirable destruction runs through the thinking and the action of our modern age.

There is a sense in which this destruction, despite having caused millions of deaths, has taken the place of death. Death as such, even the death inflicted by the assassin, can only destroy because, in the same instant—and only for this instant—it affirms the identity or the singularity that it permanently erases. The two events go hand in hand, this affirmation and this death, even if there's no mediation between them.

Yet destruction has a far more remote origin and a far more remote destination. Destruction doesn't always attack a life; sometimes we destroy more by allowing what we would destroy to stay alive. (And it should be said that this is, for example, a problem that lies at the heart of the repudiation of the death penalty—which isn't to say that this repudiation needs to be challenged, since the death penalty has also become a sign of destruction.)

Destruction, as the term itself implies, attacks what is "constructed" (or "instructed"). It defeats, breaks, devastates, pillages, and renders an edifice, a composition, a structure unrecognizable, unidentifiable. It uproots or dissolves what binds, joins, and gives rise to the whole. Destruction attacks the bond and the joint as such. (In Greek, we could say that it attacks the *system*. Which raises the question: Has destruction been the result of our various systems?)

Destruction attacks *sense* rather than life. Destruction is hatred of or despair at sense; or, what amounts to much the same thing, it abandons the relentless demand for a single sense, the demand for a single and sovereign sense—the demand, that is, for the single *self* in place of sense.

And yet how could there ever be a sense that wasn't single and sovereign? It's the inability either to avoid or to respond to this question that leads to destruction *as* sense: sense busy dismantling sense.

Doubtless the destructive assault first targets the sense of the other or the other of sense. But it also strikes the sense of the proper. Dismantling an other sense isn't possible without dislocating sense in general. The principle of destruction would harbor a general renunciation of sense, therefore, including the very sense of the act that we name thus: destroy. Again: this act is the final flare of sense extinguishing itself—its final scorched imprint. (Death would be something quite different, a flare of sense that eternalizes itself.)

To destroy would be not to support sense or to despair of it. Once we're left with broken structures, dislocated joints, displaced pieces, there is no longer any sense. There is no longer any worry over sense.

Cultures other than the modern one have all been familiar with intentional destruction. They have always known what it was to raze a village, to exterminate a tribe: to remove them from the various crucibles of sense, from the points at which a sense is either emitted or concentrated.

Successful destruction has always tended to efface even the memory of the existence that has been destroyed, and even the possibility of posterity (salt on the ruins of Carthage), offering only the assurance that this—or that, this one here, that one there—never existed and would never exist. Destruction strives not simply to annihilate a being, but to shatter the very structure that renders it possible, reaching into its origin and its end, tearing from it its very birth and death.

And yet the culture of destruction, driven by a will in pursuit of a single and unalterable sense, releases an infinite sense or a nonsensical infinity. A plan for the world, for humanity, for history, the horizon of economy and right, the generalized and circular contract-form: a hateful and desperate contempt for sense in general. Dostoyevsky's "anything goes." When *anything* goes, it is destruction, first and foremost, exclusively, even, that goes—including self-destruction.

The desire to destroy resents connection, interplay, assembly and its complexity: it resents the fold (it resents not the completed structure, but that which structures; not the assembled, but its assembly; not the folded, but the fold). And in order to destroy, we fold to the extreme, we squeeze, we break. The infant destroys because there's no question of considering or exploring the assembly of the object, of the machine. The infantile man destroys because he can't tolerate the obstacle of complexity, the subtlety of the mechanism, the detours, the delays of the process. Equally, though, he can't support the simplicity or the delicacy of the various points of contact, the spacings of interplay. As such, the culture of destruction is a culture that renders itself and other cultures opaque, dissembling the arrangement of their systems or of their sense. A culture of the opacity of sense.

Which is also to say, culture of an excessive *demand* for sense.

Excessive *because* it makes demands.

What is it that opposes destruction? Pity and compassion (Rousseau).

(Here, we'd need patiently to analyze the gesture by which Rousseau, in the Preface to the *Confessions*, pleads with us to refrain from destroying the portrait that he's painting: "I beg you, in the name of compassion and the whole human race, not to annihilate a useful and singular work.")

But neither pity nor the supposed communion with the other nor the projection of the self onto the other leave the horizon of the *self*. We need to understand this differently, as a compassion that places the self outside itself. The gap may be infinitely narrow, but it is so infinitely.

Love looks more like pity than it does destruction. Or perhaps it looks as much like one as it does the other. But this is why love is always both invoked as the principle of the social bond *and* pushed back to its periphery, to the uncertainty of its outer fringes. Love neither opposes nor supports destruction. It is merely the name of the problem, of our problem.

But what if there were a *curiosity* for the other and for the other in "itself"? Not a curiosity about the surface but a curiosity about the origin, about existing for the sake of existing? A curiosity without pathos, therefore; not a cold interest, but not a sentimental one, either. What if the other as such were simply *interesting*?

Not to destroy the other involves more and is more difficult than respect or even love for the other. It involves being sensitive to the necessary secret, to the elusiveness of the sense of both the other and oneself. It involves being sensitive to play without childishness; it involves being sensitive to separation.

We can be certain that what we destroy will no longer escape, will no longer conceal itself, will no longer make strange signals from afar. What we destroy we have in our hands, then in our fist, then under our feet— and then nowhere. What we don't destroy subsists *somewhere*. This is the discrete grandeur of tombs; they are not monuments but distinct places, and that is why they stand in stark contrast to the "mass grave."

The destroyer wants to suppress this "somewhere," this plurality of places. The destroyer dislikes places—the interplay of presences, their sense. The space of destruction is a dislocated space, a space without place, undifferentiated, deserted, chaotic. In the same way, the time of destruction is an annulled time, stretched out and empty: instead of the future, what might have been is petrified, made present as stillborn.

Put differently, the space-time of destruction would be the very opposite of the tomb; it would be the stomach in which flesh, having been devoured, digests itself. In this instance, the mass grave would become the body, the reopening of a sense. Cannibalism—which has occupied our religions, Dionysian and Christian figures, for so long—would be the structuring destruction. Whether the destruction is of the heart or the stomach of the structure, this doubtless gives us one of the most emphatic motifs for our culture: under the guise of mystery, this is actually the incarnation; under the guise of melancholy, incorporation; under the guise of finite knowing, the madness of systems or structures.

If it's true that we have produced a culture of destruction, we need to try to understand why. Clearly it's not enough to evoke the "evil" in man or his destructive "instinct." Rather, we need to consider the possibility that our culture has seized upon evil as an intrinsic possibility—neither accidental nor secondary—of being itself, or that culture has pointed out a "destructive drive," originally involved in the drive toward life and propagation, the two as one (moving toward two forms of perpetuation—but not toward *existence*).

So our culture shelters within itself the possibility of destruction. Regardless of whether this means that this culture should itself be destroyed, this is precisely what it undertakes to do. We can date—from the conquest of the Americas—the moment when the West, by revealing a new aptitude for destruction (unrelated, in this sense, to the conquests of the Romans, barbarians, Arabs, and Turks, or to the Crusades), initiated its own self-destruction. Millions of Native Americans were destroyed, along with their cultures; so, too, were thousands of Europeans, destroying themselves in the rage for conquest and gold as their culture began to gnaw away at itself with doubts concerning its validity, its "Catholicism," its very "humanity," even. It was a long time before this culminated in the self-destruction of

Europe in a "total" war whose very invention astounded itself. But, finally, we are here; and this is history, the very construction of our history.

And we've caused this thing to spread to the globalizing rhythm of a technology variously employed by war, by the control of war, by the destruction of places and of histories, by the control of this destruction—always more than destruction, always more than control, a control that, destructive in its turn, spirals, indeterminate, out of control.

Self-destruction: the mark of a culture in which suicide holds a distinguished place, from Socrates to Werther, to Stefan Zweig, to Primo Levi, to so many others. I'm not talking here about Japanese suicide nor even Stoic suicide, in which we run up against an objective limit that cuts us short. Rather, it is a matter of a fundamentally *destructive* suicide that attacks the *self,* the *proper* as structure and as interplay, an assault on the very pulse of existence.

Self-destruction indicates the stakes here: the *self,* the system that articulates itself *from within* culture. This culture is the culture of the self, of its appropriation, its concentration-in-itself. And insofar as it involves the self or the ego, it discovers the principle of evil. There's surely no Western interpretation of evil that doesn't end up imputing the ego or the egological as such (including its earliest projection into a Lucifer). No more, however, is there any interpretation of the "good" that doesn't situate it in the appropriation of the self—in the autonomy and self-foundation of the free subject, for example. The ego is both structure (the appropriation of the self) and destruction (the concentration in the self), just as it is both the singular and Narcissus, or the partner and the monad.

Everything happens as if destruction were inscribed upon the structure—as its joints *and* its fissures—precisely to the extent that the structure programs what cannot take place: the infinite appropriation of the self by itself. The certainty of the *cogito* is, as we know, constitutionally blind. Kant's "transcendental I" is an empty point. The ego of psychoanalysis suffers from a structural lack (or is *the* structural lack) of the self, a line of filiation that leads back to Oedipus's gouged eyes. And filiation itself, the dominance of the theme of filiation, indicates the blind process of an ego that pursues itself from generation to generation.

This is why the ego qualifies itself essentially as *desire,* desire itself being understood as submission to the law of lack (rather than to the law of a departure from the self). The ego is posed as the frustration or, rather, the entropy of the ego itself.

The horizon of destruction: the suppression of exteriority more than the suppression of time or space, more than the suppression of the body or of everything contained within it; the absolute concentration in itself, as much in the destroyer as in the destroyed. The *sovereignty* of the destroyer: destruction reduces the other to a null and void concentration in itself, but also testifies to the destroyer's own concentration, to the absolute character of the destroyer's own gathering-in-itself, beyond which there is no other power or decision.

What the destroyer fails to see, however, is the connection between the two concentrations. The following propositions, as much as the preceding ones, are true: the self's own sovereignty is null, and the annihilation of the other reveals in this other an unattainable sovereignty. Because absolute presence-to-self is without space and time, it is, in its detachment and entrenchment, its own cancellation.

It isn't a "strong me" that destroys; it is a me that lacks a self.

As such, it constitutes itself as the subject of technology, that is, of an operation of infinite mastery in which infinity takes the place of sovereignty. Technology has made possible the modern apocalypse—the modern revelation—of destruction. Not, however, as tends to be thought, because it has furnished the means for this. On the contrary, it has furnished the *end*, doing so under the auspices of the in(de)finite appropriation that characterizes technology (characterizes what is without work, what exceeds work [*le sans-œuvre, l'au-delà de l'œuvre*]). By itself, technology provides no end; on the contrary, it is the resolute infinitization, the incessant displacement of ends. At the same time, however, it is in the infinite displacement of the end that the Western subject has ended up recognizing itself and wanting to appropriate itself. Our problem is not technology but the desubjectivization of technology.

Technology isn't destructive, since what is un-working isn't devastation. Yet destruction is technology; that is, it is endless, like the appropriation of which it functions as inversion or despair (Schelling's "inverted God"). It is endless because it is normalized by the absolute End, the endless Finitization, the null point of the Ego in its imploded identification.

As for technology, it is endless because it is infinitely *finite*. Across all its works, its un-working isn't regulated by any particular End. Or, somewhat better (and I am indebted to Philippe Lacoue-Labarthe on this point), it has from this point on the singular figure of a finitization—itself infinite, unfinishable—of destruction: the figure of nuclear menace/deterrent. (It wasn't a coincidence that nuclear weapons were—in fact or as a pretext—at the heart of the Gulf War; destruction presented in such a way as to maintain control over final destruction. The same sort of control is at work in the transformation of the ex–Soviet Union and in a certain segment of North-South relations—which have thus become simply North-North relations more than anything else.)

So infinite nuclear finitization finishes—or completely finishes off—humanity, indeed, all living things; it is, if you like, the destruction of destruction. No doubt it'll be neither of these things. But the alternative indicates the magnitude of the stakes. In terms of the ego, the two things are identical: there is no longer anyone—or, more accurately, there are no longer any distinct *ones*—who is confronted, but a mass or an idyllic vision.

In each case, something indestructible is left behind: destruction itself or the world. Ultimately, though, it is the world that is left, because destruction takes place in the world and not vice versa. (That in which or that through which the world takes place is neither nothing nor destruction nor construction.) The world, then—at least if it makes any sense to think of a "world" without a subject.

Yet this regulating fiction touches on the very limit of what is at stake: the pure being of a world or of "something" in general. The pure *there is* as the indestructible, the gift that cannot be refused (since it has no one to give it), of a space without a subject to arrange it, to distribute it, to give it sense. A *there is* that would be neither *for* us nor *because* of us. Either that or the "sensible" world outside the "sense" given to it by a sentient subject: the very thing that philosophy has never been able to think, still less to touch, even though it has doubtless always been obsessed with or haunted by it.

All potential destruction runs up against this limit. We can't destroy the world any more than we can destroy what has to be called *being*: the *fact* that "there is" something, without this being either for us or because of us. Something in general, and us, too, therefore. Something that neither has its origin nor its end in man, and certainly not in the ego.

Granted, it's little comfort knowing that being is indestructible if this knowledge is only gained on the verge of our destruction, if there is no one to know it. In truth, though, we already know this, here and now. "Being" or the "there is" or "existence" is, in us, what happens before us and ahead of us, arising from the very step beyond us. It is the incommensurable that measures us. The indestructible measures each one of our destructions, their impotence. Existence resists. None of which either prevents destruction or justifies it; rather, it marks its absolute limit.

In this sense, then, existence is indestructible, sovereign. This sovereignty, however, is precisely *nothing* (indiscernible, in fact, from the fold or the interplay of the structure, from the spacing that articulates it). Or, rather, it *is* nothing; the *res*, the thing itself, is nothing, no actual thing; it is reality itself. *Destruction, then, is unreal or nonrealizing. Reality is what confronts us when we are confronted with nothing, that is, with the absence of possibilities of appropriation, of identification, of signification. Yet we are confronted by this absence insofar as it has all the stability and all the resistance of the worldly "there is,"* something that not only resists in "us" but perhaps also resists us.

The peculiar stability and resistance of all these ruined edifices, villages, peoples, and countries continually awaken our terror, our pity, our rebellion—those who are forgotten are remembered. This awakening and this oblivion, however, still indicate the destructive "nothing" of reality, the intimate exhaustion by which we are *in the world,* and the *sense* of this existence.

Again, this doesn't deliver us from destruction; it neither ends nor justifies it. On the contrary, we need to learn to stop dreaming of the end, to stop justifying it. That is to say, we need to take our leave of the historico-romantic mode of thinking that promises an apotheosis or an apocalypse—or both, one in the other—as well as the baroque mode of thinking that engendered destruction in the numerous shards of a shimmering, whirling universe. Each of these modes has its brilliant, joyous version and its somber, melancholy version. In each case, though, we try to conceal and make off with destruction, to carry it away to the point of overcoming or disaster. We don't stop with what resists us, or with what resists *that.*

The symbol and the paradigm of everything that is dedicated to destruction is the "temple." The temple is the structure that connects human places to the totality of the world by cutting the space of this union into this world. (The *templum* was originally the space carved into the sky by the soothsayer's staff.) The temple is the site of con-templation, the attentive gaze supported by this space, open to its spacing. We, we other Westerners, no longer have any temples; perhaps the time of the end of temples is upon the earth as a whole. And yet, as Plutarch writes, "the world is a temple."

Today, however, can this phrase have a sense that is neither meta-physical nor metaphoric? A sense that is *our own*? Either way, it cannot respond to what Nietzsche believed still needed to be said: "In order to build a sanctuary, a sanctuary has to be destroyed." Indeed, on the one hand, it is no longer a matter of sanctuary (the word itself has become rather passé in the vocabulary of nuclear war) and so no longer a matter of destroying something in order to make room for something else; instead, it is a matter of bringing the *templum* to the *spacing* of being. On the other hand, though, it is no longer a matter of "building," since one doesn't build a world; rather, one arrives there, dwells in it, departs from it. Instead, therefore, it would be a matter of allowing ourselves to contemplate the world, the spacing of its *there is*.

Not the restoration of a temple, therefore, but the consideration of worldly places as places of existing. Far from being a matter of restoration, this is revolution, properly speaking. And yet, insofar as revolution is taken to mean "revolutionary destruction," it's also a matter of revolution against destruction. Revolution as resistance, as the necessity and impatience of existence; revolution as having suddenly arisen, here and now, opening history, allowing places to "take place," as it were. But this isn't simply a revolution; it is permanent revolution, the possibility, at every moment, of opening space (and I'm thinking here of Michelet's remark that the open space of the *Champs de Mars* was the sole "monument" to the revolution).

The history of the West has revolved around four figures of the temple:

1. The Greek temple, the source of the nascent West's contemplation and thus what is doomed both to ruinous destruction *and* to artistic metamorphosis.

2. The Jewish temple—twice destroyed, then taken up in terms of its destruction, as the meaning of its own destruction and of the diaspora of those united by no determinate sense.

3. The Christian temple, the temple of infinite construction, the mastery of the spire and the dome, where technology contemplates itself.

4. The Islamic temple, whose heart, the black rock of Kaaba, is, far from a reserved space, an impenetrable, indestructible thing.

The sort of knowledge that we need—the sort of knowledge that we lack—is the fourfold knowledge of *art* and *technology*, of disseminated *sense* and indestructible *nothing*.

This fourfold knowledge would be a structural one—a knowledge of this entire fourfold structure and of the way in which it arranges a fourfold space: the Mediterranean, Europe, the West, the Earth, and a fourfold time: the "Pre-history" of the East, History itself, Decline, and the Present. This knowledge happens, though, as not-knowing, which is neither ignorance nor confusion, but is certainly no longer mastery. It is sovereign knowledge—that is, nothing, knowledge as existence.

"The world is a temple": in fact, the world is the only temple there is if there are no longer any temples, if structure has itself deconstructed temples. The world is the only carved space that remains. And what allows it to be contemplated as such is nothing—nothing but its existence, our existence, the fact that it is, appearing, disappearing.

None of this, though, is accessible to the ego. Indeed, it is always *from out of this* that the ego emerges in order to contemplate blindly the desert of what it has destroyed. Whoever would contemplate the world would, in truth, contemplate the effacement of the ego.

Let me echo the ancient words of a Muslim reviled for having wanted to unite, from East to West, the separate modes of contemplation: "There is, between you and I, a 'this is me' that torments me. Ah! Take away the 'this is me' that separates us!"³

These words and the voice that utters them bespeak the dimension of the world. But there is no one voice, since any such voice would no longer be singular. Nor can the ego and destruction be effaced in a communal invocation. What we need are voices that are singular, distinct, and that *do not properly understand one another*, voices that call to one another, that *provoke* one another.

Translated by James Gilbert-Walsh

PART THREE

DIFFERENCE

5

Elliptical Sense

I

For Kant, a pleasure that we no longer perceive is at the origin of thought. This is why thought is "originally impassioned," as Derrida puts it in "Ellipsis." The trace of this pleasure might be found in all philosophy. It is the pleasure of the origin itself: the satisfaction or joy of discovering the source, getting to the center or ground. More exactly: the satisfaction or joy which the origin experiences in finding and touching itself, the joy of originating from itself in itself.

This is also, properly speaking, the act of thought that Kant calls *transcendental*: reason discovering itself, making itself available as the principle of its own possibilities. We shall have more to say about the transcendental. But for the moment let us say that "Ellipsis," in writing on the origin and on writing as the "passion of the origin," adopts a transcendental standpoint. Or at least it *seems* to adopt such a standpoint.

From this position is derived the condition of possibility which is not itself the origin (and this ellipsis or eclipse of the origin in the Kantian "condition of possibility" is undoubtedly what sets off the whole of modern thought), but which forms, on the contrary, the condition of possibility of the origin itself. This is our history since Kant: the origin is no longer given—likewise, its pleasure is no longer given—but becomes instead that toward which reason regresses, or that toward which it advances, up to the very limits of its possibilities. The origin enters what Derrida will call its *différance.* The origin differs or defers, differs from itself or defers itself. And that is its joy or passion: *à corps perdu.*

The origin, or sense, if the origin is by definition the origin of sense, contains within itself (and/or differing) the sense of the origin, its own sense, itself being the very sense and site of sense. Nothing less than sense itself, "all sense," as is written in "Ellipsis." (This is the only occurrence of the word "sense" in Derrida's text. In one fell swoop, for the entire text and its ellipsis, *all sense.* The slightest text of thought can expose no less.)

The condition of possibility of the origin (of sense) is called *writing.* Writing isn't the vehicle or medium of sense; were this so, it wouldn't be its condition of possibility, but the condition of its transmission. Here, "writing" doesn't refer to Derrida's writing, which communicates to us the sense and the logic of a certain discourse on the origin, sense, and writing (at least insofar as this sense and this logic are communicable). This writing is not that of the *book* which this text concludes and closes (which is entitled *Writing and Difference*). Or rather, the writing of the origin is this writing itself, and this book itself: there is no other, there is nothing more to read once the book has been closed, there are not two writings, one empirical and one transcendental. There is a single "transcendental experience" of "writing." But this experience attests precisely to its non-self-identity. In other words, it is the experience of *what cannot* be experienced. Writing *is différance.*

Thus writing is said to be the "passion of and for the origin." This passion does not arise at the origin: it is and makes the origin itself. The origin is a passion, the passion of the self in its difference, and it is that which makes sense, *all sense.* All sense is always passion, in all the senses of the word "sense." (Hegel, building on Kant, was well aware of this: sense—the sense of being—is also the sense of sensibility. For Hegel, this was the crux and the passion of the *aesthetic* in general, and hence also of writing in its relation to philosophy, in the sense of its relation to philosophy.) What makes sense about sense, what makes it originate, is that it senses itself making sense. (To sense the sense or to touch the being-sense of sense, even if it were to be senseless—that's Derrida's passion. To touch the body of sense. To incorporate sense. Scratching, cutting, branding. Putting to the test of sense. I shall write about nothing else.) Sense isn't a matter of something *having* or *making* sense (the world, existence, or this discourse of Derrida's). It's rather the fact that sense apprehends itself, grasps itself as *sense.*

This means that sense, essentially, has to repeat itself: not by being stated or given twice in identical fashion, as is the case with the "reissuing of a book," but by opening in itself (as itself) the possibility of relating to itself in the "referral of one sign to another." It is in just such a referral that sense is recognized or grasped as sense. Sense is the duplication of the origin and the relation that is opened, in the origin, between the origin and the end, and the pleasure, for the origin, of enjoying that which it originates (that of which it is the origin and the fact that it originates).

Such is the passion, the whole passion of writing: sense, in order to be or to make sense, has to *repeat itself,* which is to say, in the original sense of this word, it must *make repeated demands on itself.* Sense is not given; it is the demand *that* it be given. (This implies a giving of the demand, but that is precisely what, in Kantian terms, ought to be termed the "transcendental" and *not,* of course, the transcendent, which would be the pure presence of sense, neither demanded nor capable of being demanded.) Sense must interrogate itself anew (though it is in this "anew" that everything begins; the origin is not the new, but the "anew"); it must make demands on itself, call to itself, ask itself, implore itself, want itself, desire itself, seduce itself as sense. Writing is nothing other than this demand, renewed and modified without end. Sense calls for more sense, just as, for Valéry, "it is the sense which calls for more form" in poetry. And, in effect, it comes down to the same thing. All poetry, and all of Derrida's philosophy, meets this demand. Consequently there is something missing in sense, something missing from the start. And "all sense is altered or exhausted by this lack." Writing is the outline of this alteration. Hence, this outline is "in essence *elliptical,*" because it does not come back full circle to the same. Ellipsis: the other in the return to the self, the geometral of the *pas* of meaning, singular and plural.

Strictly speaking, however, nothing is altered. It's not as if there's a first sense that would then be diverted and disturbed by a second writing, doomed to lament its infinite loss or painfully to await its infinite reconstitution. "All sense is altered [*tout le sens est altéré*]." Which means, first of all, that sense is thirsty [*altéré* as the opposite of *désaltéré,* "refreshed"]. It thirsts after itself and its own lack; that is its passion. (And it is also Derrida's passion for language; in the word *altéré* as he employs it here, an ellipsis of sense makes sense, the alteration and the excess of sense.) Sense thirsts after its own ellipsis, for its originary *trope,* for that which hides it, eludes it, and passes it by in silence. Ellipsis: the step/*pas* of sense passing beneath sense. What is passed over in silence, in all sense, is the sense of sense. But there is nothing negative in this, nor, in truth, anything silent. For nothing is lost, nor anything silenced. Everything is said, and, like every philosophical text (every text in general?), this text says everything about the origin, says the whole origin, and presents itself as the knowledge of the origin. ("Here" is its first word, and later on we read "we now know.") Everything is said here and now, all sense is offered on the surface of this writing. No thinking thinks more economically, and less passionately, than in thinking everything, all at once. No pleasure of thinking can enjoy in a lesser degree than absolute *enjoyment*. Thus this text pronounces itself, or the orbit that carries it, to be nothing less than a "system," *the* system in which the origin itself "is only a function and a locus."

Writing is the passion of this system. Broadly speaking, a system is the conjunction that holds articulated parts together. More strictly, in the philosophical tradition, it is the juncture, the conjoining of the organs of the living being, its life or Life itself (this life which, according to Hegel, is most profoundly characterized by *sense*, insofar as it senses and senses itself sensing). The adjoining or conjoining of writing is the "binding joint" of the book, or its life. The life of the book is played out—is "in play" and "at stake"—not in the closed book, but in the open book "between the two hands which hold the book," this book by Jabès that Derrida holds open and reads for us. Jabès, who writes nothing but a continuation of the book, and *on* the book; this book of Derrida's which he writes to us and gives us to read and to hold in the ellipse of our hands.

The *maintenant*, the now, of sense articulates itself, repeats itself and puts itself in play in the *mains tenant*, the hands holding the book. These *mains tenant* multiply the now (the *maintenant*), dividing presence, eliding it and making it plural. These are "our hands": it is no longer an *I* that is being uttered, but the uttering and articulation of a *we*. This juncture goes beyond the adjoining of a living being that reads. It prolongs and exceeds him. It is not someone living who reads, even if it is not someone dead. (And the book itself is neither alive nor dead.) What now holds or takes the book in hand is a system whose systematicity differs from and defers itself. "The *différance* in the now of writing" is itself the "system" of writing, within which the origin is inscribed merely as a "place."

Différance is nothing other than the infinite re-petition of sense, which consists neither in its duplication nor in its infinite distancing from itself. Rather, *différance* is the access of sense to sense in its own demand, an access that does not accede, this exposed finitude beyond which, now that "God is dead," there is nothing to think.

If sense were simply given, if access to it were not deferred, if sense did not demand sense (if it demanded nothing), sense would have no more sense than water within water, stone within stone, or the closed book in a book that has never been opened. But the book *is* open, in our hands. *Différance* can never be conceptualized, but it can be written. *Différance* is the demand, the call, the request, the seduction, the imprecation, the imperative, the supplication, the jubilation of writing. *Différance* is passion.

With a blow—because it is a blow, struck by the origin against the origin itself—"the joint is a *brisure* ["hinge"]." The system then really is a system, but a system of *brisure*. This is not the negation of system, but system itself, suspended at the point of its *systasis. Brisure* does not break the joint: in repetition "nothing has budged." Or else, the joint has always already been broken in itself, as such and in sum by itself. What joins divides; what adjoins *is* divided. *Brisure* is not the other of juncture, it is its heart, its essence, and its passion. It is the exact and infinitely discrete limit upon which the joint articulates itself. The book between our hands and the folding in of the book upon itself. The heart of the heart is always a beating, and the essence of essence consists in the withdrawal of its own existence.

It is this limit that passion demands, this that it craves. The limit of what, in order to be itself and to be present to itself, does not come back to itself. The circle which at once closes itself off and fails to do so: an ellipsis.

Sense which does not come back to itself is elliptical. Sense which, *as sense*, does not close off its own sense, or closes it off only by repeating and differing from itself, appealing again and again to its limit as to its essence and its truth. Returning to itself, to this passion.

To appeal to the limit is not to set out to conquer a territory. It is not to lay claim to boundaries or borders, for when borders are appropriated, there is no longer any limit. Yet to demand the limit *as such* is to demand what cannot be appropriated. It is to demand nothing, an infinite exposition which takes place at the limit, the abandonment to this space without space that is the limit itself. This space has no limits, and is thus infinite, though this does not mean that it is an infinite space, any more than that it is "finite." Rather, it is, not "finished," but the end, or finitude itself.

Thought of the origin: of the end: of the end of origin. An end that initiates a cut into the origin itself: writing.

Such is the last page of the book, the last line of the text—the other site of the ellipsis, after the *hic et nunc* of the beginning—which is what the book, the text, never stops demanding, calling for, soliciting. The ellipsis of "Ellipsis" closes itself off in *différance* and its own circularity, and in the play of a recognition which never returns. In the last line Derrida inscribes the final words of a quotation from Jabès. It is a signature, the signature on a fragment, a pronouncement that precedes it: "Reb Dérissa." All the authority, if not all the sense, of the text will have been altered by this move. It will have been the thirst or the passion for putting into play the *I*, the origin, the author, the subject of this text.

Closing of the text: quotation of the other text, ellipsis. This quotation, almost signature. The signature marks the limit of signs. It is their event, the propriety of their advent, their origin or sign of origin, or origin itself as a singular sign, which no longer signals anything, which cuts sense in two. Derrida signs and de-signates himself; his signature is repeatable. It owes its "sense" entirely to its repetition; it has no signification. Its sense *is* repetition, the demand for the singular. Derrida asks for himself, and is altered. Singularity is doubled and thirsts after itself insofar as it is the origin of the text. An exorbitant thirst, the thirst of one who has already drunk, who has drunk the entire text, the whole of writing, and whose drunkenness asks for it all over again. Derrida is a drunken rabbi.

The mastermind that ordains the system of the text bestows his own name on a double (itself unreal; the text has not neglected to remind us that Jabès's rabbis are "imaginary"). The double substitutes a double "s "—that "disseminating letter," Derrida writes later—for the "d "in the "da" of "Derrida." An elsewhere in the guise of a *here*, a fictitious being in the guise of Dasein, or existence. *Dérissa*—slim, razor-sharp, derisory—touches the limits of a name and a body "with an animal-like, quick, silent, smooth, brilliant, slippery motion, in the manner of a serpent or a fish," as the text says of a book that insinuates itself "into the dangerous hole" of the center, filling it in.

Fills it to bursting with pleasure: because it's a game, yes, it's a laugh. *Estos de risa*: this makes us laugh. Here laughter breaks out—laughter is never anything but explosive; it never closes up again—the laughter of an ellipsis opened like a mouth around its paired foci: Derrida, Dérissa. Mocking laughter. But mocks or mimics what? Nothing; merely its breaking out. The origin laughs. There is such a thing as transcendental laughter—and several times the text has evoked a certain "joy" of writing . . .

What would a transcendental laughter be? Certainly not an inversion of the significance or value ascribed to seriousness and necessarily demanded by thinking. This laughter doesn't laugh at seriousness, but laughs at the limit of the serious—of sense. It is the knowledge of a condition of possibility which doesn't tell us anything. This isn't exactly comedy: neither nonsense nor irony. This laughter doesn't laugh *at* anything. It laughs at nothing, for nothing, for a nothing. It signifies nothing, but it is not absurd. It laughs to be the explosion of its own laughter. It laughs derridaly, dérrissally. This is not to say that it isn't serious, nor that it is untouched by sorrow. Rissa, rrida: it is beyond any opposition between the serious and the nonserious, between pain and pleasure. Or rather, it is at the juncture where these oppositions meet, the limit they share, a limit that is itself no more than the limit of each of these terms, the limit of their significations, the limit at which these significations, as such, are exposed. We could say, in other words, that such a limit—*a limit of this type*, Derrida might say— where pain and pleasure share the joy [of their encounter], is the site of the sublime. I prefer to say, in a less aesthetic language, that this is the place of exposition. The origin exposes itself: to not being the origin.

There is a joy, a gaiety even, that has always been at the limit of philosophy. It is neither comedy, irony, grotesque, nor humor, though it perhaps mixes all these significations together. But it is also the ellipsis of these *comiques significatifs* ("modes of the comic as meaning," to adopt Baudelaire's phrase), evoking the "strange serenity" the text has named. In and by this serenity, knowledge relieves itself of the weight of knowing, and sense recognizes or feels itself to be the extreme lightness of a "departure from the identical" which "weighs nothing in itself," but "thinks and weighs the book as such." This play on *pensée*, what is thought, and *pesée*, what is weighed, this play inscribed in language itself, speaks thinking as measuring and as test.[1] Here the book, its juncture, is measured, put to the test.

But precisely this, this which *indeed says* something, and which says it through the meaningful game of a slippage of the *etymon*, says nothing or *means* nothing. It appropriates nothing of the *etymon*; it doesn't appropriate an originary propriety of sense. No more than the ellipsis "Derrida/Dérissa" lays claim to any kinship. Thought will not let itself be weighed, and weight will not let itself be thought, by it. If there is anything here at all, it is the lightness of laughter, this gossamer, infinite lightness which laughs *at* nothing, one must reiterate, but which is the lightening of sense. No theory of comedy or of the joke has been able to master it. Here theory laughs at itself. Derrida will always have laughed, with a laughter at once violent and light, a laughter of the origin and of writing.

In lightening itself, sense does not cast off its ballast, does not unburden or debauch itself. Sense lightens itself and laughs, *insofar as it is sense*, with all the intensity of its appeal and repeated demand for sense. Its lightening (which is not a relieving), means having its own limit as a resource and having the infinity of its own finitude *for its sense*.

This sense, this sense of "all sense," this totality of sense made up of its own alteration, this totality whose being-total consists in not allowing itself to be totalized (but in being totally exposed) is always too hastily translated into "wordplay," into an acrobatics or linguistic mischief, in sum, into meaningless surface noises. However, one would be equally wrong to seek to "sublate" these plays on and in language in the manner of Hegel, who sublates the dialectic itself in a play on the word "sublate." There is no spirit of or in language, no origin of words before words, that "living speech" could bring to presence. Things are infinitely lighter and more serious: language is alone, and this is just what the word "writing" means. It is what remains of language when it has unburdened itself of sense, confided it to the living yet silent voice from which it will never depart.

"Language is alone'" doesn't means that only this exists, as is naively and imperturbably believed by those who denounce as "philosophies imprisoned in language" all thinking which does not offer them—that is to say, which does not name for them—a ready-sliced "life" and "sense" of the "concrete." On the contrary, "language is alone" means that language is not an existence, nor is it existence. But it is its *truth*. Which is to say that if existence is the sense of being, the being of sense, then language *alone* marks it, and marks it *as its own limit*.

Existence is the "there is [*il y a*]" of something. The fact *that it is* [qu'il y a]—here is the origin and the sense, and in these words "there is" language bursts into flames, laughs, and dies away. But for the "there is" of anything whatsoever there is only language, and singularly so for the "there is" of any "there is" that transports us, delights us, fills us with anguish, for the "there is" that is "*there*, but *out there, beyond*." That is to say, the truth of being, existence, the immanence of transcendence—or finitude as what defies and deconstructs the metaphysical pairing of immanence and transcendence. This "there is" is presence itself, experience just at itself, right in our hands and as of now. But the *there* of "there is" can't be put "there" or "beyond," or anywhere else, for that matter, nor in the nearness of some inward dimension. "There" "signals" the place where there is no longer any sign, save for the repetition of the demand, from sign to sign, along all of meaning, toward the limit where existence is exposed. The *there* is infinitely light, it is juncture and *brisure*, the lightening of every system and the ellipsis of every cycle, the slender limit of writing. Here we touch on presence that is no longer present *to itself* but is repetition and supplication of a presence to come. (Derrida will say, will write, "Come!" as the imperative, imperious, yet impoverished, ellipsis of an entire ontology.) The text says: "the future is not a future present." This is because it is *to* come, to come from the *there* and in the *there*. And that is why "the beyond of the closure of the book is not something to wait for." It is "there, but over there, or beyond," and it is thus to be called for, here and now, to be summoned at the limit. The appeal, the repeated demand, the joyous supplication says: "let *everything come* here." That *everything should come here*, that all sense come and be altered, here, now, at the point at which I write, at which I fail to write, at this point where we read: the passion of writing is impassioned by nothing other than this.

II

In the "there is" of existence and in that which "comes there" to presence, being is at stake, as is the sense or meaning of being. In its two major philosophical forms, the transcendental has designated something put in reserve, a withdrawal or a retreat of being. For Aristotle, being is what keeps itself in reserve over and above the multiplicity of the categories (predicaments or transcendentals) through which it is said in "multiply." Being offers itself and holds itself back in this multiplicity. For Kant, the transcendental denotes the substitution of a knowledge of the mere conditions of possible experience for a knowledge of being that would subtend this experience. Being offers itself and holds itself back in these conditions, in a subjectivity which does not apprehend itself as substance, but which knows itself (and judges itself) as a *demand*.

When the question of the sense of being was reinscribed in philosophy, or at its limit, it was not in order to break through the transcendental, to transcend it and thus penetrate the reserve of its withdrawal. Rather it was, with Heidegger, in order to interrogate this *withdrawal* itself as the essence and as the sense of being. Being: that which is no part of all that is, but which is at stake in existence. Such is the "ontico-ontological difference." The difference between being and everything that exists is precisely that which exposes existence as the putting-at-stake of the sense or meaning of being (in and as its finitude).

In these circumstances, the opposition or complementarity between the transcendental (as the withdrawal of the origin) and the ontological (as the resource at the origin) loses all pertinence. What becomes necessary is another kind of ontology altogether, or else a completely different transcendental; or, perhaps, nothing of the sort, but an ellipsis of the two. Neither the retirement of being nor its givenness, but presence itself, being itself *qua* being, exposed as a trace or as a tracing, withdrawing presence, but retracing this withdrawal, presenting the withdrawal as what it most properly is: the nonpresentable. This propriety is nothing other than absolute propriety itself and the propriety of the absolute. The absolute as the absolute of finitude—its separateness from all gathering, from all sublation in an Infinite—gives itself in the event of the trace, the appropriation of inappropriable propriety (*Ereignis*, perhaps).

(Need I emphasize the historical, ethical, and political ramifications of this turning, of this torsion of the absolute? The question is nothing other than the question of the "sense of existence" now that God, along with the Idea, Spirit, History, and Man, is dead. And, indeed, even before this question, the whole passion of the sense of existence. From a circular sense to an elliptical sense: How can we think and live that? At this point, we should add that decisively, and despite what might be said, philosophy has not failed. Derrida, and others with him, in the anxiety and collapse of the age, will have beaten the path, a path that must always be beaten afresh, in the quest for the sense of existence.)

The thought of writing (the thought of the letter of sense, rather than of the sense of the letter: the end of hermeneutics, the opening and initiation of sense) reinscribes the question of the sense of being. Ellipsis of being and the letter. What happens with this reinscription? What happens when we discern at the origin, as "Ellipsis" does, a "being-written" and a "being-inscribed"? There is no question of giving a complete answer here. What "happens" there has not finished happening, Derrida has not finished making, transforming his own response. And undoubtedly the "response" comes in the very movement of writing, which we are bound to repeat, writing "on" him, but also writing on "us."

What we can perhaps say here, however, is this: that in the ellipsis of being and the letter, in the *différance* of the sense of being, being no longer simply withdraws into its difference from what exists, or into the gap of that difference. If the ontico-ontological difference was once taken to be *central* (but was it in Heidegger himself? and if so, to what extent?), if it ever constituted a *system* centered on the juncture of Being, and of a Being established in its own difference, it can do so no longer. Difference (of being) is itself differ*a*nt. It withdraws still further from itself, and from there still calls itself forth. It is withdrawn further than any assignation to a "difference of being" (or in a "different being," or in any Other) could ever remove it, and it is altogether yet *to come*, more so than any annunciation could say. Later, Derrida will write that "within the decisive concept of the ontico-ontological difference, *everything is not to be thought in one stroke.*"[2] More than one trait or *ductus* (to adopt a paleographic term designating each of the lines used to trace a single letter, suggested to me by Ginevra Bompiani): this means at once the multiplication and the ductility of the trait, its fracturing at its juncture and also, as the condition of these events, the effacing of the trait: less than a single trait, its dissolution in its own ductility. This signifies the *ductus* of difference, *in* difference and as the "inside" of a difference that has no interiority (it *is* the withdrawal of the inheritance of being to what exists). An inside which *arrives to* the outside.

The sense of the ontico-ontological difference lies not in its *being* this difference, nor in its being *such and such*, but in the fact that it is to come, to arrive, *an sich ereignen* [to emerge in the proper-ness of its event], still to appropriate its inappropriable, its incommensurability. Being is *nothing* outside of or before its "own" *folding* of existence: the folding of the book in our hands, as we hold it. The fold multiplies the traits and opens the book to writing. The only difference is in a coming equal to the infinite withdrawal that it traces and effaces at one and the same time. It is "*there,* but *out there,* or *beyond.*"

As altered sense, existence demands, calls for, intimates *there* its "beyond." Elliptical sense, existence surpassing its sense, withdrawing and exceeding it.

That's what writing is, he says.

Perhaps we should also say that, by definition, there's nothing beyond being (and its fold), and that this marks an absolute limit. But an absolute limit is a limit with no outside, a frontier without a foreign country, an edge without an external side. This is no longer a limit, therefore, or it is the limit of nothing. Such a limit would also be an expansion without limits, but the expansion of nothing into nothing, if being itself is nothing. Such is the *infinity proper to finitude*. This expansion is a hollowing-out without limits, and this excavation is writing, "a void which continues to excavate itself," as the quotation from Jean Catesson in "Ellipsis" puts it.

Thus the void nullifies itself in itself *and* brings itself to light. Writing excavates a cavern deeper than any philosophical cave; a bulldozer and caterpillar for tearing up the whole field: a terrain, a passion for the machine, a mechanical passion, mechanical and machinated. This machine, marked *J. D.*, excavates to the center and the belly. The belly is the altered void. The machine carries out an evisceration that is itself hysterical. The hysteria of writing lies in bringing to light (a light unbearable yet simple), through a genuine simulacrum of disemboweling and parturition, this limit of being that no one can stomach. Writing perseveres and exhausts itself there, *à corps perdu*.

But writing doesn't *do* anything; rather, it lets itself be done by a machinery, by a machination which always comes to it from somewhere beyond itself, from being's passion for being nothing, nothing but its own difference to come, and which always comes *there*, there where the beyond is.

This also means that, as in the question of writing, the question of sense (of being) is altered as a question in such a way that it can no longer appear as a *question*. A question presupposes sense, and aims to bring this sense to light in its answer. But here sense is presupposed merely as the appeal to sense, the senseless sense of the appeal to sense, the ellipsis which finally never closes off anything, but which calls: the "gaping mouth," there, where the ellipsis itself, and its geometry, are eclipsed by a cry. But a silent cry: nothing but altered sense.

What responds to a call or to an appeal is not a response but an advent, a coming to presence. *Ereignis*, for Heidegger, names the advent of presence proper in (and to) its inappropriation. "Writing" bespeaks the ellipsis of the present in this advent itself, this ellipsis of the present *by which* the event takes place—taking place with no other place than the displacing of "all natural place and center," the spacing of the place itself, of the "trace," and of "our hands."

Yet writing, at the limit that is its own but where it *is* not *itself*, wouldn't "say" even this. It wouldn't substitute an affirmation to the question. It wouldn't substitute anything for anything; it would operate no transformation, re-elaboration, or re-evaluation of discourse. The "system" of writing is not another discourse "on" sense. It is the movement, the passion, and the impatience which arises with sense, "all sense."

In a sense, an exorbitant sense—the ellipsis of ellipsis itself—there is no discourse, no philosophy, and thus no thinking that is Derrida's. This, at least, would have been his passion: to elide, to eclipse thinking in writing. No longer to think, but to come and to let come. Needless to say, this doesn't amount to a "project" or to a particular "enterprise of thinking." Yet might we not say that there *is* a "program" (a trace running always ahead of itself), the program of an extenuation? One that Derrida carries out relentlessly?

The sense of being differs—differs (from) its own difference, coming to be *the same* as existence and *nothing else*—and calling to itself, calling for itself, and repeating itself as being the "same," *right at* existence, its difference, always remembering itself in the letter of sense which *literally does not make sense*, the rabbi of open books and not of the *biblia*, all of this wouldn't be Derrida's discourse, any more than it would be Dérissa's or anyone else's. It would be what *comes* today, here and now, *our history*, to all discourse, in all discourse, at its fractured juncture, no possibility of this coming ever being halted—being, on the contrary, what is always coming, and to come.

What is it to *come* or to *enjoy*? What is *joy*? This is no longer a "question." It has never been a question for philosophy, whether philosophy has never wanted to know anything about it, or whether it has always known—and here Spinoza speaks on behalf of all philosophers—*that* it is not a question. But it is precisely *about coming*, coming to the limit, and the limit of coming: infinite finitude.

As for *what* it comes to and *where* it comes from, this is discourse still less; this is no longer writing—writing is the coming, and its call. But it is—all the rest, all the sense of all the rest: what we call, and what perhaps we need to rewrite totally as the world, history, the body, sense, work, technology, the work of art, voice, community, the city, and passion, passion yet again.

Let no one come to say, in any event, that this joy *beyond question*— but not beyond appeal—reeks of facile and complacent discourse. It is "happiness" that reeks. Happiness succumbed to the killing fields, to grocery stores and to crack. The stench is still with us. Its accumulation will explode, of course. Joy, the sense of existence, is the infinite but irrefutable, irrecusable demand.

III

Let's go back; let's repeat the text again, returning to the other end of the ellipse, and take up the altered ring at its beginning, insofar as a ring has a beginning.

"Here or there we have discerned writing": everything is there, in one fell swoop, in this lapidary *incipit* whose affirmation or affirmativity rests on a discreet prosody. (And *here*, we ought to re-read this sentence with its proper scansion.) Everything is there in a passion of language which has overcharged with sense this simple sentence, otherwise so anodyne; which has saturated with resonances this very brief monody, to the point that somewhere, in some obscure place, it alters itself, fissures, and noiselessly gives in. Derrida has always had a devouring thirst for language, and has always striven passionately to make it do his will.

"Here or there": the first words of the text effect a *mise en abîme*, both of this text itself and of the book it closes. What has *been* done (the discerning of writing) has been done right *here*, and so it is right here: in a present already past, just started up. *When* did we begin to read? When did he start writing? It is done; a discovery has taken place; a principle has been laid down—this *incipit* is a conclusion, the systematic conclusion of the book—but it is here, under our very eyes, between our hands, and it never ceases to be at stake, still and most especially when it is written "here." It is not a "present perfect," but the passage of the present of writing (its present, its *gift*, which gives nothing without also giving the giver, "on" whom *we* are writing); it is the coming into presence of what *is* not *present*. (What comes into presence does not *become* present.) It does not stop *coming*, and coming at a limit. Presence itself is nothing but limit. And the limit itself nothing but the unlimited coming to presence—which is also the unlimited gift, present, of presence, or its offering: for presence is never *given*, but always offered or presented, which means offered to our decision whether or not to receive it.

And the *here* is immediately redoubled: it is either here *or* there. *There*, the *there*, will come at the end of the text, and will be redoubled in turn: "there, but out there, beyond." Here or there: already the two foci of the text, already the ellipsis. It's all there. Some years later, at the end of another text, accompanying once again the form and forgery of his own signature (of the proper sense of the proper name, where all sense is altered in effect), Derrida will write that he signs "here. Where? There."[3] *Here* removes itself from its own place and *there* pierces its own place (in performing it). Derrida's entire text and oeuvre is altered by perforating and performing itself. He has, he *is*, an inextinguishable thirst for a wild and drunken pursuit of self-externalization of offering himself up where he is not, of blocking himself from being where he is. He cannot bear himself, though he is borne only by himself. And that sums up the violent, desperate, joyous errancy of the *sense* of the age, of *our sense*, disseminated in a great gust coming from beyond the West, just as it is sedimented and paved over by the thickness, and thus the speechlessness, of our words. *All* of Derrida's text is a deaf-mute text.

It is already time to inscribe an ellipsis here—as the title (Derrida's, and mine in repeating it) has already done. Or, more exactly, one can't do less, but one must go to the end, the ellipsis of ellipsis.

For Derrida has neglected, by ellipsis, in accordance with the tropological use of the word "ellipsis," which surely he could not have failed to remember, making explicit the sense of this word. (And so: "Ellipsis" as a title; the ellipsis of the title. He contrives not to entitle this text any more than he signs it.) He will inscribe it in Greek, and elliptically attach to it the double value of a lack, of a decentering, and of an avoidance. *El-lipsis*, from *ek-leipō*, I avoid: I avoid—writing what I write. I live off writing, I leave off writing.

And he will leave out saying (writing) that the ellipsis (as eclipse) has as its *etymon* the idea of fault, of the absence of precision or exactitude. The geometrical ellipsis was initially a generic term for figures that failed to be identical, before being used (by Apollonius of Pergamon, in his treatise on *Conics*) in the sense familiar to us, as designating what is missing in a circle and doubles the property of the constant radius of the circle into the constancy of the sum of two distances, which always vary. All of this, together with an entire structural, historical, rhetorical and literary analysis of the ellipsis and ellipses, has been subject to an ellipsis.

However, it is not simply a question of the specular play "Ellipsis upon ellipsis, and in ellipsis." In calling itself "Ellipsis" (which is not at all the same thing as being entitled "On Ellipsis") *and* in its display of abyssal speculation, itself simple, infinitely so, the text says, writes, or "ellipses" (eclipses and reveals) something else entirely. It indicates that something else is subject to ellipsis, something we cannot and must not know. It lets us know that we are really and truly missing something. Lots of things at once no doubt: for example, the identity *between* "Derrida" and "Dérissa," or else "*this* other hand," named, pointed to, and shown to be invisible, unnameable—and those suspension points that follow it . . . serpent's hand, or fish's . . . This text says all sorts of sensible things about writing and about sense, *and* it says that it has something else tucked away, that it's telling another story. But also it says that this exhibiting of a secret hides nothing, that there isn't another story or, at least, that he doesn't know it himself . . . This text effaces as much as it traces, effaces precisely insofar as it traces, retracing the effacing and effacing this trace as well . . . Certainly, we will have missed the sense. It will have changed us. The passion of J. D. is to alter or to change his reader. What other passion could a piece of writing have?

Once again, and first of all: "here *or* there." An ellipsis of places, of two foci, neither of which can center the text or localize the writing that we have discerned. This double focus, these two fires, two lights, two burnt patches, are shown to us, then removed from view. What is more, "two" is more than two; "two" opens onto the multiple. In the "here or there" it is the suspension, the hesitation, and the beating of the *or* that counts. Of this *or* [ou] which does not say *where* [où] writing is. Nor when, nor how. "Here or there" is without a definite place, it is also "sometimes, at moments, from time to time," and therefore "by accident, by chance, fortuitously." Writing can only be made out by accident. Even the calculation of writing, to which we see Derrida give himself over to here—a calculus that is meticulous and fierce, with all the rigor of the geometer (is he also from Pergamon, the city of *parchment?*, this little secret, scratched here?), a tenacity ruled by the *systematic* tracking down of what deregulates and disseminates sense—this very calculus (in fact, especially this calculus) is given over to the vagaries of language. Here or there language might favor the game or even make the rules. If the circle of sense did link up, the game would take place everywhere or nowhere: no more play, nothing but sense. But the game of sense implies the hazardous ellipsis of its rules.

Neither manifest literalness nor *mise en abîme*, no less manifest, makes sense of the text. Neither the "whole" nor the "hole" of sense. But always once more the ellipsis, which is to say: sense itself *as* ellipsis, as not moving around a fixed point, but coming endlessly to the limit—here or there—where signification is eclipsed and a presence only arrives at its sense: a rabbi, a fish, a piece of parchment, who and what else? This sense of a presence is the joy, the pleasure and pain of the enjoyment of this presence, exposed before or beyond all presentation and any present of a signifiable sense (of a sense present to itself?). This takes place where place has no signifying privilege, unassuming places indifferent to all presences, to all the differences between them: a constant sum, here or there.

What by chance takes (has taken) place here is a *discerning* ("here or there we have discerned writing"). That is to say, a fine, penetrating insight, a perspicacious gaze which has insinuated itself into writing, across "labyrinth" and "abyss," plunging "into the horizontality of a pure surface, which itself represents itself from detour to detour" (for where else is writing to be discerned if not here, right at the "grapheme" itself?). In the interstices of a "deconstructed" discourse, a piercing theory has seen what had never been seen before. So far, a classic *incipit* of the philosophical text. But to dis-cern, strictly, means to see *between* [to glimpse, entre*voir*], it is barely to see, or to guess, in an ellipsis of the eye. *Theorein* has been reduced here to an extenuation, to a vestige in the half-light—to a twilight vision, not one of daytime.

"We have discerned": we have divided off with a *cerne*, which in French is the contour and particularly the ring of fatigue around tired eyes; thus we have divided off from two *cernes*, tracing the contour and the division, the division as contour. (The sentence that follows in the text will "sketch" this "dividing line"—and that "dividing line" will divide and share of itself; separation and communication, exchange and isolation.) We have retraced the limit of writing, writing as limit. We have written writing: it can't be *seen*, or barely; it writes itself; it traces itself and effaces itself under the very eyes of anyone who would try to look. It sets its course by groping along its traces. But its effacement is its repetition: it is its demand and its calling forth; it is "all the sense" that traverses it, always coming from elsewhere, and nowhere, offering itself to us as it takes us away from ourselves.

But who, "we"? This *we* which has, or have, discerned writing is both the modest authorial "we" and the royal "we" of the philosopher. But it is also *ours*: the *we* of a community in its history. "We" voices the historiality of the discerning of writing. This discerning is as recent as the outline, in modernity (let us say from Benjamin and Bataille to Blanchot), of a certain title or graph of writing whose philosophical inscription Derrida has assumed and assured (in other words: where he invents "literature"). *And yet* this discerning is as ancient as the first philosophical inscription. Later, Derrida will retrace the separation of book and text back to Plato: ellipsis of the West.

Here *we* are at this limit: the waning [*occident*] of sense, the distension of its foci, frees up the task of thinking (though in what sense is it still "thinking"?) the sense of our finite existences.

Transcendental experience is right here. There is, in effect, nothing in this *incipit* that does not bear the stamp of the empirical: the randomness of place and moment, the simple facticity of discerning. The *incipit* gives the origin and the principle of the system in the register of the empirical. Here's what happened, it's happened to us. It not only opens up discourse to writing, but it already breaches it ("breach" will be the penultimate word of the book). It opens up an irrepressible empiricity, in writing it, in offering as a narrative what is, by rights, an exposition *more geometrico*, but elliptically so. Thus the transcendental experience of writing is not Husserl's "transcendental experience." Husserl's was meant to be *pure* experience, the reduction and purification of the empirical. Here, by contrast, experience is impure—and this is why, undoubtedly, the concept of "experience" is itself inappropriate, at least insofar as it presupposes some sort of experimental setup, as is the concept of the transcendental (which always lays claim to an *a priori* purity as condition of possibility).

Instead it is a question here of putting together what befalls us, in the non-purity of the event and the accident, the historical passage in which all sense of History is changed: wars and genocides, collapses of representation, the erosion of politics by global technology, the drifting of "unchained peninsulas."

In that case, experience should be expressed or thought as "wandering," as "adventure," and as the "dance" named in the text—in short, as passion itself: the passion of sense. What would pass as a "condition of possibility" here (but also an "ontology") would be on the order of passion. But passion is always destined to the impossible. It does not transfom it into the possible, does not master it; rather, it is dedicated and exposed to it, passive at the limit where the impossible comes, which is to say, where *everything* comes, all sense, and where the impossible is reached as the limit.

The impossible is the center, the origin, and the sense. Ellipsis is the ellipsis of the center, its lack, its failing, and the presentation of the "dangerous hole" into which the "anxious desire of the book" seeks to "have insinuated itself." But when it insinuates itself there it discovers or discerns that it has plunged into nothing other than the "horizontality of a pure surface." The circle gapes; the ellipsis surfaces. Touching the center, one touches writing. All sense is altered—but what glides across the surface (brilliant, slippery fish . . .) and what plunges into the hole (tightly rolled parchment), would these not be the same? The same which alters, and all sense, once again, without end? And is it the same passion to touch the center and to touch writing? Is it the same machine which digs, fills in, and traces anew?

IV

Undoubtedly it is the same machine: has there ever been more than one passion—more than one anguish, more than one joy, even if this unicity is in essence plural? The passion for the center, for touching the center, and for the touching of the center has always been J. D.'s passion—the passion of philosophy *as* the passion of writing. The one and the other, according to the two senses of the genitive, and one in the other, and one for the other. Both completed, raised up, or cast into the depths by the passion for touching language, as he will have repeated. To touch language: to touch the trace, and to touch its effacement. To touch what moves and vibrates in the "open mouth, the hidden center, the elliptical return." To touch the ellipsis itself—and to touch ellipsis inasmuch as it touches, as an orbit touches the edges of a system, whether cosmological or ocular. A strange, orbital touch: touching the eye, the tongue, language, and the world. At the center, and in the belly.

It is the same passion: *to discern* is to see and to trace; it is to see or to trace at the point where the rings around the eyes touch—between the eyes. Discerning is where touching and vision touch. It is the limit of vision—and the limit of touch. To discern is to see what differs in touching. To the see the center differing (from itself): the ellipsis. There is a certain narrowing in all discerning: sight narrows to the extreme, and becomes sharper and more strangled. It always has its two hands clenched around the book.

It is the system, again. It is the will to system. (But what is will? Who knows, or thinks he knows? Doesn't will differ in its essence?) It is the will to touch: the wish that the hands touch, across the book, and through the book; that its hands touch, reaching just as far as its skin, its parchment; that our hands touch, always through the intermediary of skin, but touch nonetheless. To touch oneself, to be touched right at oneself, outside oneself, without anything being appropriated. That is writing, love, and sense.

Sense *is* touching. The "transcendental" of sense (or what is "onto-logical" in it) is touch: obscure, impure, untouchable touch, "with an animal-like, quick, silent, smooth, brilliant, sliding motion, in the fashion of a serpent or a fish," even more than hands, the surface of the skin. The skin repeats itself, here or there. The text says nothing of this: it will have effected an ellipsis of the skin. But that is why there is no skin *as such*. It is missing and always being undone, and this is how it covers up, unveils, and offers.

Always an undoing of sense, always an ellipsis in which sense emerges. It is the passion after a skin to write on. He writes endlessly on his own skin, hand to hand, *à corps perdu.* (This means that whoever writes "on" Derrida is no different from Derrida writing "on" sense and "on" writing, or from anyone who writes on anything at all. We always write "on" some*one*, on some singularity of the skin, on a surface scratched and tattooed yet smooth and slippery, on a piece of parchment, on a voice. An epidermic writing, mimicking the movements, contortions, and alterations of a skin of sense stretched tight and perforated, intact and enacted, miming a writing which imitates nothing, no sense having been given to it. One always writes as if overcome by a sovereign, sublime Mimesis of Sense, and by its inimitable Style; in writing one is always mimicking the gestures and dances of this senseless model, *à corps perdu.*)

This *corps perdu,* this lost body—Derrida found it one day written in French in Hegel. (See the beginning of *Margins.*) It is the passion of writing. Writing can do nothing but lose its body. As soon as writing touches the body, writing loses touch itself. Writing has only to trace it or efface it. But the body is not lost in the simple exteriority of a "physical" or "concrete" presence. Rather, it is lost to all material or spiritual modalities of a presence full of sense, charged with sense. And if writing loses the body, loses its own body *à corps perdu,* this occurs to the extent to which it inscribes its presence beyond all recognized modalities of presence. To inscribe presence is not to (re)present it or to signify it, but to let come to one and over one what merely presents itself at the limit where inscription itself withdraws (or ex-scribes itself, writes itself outside itself).

Derrida—under the name "Derrida" or some alteration of this name—will not have stopped inscribing the presence of this lost body. He is not trying to make some new power arise through language, to erect any system or nonsystem of some new disposition of sense. On the contrary, he has always played—on stage and at stake—the body lost at the limit of all language, the foreign body, which is the body of our foreignness.

That is why this body is lost in the very discourse of writing and the deconstruction of metaphysics, insofar as that is a discourse (a philosophy or even a thinking). The experience named "writing" *is* this violent exhaustion of the discourse in which "all sense" is altered, not into another or the other sense, but in this exscribed body, this flesh which is the whole resource and plenitude of sense, even though it is neither its origin nor its end, yet still place and the ellipsis of place.

This body is material and singular—it is also the very body of Jacques Derrida—but it is material in a singular way: one cannot designate it or present it as a "[subject] matter." It is present with that presence of the unavoidable withdrawal of writing, where it can be nothing but its own ellipsis, there, out there, and beyond.

There, out there, beyond "Derrida" himself, but nonetheless here, on his body and his text, philosophy will have moved, materially, and *our* history will have moved. It will have inscribed/exscribed something which has nothing to do with any of the possible transformations of ontology or of the transcendental (even if the discourse frequently proves susceptible to being brought back to such transformative operations). Philosophy will have moved with a movement discreet, powerful, and trembling: the movement of a lost body presented at the limit of language. This body is made of flesh, of gestures, forces, blows, passions, techniques, powers, and drives; it is dynamic, energetic, economic, political, sensuous, aesthetic—but it is none of these meanings as such. It is the presence which *has* no sense, but which is sense, its ellipsis and its advent.

Derrida "himself"—or his ellipsis—is a wild singularity of this body, crazy for it, crazy with its presence, crazy with laughter and anguish at the always-retraced limit where its own presence never stops coming *à corps perdu*—discreet, powerful, trembling like everything which is to come.

Translated by Jonathan Derbyshire

6

Borborygmi

I

"Borborygmi" was a nonchalant and hasty response, premature as always, to the request to provide a title for this talk. I thought: I don't know what to say. I was mumbling and stammering. Then this word came to me: a Greek onomatopoeia, now a medical term for a rumbling in the bowels, which has, in turn, developed a figurative meaning in French, connoting "incomprehensible and inarticulate remarks."

As it happens, this sort of response isn't restricted to this particular request—the request to speak about Derrida.[1] More and more, I find that each request to speak arouses in me an anxiety—but also, paradoxically, a need to respond with an inarticulate grunt. As if each time it became clearer to me that the response, indeed every response, must lead back to the edge of language, exhausting its semantic resources in order to let something that is, immediately and materially, the unheard sense of which we are the hearkening, murmur and creak, albeit at the price of any possibility of identifying this "we."

So, at the very moment that I let you in on this insignificant anecdote concerning my title, doing so simply in order to avoid having to come back to it, I am confirming its structural or transcendental, which is to say historial, necessity. What behooves us—us other philosophers—is to articulate the inarticulate remarking of a sense more powerful and more remote than all configurations, constellations, or constructions of sense.

What falls to us in this way is the job, precisely, of articulating sense, its power and its withdrawal. It is a matter of articulating the inarticulable, not of lapsing into mumbled incantation (poetry in the worst sense) or of settling for the displacement, reversal, and perpetual relativization of concepts (of settling, that is, for nihilism). It is the inarticulable *as such* that has to be articulated, with the proviso that it is precisely the "as such," in withdrawing, which is the problem here, though in such a way that this withdrawal is seen to belong essentially to the "as such" as such. In short, we need to express the fact that truth, each time, opens and inaugurates the outside of all truth, but in a way that is, each time, proper to itself, absolutely proper, exact, clear, distinct and distinctive, unique, certain, and present.

Or, to put it another way, we must name that which has no name, name that which, by definition, witholds itself from nomination. More exactly, we have to name de-nomination itself, put a name to the very withdrawal of the name, as opposed to naming a "that" which would have no name. The tradition has always sought to give the name "God" to what has no name. God is the (nick)name of the Name taken absolutely. It is the nominal essence of what is beyond all names. If the "death of God" means anything, if we are at last to find a sense of ourselves in it, it is because we need to learn to stop naming a "this" or a "that" which would be beyond all names (but which would be, for this very reason, the repository of an ultimate nomination and propriety) and instead to name properly, for every "this" and every "that," for all things, the deprivation of the proper and the name: the most essential origin in the midst of the inessential fragility of being.

Naming requires that a name be made. In Greek this is called *ono-matopoeia*, the production, creation, or *poiesis* of the name. We know that there is never genuine onomatopoeia in languages. Its very concept is contradictory: either there is a noise, which is precisely not a name, or there is a name, which imitates a noise without being the noise itself. A contradictory or limit concept, then, but one that language nevertheless brushes up against incessantly: the thing making a name for itself, rather than the ostension of its sense by its name.

Not a proper name then, but the thing itself, materially, being the singular stamp of its truth and, at the same time, the syncopated withdrawal of its name, and this very withdrawal, moreover, being the truth of the name. Is it possible to think of an onomatopoeia of truth? Of truth naming itself with its own sound, so that what is proper both to it and to us can resonate or ring out? But truth is essentially self-presentation. Truth presents and names itself. All the while truth turns itself inside out, as a relation to itself, as the enfolding of the innermost distance which forms it, just as it presents itself to itself and as it presents *self*. Can we thus imagine a borborygmus for truth's "intestinal difference"?[2]

This self-presentation is so intimate and intestinal that it is also entirely foreign. Is it a question, then, of a barbarism, of the language of truth being a language of the other, of the wholly foreign, and, as such, being badly formed, mumbled, and stammered? A barbaric idiom? Does Derrida think about anything else? Is Derrida naming anything else when he writes his own name, "Derrida," when he writes this name and about this particular proper name beneath his signature? Throughout his work autobiography is at issue to such an extent that all other questions appear secondary or derived.[3] The philosophical order itself seems to dissolve, to capsize, or to run mad in the erratic empiricalness of a name beyond all question or concept. But beneath autobiography, and beneath this "outside," if not *as* this outside, could it be that what is really at stake is an auto-hetero-graphy of truth?

II

What or who is there behind Derrida [*derrière Derrida*]?

There is more than one question here—as we might suppose he would say himself. This question cannot be made univocal, for it could conceivably contain questions of genealogy, antecedence, foundation, or substance, as well as a suspicion about a disguised presence or motive. Similarly, there are several ways of construing that "behind" as a meaning or direction: backwards, forwards, as already given or to be discovered up ahead; as "behind," *de retro*; as an antecedent or a return, as already there or as the coming of a return. But always coming from behind, never frontally. We could say the same about the object of the question: *what* is there or *who* is there, two possibilities that leave open the elision crossed by "there," the "there" that stands there for the "there" presupposed by "behind" or "after," precisely. Finally, the question leaves open the very subject of its questioning: Derrida the individual, the philosopher, the signatory, the signature, the name, the signifier, or the improbable signified of a proper name, in general, the sense of a "derrida," like that of a rudder, a riddle, or a drawn-down—*but in what language?*

Consequently *such* a question must be handled in accordance with the use he himself—he, Derrida, the one in question here—makes of the *such* [tel], of a *such* without an *as* or a *that*, of this archaic *such*, which he has made into one of the singular features of his lexicon and syntax (precisely, of his syntactical lexia). His fanatical use and abuse of the *such* shows just how much he values the ability to upset demonstrative, indicative, or indexical determinacy—of *this, that, or the other*—to make resonate there both under- and over-determination.[4] A *such* that is not *as such*, a *such* which stands alone, the subject of an ostension rather than a designation, without reference or referent, comparable only to itself and therefore incomparable, incommensurable, with no gap between the similar and the same. Neither as such nor such as it is, but *such* without relation to any genre, or else strictly unique in its genre and thus without generality or genus. The idiom of a unique singular, *one such, such a Derrida*. The real Derrida or the truth of Derrida, or even such a truth of *such*. What is there behind that?

In putting these extremes of the idiom together—on the one hand, the extremity of the syntactical operator which connects nothing (the "such") and, on the other, the nominal form which signifies nothing and names only the name, as the proper itself, "Derrida"—we are brought to the outermost limit of the idiom. There is nothing behind it. It refers to nothing, it makes no sense or connection, it merely echoes itself, like a shot or a noise, like the emphasis of a pure *phasis*. And yet it is already implied in reference; it relates to relation and names naming. In a vacuum, granted, but a vacuum which creates a gulf, an appeal for sense that is like an intake of air, a pure and vertiginous aspiration. Idiom is impossible, we know. It *is* the impossible, as he (Derrida) never stops repeating: it must be understood that we stand face to face with the impossible, faced with the question: "How does the impossible express itself, what does it mean?" How the expression of the impossible is an impossible meaning. But this same wanting-to-say-the-impossible makes the impossible itself snap or crackle, a barbaric idiom whose very barbarity can be heard at least by those with an ear for it. Against such a name, sense or truth itself resounds: its sound, its echo, its muffled cry, its rustle, its murmur, or its shout.

Just at [à même]: that is the law of idiom, in the double polarity of the *such* and the *proper name*. No relation, no signification. What is said, if it is said, what is stammered, mumbled, or murmured, is just at the idiomatic word, just at the onomatopoeia of the impossible. There is nothing behind, therefore: no depths or reserves of sense or of truth. There is nothing behind *Derrida as such*, evidently and eminently, nothing. All background, all *hypokeimenon* or *subjectum*, disappears *ipso facto*: the idiomatic gesture or tone is responsible, by itself, for this disappearance and abolition of all wishing to speak, all intentionality, and all plan. Nothing behind and, in consequence, everything up front. Everything pushed forward, but a forward with no backward, not even a phenomenon, not even a surface.

If there is nothing behind, there is nothing in front, either: nothing ahead of itself or of us, nothing which relates to itself or to the other. Not a manifestation or an event, not a story and thus neither a process nor a narration. No autobiography, therefore, but the scratched outline of an autograph, an event, if you like, though with nothing occurring or arising but the most extreme sense or truth of all sense and truth.

And all this only in a sense, of course, for there could never be sense without the alterity which works over sense as such. That is its truth, in fact, the truth of sense. If I say *such* and *Derrida*, and if I say *One Such* in general, I could very well be said to be saying nothing, but it could not be said that I am not saying. And that is what cannot be affected by even the most extravagant claims of the skeptic. The most obscure and barbaric idiom can indeed take language to the limits of meaning and communication—but it is still language, it is language which is thereby stretched to the limit. It is language that has become a thing, withdrawn from any relation to sense. But this thinglike language, this noise or mark, itself *means*, even if it expresses nothing, if it wills to say nothing, or even if it wills not to will. It is beyond the will. It seeks neither to communicate nor signify, but is the pure expression of that which puts itself forward without going outside itself, stamping its own truth on itself. Dividing itself without going outside itself, necessarily an auto-hetero-graph. An expression so pure and so in tune with itself that it is precisely the annihilation of the will as representation and as power to present representation. It is, in its tension, just the triggering of self-presence.

The click of the trigger. "I cl'," he says:[5] clack, lack, alc, gl, tr, infra- or intra-verbal phonemes, like the inaudible "a" of "differ*a*nce" or such parentheses, onomatopoeias, such glug-glug, tic-tak, trrr, or words that might one call, in their way, phone-emphatic, wink, gul, hinge, thence, dike, tint, sing, an obsession with resonance and assonance, a poetics that is above all sonorous, infra-significant, where one blows out of all proportion sonorities slipping outside the sign, drawing out the sound of the sign, angiospermic, androeciumic, epigynetic, petroglyphic, heliotropic, and thus communicating with a philosophical beyond of signification, portmanteau-words and concepts multiplied almost to the point of exhaustion, untenable yet retained, hurled, lost in the profusion, destinerrance, emasculation, peniclitoris, logoarchy, signsponge, the jerky spasm of an eructo-jaculation, *logoroperatergo*. This is not all: one must then consider the whole sentence, and then the set of sentences making up the book, and then the indefinite sequence of books and the fearsome, irrepressible manner in which he piles them up and arrests them, allowing questions or hypotheses, references and allusions, to proliferate, making them each other's guardians until he decides to banish them or send them all flying, to the point that he pulls the rug out from under his own feet or takes back what he had already given away up front.

A tergo, here we go again. It is from behind language—from behind by letting oneself slip to the bottom, to the rear, or indeed from behind it by turning around back to the front, by twisting all the front to make it turn back in the rear—that his frenzy of language seeks indefatigably to make idiomatic the barbarous, thus making a language purely wordbound, but also, cut off from any tongue, purely the thing itself, a characteristic that would no longer be Leibnizian because of no longer being symbolic—at unless it were so absolutely, purely, and simply: a pure division of the symbolizing thing from itself, splitting so as to let its fracture sound and thus let itself be recognized, by and to itself. For and in itself—but then, necessarily, such that to the other, in the other, and for the other this language engraves or has engraved itself on itself, a mark that at the same time sets language going behind and in front of itself, always in retreat and always sent up ahead and behind: and thus, properly.

And what is behind all this, at the very least and in a first approximation, what if not what is proper, what is its own? But what is properly the alterity of the proper? What haunts the proper, as he likes to say, as he likes to haunt himself with haunting and the sound of the word "haunting"—is that it is not enough for the proper properly to be the proper.[6] What is most properly the proper is the development and sequence in itself of a formidable logic of self-marking, self-reference, and self-expression. There is no proper, no own, without appropriation, and the "I" is nothing, not even a Kantian empty "I," without such an auto-graph, the very auto-mark by which alone the "auto" sets itself in motion: the originary trigger, or starter of self-presence, stemming originarily from presence to itself. A heterogeneous auto-mark, generated from the other in the most intimate or intestinal reaches of the *auto*. But what is this trigger if it is not truth? What else could it be but this alterity of the true, which grasps the thing *as such* and properly names it, not in order to signify it, but to make of it the senseless origin of sense?

The truth is that the thing names itself properly in such a way that nothing precedes it or subordinates it; it says itself in being, if not this side of or beyond being, but always saying *itself* with a saying before or beyond discourse, saying or manifesting the *itself* of the proper and the proper as *itself*—the to-itself which opens sense itself.

Without that, would there be anything there at all? Would there be some*one*, a thing or a person? In allowing the impossible idiomaticity of the proper to proliferate in a starry madness of sub- and sur-nominations, of hyper-nominations, like galaxies expanding around a black hole of the proper name absorbing all sense, it is the proper which "Derrida" is stalking and tracking, and trying to make melt away and implode on top, underneath, behind, or in front; nothing less than the totality and the architotality of the proper in truth, thus its absolute, singular, irreducible, incompressible, irrefragable, irrecuperable uniqueness, but also its absolute, indefinitely plural, multipliable, extendable, communicable, exchangeable generality. Such a Derrida = One Such = all origin, any living present of sense, the birth and death of each one as every one which recognizes itself as *such*, as having nothing to recognize but its uniqueness without unity.

III

Let's leave Monsieur Derrida there, as we must. Let's abandon him to that for which he is merely the borrowed name: the self-naming-in-truth of everyone, of each entity unique in itself. This today is the absolute need, the most pressing requirement of philosophy (and/or poetry, of their intestinal difference) in the age of suspended assumptions and abandoned figures: that everyone be truly named and that sense emerge afresh from the heterology of all these singular nominations.

Let's immediately move behind Derrida, straight to this truth. We can expect to do so, however, only by passing through his eponym (as if there were ever a name that wasn't borrowed . . .). What is behind him is behind *there*: truth does not reside in a generality, or, at the very least, this generality does not have the consistency of a homogeneous other world or of a subsumption. On the contrary, its "consistency" is that of the discrete, singular disjunction of all in one and one in all, at once the same for all, just like that identical for all, and each time identical to itself alone. (It's the same question: neither "the people" nor "the individual"; neither "the community" nor "the hero"; and indeed, neither "philosophy" nor "the thinker"; neither "language" nor "the poet." Rather, the question is how one distinguishes itself from the other, and how to pass from one to the other without referring or reducing one to the other.)

Behind there: in the same spot as the name "Derrida," a random place like any other, but also the unique, the most unique place to which he accords the exorbitant privilege of revealing what truth truly amounts to—that there is no truth which is not, each time, exorbitant.

"What or who is behind Derrida?" is the only autobiographical question worth asking, so long as one hears it as a question about auto-constitution or auto-manifestation, not so much a question, in fact, as a wish or a drive to search behind the self for what moves the self and makes it come to itself, as itself. (Posed from outside, it is in effect a false question, one that belongs on the side of the antithesis in the Kantian antinomies, reaching back all the way along the infinite regress of causes. But it will be understood that the truth I am speaking about is inseparable from freedom, from its singular and absolute beginning, from its liberation before each and every particular "freedom.")

The autobiographical question—or the autobiographical urge, curiosity, attraction, instinct, compulsion, and indulgence[7]—can only proceed from this interrogation: What is there behind the self, and what ensures the advent of the self, something hidden from the self but which it searches after in order precisely to be this very self? This questioning or drive must inquire after what precedes it: it, the question, or the drive, but that is to say the *autos* itself, which is not there unless it seeks itself, demands itself, and pushes itself (marks itself or implodes), and, preceding, is conjured up, that which is pre-dicted in being pro-duced, is made to resonate before it finds its own voice and indeed so as to let be heard in advance what is proper to its voice (the proper of a voice in general; that is to say, a unique resonance and an inimitable timbre, or that which wants to express itself *as such*). Strictly speaking, therefore, the autobiographical question can be nothing but the question of the heterological antecedence of the *autos* itself, or in the *autos* itself, or in its ownmost behind. And it is there, after all, this behind that gives to this question or compulsion, this compulsion to question, at once its absolute, vertiginous necessity and its constitutive trait of impossibility: it always fizzles out at the very point at which it is being put together. But perhaps it's precisely the sound of this fizzling out that it wants to be heard, even if that means bursting the ear drum or putting up with the echoing of the void.

Derrida hasn't failed to amplify the question. In a frenzied autobiographical turn, he has not only answered the question "What or who is behind Derrida?" but has given, prescribed this response in inscribing "Derrida," already, right at the back. Thus (and here I'm cutting, extracting from, a text that's arranged precisely to prevent such abbreviation; I've supplied enough of the context, though, so as to give a whiff of the chords and harmonies of the autobiographical music in play here):

A fleet of screens [*paravents*] with purple sails, purple veils [*voiles pourpres*], a fleet ready for the attack, the defense, a fleet guarding itself at the prow and the poop, gold spurs for the parade.

The parade always stays behind [*derrière*].

Derrière: every time the word comes first, if written therefore after a period and with a capital letter, something inside me used to start to recognize there my father's name, in golden letters on his tomb, even before he was there.

A fortiori when I read *Derrière le rideau* [*Behind the curtain*].

Derrière, behind, isn't it always already behind a curtain, a veil, a weaving. A fleecing text.[8]

Behind a veil, the truth. The truth of what is behind, of what either can be unveiled or remain hidden, a promised and intangible nudity, and at the same time the back or behind of truth, the back side of the fabric, texture itself, itself and spun out of itself, not something to be veiled or unveiled, but something set out—something that sets sail, in the sense of taking to the high seas and making for clear water, without limits, a showing that is both exhibition and protection, ostentation and dissimulation.

What is he showing here, what truth? He shows how he already grabs hold of himself from behind himself, or rather, he says how "something in me" grabs hold of itself, how the very thing of the self grabs hold of itself by itself, a self behind the self, a self like its own origin or provenance. Not just the active origin of the father, but an origin already originated ahead of time and before its hour, ahead of its own emergence, already, properly speaking, conveyed to its properness of immemorial provenance. The deathly inscription of the name, the inscription of the death of the name, of the name as death, my own death, then, in my name, though a death seized from behind as what was already behind the origin itself. Before me the tombstone allows me to see the name as the obverse, as the reverse of the origin—of its *own* origin, which it will never grasp or recognize, except from behind and *as* the behind.[9] "Derrida," therefore, picked up and turned upside down, turned upside down and cut off from his *da*:[10] *da* without *da*, like *Sein*, or, who knows, like *Mit-Sein*. Being alone, and being-with, being-alongside-oneself, being-with-what-is-before-oneself, and not being-there, nor even being-the-there, but being what is behind the there, what is not there, offered, indicated, or localized, but inscribes itself beneath.

Isn't that the truth of the *there*, however? The truth of each *there* in and as such? For *there* is not one encircled locality, determinate and opposed to another (not the *da* as opposed to a *fort*, but rather the *fort* of all *da*). *Da* is the opening up of place before the place itself, the already-open without which there would be no place, no site of being: the hinterland of place. The *da* cannot be occupied. Rather, it is a matter of being; that is, instead of presupposing it as a given locale, presupposing oneself in and as the ownmost presupposition of the *da*, in and as its taking place before and behind the place. *Da* is the "essential openness" which Dasein "carries in its ownmost Being":[11] it does not carry it in front of it, like something it might present. Rather, it literally brings it along "all the way from home" (*von Hause aus mit*), which is a way of saying "originally" or "in its ownmost being," and which implies a house behind or from which one emerges, even if, at the same time, it is the emergence which makes the house (as the assonance *Hauslaus* suggests): the emerging which makes the opening or clearing in which the house consists. The house or home: the family, the name of the father, and, first of all, the genetic outpouring, emergence, genealogy.

Hence *da* is behind as the up-ahead of the clearing which always precedes, which is precedence itself and thus the essence of pre-sence. A dwelling place, in which dwelling consists in opening and opening oneself, opening a "self [*soi*]" as such, which is to say, again, a "home [*chez soi*]"which is always, infinitely, behind itself and, in consequence, also always ahead of itself.

Derrida cuts off his *da*,[12] he scotomizes it in order to substitute for it, like a delocalization and an alteration (er, *"he" in German; erring* of the trace and of errance; *era* of the great temporal openings): thus, he gives his *da* over to its truth, he reopens it and reinitializes its ending—and this gesture is none other than one of collecting, by which he inscribes on the stone or weaves into the curtain the paternal *da*, on the era cut off in its turn. The exchange is impeccable: derrida is always already behind [*derrière*], which is always already behind derrida always already behind.

Derrida is always susceptible to surprising himself from behind. He watches himself, watches out for himself, gets himself caught. He is on the trail of the trace, which he effaces insofar as he leaves its imprint behind him. He is on the scent of effacement itself: he effaces an enormous overload of traces, marks, and gilded letters. His mania for marking is the madness[13] of effacing the mark in marking effacement, in one fell swoop always knocking himself out, from behind.

But this "Derrière" with a capital letter, this "Derrière" "coming first"—not as a substantive, therefore, not as Monsieur Derrière, but first in the syntax, thus coming about in the course of the sentence, raised through a dot and through a blank space behind it—this "Derrière" that he cannot encounter without recognizing what is his own, what is proper, his proper provenance, birth-and-death, by writing it is he appearing to himself, holding himself up, or objectifying himself? Has he sent this back in advance? He didn't miss the opportunity.[14] See, for example, a double occurrence in *The Post Card* (which comes after *Glas*, and is duly legible by any well-informed reader).[15]

The first occurrence, one line at the top of a verso page, begins with the last words of a sentence that remains invisible behind it: "cup. Behind the great man the dwarf with the flat hat, the slave or the preceptor seeks to hitch himself up." "A dès" concludes "a dice cup," as if to make more plausible that this cast of assonant words that ends in a beginning that stammeringly repeats—dé-dé ["à dès. Derrière"]—was a matter of chance, when it reveals itself as what he so visibly calculated (and with that mark, of course, he disguises his own track, if ever a throw of the dice . . .). The second occurrence, this time at the beginning of a paragraph, is "Behind Socrates he is as stiff as justice."

I won't try to dissect what is so clearly presented to us in disguise, the open secret that he wants us to ignore yet to recognize in the same blink of an eye: Derrida behind and ahead of everyone, ahead of an entire genealogy and lagging behind the whole of philosophy, the philosopher cut off, by default or excess, from the self-engendering which defines the philosophical as such, defines the philosophical family and ancestry in the idiomatic logic of the proper (which is perhaps only a double tautology, and of which the whole of Derrida's text, the whole text of every Derrida, would wish itself to be nothing but a gigantic tauto-phono-grapho-crypto-phaner-ology, biting its own tail, in all senses and with all imaginable effects simultaneously, fireworks and cold ashes, a madness watching over itself in the moment that it unwinds, but arising also from this very close watch.

IV

Once more, and very logically, we need to leave Monsieur Derrida there. Not only, in effect, better compulsively to show that he hides himself behind, but also better frantically to emphasize that he puts himself forward, in order to turn round and be nothing but his back, as if showing a clean pair of heels. Not only to be seen only from behind, but in order to *be* simply the back, in the absolute sense of *being*, in order that the *sein* of this *Dasein* be nothing other than this *da* which precedes it, but which it has to be in opening itself up, not yet being, then, only opening itself to being, not being, not being an entity there, but instead withdrawing so as to emerge from behind any allocation of being, substance, or subject, so as to burst forth in the *sub* or the *hypo* which no longer refers to anything, is no longer predicated of anything: an absolute *incipit* gaping at the origin of what is properly or improperly called "metaphysics," that is to say, the intestinal difference of the *phusis* and technology of its reversal.

Everything comes back, you see, to the capital letter: the whole affair of the behind, and what went on behind, comes down to the capital letter or, at the very least, goes by way of it. It is the capital letter which triggers the propriety of the name in the impropriety of the behind. There must be the *incipit* of the sentence: there must be the sentential or phatic opening, the affirmation, the declaration, the leap without consequence or subsequence, before all sequence, the casting into words, speaking as a cast, and perhaps a cast before all of speech, the blow or throw.

But first, at the *incipit*, the capital letter is undecidable: Derrida gives this situation a sort of general formalization when, proposing this leading (*princeps*) sentence "He will have obligated," he asks "Who is the 'He' in this phrase. . . . by what right *He* carries a capital letter"? He replies, "Perhaps not only as an *incipit*," since one must allow the hypothesis "of another capital letter or the capital letter of the Other."[16] The capital letter can simply be the mark of the *incipit*, "he" may be anyone, or perhaps the mark of the absolute distance of the Other—a hyper-*incipit* more with-drawn, buried deeper, than any primacy of the logico-grammatical subject. It is both at once, it carries both at once and one in the other, it replaces or covers over one with the other indefinitely. The covering up of "Derrida" by "Derrière" effects nothing else: at once any "behind" [*n'importe quel 'derrière'*], which is also to say any proper name, and anything as a proper name, simply the mark of this absolute limit: naked propriety, which, as such, has nothing proper about it and, at the same time, the absolute, unique "behind" which subtends all possible presence, the opening and withdrawal into the other of all identity and all presence; but also, and again at the same time, any "derrida," the son or the father, and of course with that the father's father (which process, from son to father, one thing leading to another, will soon end up scrambling all proper names in the complexity of genealogies), and at the same time the one and only Derrida, the madman who signs all that, absolutely, though by doing so he makes himself something other than all identity, something which passes behind all possible identification (or else echoes like the trigger or the echo of the faint timbre of the other at the very heart of its own identification).

All this is not as vertiginous as it appears—or rather, this very real vertigo is basic or elemental. The appropriation of the proper (reaching be-hind oneself in order to endow oneself with the proper) can only take place in the properly untenable conjunction of an absolute "Illeity" (the Other, the Most High, the Most Distant) and a common, indifferent and inter-changeable "he" (the other, always an other, yet an other).

What occurs in this conjoining or conjunction is nothing less than the conflagration of sur-significance and in-significance: the one can only emerge by way of the other, the one opens out in the other. This mutual opening opens meaning or significance in general: that it has sense, or the truth of sense, is something absolutely proper, unique and originary, and thus indistinguishable from its own substitution by every other. To put it another way: the absolute Narcissus can only grasp himself, if he does so, as identical and equal to all others insofar as he is the Unique itself. That, after all, is the most enduring lesson we have learnt about the constitution of subjectivity—going back at least as far as Saint Augustine and then right up to the *Jemeinigkeit* of *Dasein*, by way of the *ego sum*, the universality of the Hegelian *I*, and the Husserlian *alter ego*.

This lesson forces us to confront what is perhaps the most significant fact, certainly the most powerful constraint, the one richest in resources and aporias, in our entire tradition: namely, that autology is intrinsically heterology. Logic, ethics, aesthetics, poetics, and politics are all subject to this axiom, and to its double condition or double bind: that I must always, inexorably, retreat both forward and backward, into what is more intimate and internal, even intestinal, to me than my ownmost innerness; and that there is sense, in all truth, only to the extent that I go outside myself, am exposed to other origins and to the other, to all others, at the origin. This requirement owes as much to the erratic, incalculable, and inappropriable luck of others as it does to myself. The singular has no necessity: it *is* each time its singular necessity. I occupy necessarily the indifferent site of an absence of necessity which I share with everyone, and where sense opens out. The retreat behind myself is the same thing as voyaging out among others: both are plunged into the proximity of an infinite distancing. They *touch at a distance*: this is what is called "being in the true."

In this connection, what purpose does the detour by way of "Derrida" serve? Why should such a general lesson have to pass through there? Through "there," through "Derrida," which, of course, also means: through anywhere and through anyone, *but* anywhere and anyone insofar *as* the "any," *here, signifies each time in its singular occurrence.*

The generality of this lesson—and, I repeat, there is perhaps nothing more general or more generic in what passes, in the widest sense of the term, for "our tradition"—lies precisely in its nongenerality: the heterology of autology constitutes autology *itself* in singularities whose difference constitutes, institutes, and opens the "auto" as such.

In the singular—*singulus*, one by one—generality is not arranged in discrete units carved out of an overarching, transcendental or original homogeneity: *the genus*, here, is from the outset the differential uniqueness of each "one." Without doubt, each "one" is as such in-significant and substitutable. But, in order to be substitutable or substituted for, it must be given in its uniqueness, without which there could be no substitution. Without that there would just be indistinctness, the mere, massive conservation of a *substantia noumenon*. Nothing would happen and no-one would come on the scene, there would be neither birth nor death. No Derrida, no Plato, no Dupont, no Schmitt, and nothing behind, everything quite simply put up front, *vorhanden, objectum*. What happens, on the other hand, the *subjectum* surging and bursting forth, is that everything happens, everyone comes on the scene. It comes from nowhere—from behind, ever farther behind—given, thrown rather, like nothing so much as a uniqueness empty of sense: this emptiness, in truth, is the opening of all sense, in and to all senses and in all directions. But the opening has to be opened, slit, launched, burst apart, or cracked, *each time*, incessantly.

V

Opening has the character, simultaneously, of something entrenched and of generality or universality. Entrenchment because it (*ça*) opens, it snaps apart, the depths or the whole is undermined (those depths or that whole which will therefore never have taken place, which subsist nowhere, which are neither depths nor whole). Universality because once that snaps open, it opens in every sense, communicates opening to all points and in all directions (it is that which opens points and directions as such).

All our concerns are gathered together there, those belonging to us latecomers and early risers: we emerge from the depths and the whole, and we call this emergence history, Occident or world, technology. We spring up, strange and frightening, from an opening which gapes everywhere and which refers all cohesion of ground and of totality to the nonplace. Thus from behind ourselves, from beyond all identity, we come on the scene, which is to say, we bring *ourselves* on the scene, unspeakably new. *They* come on the scene, over there, up close, just behind or ahead of us. This violent torsion exhausts and dazzles us.

In a flash, an entrenchment is communicated throughout. Its absolute uniqueness (its infinite value and dignity) is distinguished absolutely: this distinction is nothing but the negativity of entrenchment, a negativity which is itself the most complete affirmation, the unique and its propriety,[17] the unique appropriating itself properly. All distinctions are equal, they each merit, equally, the passion of the origin, an excessive love which signifies nothing less than the recognition of unrecognizable uniqueness. They are equal, and substitutable, though this equality is the equality of what is most unequal in the world: equality of the incommensurable, equality of an appropriation which is each time an infinite overflowing of self into self.

The *proper* is not only what digs itself in, entrenches itself against the rest: it is also what digs itself in and retreats into itself infinitely in order to open there the space of appropriation. The advent of self is behind every self. The proper pushes the self back beyond all propriety, so as to let it emerge. *Proper* is *pro privo*, it is a movement, not a given but a giving: a giving of itself to itself, which in fact means giving itself up to what has no other place or consistency than the "itself" of the "giving itself up" itself. To appropriate oneself: giving oneself up, or devoting oneself, to giving oneself up or to devoting oneself—and always, in the final analysis, surrendering to the infinite turning back which constitutes the structure and the sense of *self.*

Behind, consequently—not what would be behind, but the being-behind-itself of the unique. Behind there is nothing for sense, but this *nothing* itself is like a hard, impenetrable, resisting thing: the being-back of the back itself, which attaches to nothing and through which nothing, coming from elsewhere, can penetrate. Behind each "one," as its behind, there is the *primal matter* of the unique: uniqueness itself, insignificant and as if reduced to its impenetrability. Primal matter is the back side: that is to say, that which has no face, that which one cannot face up to, but which opens and which comes into the open, or as the open itself. The open *as such*: that which cannot be indexed "as such," being comparable to nothing, not even itself, since the "self" itself is still, infinitely, to come. The open *as such*, incomparable, but which, barely open, resounds in itself *as* itself, the echo of its idiomatic creaking, cracking and straining.

This is why it must be one, each time one, which impossibly passes behind: it doesn't pass behind as one might journey to the depths, behind appearances or into the supposed consistency of a whole. Rather, it must pass uniquely to the unique reverse of the unique. This reverse is neither present nor absent, it is, properly speaking, neither form nor matter, though it has the irreducibility of matter and presence, and it has the alteration and torsion of absence and form. This torsion of the irreducible, this splitting at the bottom, which does not arise from it but nonetheless belongs to it just as it breaks it to pieces—this splitting which consequently withdraws into the depths, as unobtrusive as disruptive or difficult—is a "kernel," not as a hidden presence, but as something which escapes from "the laws of presence itself."[18] It is the hard kernel which is not some other thing behind the thing, but the thing itself behind itself, withdrawn into its reality. It is here just a question of the real: *res*, the thing itself in its own detonation. Derrida's thinking is an absolute realism of the pure real, that is, of the real which springs forth from behind everything: *realizing* everything, while being nothing realized, being *nothing*, the *res* of realization itself. Not only does this realism affirm the real, it touches it. To touch it is not to merge with it: it is to come into contact, to experience the resistance of the impenetrable, of the thing or being as the hard blow which rings out.

This is why Derrida wants to touch himself as if touching this real, he wants to touch the real as if it were himself: to be himself the inexpressible kernel from which sense originates in what is beyond sense, in a behind of sense or, rather, in a sense behind which is neither the reverse nor the excess of sense, neither its hyperbole nor its exhaustion, but merely its opening and its gaping wide. This is simply being-to-self, but being-to-self turns out to be nothing but a being-to-that-which-is-not-already-there: *self*, the real, is a hard kernel because it is not given, because its being as kernel consists in an endless recoil or retreat, though this recoil without end, far from implying flight, is its most proper stance, its emergence in a combination of anxiety and joy.

When I say that he wants it, I mean: he wants to get behind the will, he wants to wish just that its breath is taken away, anxiety and joy mixed together, in the jubilant mourning for his name, which resounds as a lost name. Thus he wants to touch the secret of his name,[19] which is the secret of all names and is the secret par excellence: what remains secret even when one unveils it, especially when one unveils it, that about which there is nothing to say, except to say its name again and again, a bizarre and barbaric background noise.

(Music deprived, at bottom, of art and of articulation in general, of discourse, of form, and of sense, a proffering of the unnameable, archi-tracing trait of the sonic rip around which the air wraps itself, vibrating: the spirit of philosophy out of the matter of music, this is our entire history.)

Being-to-itself: being-thrown—but not simply precipitated into an abyss, but thrown into the splitting which opens it, and out of which it emerges in falling. Thrown, then, as if *rhythmed by its going-to-itself, in itself*,[20] which takes it out of itself, wrenches it from the depths and the whole in order to hurl it toward the inexpressible unique which, in turn, hurls it back into the general communication of all uniquenesses in the very rhythm which disjoins and conjoins them one to the other. Rhythmed autoheterography of existences.

The *itself* of the *self* is just the step and the echo of this rhythm, where the real properly refers to itself, across its opening, the absolute and original impropriety of the thing itself; the syncopated beat of being, to which being is reduced. Already and not yet language: the back of language, a barbaric glottal stop at the back of the throat, the rough crashing and the ending of a song, growling and grunting, a nonspeaking animal which gives voice.

In order to touch this rhythm, one must never stop "effacing all the traits of language," toward "'words' that are so 'true' that I can no longer recognize them myself."[21] Words which no longer name anything, or rather which name only the behind of all naming, which articulate what is inarticulated in the opening of the real, a song which sings nothing but which modulates—or even silences—this opening itself. A proper name, then, like the rhythmic and melodic idiom of the origin itself, its unique poem.

All proper names are common nouns and, reciprocally, all common nouns are proper names: names and language are born in this vacillation.

Any which, consequently, any *such* and any *da*, making any sound, indefinitely substitutable, a simple exemplar at the heart of the innumerable: but at the same time, necessarily, not any one but this one alone, the unique and inimitable example of self, "Derrida" in this case then and behind Derrida still Derrida rather than a bottomless behind. There must never be any exemplarity: the unique must begin (itself) again each time. The example of the inexemplifiable must bury itself in and re-emerge from each uniqueness.

Right at the insignificance of a name, in the vagaries of its assonances, and by their very coinage, is coined the absolute significance of one *for itself as much as for every other*. It resonates dimly, it creaks or grinds, chokes even.

It's not something that can be heard, it hovers as if between unnameable sounds and the inimitable timbre of a voice, like the echo of one to the others, which a hiccup would suspend. This does not make itself heard, but the whole of the real resonates there.

Translated by Jonathan Derbyshire

PART FOUR

JUDGING

The *Kategorein* of Excess

Stark violence
Lays all walls waste; private estates are torn,
Ransacked in the public eye. We forsake
Our lone luck now, compelled by bond, by blood,
To keep some unsaid pact; perhaps concern
Is helpless here, quite extra, yet we must make
The gesture, bend and hold the prone man's head.[1]

Might not the categorical imperative be something that we can no longer avoid? Might it be—in Kant, certainly, but also in what is a long way from Kant—an obligation for our thinking? An obligation, moreover, that is indissociable from what most urgently obliges us to think, an obligation that is not the self-reproduction of the philosophical exercise but, if we can seriously say this, a *worldly demand*? And, over and above its being indissociable from this demand, might this obligation not be *inalienable*, not merely as something proper but also wholly otherwise?

Nothing is more foreign—or stranger—to us than the categorical imperative. The phrase itself is one of those rare technical expressions that have passed from philosophy into everyday speech, as if our language had been exposed [*impressionée*] to it, in both a moral and a photographic sense. And yet, perhaps it only *seems* to have been thus exposed; our language holds this phrase at a distance, never uttering it without invisible quotation marks. Indeed, although this phrase does haunt our language, our language strives to exorcise it. "Categorical imperative" evokes, on the one hand, the unreserved sovereignty of a moral absolute, the formidable majesty of an unconditional order; at the same time, however, it evokes the inaccessible character of such a commandment, the impossibility of its execution, which is ultimately to say the impossibility of obeying it or the vanity of trying to submit to it. Moreover, its majesty is soon cloaked (and this has long been the case) in a degree of absurdity or, in any case, comports itself in a manner that is decidedly obsolete. Insofar as Kant's signature, included between parentheses in the quotation marks, is not effaced (and it never is completely effaced), it is the Kant of a rationalist and formalist *Schwärmerei* that shows through, the Kant in whom pietist hypocrisy competes unstintingly with a catatonic understanding. Two choices: either we smile at this or we become enraged by it, from Hegel to Nietzsche, from Hegel to ourselves.

Above all, however, the "categorical imperative" carries with it the values or the determinations that we hold to be most loathsome for our culture and our moral sensibility (something that stems from there no longer being any moral *philosophy*, without which the nature and scope of this fact cannot be put to the test). What the imperative brings with it, then, is not only the famous "respect for principles" that takes matters "out of our hands," so to speak (echoing the famous "dirty hands" of culpability), but, first and foremost, the notion of absolute commandment, the urgent tone and the coercive gesture, referring sometimes to the beautiful soul, sometimes to an unqualifiable tyranny. Moreover, the imperative brings with it something that inverts all of this: obedience, submission, being-obliged or being-constrained, manifest and inadmissible antitheses of the freedom whereby we define or assert ourselves.

The *imperative* suppresses the freedom of initiative, and the *categorical* imperative suppresses the freedom of deliberation. Together, they suppress the freedom of self-determination, that is, they suppress what is, for us, the Good itself, the "Good" that we no longer designate as such but that consists for us in an absolute self-determination that nothing ought to be able to command. Nothing is stranger to our modern *ethos* than obligation, and it cannot be engaged without there being singular confusions; this sensibility no longer discriminates, for example, between Rousseauist and Nietzschean motifs; or, again, it continues to eye Stirner and Feuerbach in the same glance. Humanity and the individual are self-determining; freedom is both project and nature. One thing is clear, however: freedom is contrary to all obligation; it gains its authority from itself alone and gives itself its own law. Lacking the ability to assign this act of self-giving, our ethics and our politics lose all sense of direction and wander aimlessly, from Nature to History, from Man to God, from People to State, from Spontaneity to Values . . .

And yet it is always possible that the categorical imperative is, at the same time, rather closer to us than we might suspect. Freedom itself, this freedom conceived as a state—or as a being—withdrawn from every power and from every external command, this freedom is posited as a "categorical imperative," by which we mean, at the very least, that it is not open to debate. (This is, for instance, the explicit or implicit motif in our most general practice of defending "human rights.")

This being so, we somehow tap into and divert a certain aspect of the word "freedom." We claim that freedom is imposed by freedom itself, absolutely and unconditionally. In one way or another, we pose or suppose that this freedom (or, if we no longer want to run the risk of determining it in terms of an essence, then this or that collection of "freedoms" or "human rights") is given, conceived, recognizable, or assignable. If freedom, for Kant, is the *ratio essendi* of the moral law, this law is, in turn, the *ratio cognoscendi* of freedom (which turns the imperative into the singular authority of this "knowledge"); for us, by contrast, freedom is thought and is only thinkable as being simultaneously the *ratio essendi* and the *ratio cognoscendi* of all moral law. *Self*-evidently, therefore, freedom imposes or has to impose itself. But this *self*-imposition is no longer really an imposition; if it were not imposed on those who ridicule and degrade it (or if its imposition were not sought), freedom wouldn't impose itself; it would flourish, it would bloom spontaneously, since its nature is ultimately that of an essential and pure spontaneity. The imperative, then, is not exactly an imperative. The imperative of our imperatives is that true imperatives *must not* have the character of constraint, of externality, nor must they be tied to the exercise of an injunction, an obligation or a submission.

(At the same time, an abyss opens up between what we oddly persist in calling a "subject," between what we represent as being stripped of its spontaneity by economy, history, the unconscious, writing, technology, and what is, in fact, the true metaphysical concept of the subject—to which, in the last analysis, we no longer even realize we have been subjected in the name of freedom.)

Yet it still falls to us, like a muffled and obstinate demand, to think something (freedom, for instance) as an unconditional prescription. Perhaps we cannot even think without insisting, in one way or another, that this very thing—"thinking"—immediately obeys some secret intimation. So, through or because of its very withdrawal, the imperative draws nearer to us. And this proximity may well be closer than everything that, under the guise of proximity, we think of in terms of familiarity or intimacy. It would be the proximity of that with which we are obsessed but that is lost to us, the proximity of that whose loss haunts us.

Now, what haunts [*hante*] is, according to its accepted etymological origins, what inhabits or occupies [*habite*] or, on a more knowing etymological reading, what returns to the stable, to the hearth, to the home. *Haunt* is from the same family as *Heim*. The proximity of the imperative might well be the *Un-heimlichkeit* that haunts our thinking, a disturbing peculiarity that disturbs only because it is so close, so immediate in its estrangement. But to return to the familiar abode is still to return to the *ethos*. The stakes here are none other than those of an ethics, therefore[2]—not in the sense of a science or a discipline, however, or in the sense of a moral sense or sentiment, but in the sense, precisely, of a haunting.

Now, it cannot be a matter of taming the peculiarity of the imperative or of pacifying its haunting. Even supposing that the imperative were able to anticipate our future—to predict the return or the advent of an imperative ethics—we have known since Hegel that such anticipation is not the job of philosophy, which cannot pass beyond its own time. Which means what, precisely? Simply that time—the element of thinking—does not overstep itself; this limit, in short, defines it. To think is neither to predict nor to prophesy nor to deliver messages, but to expose oneself to what happens with time, in time. In the time of haunting there can and must be a thinking and an ethics—if ethics it is—of haunting.

But assuming, despite everything, that such anticipation were possible, it could never be the anticipation of a tamed imperative, an imperative rendered familiar and natural. If we have indeed lost the imperative (assuming that such a remark makes any sense), we can rest assured that, at the very least, we are unlikely to recover it; its essence runs counter to or avoids this. The imperative cannot be domesticated—and this is again one of the hallmarks of haunting: it is, by definition, something domestic that cannot be domesticated. It does not enter into the economy that it haunts. It leads us back to an abode that, as an abode, doesn't allow us to settle comfortably into it. And yet it is still an abode. We certainly don't dwell in the imperative, but we do dwell *under* it.

As such, it isn't a matter of recognizing, reevaluating, and reappropriating the categorical imperative, whether as a reactivation of Kant's philosophy or as a "resource" within it (philosophy cannot go beyond its own time), nor even as a way of appeasing the ghosts that haunt us. It can only be a matter of indicating the imperative's *insistence* for a thinking, our thinking, that is less a "tributary of Kant" than it is one that submits to an imperative necessity whereby it is referred back, initially, from its very opening, to Kant.[3]

~

Why, for Kant, the imperative, therefore? Why does the expression of the moral law take place in the imperative voice? Why a prescription rather than a description? Why an order rather than a recommendation or an exhortation?

Kant's reply is simple: the imperative exists because *evil* exists in man. There *has* to be the imperative because there is evil.

Immediately, this reply is one that disturbs our moral sensibility. We're not about to tolerate Kant's imputation to man and in man of a wholly *radical* evil. To the evil the spectacle of which the political scene (and can there be, henceforth, any other scene? isn't every scene political?) gives us a glimpse, a spectacle that we can agree is unparalleled in our history due to its constancy, its technical nature, its rationality, to this evil we want to concede only the nature of an accident (and, reciprocally, the very category of "accident" has ended up inheriting the intrinsic value of an "evil" or a "misfortune"). Those who do not see history as the necessary and perhaps asymptotic process of this accident's elimination see it instead as an accident in general, as a catastrophe having taken place on a prior or ideal register. In either case, wouldn't the accidental character of evil be the hidden metaphysical resource underlying our paradoxical capacity to *resign* ourselves to evil as such—the evil that we tend to call "banal"—so that we can have done with it once and for all?

Here, though, I'm not so much raising the question of evil—which is basically the question of its Kantian incomprehensibility—in itself as I am evoking it from afar. Any such examination would demand a great deal of groundwork since, in all likelihood, it couldn't really begin without sustained and prior consideration of the imperative. As is the case with freedom, the imperative is the *ratio cognoscendi* of evil. Concerning the latter, let me merely say two things: first, that its question (if it is still a *question* in the classical philosophical sense) is there at the very horizon of our questions and, second, that its presence as a question does not, in the face of the accidentality of evil, posit something that amounts to its pure and simple essentiality, and thus to some modern avatar of "original sin." Not that I want to make concessions to our sensibility, which recoils from the evocation of an "original sin" (without ever going on to ask what we might mean by "origin" or by "sin"). No, I merely want to say that our sensibility—whether "pessimistic" or "optimistic"—is incapable of measuring up to the question of evil, and that this inability itself provides the measure of what falls to thinking (here, the "thinking" for which we are calling requires not simply a *dispassionate* or *cold* consideration but, perhaps, a wholly different sensibility for thinking).

~

There is the imperative because there is evil. There is evil, and that is to say, the possibility of transgressing the law—and the tendency to do so. The law exists as a commandment because it can be violated. Now, this does not mean that there is, on the one hand, the law itself (in the way that there are physical laws, for example, laws of nature) and, on the other, the imperative addressed to someone who, accidentally, might not direct him- or herself spontaneously according to the law. Were this the case (and this case is typical where laws are concerned), the imperative would not be the law itself; *as an imperative*, it would not be identical with it. As such, it would have a decidedly supplemental corrective and pedagogic function. It would address itself to the infant in man, and not to man. But the imperative involves neither punishment nor reward: and it's in precisely this that we find its *categorical* rather than its purely hypothetical character (a distinction equivalent in Kant to the distinction between moral and *technical* imperatives). The law takes place *only* as the imperative. And so the imperative does not prescribe that we act *in accordance with* the law, since "the law," in this sense, is given neither by the imperative nor prior to it. Rather, it prescribes *acting legally*, in the *legislative* sense. It prescribes that the maxim of action be the founding act of a law, of the law. Without dwelling on the formidable implications of this state of affairs, let us suppose that the imperative prescribes *the act of legislation* (hence it prescribes "universally").

Let us leave to one side the metaphysical or ideological model of legislative sovereignty—whether originary, institutive or constitutive—which is also involved in this thinking. The effects of this model, incontestable though they may be, are submitted by Kant to an essential limitation: it can never be a matter of either producing or presenting this originality itself. Here, it is enough to recall, as a clue, that in the political realm Kant explicitly renounces any search for the originary institution of the legal state. On the contrary, the political order is itself submitted to the imperative:

There are thus three distinct authorities (*potestas legislatoria, executoria, iudiciaria*) by which a state (*civitas*) has its autonomy, that is, by which it forms and preserves itself in accordance with laws of freedom. A state's *well being* consists in their being united (*salus rei publicae suprema lex est*). By the well-being of a state must not be understood the *welfare* of its citizens nor their *happiness*; for happiness can perhaps come to them more easily and as they would like it to in a state of nature (as Rousseau asserts) or even under a despotic government. By the well-being of a state is understood, instead, that condition in which its constitution conforms most fully to principles of Right; it is that condition after which reason, by a *categorical imperative*, makes it obligatory for us to strive.[4]

Contrary to appearances, this doesn't concern a thinking "of the state" in the usual sense in which we understand the term. The "state" designates, rather, the space necessary for the legislation that demands the imperative.

The imperative wouldn't be able to prescribe if the legislation were given. That is to say, it couldn't prescribe what it prescribes if the legislation were given independently of itself; it couldn't prescribe if evil were inscribed in this legality independent of it. We need to distinguish between recognized evil, localized by a law that takes it into account as a fact, and the evil disposition implicated in law by the imperative law. If evil were a law of nature (we tend to view it this way when we confuse the ferocity of an animal or the devastating force of a volcano with the cruelty of humanity), the prescription of the good would be absurd, and futile. Besides, the possibility of violating the law has to be imputed to us.[5] In the necessity of this imputation, evil is incomprehensible. But this is why evil, as an incomprehensible possibility, is *evil*, which is to say, *free*. If it were not free, it would not be "evil." (But this does not mean that without any evil act there would be no freedom, since freedom would then be confused with free will; instead, it means that without the *possibility* of evil and so without a disposition toward it, there would be no freedom. Freedom isn't the free choice between "good" and "evil" since, ultimately, for such a choice, everything is *good.* What freedom is remains as incomprehensible as evil itself: at the very least, however, this means that freedom is *addressed* only to a being disposed toward evil.)

As such, the imperative corresponds to *radical* evil, to the evil that corrupts the very ground of maxims.[6] That this evil is not that of a "propensity" is evident in two respects: it doesn't originate in a natural inclination, and it doesn't correspond with a slip, with a deviation from the maxim (in this case, the deviation would perhaps be no more than an error and perhaps there would be no possibility of voluntary evil; here, however, the will itself has to be radically corruptible). Evil is the corruption of the ground of the maxim and a maxim thus corrupted is a maxim that is no longer law making. Evil is not a contrary law; it is the disposition contrary to the law, the il-legislative disposition.

And yet it is because the law is the law *of making the law* (or of law making) that it reveals of itself—and, in a certain way, in itself—the inscription of this possibility. By definition, an ordinary law sets the "outlaw" outside the law. Yet the law of the law includes the outlaw as the one to whom it is necessarily addressed—the one to whom, in this sense, it is *abandoned,* while its addressee is, in turn, abandoned to the entire rigor of the law.[7] "*Act in such a way . . .* " only makes sense if it is addressed, not only to one who is *able* to refrain from acting in such a way, but first and foremost to one who, radically, in his or her very disposition, does *not* act in such a way. The law prohibits the one to whom it is addressed from obeying it from the outset, without stumbling. It is the law of freedom, therefore, and this is why it takes the form of an imperative. This latter isn't an expression derived from the law, its mouthpiece, as it were. As the imperative, it *is* or makes the law.

~

The imperative law thus differs from right. Right never says "Act!" It articulates a rule and asks that a particular case be submitted to it;[8] as such, however, it does not command. Or, more exactly, it commands to the extent that it is recognized as right, to the extent that it has the force of a law, which presupposes the parceling out of a scope proper to law as such (collectivity, state, church, etc.). Here, though, we are dealing with the law of all reasonable beings, all beings capable of law. The imperative states—but is this still a matter of "stating" or of "saying"? And if so, in what sense?—the law's case, absolutely.

And yet, for all that, it is not an *order.* As with right, it differs from the orders with which our sensibility continually confuses it. At the very least, it differs if we understand the order as Canetti, for example, understands it: as the gesture or relation whose most primitive form would be that of the threat of death that guides the fleeing deer. In fact, it could be that every human exercise of the order arises from such a menacing commandment. But the imperative contains neither threat nor promise. Indeed, its essence lies in the fact that it contains neither. Such is the sense of obedience *out of duty*, as opposed to an execution that only *conforms to* duty. To obey because of duty is to obey in the interests of duty itself alone, which is what has no interest. Moreover, duty obliges us to nothing other than duty itself, whereas the order requires its being carried out. (Do we really need to be reminded of the fact that, for Kant, this has nothing to do with a morality that is satisfied with good intentions, with a morality exempt from doing everything possible in order to carry out its duty?)

Duty obliges us to duty. In other words, it prescribes the legislative act, and this act, by itself, has no option but to *obligate itself* to the universality of the law, since it is obligated to a universality which is precisely not the universality of the particular contents of the law but that of its legality or, more exactly still, that of the being-law of the law. The law of duty obliges us to the duty of the law, this law that is not given.

Hence, although the law lies outside of the realm of orders, it does not lie outside that of duty. The former is limited to the application of a law with which it cannot, by itself, identify. On the contrary, it presupposes that such a law is known, whatever it might be (for example, the law of the strongest . . .). In the same way, and for the same reason, the order isn't identified with the utterance of the law, and the act of ordering can generally do without speech: "The order is older than language, otherwise dogs would not be able to understand it."[9] On the other hand, it makes no sense to imagine the imperative as other than being uttered.[10] The imperative is *only* a verbal or discursive form. *Duty* is not a mode of being—at least not in the classical sense of the term—but a mode of language—although perhaps in a radically new sense. *What* I have to do can be presented nonlinguistically; *the fact that I have to do it* can only ever be said. Ultimately, moreover, the fact that I have to do it can only be said to me. "Act . . . " This has to be *addressed* to me.

The duty of the law is no more a duty of love than it is an order: "There is no feeling of duty, although there is, indeed, a feeling from the representation of our duty, for the latter is a necessitation through the categorical moral imperative. Duty of compulsion not duty of love."[11] Indeed: "One can demand of man that he do what the law commands of him, but not that he do it *voluntarily*."[12] If duty depended on seduction, it would no longer be duty, strictly speaking, but would possess a power whose effect would be a matter of what Kant calls the "pathological." In this respect, such an effect could no longer distinguish duty from the threatening order.

When Kant writes that "in man there dwells an active principle . . . accompanying him not as soul . . . but as spirit, one that . . . commands him irresistibly according to the law of moral practical reason"[13] he means that the imperative does not exist in the psychic substance known to us only phenomenologically (and so never really as *substance*), but only in this *Gemüt* whose main job is to be the unity of transcendental constitution. The imperative does not belong to the nature of the subject; rather, it belongs to what, although resembling a subject, exceeds, in the strongest sense of the term, its subject status: it belongs to reason's condition of possibility, to the condition of possibility of a reason that is itself practical. More precisely: a reason that is *practical in and of itself.* Not, however, in that it shows itself to be such (it does not "reveal" itself); rather, this practicality happens to it as a fact, as the *factum rationis* of which it is not the subject. (This fact has no subject; it is not a subject).

The imperative provides the conditions of possibility for praxis or is itself the transcendental of praxis. As elsewhere, yet here, perhaps, more than anywhere else, this transcendental indicates nontranscendence. The principle of praxis isn't a transcendent reality; rather, it consists in reason's being practical in and of itself or in the *a priori* practical condition of reasonable beings as such. For Kant (who turns back, in this respect, to the Aristotelian tradition), praxis isn't in the first instance the order of actions insofar as they demand submission to evaluations and norms; rather, it is the order of action itself insofar as it imposes itself as the order of reason and insofar as it imposes praxis, that is, action whose result is not distinct from the agent (unlike—or as opposed to—*poiesis*, which *produces* a distinct result). Or, if you prefer, the stakes are not primarily the rationalizing of action but the discovery that reason as such, as pure reason, has to act. To act as pure reason means to make law. Such is the *duty* of reason. On this account, and for the first time in its history, reason no longer consists in a given rationality in terms of which acts have to be measured; rather, as pure practical reason it is identical with the *a priori* duty of being—that is, of acting out—what it is: pure practical reason.

No doubt *pure reason* is not only an expression that is foreign to our sensibility but one whose concepts need to be submitted—perhaps more than any other concepts—to critique or to the deconstruction of metaphysics. Yet it could well be that a new task announces itself thus: the task of thinking "pure reason" *in terms of* its being-practical, *in terms of* the duty that constitutes or enjoins it.

If the imperative is not an order in the aforementioned sense, it nevertheless *prescribes* effectively. That is, even before giving instruction relative to the modality of action,[14] it prescribes action; it obliges us to act. This means that the action is not just an empirically determined contingency but something that possesses an unconditional necessity. In all hypothetical (or technical) imperatives, action is a means submitted to the condition of an end. By contrast, the categorical imperative makes action an end—not in the activist sense of "acting for the sake of acting," but in the sense that the action that holds here as an end is the unconditioned (or free) action of pure reason. Since this end is unconditioned, however, it cannot be presented as a necessity derived from a prior law—from the law of nature, for example. This is why freedom is not, as in Hegel, reason or the rationality of reason, and why it does not constitute an end in the sense of a *telos* programmed by an *archē*. Free action as end is never anything more than a beginning, an initiative or an initial move without any end (and, as we know, Kant defines freedom as the power of beginning something from out of oneself). What's more, freedom isn't prescribed in the sense of having been pre-inscribed; it is *enjoined*. Reason or the rationality of reason (engaging thus, perhaps, in its own deconstruction) takes places at an injunction.

This injunction is both more and less than an order. It does not threaten, does not force an action to be carried out—and the imperative as such is deprived of all executive power. Equally, though, it imposes, it applies, it joins to reason the prescription of a free action, a free legislation of which nothing, not even its mere possibility, can be *known* by or *revealed* to reason. The imperative injunction forces reason in the direction of what exceeds it absolutely.

This is why the imperative "is impressed upon us [*uns aufdringt*] as a synthetic a priori proposition that is not based on any intuition, either pure or empirical."[15] It imposes itself as a fact imposes itself, and it imposes itself as *factum rationis*. The *factum rationis* is not an empirical intuition: if it were, it would submit the imperative to a sensible condition. This, moreover, does not constitute an argument grounded on a moralistic disdain for the sensible (nothing could be more foreign to Kant), but an argument grounded on the *condition* that is thus imposed on an unconditioned injunction. The *factum* is that the imperative doesn't depend on any fact. Where would duty lie, and where freedom, if I have to act because, here or there, in the other or in myself, I am obliged to encounter something in the experience of action?

No more, however, is the *factum rationis* an intellectual intuition; it occupies, in the synthetic *a priori* proposition that the imperative is, the place of the *a priori* forms of pure intuition. It is, we might say, the space-time of pure practical reason. This perhaps means that it at least shares with the *a priori* forms of pure intuition a position that is *derivative* rather than originary, and that, for this very reason, it is a *factum*.[16] Its factuality is not such that, in it, reason can present itself as the originary power of its praxis; rather, its praxis enjoins it. And in this sense, its praxis is given to it, just as objects are given to it in pure intuition. ("Intuition . . . only takes place insofar as the object is given to us; but this in turn is possible only if it affects the mind [*Gemüt*] in a certain way.")[17] The *factum* is the practical mode of this *a priori* gift. The anteriority of this gift is irreducible and exceeds absolutely every self-positing act of reason, every self-representation and every self-mastery. It is also the practical mode of reason's *being-affected*. The imperative affects reason. Yes, this does mean that it humiliates reason (and might it not be precisely this that our sensibility is unable to tolerate?), but what it means before all else is that it befalls reason from the outside, as it were, from an outside that, although exceeding all passivity, is far from being identical with activity (which, remember, is prescribed; activity is the end). The imperative is inactive; it is imperative. It exceeds any relation between active and passive, between spontaneous and receptive.

Hence this excess reconstitutes neither an "originary intuition" nor (for this would amount to the same thing) an originary act. The imperative does not dialectically *sublate* the critical distinction between spontaneity and receptivity or between subject and finitude. It is not, like Hegelian *ethos*, the being-finite realizing the moral Idea by denying itself and thereby raising itself to the level of subject (the subject of philosophy or of the state). It is—or is *given*—differently.

In this difference—which, being absolute, is also not the Absolute—the imperative *repeats* this distinction: since it is the imperative, the imperative imposes the separation of a passivity (to which it is enjoined) from an activity (which it enjoins). What it does not do, however, is impose this separation as if it had produced it; rather, separation is imposed upon it, and the imperative only imposes separation insofar as separation is imposed upon it. Put differently: there is the imperative because this unsublatable distinction is imposed.

Now, the *factum rationis*, far from corresponding to rationality as a fact (posited, established, available), designates a factuality heterogeneous to and incommensurable with the reason from the heart of which, nonetheless, it emerges. This incommensurability measures us; it obliges us.

～

What does it mean to be obliged? What does it mean to be enjoined? This question, understood as an ontological question (one that perhaps repeats and displaces the Heideggerian question of the ontico-ontological difference and the Derridian question of *différance*), constitutes the horizon of this section of the present volume,[18] a horizon that has not been reached, much less surpassed. Still, we can at least indicate this—even if this indication carries us beyond any *question* in the conventional sense of this term (can a *question*, for instance, be transformed into an *obligation*? This is not impossible; in any case, this problem belongs to the horizon of our "question").

We are obliged—reason is obliged—to respect the law. We are obliged not by force of an authoritarian order but by force of a constitution that is nevertheless neither a grounding nor an institution: "The restoration of the original predisposition to good in us is . . . the acquiring of a *lost* incentive for good, for the incentive that consists in the respect for the moral law we have never been able to lose."[19]

We have been unable to lose respect, for the loss of respect would signal the loss of any relation (albeit negative) to the law. Respect, even before being qualified as "a feeling of reason" (an aspect that I do not want to consider here), forms the very relation to the law. The imperative cannot take place without respect, and it is not the imperative as such, in isolation, that gives the law (always providing that it is even possible for us to isolate it; if a descriptive proposition can be posited separately, devoid of relation— "there is [or there is not] a universal law," for example—does this make sense for an injunction alone . . . ?). Without this relation, then, we could speak neither of "good" nor of "evil."

Equally, it isn't out of respect for any particular law that respect as such cannot be lost. I can indeed lose respect for all sorts of laws; they can become irrelevant to me; they can no longer oblige me; I might see no harm in refusing to follow them. And if, moreover, I consider it to be "good" not to follow them, it is because I am bound by some other law. Respect, however, binds me to the law of obligation itself: "Despite this fall [into evil], the injunction that we *ought* to become better men resounds unabatedly in our souls."[20] Losing this respect would signal our submission to another law, another obligation, one for which the good itself would be the law of an absence of law or the law of a pure self-giving of the law. Anarchy or absolute sovereignty oblige themselves; they are obliged to be obliged. "*It is prohibited to prohibit,*" for example (which, moreover, proves that the imagination of May '68 had an acute sense of an imperative *ethos*). The law of obligation is not a particular law; it is the law of the law, prior to any legislation and more archaic than any legislative subject. It is, paradoxically, the law of what has no law. "Nature" has laws, "man" does not. And he cannot lose respect.

We are obliged by and toward what obliges us, by and toward this obligation's injunction. Not because such an injunction has the power to command us but because it is incommensurable with any power of constraint or propensity. Ultimately, what we call the empirical proves nothing more than this: the force of a constraint always ends up by resisting the respect for a higher obligation, for the true authority or for the authority of truth, at least insofar as it manifests itself as a challenge to violence (which, as we know all too well, doesn't mean that respect is something that sweeps violence away; here, it is a matter of a "resistance of what does not resist—ethical resistance," as Levinas has it.)[21] The price paid for this in time, lives, dignity, is appalling. It is unstoppable. The protestation of respect thus constitutes a dimension of experience without which we would have no experience of evil. Respect protests in the name of what is incommensurable about obligation, and the relation to this incommensurability constitutes us, makes of us the *factum rationis* that obligates us. Yet this isn't to say that we give ourselves over to the law, still less to say that we have to give ourselves as law (it's not through "humanity" that the law has to be determined but vice versa, as we shall see).

Respect isn't addressed to a good, since the law doesn't prescribe the appropriation of a good. The law prescribes the act of legislating according to the form of the law, that is, according to its universal form. Universality, however, is not given. Neither its criterion nor its nature are given inasmuch as the law is not decreed by my maxim. If they were, universality would not be given but imposed; it would do violence to us rather than enjoin us. The gift can be tied to the injunction, not to violence.

Hence the moral law—the imperative—withdraws from the rational law that exceeds it. The moral law prescribes universality and, with it, rationality as a task and not as a good that has been assigned to it. Inversely, the law decrees (this is even its only decree) that universality should not consist in the establishment at the universal level of a singular will.[22] The *task* of the universal lies in an entirely different direction from its appropriation through subjective particularity. The moral law is not only in excess of what ought to be a rational subject, it also enjoins a beyond of subjectivity in general. The law traces a single trajectory—the trajectory of the imperative—from this side of the subject to beyond it. (Which isn't to say that it can't be *my* law; on the contrary, it *has* to be the law of *my* maxim. It doesn't prescribe *submission* to the universal but prescribes that I make universal law. But this doubtless demands a singular status that is no longer that of subjectivity.)

This is why respect is simultaneously admiration or veneration for the law *and* the humiliation of the subject before it: the law enjoins the subject, joining to it its fundamental inability to satisfy the law—which disjoins it.[23] Respect is the very alteration of the position and structure of the subject; that is, the latter faces up to (but without being able to look upon) or responds to (but without *responding*[24]) the alterity of the law. This alterity isn't the fact of some assignable other, whether a great Other or a small one, even though it determines the being-other of every other. It is the fact of reason, the fact that there is a factuality or a facticity of the injunction in reason to reason, the fact that reason's other is inscribed within reason itself. This "*in . . . to . . .*" provides the incommensurable structure of the law: it is not a matter of the subject's giving -its -law to itself; rather, in reason itself, an injunction is addressed to reason, from without, therefore, from a doubly other outside that demands, addresses, and enjoins it.

Respect, then, is to the consideration of a good as the imperative is to the self-legislation of the subject. And this is why the good that is in here in play, since it still falls under the name of the *Sovereign Good*, needs to be understood less in terms of the *good* than in terms of *sovereignty*: that is, according to a difference that is incommensurable with anything that could be or make a "good."[25] The Sovereign Good not only reduces to nothing goods in general, it also consists in nothing other than this reduction to nothing. This leaves no room for a more elevated sense of the good and points instead to the immeasurable extremity of this elevation: *das höchste*

Gut, the highest, supreme, or sovereign good, which, in fact, is no longer measured in terms of "height" of any sort. The Sovereign Good is this extreme: not the "highest" good, in other words, but the excess of extremity beyond all height and measure. The Sovereign Good also, and perhaps ultimately, means that *we cannot measure its excess*. And that, by the same token, it obliges us:

What is it in us (we can ask ourselves) whereby we, beings ever dependent upon nature through so many needs, are at the same time raised so far above these needs by the idea of an original predisposition (in us) that we count them all as nothing, and ourselves as unworthy of existence, if we cater to their satisfaction (though this alone can make life worth desiring) in opposition to the law—a law by virtue of which our reason commands us potently, yet without making either promises or threats?[26]

Equally, the Sovereign Good cannot both exclude goods (or happiness) *and* require, as its very sovereignty, what can no longer be thought as a "good," namely, being-obliged by the law. Kant writes:

This ultimate end of pure practical reason is the highest good, so far as this is possible in the world, which good, however, is not merely to be sought in what nature can provide, that is to say, in happiness (the greatest amount of pleasure). Instead, it is to be sought in the supreme requirement, that is, the only condition under which reason can award it to rational beings in the world and, of course, at the same time in the ethical, law-abiding conduct of rational beings.[27]

~

Respect for the law concerns its sublimity: "The majesty of the moral law (as of the law on Sinai) instils awe (not dread, which repels, nor charm, which invites familiarity); and in this instance, since the ruler resides within us, this *respect*, as of a subject toward his ruler, awakens a *sense of the sublimity* of our own destiny which enraptures us more than any beauty."[28] The feeling of the sublime in general (always assuming that it can be distinguished from the feeling of the sublime involved in our destiny; in reality, there is only one sublime) is the feeling of the limit of our faculties. The law exceeds absolutely the farthest limits of representation and measure— and, if it needs to be constructed, according to the second formulation of the categorical imperative, in terms of the *type* of a universal law of nature, it isn't in the sense of a phenomenal law but in the sense of a law of the phenomena that does not itself appear in the phenomenal sense. In his own copy of the Bible, next to Luke 17: 20: "the kingdom of God cometh not with outward show," Kant wrote these words: "visible (form)."[29] The feeling of the sublime is addressed to what exceeds form.

And yet the universal character of the law is not given as something invisible. What exceeds form doesn't take on a superior or supersensible form. Rather, it denotes the very formation of form, concealed in every form that appears and delivered over to reason as a task.[30] This task is enjoined because it can be neither represented nor taught in the manner of a technical task. There is no natural law of formation (in the same way that life is unrepresentable for us). There is simply the law of legislating in this absence of law; that is, there is the law of making an ethical world, of forming an ethical world—making it or forming it *as if* there could be a natural one, in which we could live. So far as the formation of this ethical world—of this world under moral laws—is concerned, there is no law if not the law of forming it.

Understood thus, the sublime character of the law indicates humanity's "divine destination." But the "divine" doesn't name a subject (or a project) of law. Granted, God is the legislator, but God exists because a categorical imperative exists: "the idea of such a being . . . emerges from this imperative and not the reverse."[31] "God" isn't the God of nature—any more than, for the same reason, He is the God of religion. No, "God" *is* the divine destination of man insofar as this destination is enjoined by him. "God" *is* not *beyond* representation. On the contrary, the beyond of representation—the limit beyond which we cannot pass since, rather than opening onto a limitlessness of form that would somehow lie beyond form, it marks the *end* of form and of the world insofar as it exhausts or withdraws the very formation of form and of world—this beyond of representation (and of the subject) makes the law. And the law *destines* to this end in a manner that is both "divine" and "sublime."

This mode of *destining* is not a way of promising nor of fixing an end or an accomplishment. Rather, it is a way of *abandoning*. Perhaps the categorical imperative is only a transformation of tragic truth, a truth that destiny has essentially abandoned. The law abandoned—to itself. What *haunts* us, what has haunted us ever since our loss of tragedy's representation or since the imperative began to present us with its irreducibility, is this abandonment.[32]

Hence there is a destination, an ultimate abandonment to the sense of finitude. The sublime character of the law—which depends strictly on its imperative nature—stems from the fact that it destines to the universality, to the absolutely grand and to the incommensurable *in* finitude. On the other hand, there can be no destination to an end thought as the absolute *telos* of the infinite development of a finite being.[33]

What still counts here is the beginning, then, the *sending* of the imperative. The law is unsurpassable as the imperative law because it is not the self-legislation of the subject. In the self-legislation of a substance, which turns the substance into a subject—God, Nature, or Man—the law *sublates* itself, conserves itself by *suppressing itself* as a law into a submission to its only freedom, a freedom that, moreover, it thus confers upon itself. Now, to this thought is joined the corollary of a (Christian and speculative) conception of the law as slavery. By contrast, the imperative imposes the law as the outermost, unrecoverable limit *on the basis of which* the injunction is addressed.

Hence the law is *addressed to* a freedom and not *founded by* it. Reciprocally, freedom does not consist in obedience to its own law—to the law proper to its nature—but in beginning from itself: it is an inaugural freedom, therefore, prior to all law. And yet this freedom is, before anything else, the recipient of the law. Here, there are always two "origins," neither of which is recoverable and each of which seems, indefinitely and in turn, to step over the other: the address of the law and the free beginning. Put differently, there are two "principles," neither of which responds strictly to the status of a principle: the imperative and freedom. And everything unfolds as if the law prescribed to freedom the job of beginning this side of the law. And yet, it prescribes this to freedom, enjoins it to it, and this is itself the ground of the imperative: there is an imperative because freedom is the recipient and not the self-positing and self-legislative freedom of the subject.

True, we could go with the opposite by invoking the well-known passage from the *Critique of Practical Reason*: freedom is the *ratio essendi* of the moral law and the moral law is the *ratio cognoscendi* of freedom. But does the expression *ratio essendi* actually indicate that freedom is, in some way, beyond the law, that it is the inventive power behind it, that it is nothing other than its autonomy, its self-positing? In reality, it is nothing like this: freedom is the *ratio essendi* of the moral law, not as the condition of existence or manifestation, but as the condition of realization in the sense that a moral law addressed to a will not subject to the law would be a contradiction.[34]

∼

The imperative is essentially addressed to freedom. "The ground of the possibility of categorical imperatives is this: that they refer to no other property of choice (by which some purpose can be ascribed to it) than simply to its freedom."[35] This means that the imperative is imperative because it is addressed and because it belongs thus to a more general group of *addresses* (interpellation, prayer, order, call, demand, exhortation, warning, etc.), unless it defines a constant underlying this whole group, a constant that is modified accordingly in various ways or able to take on different tones. And what this also means is that the imperative is categorical because it is addressed to a freedom and so cannot in advance submit the maxim of that to the condition of an end.

What this ultimately means, then, is that freedom is essentially and not accidentally or provisionally the addressee of the injunction. As such, this freedom, which is not the self-position of the Subject, is no longer to be seen as the free will of the individual subject. It concerns what, in the individual, is not individual. And what is not individual—but also not "collective" as such—is the possibility of being "addressed" by the other, from out of the alterity of the other (and not of being in some way ratified by the sameness of the other); it is the possibility of being interpellated or, even, according to the Greek sense of the term, of being *categorized* by the other. *Kategorein* is to accuse, to speak the accusative truth about someone and so to affirm, impute, and attribute. *The imperative categorizes its addressee*; it affirms the freedom of the addressee, imputes evil to it and intends or abandons it to the law. In this way, the imperative categorizes the essence or nature of man, doing so in excess of every category, in excess of what is proper to man.

To treat humanity as an end is to treat it as just such an addressee. It is to avoid the conditional submission to any concept of man whatsoever, but only to the injunction that is destined for him and that destines him. This injunction destines man to nothing but being such a destinee: one to whom, in the finite space that he never exceeds, the *kategorein* of excess is continually addressed.

Translated by James Gilbert-Walsh and Simon Sparks

8

Lapsus judicii

What happens when philosophy becomes juridical? What happens when philosophy becomes juridical, *not* in the sense that it takes right as one of its objects and assigns itself the task of a reflection or meditation on it (although philosophy cannot legitimately neglect this sort of work . . .), but in the sense that philosophy itself, as such, would be instituted, determined, and presented according to the concept and in the form of a juridical discourse and practice? In the sense, then, in which philosophy would be *legitimated* juridically. What would be the stakes, the nature and the validity of this operation, which goes beyond anything that we might term a "philosophy of right"? What then of philosophy? What then of right?

Such questions might seem a little odd, but posed in terms of historical figures, they could be stated thus: What would happen if Athens were presented in Rome, and as Rome? That is to say, if Rome were only Rome in order to be the very thing whose exclusion constitutes it? For Rome can no doubt be seen as the substitution of right for philosophy; leaving aside the officially recognized history of philosophy, the history of its teaching would be more than enough to make the case.

Posed in historical terms the question would therefore be: What happens when, in Rome, philosophy *passes* into right?

It's no coincidence that the very philosophy that seeks to know itself through its own history—namely, Hegelian science—sees, in the moment of the Roman discourse on right (the corollary of which can be found in philosophical skepticism—and so in what can scarcely be said to belong to philosophy), the very negativity of the Self, something that needs to be understood here as negativity turned in upon itself and deprived of its dialectical richness: the Self knows "the loss of its essence" in "the equivocal universal exclusion" and the "reciprocal dissociation" of consciousness that right designates by the "disdainful expression" *persons* (*Person* in Hegel's text, the German rendering of the Latin *persona*: mask and anonymity).[1] The Latin concept (the Etruscan word) *persona* provides the strange figure that undoes the figure or the *Gestalt*—the form and the content—of the Self. Although the Life of the Concept, here as elsewhere, is sublated, the "state of right" is still a pure or, rather, wholly *im*pure loss of substance and consciousness. Spirit—philosophy—passes it by rather than passing through it.

Yet in the run up to Hegelian science, Rome had already repeated itself. Philosophy had already become juridical. It had already become so with Kant. So common has this currency become (with and since Hegel), that it's sometimes even said that, with Kant, philosophy becomes legalism, an entirely formal, formalist, and procedural discourse. For a while, Kant would have been the Chicanneau of philosophy[2]—and for many he still is. In philosophy, it's Kant who prompts the question: What happens when philosophy becomes juridical, when it's articulated as jurisdiction?

The question is a double one, therefore, and doubly heterogeneous. If philosophy is Greek, it's the *Latin* question of philosophy; if Rome is the dissolution of philosophy, it's the *philosophical* question of Rome. I want to try to broach this question by explaining as briefly as possible this reciprocal implication, even if my explanation will have to take the form of an assertion rather than an argument. To the extent that it will ever be possible to *justify* this sort of assertion, that's something that will have to be done later on by examining the Kantian operation in and of itself.

If the Roman discourse on right is substituted for philosophy or imposes its mask upon it, then this is perhaps because it's in Rome, and on the basis of this, that metaphysics sets about declaring itself by right. Intimately tied up with the specifically *Greek* discourse of metaphysics, therefore, would be a *Latin* discourse:[3] juridical discourse. (Of course, we would need to complicate matters still further by addressing the fact that "discourse" itself is a Latin concept, but we must take one or two shortcuts here.) Befalling *logos* both from within and without, "within" as "without," Latin jurisdiction would say something quite different. Precisely by way of this substitution, however, Latin jurisdiction holds its ground and affirms its right: no *jus* without *ratio*. As such, it has (always?) already been claimed by *logos*. And, to the extent that *logos* must pass into its own history, *logos itself* is articulated by it.

But what is juridical discourse? In the Latin world—or, as we saw earlier, here and now, *hic et nunc*—the very notion of "juridical discourse" borders on tautology. (Almost inevitably, we will repeat some well-known facts here.) Jurisdiction is the fact of *saying* right. Such saying is inherent to right—just as, reciprocally, right has to be inherent to its saying, to its being said, if an element of a *code* is going to be determined for language and if the statements formed within it are going to be *just* or even *judicious*; such, indeed, is the logical duty, office, and right of "saying" . . . The basic entanglement of speech (and language in particular) with right constitutes Latin discourse. *Discourse*—in the language of the sixteenth century, both statement *and* reason—takes the place of *logos* through the coupling of *jus* and *dictio*, in the twin production of the judicial and the judicious.

Hence *dictio*, by itself, in some way comprises a judgment even before it's actually formulated. *Dicere* means to show and, in order to be able to show, to discern or to fix, to establish and to point the finger at whatever it is that is being determined (*indicere*). Latin saying operates by judging; it is constitutively judicial: *causam dicere* is to establish and to show the cause, to plead. From this point on, discourse only shows things by pleading their cause; and such is the program that it falls to Kant to carry out.

Jurisdiction is not added to *jus*. At most it explains it, but only as a last resort does it establish it. In itself, we might say, if we wanted to resort to a more Hegelian vocabulary (as if that wasn't precisely what's irrelevant here), *jus* is doubtless not a word; it is the "area [*l'aire*] of the action or the maximum claim resulting from the natural definition or conventional status of an individual or a group."[4] Yet this area needs *ipso facto* to be "defined, in each case, extremely precisely." Equally, "the explicit articulation of every *jus*, the formula that articulates its limits and, within these limits, secures it, is essential." Yet the form of this (other) determination of *logos* is not the *idea* (or the *concept*), but the *formula*, the "minor form." *Formula* is itself a juridical term. It is the *mise en forme* needed in order to engage an action that conforms to the terms of right. To formulate, to articulate, is to ratify in accordance with right. In itself and *for itself*, however, right exists only through and as formulation.

Essentially, then, *jus* is articulated as a subject, but as a subject that is less substance (rather, and as Hegel points out, this is what it loses) than a power (an ability, will, desire, potential, faculty—always, though, in terms of right) of "action" and "claim"; a subject that shows itself less through its presence (its figure, what is proper to it, its *Gestalt*) than through the contours of the area that defines its figure and its identity: the outline of the *persona*. This (juridical) person, this persona, is still one who formulates, assuming that we can indeed map onto its Etruscan origin (which carries the sense of "mask") the popular etymology of the word: the mask *personat*, it amplifies the voice and lets it be heard from afar. (The subject of) right is the one the power of whose voice (or, more precisely, whose megaphone, whose artificial voice) establishes and circumscribes propriety. This power itself is artificial and theatrical: (the subject of) right is established—or stated—on a nothingness of being and nature.

What is stated by the judge—*judex*, one invested with jurisdiction—is the formula that says or makes right by setting out the relation of the law to the case *hic et nunc* in question. The fact that enunciation [*le dire*] is inherent to right corresponds to a specific status that I'd sum up in the following way: casuality constitutes the essence of right; casuistry, the essence of jurisdiction. *Casus* denotes the fall—the fall in or through chance, through contingency, the fall according to *opportunity* (an opportunity that constitutes the judge as much as the criminal); the fall, then, as *accident*. The "essence" of right stems from the singular relation of accident to essence. *De jure*, the law ought to be the universal code whose very definition implies the annulment or the reabsorption of any accident. *De facto* (but this fact is itself constitutive of right, is itself the very fact of juris-diction), cases ought to be referred and legitimated case by case. This necessity doesn't stem from the pure and simple accident of an indefinite diversity of empirical conditions (of *personal* situations) that would always overflow the inevitable limitation (itself entirely empirical) of the various forms of right. Here, it is a matter of the necessity of the accidental. Or rather (since what's doubtless involved here is a certain aporetic relation of metaphysical necessity to the empirical, to the factual, to the actual or the evidential as such), the juridical order is the order instituted through the formal—in every sense of the term—taking into account of the accident *itself*, without ever *conceiving* its necessity.

Jurisdiction is articulated around a double structure, therefore. On the one hand, it states the right of the case, thereby making it a case: it subsumes it, suppresses its accidental character; *picks it up* [relève] after its fall;

sublative (*aufhebend*) jurisdiction proceeds thus in the same way as the Concept of Hegelian science. On the other hand, though, it states the right *of* this case and so states right itself *through* this case: in a sense, right exists through the case alone, through its accidental character; even if the case is settled [*casé*] and domesticated (*casa*, house, has nothing to do with *casus*), it has to fall down once it is picked up or sublated. The logic of the case is one of falling or sliding in on itself, a logic of falling back. In terms of the model established by right, the case, even the case that has already been judged, is always *lapse* and *relapse*. And it carries, too, as I shall want to show, the other Latin name for a fall: *lapsus*.

The Latin discourse of philosophy would be a way of taking the accident as such into account: therefore, never completely Greek (logical); never completely German (speculative). Kant's predilection for Latin seems less and less an accident.

~

Since the case is not only unforeseen but has to be so, and since right is given as the case of its own utterance, so juridical discourse shows itself to be the true discourse of fiction. The prominent part played by the notion of "juridical fiction" in and since the Roman discourse on right is well known, and I don't want to deal with it here. It should be enough to indicate the three registers on which this notion can be invoked: first, the academic exercise, in which the treatment of fictitious cases (possible cases, in other words, however counterfactual and improbable they may be: anything can happen) forms the handling of jurisdiction; then, the constitution as a juridical *case* of a reality that is in itself concealed (the creation, if you like, of a reality of pure signs); finally, the action of the so-called *fictitious* Roman discourse on right through which the law is extended to a case to which it does not actually apply (the illegitimate extension of the legitimacy of a sign). According to this summary division, fiction would represent little more than a certain number of typical cases in the exercise of right. In order to produce them, however, right will have to have the generic ability of fiction.

In fact, the relation of law to case—the relation of jurisdiction— means that no case is a law and that a case only *falls* under the law once the law speaks of it. The accident—what happens—has to be struck by the seal of the law (of its utterance) in order to be not simply judged but constituted as an instance or case of right, modeled or sculpted (*fictum*) in terms of right. Juris-diction is or makes up juris-fiction. Law and case come before right only if they are modeled, shaped, fashioned—fictioned—in and through one another. The implications of this necessity are quite radical, however: the installation or inauguration of right must of itself be fictioned. Jurisdiction as such needs to be uttered: the "Praetorian Edict" was the yearly manifesto formulating the principles for right saying. Right repeats its installation with the investiture of each person who receives or takes the right to state it.[5] The *persona* of the judge and his *edictum* are forged from the same *fictitious* gesture: right is said here of the case for which there can be no prior right, and which is *the case of right*. (When Hadrian laid down a "perpetual edict," there was no longer the fiction of judging: in fact, every installation of right would henceforth be handed over to the state . . .)

Now, although we can hear the *fiction* in Latin discourse, this has, in principle, nothing to do with the values that are normally associated with that word—the mixed values of the Greek *poiesis, mimesis,* and *phantasia,* which come together in German *Dichtung. Dichtung* makes up a world; by definition, it excludes anything like a causal or accidental "structure"—just like the world of metaphysical *theoria.* If poetry fictions, it does so as a theory: a vision that produces visions. By contrast, (juridical) fiction works *with* a world, with the accidental, eventful actuality of a "worldness" that the law neither produces nor sublates. If anything and everything can happen in *Dichtung,* that's because it produces the unlimited field of its own production; if anything and everything can happen for right, it is because there's always something that exceeds the limits of its spaces. Fiction always shapes the meeting of the universal and the particular, of necessity and contingency, doing so in such a way that what is shaped carries the indelible mark of the *case,* a situation that stands in sharp distinction to Hegelian synthesis, where the mark is always already led toward the dialectical erasure of each one of its distinctive traits, right up to its complete resolution in the Concept, beyond any figure. The figure (which, like *fictio,* comes from *fingo*) can in no way move past or be surpassed; it constitutes the specific order of the *persona,* the *formula,* and the *dictio.* By saying right, the *judex* always says at the same time that the reality of the case is included in law *and* that saying it fictions or figures the very "being" of the case. Indeed, we might well be forgiven for saying that the juridical order essentially arises from a "cynicism" of fiction, from a "bare-faced lie." We pro-

ceed *as if* (and the Greek word for fiction, remember, is *hypokrisis*), this being one of the central motifs that Kant introduces into philosophy.

The poetic operation—at least in the way that it's thought by metaphysics—consists in a putting to work (*energeia*) of sense. Its very principle dictates that it involve the resolution of figures, that is, the signs of
sense—or, what amounts to much the same thing, the creation of a pure
and autonomous sense beyond all signs. "Veritas nullo egeat signo,"[6] declares Spinoza, and, in this regard, Leibniz, Hegel, and Mallarmé all stubbornly insist on the same sort of poetry (poetry itself). This is the autonomous operation (and, in Greek, *autonomy* is what gives itself its law)
par excellence, and it presupposes the sovereign autonomy of its subject.

The juridical act—it scarcely merits the name "operation"[7]—forms
or figures a fact whose essence or whose own sense falls, on principle, outside of this form. It deliberately institutes the break between the sign and
the thing; more accurately, it is the act of this break or this breaking, and
it is so first of all insofar as its agent fictions or fashions him or herself into
the person of the right to utter right.

It's tempting to conclude that, because of this self-saying, this "auto-
diction" (but can we actually speak Greek and Latin at the same time?), the
judex is equivalent to the poet and so to the theoretician. Indeed, we might
well say, a little more precisely, that the juridical person figures what happens—*accidit*—to the subject of the poem (or) of knowledge, even to the
extent that this subject wants to be and thinks itself accordingly as the absolute origin and propriety of an absolute right: that of creation or of truth;
of a right, in other words, whose "area of action or claim" would be total,
unlimited, always escaping the limiting, localizing conditions of right.[8]
Right always proceeds from a delimitation to a localization, that is, by way
of a dislocation. The subject undergoes a dislocation; this is the limit of its
own figure. The accident that affects it or the occasion that befalls it is the
case of the absolute subject itself. Jurisdiction implies that *the origin is a
case* or that the inaugural gesture of right involves an "area" and thus a delimitation, thereby contravening the *logic* of the subject. The loss of the
substance of the Self is equivalent to the de-finition of the person; to finitude, in other words. In much the same way, the person is neither the subject nor the seat of right, unless the magistrate, on the basis of the particular case, concedes the judicial *action*: not *jus in personam*, therefore, but
actio in personam.[9]

The juridical person is determined by way of the accidental, the fictional, and (so) by way of finitude. This is why such a person is the precise opposite of the subject.[10] And this is also why its determinations are gathered in that of the "subject" *of the statement.* (We've already seen that since right is what is said, the subject is only ever going to be the subject of what is stated.) The *person* is the one who states—whether on the level of accusation, defense, or sentence—and who states him- or herself thus; yet he or she does so in such a way that this "self" is not a substantial identity, not a "personality" per se; rather, it is the *judgment* of the person.

With judgment, right brings us back into the sphere of philosophy. Or, rather, at the same time that right was busy being substituted for philosophy, philosophy had already begun discreetly to saddle it with a problem taken from Greek discourse.

Judgment—logical or philosophical statements as well as juridical ones—is distinct from the concept. The subject of conception is the physical or metaphysical, poetic or theoretical subject; the subject always *conceives* the thing and, by conceiving of it, thereby conceives itself. Rather than signifying the thing, however, the subject engenders or produces it, and if it does "see" it (in the sense of *theoria*), it is still, as Aristotle says, in the sense that light produces colors.

Greek discourse has no real term for judgment. As we shall see, the *judicium*—the juridical word, the *term* of jurisdiction—might well pass for the Latin philosopheme par excellence. Its Greek precursor is *krisis*, a notion that is more "practical" than "theoretical," denoting discernment, choice, and decision, with connotations that are always more moral and political (or technical, and medical in particular) than they are properly gnoseological.

Now, *krisis* only becomes a gnoseological notion—even to the point of determining the "gnoseological" as a whole—with the Stoic theory of the sign. The *kritērion* is the distinctive sign, the mark or the imprint that actually corresponds to the character of the thing. The thing isn't given or produced in or through the subject; rather, it is known through its criterion, through those criteria that mark it out, distinguish it, and thereby make it known. This is the *phantasia kataleptikē,* the "comprehensive representation." Yet we still need to gain or to recognize this criterion itself; we still need to avoid mistaking it, under the effects of a *pathos,* by reading the signs incorrectly and so by running it together with *phantasia*'s evil double, *phantasma.* What we have to do, therefore, is *krinein,* to discern correctly the signs specific to it (its *idioms*). Three things emerge with the theory of the sign. First, the *pathological* possibility of error; that is, the possibility that the accident might actually happen to knowledge rather than simply as a lack of it. Second, the role of the *decision* (of a gesture "over and above" the *logos*) concerning the precision of the sign. Third, the role of the *statement*, at least as the attribution or predication that relates the sign to the thing.

The decision that is stated in order (in principle) to separate out *logos* from any sense of *pathos* will be transcribed by the *judicium*. It is right that prepares the concept for the absence of conception—or for unnatural or nongenerative conception. The "concept" furnished by the sign isn't the opening of the thing itself but the imposition of its idiom, won against the danger or the risk of a fall into phantasy—a victory that always needs to be gained and thus a risk that always needs to be run. Uncertainty is constitutive of judgment, since its job of *adjustment* needs to be understood as essentially a division: "Judgment is an expression of *finitude* and, from this point of view, things are said to be *finite*, because they consist in a judgment, because their being present and their universal nature (their body and their soul), though certainly united (were this not the case, the things would be nothing), are still elements that are already different enough to be separable."[11]

The *judicium*, then, will be determined—through the Augustinian tradition and the interpretation of the figures of Scripture (an interpretation that, in turn, has Stoic origins)—as the specific part of an appreciation, of an estimation that, in order to be ultimately certain of its result, will have to be no less changeable and personal in the manner of its establishment. Through scholasticism and the *critica* (the part of the *dialectica* that treats of judgment), the *judicium* will be determined as the intellectual act of a *compositio* as opposed to the *intelligentia indivisibilium* that properly comprises conception. *Compositio* implies first and foremost assemblage, fashioning, fiction; *krisis* always involves a *hypokrisis*;[12] then (but this is one and the same thing) it implies the position or the imposition of the sign for the thing figured thus, the investiture through the sign and conferred by the sign of the right to say the thing.

The order of judgment is made up of the multiple, the uncertain, and the unequal. *Opus incertum*, as we say in Latin to designate architectonic works built of irregular stone. Since the order of construction isn't given in advance by the materials used, we're going to have to judge the possibilities of adjusting them ourselves. Judicial work is essentially an *opus incertum*. And Kant's notion of critique, constructed as it is on judgment, is *opus philosophicum incertum* par excellence.

The *judicium* is always unequal; more accurately, it is "founded" on inequality. If *ratio* is unequal for each and every one of us, then judgment is going to vary from one person to the next.[13] Descartes's *Discourse on Method* opens onto this shared division, installing a hitherto unknown metaphysical rule of truth as certainty—of truth as a subject's own statement of its own substance and of this substance *as itself constituted by the statement of the ego.* The *opus incertum* is at work well before Kant appears on the scene, from the time of *certitudo*, therefore. What happens to *logos* can be seen from the *Logique* of Port-Royal (". . . or the *art* of thinking," remember): it becomes entirely a logic of judgment, of its fragility, of its errors, of its education and rectification, in short, of its misconception. The entire treatise of reason becomes a review of its case, an enterprise designed to correct *lapsus judicii.* An enterprise *de jure* infinite, therefore, since the *lapsus* belongs structurally (if not essentially) to the *judicium*—and judgment henceforth qualifies the essential nature of man. Hence this, from the first discourse of the *Logique* of Port-Royal: "Our principal concern should be to form our judgements. . . . That men have little love for truth means that most of the time they make little effort to distinguish what is true from what is false." Through the history of judgment, right has in some way given back what it has taken from metaphysics. It has given back *ratio*—the reason that henceforth needs to be referred back to the separation of signs and the composition of figures—and the *judicium*, the masked statement of the law of its fiction and of the limits of its validity.

Hence, the Latin discourse of philosophy comes into its own: Kant opens the tribunal of reason.

This expression needs to be understood literally. As we know, there can be no question of seeking *metaphorical* values in the judicial apparatus with which Kant fits out his discourse. Quite the contrary. Indeed, despite the fact that the notion of a "tribunal of reason" is still often seen as little more than a discursive ornament, it ought not to be seen as a mere figure; instead, we need to see it as the very conceptuality that Kant puts into play. And if we can't avoid thinking here in terms of figures, this will have to be in the sense that the entire discourse of metaphysics is determined according to the fictioning structure of Latin right.

Indeed, it is actually not the celebrated text concerning the "tribunal of reason" that should occupy all our attention. It is mentioned here only because this idea opens—both figures and formulates—the entire procedure of the *Critique of Pure Reason.*

The Preface to the first edition (1781) introduces the *Critique* by way of a judicial history of reason. In its dogmatic age, metaphysics began as despotic, before its internecine struggles cast it into anarchy (two forms of illegitimacy, then); Locke's "*physiology* of the human understanding" was thought to have put an end to all this, but once it was usurped (because purely empirical) "metaphysics fell back into the same old worm-eaten dogmatism" before drifting into indifferentism.[14] Such indifference, though, is "the effect not of the thoughtlessness of our age, but of its ripened power of judgment,"[15] and it is this that calls for us to have done with illusory knowledge. This judgment, Kant writes, "demands that reason should take on anew the most difficult of all its tasks, namely, that of self-knowledge, and to institute a court of justice, by which reason may secure its rightful claims while dismissing all its groundless pretensions, and this not by mere decrees, but according to its own eternal and unchangeable laws."[16] The history that Kant relates consists, accordingly, in rejecting the models of power and nature in favor of the model of right. Right is neither *archē* nor *phusis*; it is essentially *reason.* Yet reason matured into old age (and this maturity can't simply be seen as something natural) is itself essentially *judgment.* In this instance, judgment comes before all else; it is judgment that evokes the tribunal. And yet judgment isn't just a founding or originary instance, but the belated and derivative product of the errors of metaphysics. Now, it is in precisely this regard that the founding *logos,* the *logos* that says "know thyself," submits to a radical conversion: its roots are torn up and severed. Knowing ourselves becomes a matter of judging ourselves; judging ourselves presupposes that we have at our disposal our own "eternal and unchangeable laws." The problem, though, is that the history of reason—and here, no doubt, the very fact that reason presents itself *as a history*—belies the fact that these laws have only ever been given within metaphysics. The tribunal can only put to work a sentence passed according to these laws *at the same time* as it puts to work these laws themselves. This judgment of judgments is the praetorian edict of metaphysics: it says the right of the right to say. And yet, setting itself thus in the position of absolute praetor,[17] reason is also touched by juridical casuality, in two ways:

1. Since it has to judge *itself,* reason is itself a *case* in the sense of a default from, or a lack of, right;

2. To this extent, and to the extent that reason ought to draw right from itself alone, its jurisdiction can only be "absolute" in the paradoxically accidental institution of its tribunal: it arises from a history that is neither natural nor metaphysical, from a history that, far from being regulated by the growing richness of the Concept, seems, rather, to be deregulated by the growing entropy of reason itself (a true *History* can only open out on the basis of critique).

Rather than having an essence, therefore—which would involve knowing itself—reason has an accident, which involves having to judge itself. Reason stumbles over its own case—the case of the judge.

Surely, as the Preface to the *Critique*'s second edition points out, there *is* a model for the tribunal, or at least a criterion according to which it is possible to judge. The "secure course of a science" is signposted by mathematics, physics, and chemistry, and the job of critique lies in leading metaphysics down this route. However, the law thus invoked doesn't make jurisdiction as such obsolete.[18] It doesn't *found* the tribunal but leaves it the—infinite—task of *justifying* itself. All of which can be shown schematically in the following three motifs:

1. The mathematico-physical sciences *are not* and *do not constitute* metaphysics. Kantian philosophy isn't geared toward epistemology (a discourse that aims merely to reproduce the rigor of scientific discourse). Equally, it is entirely different from Cartesian *mathesis,* which, through the "envelope" of "vulgar mathematics," denotes the universal science that makes up their soul or their core. Instead, then, Kantian metaphysics is *another* science altogether, one that appeals to the established sciences as analogical models (in the Analogies of Experience, remember, the mathematical analogy is able to provide no more than a model that is *itself* analogical to the philosophical analogy charged with thinking the unity of experience). The exemplary character of the sciences doesn't prevent them from being heterogeneous to metaphysics. Analogism runs all the way through this heterogeneity—but this gesture is a fictioning one, not one of identification. Kant has no real theory of knowledge; rather, he addresses theory insofar as it is bereft of knowledge.

2. Reason doubtless sees *itself* at work in the sciences. In this sense, it has always already recognized itself; it has always mastered from the outset its own rationality; hence it has no need to *judge.*[19] And yet the fact still re-

mains that these sciences are always going to be lacking in reason. This isn't to say that, in order for them to be sciences, they need to see themselves as founded by philosophy (this interpretation is the parallel double error made by the neo-Kantians, on the one hand, and the "epistemologues," on the other, who commend or blame Kant for one and the same bad reason).[20] No, precisely the self-legislation of the sciences and the consistency proper to them qualify them as models; mathematics, especially, finds itself qualified as the only adequate and autonomous presentation of the object that can actually take place, a presentation that philosophy can accordingly never hope to equal. The sciences lack reason because reason *as such* cannot be found in them; from this point on, reason has to judge, to decide as to its own rationality, both insofar as it isn't at work in the sciences and insofar as it is not, in itself, a science. This is the *properly juridical* sense (a sense that's neither foundational, nor explanatory, nor interpretative, nor justificatory, but all of these senses doubled . . .) of the critical question: How are synthetic *a priori* judgments possible? Given that, *de facto*, there are such judgments, this is both the question of right and the question raised by it. The famous *Quid juris?* with which Kant opens the Deduction in no way means that the sciences are going to be legitimated (something of which they have no real need).[21] Rather, it means that reason is going to be given a figure—from which it doubtless follows that reason doesn't actually have a figure, or that it has lost it, or that it has not yet found the figure proper to it.

3. The analogical model that reason finds in the sciences—the model on which it *falls*—is already that of the tribunal. What Thales, Galileo, Toricelli, and Stahl (to recall merely the most celebrated page of the Preface to the second edition) bring to light is the judicial figure of reason: "Reason, in order to be taught by nature, must approach it with its principles in one hand, according to which alone the agreement among appearances can count as law, and, in the other hand, the experiments thought out in accordance with these principles . . . like an appointed judge who compels the witnesses to answer the questions he puts to them."[22] As we can see, what's at stake here isn't the functioning of scientific laws as such, but the gesture through which the "subject" of such laws is established— precisely insofar as this "subject" is not the subject of Cartesian metaphysics (a subject that is science) and so insofar as this "subject" is not absolutely but merely established by saying right.

The stakes of this jurisdiction are double:

1. It leads to a fictioning whose principle is furnished by the first of these analogical models: the model of mathematics or, more precisely, of geometry, whose "shining example" finds a permanent place in the critical enterprise.[23] By "demonstrating the isosceles triangle," Thales in fact found "that he had to produce this figure from what he himself thought into the object and presented (through construction) according to *a priori* concepts."[24] The *construction of the figure* thus forms the nexus of the legitimacy that has to be assigned to reason. Yet it would be wrong to understand all this as a simple play on the word "figure" (unless the whole of Kant's text is seen as a thoroughgoing play on this word); through its trace,[25] through the tracing or the modeling of its "representation *a priori*," the geometrical figure as such provides what is needed by reason: the presentation of the concept in intuition. Figuration is the basic prerequisite. Equally, the triangle will still be the first model for the *schema*, that nonempirical figure charged with giving concepts their signification and so with bringing judgment into play. Yet however nonempirical the figure of the schema may be, it is still a *figure*: it is precisely *not* the intelligible property of an empirical image, and calling it a schema involves no recourse to "imagery." It is or forms the condition of a cognition that can only take place with respect to the figural or whose right is coextensive with the outline that models figures. Signific*a*tion operates within a signi*fiction* (the reunion, fashioned in and as a figure, of the concept of intuition). Signification makes jurisdiction; it assigns or it states (and does so first of all and in each case by stating the very nonempirical possibility of statement) the concept's area of legitimacy, the area that traces the sensible, phenomenal condition of its figurability. In the *Critique* (in philosophy become juridical), saying right is a matter of saying the area of the figure in general, of phenomenal fiction (and phenomenal fiction is what replaces the *poiesis* [or] *mimesis* of the "thing itself"). It is, then, to say the area as such and for itself (to say the outline, the contour, the *limes* of and in reason); it is to say the *areality* of the rational *area*. This jurisdiction says juris-diction itself.

2. Yet the jurisdiction that needs to be established here is that of philosophy. Now, philosophy cannot hope to attain the pure and direct presentation of mathematics, a presentation that is only possible because mathematics doesn't involve the existence of things. The fact that philosophy, by contrast, has to deal with that existence—with its actuality and multiplicity—would imply, in the first or last instance, that it could present the totality and unity of experience. This, indeed, is precisely what it

ought to do and what, in principle, it cannot, since reason isn't *intuitus originarius*, that for which the production of the thing and the presentation of it face on, as it were, are one and the same. Philosophy can never attain the "demonstrative construction" of geometry, therefore, the pure *a-realization* (or figuration) in which intuition is isomorphic to and contemporary with the concept. Philosophy has to judge the legitimacy of the figure; put differently: reason has to trace the area of its own right. This gesture is indiscernible from the sovereign gesture of the absolute establishment of right in general (its foundation in being), or it would be were the condition imposed on it not precisely that of the nonoriginary position of reason. Reason is subject to the "*a priori* forms of sensibility," namely, time and space. Time itself, the *a priori* form of the subject, does not present itself; it can only ever be figured by space ("because this inner intuition yields no figure [*Gestalt*] we also attempt to remedy this lack through analogies, and represent the temporal sequence through a line"):[26] these remarks, from the Transcendental Aesthetic, which opens the *Critique*, sum up the whole problem. They suggest that reason is subject in advance to the condition of the figure; that reason cannot create its own *limes*, merely delimit itself from within a limiting structure. As such, the ontology of *finitude* is engaged in this precise case: ontology falls under juris-diction.

All of which explains why the decisive moment of the Analytic is the Transcendental Doctrine of Judgment. So far as judgment is concerned, the Introduction ("On the Transcendental Power of Judgment in General") distinguishes transcendental logic from its merely formal aspect. Merely formal or general logic "contains no precepts at all for the power of judgment,"[27] since it deals with formal rules alone and not with their application to the content of cognition; it cannot, in other words, "distinguish whether a case *in concreto*" belongs under them.[28] The judgment of the case, and hence judgment properly called, thus depends on "a special talent that cannot be taught but only practiced." Defined as a "logic," judgment—and the judgment uttered by the person who judges—itself constitutes a case; it is neither necessary nor foreseeable, therefore, neither programmable nor teachable. As such, it cannot be insured against accident, against the errors of judgment that "a physician, a judge, or a statesman" (the practitioners of *krisis*) might easily make;[29] in short, it is only by *chance* (a word that comes from *casus*) that a case is properly judged.

Transcendental logic repairs this fault. It alone can "secure the power of judgment in the use of the pure understanding through determinate rules,"[30] thereby defining and concentrating in itself the very task of philosophy. Philosophy cannot "expand the role of the understanding" (it cannot win territory or an area) but "as critique, in order to avoid errors of judgment (*lapsus judicii*) in the use of the few pure concepts of the understanding that we have, philosophy with all of its perspicacity and art of scrutiny is called up (even though its use is then only a negative one)."[31] The role of the *Critique*, therefore, is to occupy the place of the foundation of right; it is, in principle, charged with saying the right of right and of sheltering *jus* from the casuality of its *dictio*.

Now, *it is precisely this foundational operation that shows itself to be the juridical act par excellence*: with this, we come before the tribunal itself, at the very heart of *critique* as such. For this reason, as much as the jurisdiction of all jurisdiction disengages from all juridical statutes (as much as it sets itself up as the site of *privilege*), *with this same gesture* it carves into itself the infinite flaw that leads it to fall continually upon its own case. In other words: since philosophy thinks itself—*says itself*—in terms of right, it inevitably thinks in a way that is structured around (or affected by) *lapsus judicii*, by the slipping and falling that are an intrinsic part of the lack of substance within which jurisdiction takes place.

By way of conclusion, let me simply try to address the first function of this constitutive and permanent *lapsus*: the one that concerns the very principle of critical jurisdiction.

Because of the claim that it makes (the rights that it assigns to itself), transcendental logic is the faculty of indicating, beyond any rule, the *a priori* case to which the rule can be applied. As such, it eliminates the casuality of the case and forges the contradictory notion of a jurisprudence that owes nothing to experience.

And yet, although this operation will already have been carried out in the *Critique*, it is not under the motif of jurisprudence, but under the juridical concept of *deduction*.[32] Now, for "jurisconsults," "deduction" is proof that responds in a cause to the question *Quid juris?* Deduction is the establishment of right. Hence the transcendental deduction of the pure concepts of the understanding ought to establish the right of reason in *every case*.

In fact, this is what it does, finally establishing that the understanding "is itself the legislation for nature."[33] Sheltered thus from any external limiting condition, the understanding, from the moment that it comes to judge, ends up falling upon its own case, on the case of its investiture as "legislator." If, in the schematism, judgment demands the reunion of intuition and concept, if it demands figuration, that is simply because the very subject of legislation is able to present itself (to itself) only as represented, as figured, as *a-realized* in general. All cases are absorbed by right *a priori*; here, though, *the a priori*, right itself, is formed by the condition of sensibility—only in this way can it allow jurisprudence to take place. The *a priori* is essentially dis-locative. Right consists in the statement of its subject's *areality*. For this very reason, the subject is nothing more than the statement: I "am" right; I "am" the limitation of my own statement. The right of this subject refers to the figural, delimiting outline of signification in general. This outline is the outline of a limit that is internal to itself, a frontier that falls within reason, the frontier between concept and intuition (that is, between the concept and its conception). It is the outline, then, that infinitely separates the subject of right from the whole of its interiority, that stamps it with its figure, and that subjects it to this figure by sketching out its *persona*: in the case that says the right of every case, it is the *persona* of the judge that speaks.

The end result of the Deduction is the unity of apperception (of the I) to which representations have to be related if they are going to constitute a unitary experience and be capable of making *sense*. Here, right calls for the condition *sine qua non* of its subject (the tribunal judges that there has to be a judge presiding over it). Critique can only adequately meet this demand through the (re)presentation of a *persona*. In fact, Kant declares a propos the transcendental consciousness thus evoked: "It matters little whether this representation is clear or obscure; it is not even a matter of the reality of this consciousness. Instead, it is a matter of the possibility of the logical form of all consciousness necessarily resting on the relation to this perception as to a *faculty*." *I*, the judge, is the fiction of a legislative figure—of the figure that fictions and traces areas in general.

We don't need to worry, then, about the *lapsus* of signification to which the word *areality* lends itself. To say the subject of right is to say it as an area, as a limit, and as a figure. Equally, though, it is to say the modest reality or the essential un-reality of the person who represents it, who stages it or puts it into play. The transcendental unity of the judge that reason *is* lies in the *saying* of that *person*.

De jure, every step is taken to guarantee against *lapsus judicii*. *De facto*—but this fact is itself the fact of right—the guarantee itself only ever guarantees its figure or its fiction as guarantor. Moreover, the *Critique* will never be able to stop reason from abandoning itself *de facto* to the *Trieb*, the impulse that leads it to judge outside the limits of experience and to forge dangerous and dogmatic fictions (God, the self, the world). Equally, though, and by the same token, the irresistible character of the *Trieb* of reason will be recognized and stated by the tribunal itself, as the factual limit of its own jurisdiction. The moral imperative alone will be capable of making this impulse "see reason." Yet this "categorical" imperative, in which the ultimate jurisdiction resides, can only ever offer itself up as a *factum* of reason. The pure fact of a pure moral person will say the last rights of a figured subject. It will say it as *duty*. The imperative says the duty of constituting oneself as a *judge* (of the universality of my maxim), even though there's perhaps no case conforming to this judgment that could be presented in experience. Yet it is precisely *because* no such case exists that *we have to judge* in all cases. The imperative is factual; it takes the form of an *accident* (of reason) because it is the only form that can be taken by an establishment of right that is neither a foundation nor a self-foundation. The imperative is *illegitimate*. Only thus does it make the law.

When philosophy becomes juridical, when it passes into right, its judgments can only be passed through the mouth of a person ceaselessly falling prey to the same *lapsus*, this *lapsus* through which philosophy is revealed in its entirety (it reveals the cause, its cause, its thing, *res*—nothing)—saying, in the way of all Latin discourse, *fictio* for *dictio* or *dictio* for *fictio*, but always signi*fic*ting its right to say.

As we know all too well, right furnished the model and the ideology of the bourgeois State. Yet it did so at the cost of hypostasizing juris-diction, of making it an Essence and a Sense. At the cost of forgetting or repressing its "essential" *lapsus*. And it's hardly surprising, then, that the State engenders a sometimes open, always latent revolt over the *right to say*—the ultimate demand of *the right to say the right of what is by rights without right*.

And yet, at the same time and place at which the State was born, what also opened up was the resistance of a dislocation. In philosophy and as philosophy, it is the resistance anticipated from Kant to Hegel. We've doubtless not seen the back of it, although this doesn't mean that it's a matter of waiting on some sort of a "return" to "juridical reason." Reason has doubtless not yet finished falling on its own case. Anything can happen.

Postscriptum

Jean-François Lyotard has honored this essay with a generous note to which I must return (and salute in passing the rare occurrence of a genuine *disputatio*).[34] Lyotard wants to break with the motif of "fictioning," which in his view is indebted "to a problematics of founding or origin." That Kant, in his account of judgment, dethrones the issue of origins "in favor of the question of ends" I wholeheartedly agree (and let me refer here to the text "The Free Voice of Man," written for and in the spirit of the colloquium *The Ends of Man*).[35] But it does not necessarily follow that the *juridical* fiction (which I was careful to distinguish from poetic fiction, i.e., *Dichtung*) has to play the part of the "substitute" or "proxy" for a dislocated origin (I would suggest, rather, perhaps provocatively, that there *is* an origin, and it is *this* that comprises the dis-location), and that it therefore leads back surreptitiously to the general metaphysical thematics of origin.

On the one hand, we need to determine precisely the role of proxies in general (here we might revisit Derrida's exploration of the logic of supplementarity). Does proxy "conjoin . . . the fragments of an origin, whether being or subject" or does it expose, *qua proxy*, attesting to its proxy character, a fragmentation that it does not actually "conjoin"? (In saying this, I confine myself to the Kantian version of supplementarity.) At the same time, Kant's version strives to exorcise fragmentation: Kant does everything he can to wish away the crisis that he himself opened, or that opened itself before him. (Incidentally, I do not think that Kant can be divested of his Enlightenment spirit to the degree that Lyotard believes he can; the thing is to know which "Kant" we are talking about.) But then— and this is what we might call the Kantian slide of ontology—proxy inscribes in being its own fragmentation, that is, its end or ends: the question of ends, the end as a question, and maybe as what lies beyond questioning; the end inscribed as the judgment of being.

This supposes, on the other hand, that we are never quite done with being. Lyotard himself certrainly is not. He charts "passages among 'areas' of legitimacy" such as "language (which, if you like, is being minus the illusions) *in the process* of establishing various families of legitimacy, a critical language, without rules." Language—which means, if I understand it rightly, the differences between phrases—is defined "if you like" as "being without illusion." That means that it is an illusion to speak of being, but that speaking is being "without illusion." Lyotard stands at the hub of being, of the naming of being. Who would not take that position? And how to can *illusion* be determined, if not from an exact and adequate point of view? Next, Lyotard underlines "in the process." This "in the process" (with everything that it entails) is unmistakably, irresistibly, a proxy: he is under way, he has not yet finished, nor has he yet begun, but *instead*, in place of his, in the process . . . he is. But what is this place? Lyotard would doubtless say that the question is illegitimate. Let's concede that he's right. But what *is* it to be right? Ultimately, no "play of sentences" is going to decide or articulate that. If it isn't "being," then at least it is what happens, factually, to being, the truth of an experience, the judgment of a history. It's not "phrases" that are "right" (although there is no being "right" without "phrases"). Truth is not a phrase—and yet truth happens. That means that truth *is*, while "being *is* not," as Heidegger points out.

But Lyotard basically knows all this—and that's what makes this *disputatio* possible: the debate is regulated by a common concern (or a shared imperative) that is both more and less than what our respective "sentences" say. But this does not mean that these sentences are indifferent or interchangeable.

Translated by Simon Sparks

9

Originary Ethics

There is a threefold difficulty involved in presenting Heidegger's thinking about ethics, whose terms inevitably need to be set out, at least briefly.

First of all, Heidegger's Nazi engagement, followed by his almost complete silence about the camps, have marked him (even aside from any properly political judgment) with a moral taint that many have seen as invalidating any ethical proposition on his part, if not the whole of his thinking. It isn't my concern to analyze these particulars (and the case has already been well investigated in the important work of Pierre Bourdieu, Jürgen Habermas, Jean-Pierre Faye, Otto Pöggeler, Philippe Lacoue-Labarthe, Jacques Derrida, Gérard Granel, Nicole Parfait, Dominique Janicaud, Richard Wolin, Hans Sluga, etc.). Instead, I want to restrict myself to saying this: while it is certainly correct to infer from Heidegger's moral error a certain style or a certain professional intellectual conduct (across all his works), it is wrong to draw such an inference when what is at issue is the logic by which his thinking sought to analyze what it is that constitutes man as the being through whom *being* has as its original *sense* (or *ethos*), the choice and conduct of existence. That this thinking wasn't equal to the dignity (*Würde*) which it took thus as its theme is something that ought to give rise to further thinking. But that is only possible if we take Heidegger's thinking as our point of departure (not forgetting to ask ourselves about to the precise ethical expectation to which his political engagement was intended to respond).

Second, over and above all this, there are those who think it's possible to deny any ethical dimension to Heidegger's thinking, basing their claims on his own objection to ethics as a "discipline," on the corresponding absence of a "moral philosophy" in his work, and on his refusal of any moral interpretation of the analytic of *Dasein*. Now, in order for the present essay to have any relevance whatsoever, we would need to begin by demonstrating the falsity of this argument, and by reconstructing the possibility of a properly ethical approach to Heidegger. However, not only is there no space for this here, but it can even be considered quite unnecessary.[1] Only those who have read Heidegger blindly, or not at all, could think him a stranger to ethical preoccupations. Moreover, there are already enough works in existence to refute this prejudice. It should be enough, then, to spell out the following (which will be complemented by what I have to say): there is no "morality" in Heidegger, if what is meant by that is a body of principles and aims for conduct, fixed by authority or by choice, whether collective or individual. In fact, however, there is *no* philosophy that either provides or is itself a "morality" in this sense. It isn't philosophy's job to prescribe norms or values: instead, it must think the essence or the sense of what makes up *action* [l'agir] as such; it should think, in other words, the essence or the sense of what puts action in the position of having to choose norms or values. Perhaps, incidentally, this understanding of philosophy is itself already Heideggerian or, at least for us, today, necessarily Heideggerian in tone. Of course, this wouldn't prevent us from showing how appropriate it is to Spinoza or to Kant or to Hegel or to Husserl, or prevent us from showing how, and doubtless for specific historical reasons, it chimes with Heidegger's contemporaries (each very different from the next) Bergson, Wittgenstein, or Levinas. All of which amounts to saying that, in general terms, there would be a case for showing how, with Heidegger and with Heidegger's period, philosophy understood itself (once again) as "ethics" and not, let us quickly say, as "knowledge," presupposing, in particular, a distinction between "ethics" and "morality" inherited (if at times confusedly) by the whole of our own time. But this isn't my concern here; rather, I want to sketch out an internal interpretation [*explication*] of Heidegger himself, striving to be as faithful as possible while avoiding piety.

The third difficulty runs counter to the second. If, paradoxically, ethics constitutes both a discreet and unobtrusive theme in Heidegger's work *and* a constant preoccupation, an orientation in his thinking, then we would need to undertake a general examination of that thinking. We would have to show the extent to which the "thinking of being"—which is, after all, the main or even the exclusive title of Heidegger's thinking—is nothing other than a thinking of what he called "original ethics," and that it is so throughout, in all its various developments. In particular, it would not be difficult to show that the celebrated "turning" (the *Kehre*), characterized most succinctly in the words of the *Beiträge* as a "passage from onto*logy* to *onto*logy," basically corresponds to an accentuation, a reinforcement or a "folding" of the ethical motif. And this, we might suppose, wasn't wholly unrelated to a reflection silently tensed and perturbed by the National Socialist aberration. In much the same way that constraints of space mean that we cannot *de facto* cover the whole of Heidegger's work, then, so *de jure* there can be no isolation of a Heideggerian "moral philosophy." Instead, let me confine myself to addressing the basic intention of the text in which the motif of "original ethics" is brought to light, namely, the "Letter on 'Humanism.'" Linked to this will be some essential reminders of what paved the way for this motif in *Being and Time* and *Kant and the Problem of Metaphysics*. As for the rest, suggestions will have to suffice (and by "the rest" I mean: 1. The thinking of freedom as an "ungrounded foundation"; 2. The thinking of language and poetry as a true *ethos*; and 3. The thinking of "technology" as a retreat from moral foundations and the delivery of a different ethical demand.)

To sum up the situation, two overwhelming objections could be raised: "Heidegger has a bad morality"; "Heidegger has no morality." These are not so much ruled out here as reserved for a different sort of analysis. Instead, the only kind of analysis that is appropriate here needs to take as its theme Heidegger's thinking itself conceived of as a fundamental ethics.

The "Letter on 'Humanism'" announces itself forcefully and distinctly, in its very first sentence, as a reflection on *Handeln, action*.[2] It is very clear that the question of humanism is, for Heidegger, the question of what man is (of his *humanitas*) insofar as he has to act or to "conduct himself." (*Conduct* or action, insofar as it is its own end, action that does not "cause an effect,"[3] seems to me an appropriate term with which to render the German *Handeln* as well as the Greek *praxis*, especially in the present context.)

But what man is insofar as he has to act is not a specific aspect of his being, but his very being itself. If Dasein—according to the opening formulations of *Being and Time*—is the being for which, "in its very being, that being is *at issue* for it,"[4] it is because this "is at issue," this *il s'agit de*, this *es geht um*, this "it is about," doesn't bring into play an interest that is merely theoretical or speculative. Rather, it destroys the supposed autonomy of such an interest. If, in Dasein, it is being that is at issue [*il s'agit de l'être*] (and if, without playing on words more than language itself does, being is a matter of action [*l'être est de l'agir*]), it is because being, as the being of Dasein, *is* what is at stake [*l'enjeu*] in its conduct, and its conduct is the bringing into play [*la mise en jeu*] of being.

This point of departure—and more than that, this axiom or this transcendental absolute of all thinking of being—could also be expressed as follows: because the difference between being and beings is not a difference of being (it is not the difference between two kinds of being), it is not a difference between two realities, but the reality of Dasein insofar as it is, in and of itself, open and called to an essential and "active" relation with the proper fact of being.[5]

This relation is one of *sense*. In Dasein, it is a matter of giving sense to the fact of being—or, more exactly, in Dasein the very fact of being is one of making sense. This "making sense" is not theoretical, nor is it practical in a sense somehow opposed to the theoretical (on the whole, it would be more in keeping with Heidegger's thinking to call it practical "in the first instance"). Knowledge or the understanding of being as sense is identical with the action of sense or with action *as* sense. To be is to make sense. (In a direct line from Kant: pure reason is practical insofar as it is theoretical.)

This "making," however, is not a "producing." It is, precisely, acting, or conducting oneself. Conduct is the accomplishment (*Vollbringen*) of being. As sense's conduct, or as the conduct of sense, it is, essentially, "thinking." The essential act is thinking. But that doesn't close action back up on "a (merely) theoretical practice." If the "Letter on "Humanism,'" along with many other texts, appears to restrict action—and with it original ethics—to an activity that we might be inclined to call abstract, speculative, and only metaphorically "active" ("active" through the metaphor of the "thinkers" and the "poets"), then this is the result of an inadequate reading. In reality, "thinking" is the name for action because sense is at issue in action. Thinking (and/or poetry) is not an exceptional form of action, the "intellectual conduct" to be preferred to others, but what, in all action, brings into play the sense (of being) without which there would be no action.

This is indeed why action *qua* thinking—the bringing into play of sense—is "desired" by being. This desire is love thought as ability (*Mögen*),[6] in other words, as having a taste, an affection, or an inclination for, as wanting something, as having the ability to do something. Being desires thinking (and here we might draw a direct connection with Hegel: "the Absolute wants to be close to us"). Being desires thinking insofar as thinking can accomplish the sense that it is. What thinking names is this: the fact that sense desires itself as its own action. (And we would need here to develop the question of how the concept of such a "desire" is not that of an object-desire.)

This means that being as the fact of being—the fact that there is something in general—constitutes by itself the desire that this fact be accomplished (unfolded, acted) as sense. But this proposition needs to be understood in all its radicality and originariness. There is not first a brute fact (the being of beings, the "there is"), *then* a desire for sense (for this being). If this *were* the case, sense, action, and ethics would have to come after and from somewhere other than the fact of being. Now, on the one hand, being is not a "fact" in this sense—it is not something given, the "fact" that there is a gift—and sense cannot be conferred on it as an external signification. (Moreover, such a problematic is never truly encountered in any great philosophy. It shows through only wherever it has been possible to posit being as a brute fact of existence "in itself," in the face of which a subjectivity has to assume a giving of sense "for itself." This is true of Sartre's thinking—explicitly targeted in the "Letter on "Humanism'"—or of philosophies of the absurd. The specificity of Heidegger consists, however, in thinking being as the fact of sense and sense as the gift of being.) On the other hand, sense conceived as signification conferred on or found in addition to being itself could not properly be the sense *of* being, still less being itself as sense, Heidegger having established in *Being and Time* that "the sense of being can never be contrasted with beings, or with being as the supporting 'ground' of beings, for a 'ground' becomes accessible only as sense, even if it is itself the abyss of senselessness."[7] The fact of being—as Dasein—is *eo ipso* the desire, ability, and love (ability-love) of sense. But what is given [*donnée*] or "handed out" ["*donné*"] is precisely the "gift of essence" in which being gives itself essentially as the action of sense.[8] The "given," therefore, is the making-sense of being and what is given or desired thus, given as what is desired (even if, once again, the sense of these words would need to be reevaluated), is for the "truth of being" to be said,[9] for it to be "brought to language."[10]

Making-sense is not the same as producing sense. Let me say, in order to make things absolutely clear, that it isn't an activity that could be compared to that by which, according to Lévi-Strauss, an existential given, itself reducible to a senseless materiality, is turned into an operative sense. (To which we might add, still by way of clarification, that in a world that is not related to the other world of a principle, a donor origin, a creator, or a world-subject in general, there is, strictly speaking, no other "fundamental" possibility than the alternative represented in these ways by Heidegger and Lévi-Strauss. Unless there is a different way of going beyond both formulations of the alternative, which is another story—ours, perhaps.)

If action is an "accomplishing," that is because being itself accomplishes itself in it as the sense which it is. But being is itself nothing other than the gift of the desire of or for sense. So making-sense is not of sense's making; it is making being be, or *letting* it be[11] (depending on how we want to stress the ambivalence of German *lassen*: *bauen lassen*, to have something constructed, also means to let or to give to the constructing activity as such; *sein lassen* means to let be, to give, to entrust to the activity of being as such).

Letting be isn't passive; it is action itself. It is the essence of action insofar as action is the essence of being. It is a case of allowing being to be or to act the sense which it is or desires. Being as such—the fact that there are beings in general—is no more "present" in Dasein than anywhere else (the being of beings in general is no more present or absent in one place than another); rather, it is the "that there is" of being as sense. This sense is not a property *of* the "that there is." It properly *is* (or *makes*) the "that there is" as such. It engages it and engages itself in it: "that there is" is what is at stake in sense. Being, absolutely and rigorously considered as such (which also means, to allude to other developments in Heidegger's thinking, considered according to its unnominalized value as a verb—being *is* or *exists* being, it "makes" them be, makes them make-sense), is essentially its own "engagement" as the action of sense, therefore:[12] such is the decisive axiom of this thinking. From which it follows that ontology is, from the outset, within or beyond itself, being's *conduct of sense* or the conduct of the sense of being, depending on which of these two expressions has the strongest value (the most ethical and least directional value).

Sense's conduct—or the conduct of sense—makes being as being acted by and as Dasein. Dasein is being insofar as it is at stake as the being that man is. The conduct of sense is indissociable, then, from a "liberation of man for the dignity of his *humanitas*."[13] Dignity (*Würde*) exceeds any assignable value, any measure of action regulated by a particular given. *Humanitas* needs to be measured against this measurelessness of action or, rather, against action itself as the absolute measure. The inadequacy of humanism stems from the fact that it rests on an interpretation of beings that is already given,[14] on an interpretation that has already fixed sense (through a definition variously characterized as Christian, Marxist, etc.). By fixing sense—the signification of sense—humanism conceals or loses sight of the importance of Kant's fourth question—*Was ist der Mensch?*—as a question concerned *not* with a determinable essence of man but with what is more originary in man than man, namely Dasein *qua* finitude.[15]

The finitude of Dasein is the finitude of being as the desiring-action of sense. "Finitude," then, does not mean a limitation that would relate man—negatively, positively, dialectically—to some other authority from which he could derive his sense, or his lack of it. Instead, it means precisely the non-fixing of such a signification: not, however, as the powerlessness to fix it, but as the power to leave it open.

"Finitude" thus means: unaccomplishment as the condition for the accomplishment of action (or for the accomplishment that action *is*) as sense. This does not mean a "loss of sense" or a "sense produced through the mediation of its loss." Rather, it means that sense itself has to be seen as "the relation of being to the essence of man,"[16] that is, it is being that is at issue in man, or that man consists in (has his *humanitas* in) the making-be of sense, and the making-sense of being, which could therefore never be reduced to a fixing of the sense of being. For such fixings (significations) to be brought about (to be determined, to be chosen, and to regulate conduct), being still has to be exposed to—and as—the action of sense as such, or as the gift of the desire of and for this action, as, in other words, the *non-given of sense*, which is the very fact of being as sense—and thus as finitude.

This is why "there is and has to be something like being where finitude has come to exist."[17] But existence is not the factual given. One could say: there precisely is no "factual given" before there is the gift of the "there is" itself. There is no "fact" before the gift of being, which itself constitutes the gift [*le don*] of or the abandonment [*l'abandon*] to sense. Nor is existence *actualitas*, the entelechy of an essence.[18] It is "ek-sistence," the way or conduct of being as being "outside" of itself: in other words, as being-to-sense, or, again, as making-sense or action. (We might try saying: ek-sistence is the entelechy of what is neither essence nor power but the sense of being.)

Yet for all that, we mustn't think of ek-sistence as an ontological category alien to concrete existence. Just as this word is but a different way of writing "existence," so the structure it designates takes place only right at concrete existence. What *Being and Time* calls the "facticity" of Dasein is doubtless not the *factum brutum* of some being that lies "within the world,"[19] nor is it detached from the simple factuality of a concrete existence. The "fact" *that* Dasein *is* in that it is desired as the action of being takes place *right at* the fact *that* such and such a concrete human, in each case, exists, and that his "ontical" existence *as such* has the ontological structure of Dasein. In general, what people have gotten into the bad habit of translating "authentic" but which is, in fact, the "proper" (*eigen, Eigentlichkeit*), takes place nowhere other than right at the "improper," right at everyday existence—and, what's more, in the very mode of the improper's "turning-away" from the proper.[20] Put in another way, factual existence is "proximally and for the most part" constituted in ignorance of the facticity of sense that is the ontological fact of existence itself. "The pure 'that it is' shows itself, but the 'whence' and the 'whither' remain in darkness."[21] But it is precisely this darkness, this being-not-given of sense, that leads onto the proper dimension of sense as what is, in being and of being, desired and to be accomplished (acted out). In the ordinary impropriety of simple existing, being's propriety of sense—which consists precisely in having to make sense, and not in the disposition of a given *proper sense*—both dissimulates *and* reveals itself.

From which it follows:

1. that ontic existence has, as such, the structure of ontological ek-sisting;

2. that, correlatively, the fact of being (of Dasein) has, as such, the structure of making-sense or of action.

In principle, the ethics thus announced refers to nothing other than existence. No "value," no "ideal" floating above concrete and everyday existence provides it in advance with a norm and a signification. But this everyday existence finds itself asked to make sense.[22] This request, in turn, stems neither from heaven nor from an authority of sense: it comes from existence, being the proper request of its being. Only on the basis of this original request will it be possible for beings, in their action, to give themselves ideas or values—and, what's more, this will make *sense* only according to the original action which is at issue in the request.

Hence, this thinking strives to take most rigorously into account the impossibility, which has arisen with and as modernity, of presenting an already given sense, with the evaluations which would be deduced from it. (And although this is not the place to do so, we ought to ask ourselves whether this problematic is not in fact that of the whole of philosophy, already present in Plato's *agathon* and first radicalized in Kant's imperative.)

To clarify, we could say: the ethics engaged in this way is engaged on the basis of nihilism—as the general dissolution of sense—but as the exact reverse of nihilism: as the bringing to light of making-sense as action requested in the essence of being.[23] So it also engages itself according to the theme of a total and joint responsibility toward sense and toward existence. (I can only signal in passing the importance of the motif of responsibility. Discreetly explicit, like that of ethics itself, this motif tends toward nothing less than "being's being-responsible towards itself, proper Being-itself,"[24] the latter having, in principle, nothing solipsistic or egoistic about it but, on the contrary, containing the possibility and the necessity of being-responsible toward others.)

Ek-sistence, then, is the way in which Dasein *is* as Dasein, its way of being.[25] This way of being is immediately a conduct: the conduct of being-open to making-sense, a being-open that is itself opened by (or whose opening consists in) the desire/ability of sense. Insofar as it is opened in this way, this conduct is a setting-outside-itself or ex-position as the very position of the ek-sistent. This being-outside-itself, this "ecstatic essence,"[26] doesn't happen to an already given "self." On the contrary, through it something like a "self" (a subject, and a responsible subject) can come about. "Ecstasis," as it needs to be understood here, is not exaltation beyond the bounds of the ordinary. (Besides, *ecstasis* as exaltation is in no way the hallmark of an accession to authenticity.[27] This is why the word "ecstasis" also undergoes a modification into "standing-out."[28])

Being in ek-sistence consists in "being the there."[29] Dasein has to be understood not adverbally and locally, as being-there, but verbally, actively, and transitively, as being-the-there. Hence, Dasein is definitely *not* the name of a substance but the sentence of an action. "Being-there" in fact presupposes the prior given of both a being and a place. "Being-the-there," however, implies that being properly ek-sists as its "clearing."[30] By this "clearing" we need to understand not, or not in the first instance, an illumination or revelation that brings being to light, but being itself as an opening, a spacing-out *for* possibilities of bringing to light.[31] Being ek-sists (is) in that it opens being. The *there* is the open in which, right at an existence *hic et nunc*, making-sense is at issue. The *there* is the place in which, on the basis of it, on the basis of its opening, something can take place: a conduct of sense.

The *ek* of ek-sistence is the conduct proper to being the there in full measure (indeed, it is itself to be understood as measure insofar as there is no ethics without measure), in which, by being the there, by being *that there is there* an existence, being *is* sense. Sense, indeed, is "the structure of the opening."[32] But such a structure is not the setting up of a distance (like the given opening of a source, for example, from which sense could spring); it is the activity of opening or of opening oneself as making-sense. (Let me note in passing that action as essentially opening implies "being with one another" as its "foundation." The opening of making-sense is utterly impossible in a solipsistic mode.[33] Nonetheless, we cannot take from this the prescription of an "altruistic" morality. What is established, rather, is that, whatever the moral choice, the other is going to be essential to opening, which is essential to sense, which is what is essential in the action that makes up the essence of being.)

Essentially, then, being is a making-sense(-of-itself) and we can specify the scope of this expression by considering all the definitions that have now been acquired. But the fundamental definition is undoubtedly this: the sense which it is a matter of "making" is no more a sense that can be assigned according to something other than being than one can make sense of being by simply positing a being-there. There is, in principle, neither a simple transcendence nor a simple immanence. If it is entirely legitimate and not simply verbal acrobatics to say that the sense of being is the being of sense, this means that sense (the sense of human existence, but also, and along with it, the sense of the world) is in principle nothing other than action, or conduct. Conduct is thus the proper transcendence of the immanence that is.

Now, let me pause for a moment in order to address the objection that will doubtless be raised at this point: sense is thus identical and coextensive with all action, whatever its signification and whatever its value. As such, this supposed "ethics" leads to an indifferentism (a subjectivism or a moral relativism), even if that indifferentism is of the kind "morality of action." To this objection, two responses:

1. In fact, the determination of being as the desire/ability of making-sense is ontologically and logically prior to any evaluation of a determinate sense. This is indeed necessary if what is at stake in the first instance is an absolute *dignity* as the character of Dasein. Transposed into different terms: only a subject which is entirely responsible for sense, and for its own existence as making-sense, without prior subjection to any fixed sense, can be a fully-fledged ethical subject. Already, nothing else was at stake in the Kantian notion of dignity, for which (setting aside the model of a "law of nature," which precisely is *only* an analogical model) the "universality of the maxim" meant the totality of responsibility, while the condition of "respect" meant engagement by and before oneself as *"acting* self."[34] There is no more subjectivism in Heidegger than there is in Kant. For subjectivism, in fact, evaluative moral decision making is represented as a good in itself (the "freedom to choose"), the only real "good," already appropriated by every subject as such: fundamentally, subjectivity itself as good. By contrast, the dignity of Dasein consists in needing, in each choice, to engage what can be called, for want of a better term, the objectivity of being (and, so of humanity and the world). Remarkably, what is undoubtedly one of the most significant contemporary ethical investigations in the Anglo-American context, Charles Taylor's investigation into the "ideal of authenticity," is left as though hanging halfway between these two directions. To the extent that it challenges subjectivism without invoking a transcendent authority, it actually indicates—albeit unconsciously—the necessity of an ontology of making-sense. In general, it is instructive to note the extent to which the contemporary Anglo-American debate on the (non-)foundation of morality (between Aristotelian-Thomist proponents of a determinable "good" and liberal proponents of "justice" concerning individuals with differing subjective "goods") has the same ontological demand unwittingly behind it. What is at issue here is nothing other than the end of a metaphysico-theological foundation to morality *so as to arrive at ethics as the ground of being.* So Heidegger will at least have marked out the particulars of the problem.

2. Even though no norm or value can be determined on the fundamental level, where what is at issue is valueless value, the unevaluable dignity of making oneself the subject (or the agent) of possible evaluations, we

can, by contrast, take this to indicate a positive hint in the direction of what can quasi-orient action as such, if I may put it that way: nothing other than the truth of ek-sistence. But we must not fail to remember that this truth takes place right at existence, or that it is its very event (its every event and appropriation, *Ereignis*—a theme that I can't develop here). The imperative, we might be tempted to say, is this: *respect existence.* But this imperative provides no sense or value. What it does require, though, is that we make sense of existence *as* existence. It cannot be reduced, for example, to a "respect for life," as though the sense of life or life as sense were something given. On the contrary, talk of a respect for life immediately exposes one to all the problems of determining what "life" is, what "human life" is, and how it does or does not differ from "animal life" (or "plant life"), what its conditions of recognition, dignity, and so forth, might be. From this we can grasp how all the problems being raised today by bioethics as well as by human rights bring to light the necessity of heading back toward an ontology of action: not so that they can be resolved once and for all, but so that we can apprehend the absolute making-sense of the action that puts itself in the position of having, for example, to decide what a "human life" is—without ever having the ability to fix this *being* as a given that has been acquired once and for all. (I'm well aware that these considerations are wholly extrapolated from Heidegger, but we need at least to indicate that such an extrapolation, of which Heidegger will doubtless have been unaware, is not only possible but necessary.)

The "proper dignity" of the human,[35] which doesn't depend on any subjective evaluation,[36] derives thus from being having entrusted itself to him by ex-posing itself as the opening of making-sense. Man, no longer the "son of God," the "purpose of nature," or the "subject of history"—no longer, in other words, a being that is or that has sense—is the being through which being ex-poses itself as making-sense. Indeed, we could even risk an expression such as the following: the human is no longer the signified of sense (that would be the human according to humanism), but its signifier; not, however, in the sense that man designates its concept, but in the sense that he indicates and opens its task as one that exceeds all assigned senses of the human. "Dasein" means: the making-sense of being that exceeds in man all significations of the human.

Exposed in this way, being properly *is* the entrusting to Dasein of the "guarding" of its truth. In this sense, Heidegger calls man "the shepherd of being."[37] We ought to pause here for a moment, since this sort of "pastoralism" has often raised a smile. Granted, terms like "shepherd," "guarding," and "protective heed" aren't entirely free of evangelistic, backward-looking connotations. They evoke a sense of preservation, a conservation of what ought to be open and to be risked. There's a reactive if not out and out reactionary tone here, one that Heidegger wasn't alone in taking, a tone that often befalls moral discourses ("preserving values," etc.). It is as though inaugural dignity were brought to light without any acquired protection, without the reassurance of any given sense, itself needing to be protected or safeguarded. Now, what has to be "guarded" is the open—something that the "guarding" itself risks closing back up again. For the dignity of the open we might then substitute the emblematic value of its guardians, which will soon be identified, moreover, in terms of the determinate figures of the "thinker" and the "poet." All of this has to pose a problem, one that needs to be addressed. For it's still the case that, quite logically, the "guarding" of the "open" can only ever be the opening of the open itself, and that the pastoral tone ought not to conceal the indication of an absolute responsibility. Here we doubtless find the crux of a radical thinking of ethics: in the possibility of confusing original making-sense with an assignable origin of sense, an opening with a gift (and, again, what is lodged here is the whole ambiguity of the "gift"; I will come back to this). Thinking the origin as *ethos* or conduct isn't the same as representing an originary *ethos*, even though it is all too easy to slide imperceptibly from the one to the other. (The difficulty here isn't specific to Heidegger and could probably be found in Levinas or Spinoza as well.)

Be that as it may, let us recall for the moment that these very terms—guarding, protective heed, the solicitousness of the shepherd—indicate the order of a *conduct*. It is less a case of leading [*conduire*] a flock than of conducting ourselves in such a way that "beings might appear in the light of Being."[38]

This "appearing," however, isn't the effect of a production. Man doesn't produce beings, nor does he produce himself; his dignity is not that of a mastery (which, in general, is not susceptible of dignity, merely of prestige or impressiveness). In fact, "man does not decide whether and how beings appear." This is a matter for the "destiny of being."[39] *That* there is something, and that there are *such* things—*this* world—is not for us to decide. This, then, is given. But what is properly given with this gift, or what is properly the destination of this "destiny" (and without which

there would be neither "gift" nor "destiny," but *factum brutum*) is what *is*
not, in other words, the being of beings as the desire/ability of sense. What
is properly given—what being gives and that as which it gives itself—is the
need to make sense of and in beings as a whole (their "appearing in the
light of being"). It is in this sense that humans are responsible for being, or
that the Dasein in them is the being-responsible of/for being itself.

We need to replace for "being is" the expression *"Es gibt" das Sein."*[40]
"The essence of being" is an essence "that is giving, that grants its truth."[41]
What being gives is being itself. Being gives of being. (The) being (of beings) is not a "gift" that it "gives," therefore. And therein lies the whole ambiguity of the theme of the "gift," and it is for this reason that we might
well prefer the term "letting" to that of "giving." Being lets beings be. Being does not "give" anything: being is the letting-be through which something is. Hence the very being of beings, their essence, "gives" itself, "lets"
itself or "transfixes" beings as "truth," in other words, as that which opens
onto sense—and precisely not as a sense or as an appropriable horizon of
signification. The "gift" is inappropriable *qua* "gift," and this is exactly
what it "gives" or "lets" (hence, what we receive as a present doesn't become our property in the way that something we have acquired does; the
gift becomes "mine" without alienating its inappropriable essence *qua* gift;
for the essential reason that what, on account of the idiomatic expression
es gibt, tends to be called the "gift," cannot designate "a gift"). The gift becomes "mine" without alienating its inappropriable essence *qua* gift. Conversely and correlatively, what is "let" becomes "mine" without retaining
any sense of a giver; where this not the case, it would not *let*—or *make*—
be its own letting-be.

This is why it is a matter of corresponding to this "gift," to this "let-
ting-be/-make" as such. It is a matter of responding to it and of being responsible for it, of being engaged by it. It is a matter of finding the fitting
gesture, the right conduct (*das Schickliche . . . , das diesem Geschick ent-
spricht*, as Heidegger says) toward the giving or the letting-be/make as
such.[42] Toward being, in other words, since being is definitely not the
giver of the gift (*es* gibt—however we look at this, the gift has no owner;
and let me say that throughout our dealings with the motif of the gift in
Heidegger, Derrida's analyses must be borne in mind). Being is the gift itself; or, rather, being *is* letting-be, just as it *is* "the clearing,"[43] just as it ek-
sists beings. Being doesn't "give" being existence, therefore; being *is*, in a
transitive sense, ek-sisting.

The fitting gesture is one that "touches" on being.[44] (Here, we would need to develop the difference between touch as a mere sense—in German, *Tast, tasten*—and the *rühren* that Heidegger uses to denote a sense of stirring, affecting, moving.) If it is a matter of "touching" on being or of touching it, this is because being is "the nearest,"[45] and insofar as it denotes the transitivity of ek-sisting. If, in Dasein, it is being that "is at issue," it is because of this intimate nearness: existence touches itself; in other words, it "moves" itself, sets itself moving outside of itself and affects itself with its own *ek-*. Action, this action of "touching," is what is at stake, therefore, in the being "that is at issue." (We could also say that the theme of originary self-affection is reawakened here, beyond the sphere of consciousness and affect, as the theme of an originary *ethos*.)

"Nearness" and "touching" evoke what would we would have to call the intimate distance according to which "being" is related to "the essence of man," in other words, according to which "being itself is the relation,"[46] Being *is* the relation of existence to itself as the action of sense. For beings, being is precisely not being-there, Dasein pure and simple, but the opening to an accomplishment of sense.

The relation of existence to itself as the opening of and to sense is nothing other than the relation of the "improper" to the "proper."[47] The improper of ordinary existence reveals itself as "improper" insofar as it has an essential relation with the "proper"—even if only in terms of fleeing or avoiding. Which means: it has a relation with its own "proper [*son propre "propre"*]," with what is most proper and nearest to it, the call to make sense. One could transcribe this thus: nothing is more ordinary than the call, most often an undeceived one, to the "sense of existence," and nothing is rarer than responding to this call in a fitting ("responsible") way, in other words, without being deceived by a "sense" supposedly given to existence, as if from within or beyond it, instead of confining ourselves to the making-sense of ek-sisting.

The fact that this sort of response is rare doesn't mean that it is a privilege reserved for a few or that it is very difficult to obtain: rather, it means that it belongs to the essence of the sense of being *not* to give itself as a laid-down sense (and so, to make the point again, to be *not* properly *given*), and that the dignity of man comes from his being exposed to this essence of sense as that which touches him most closely. What touches him—or that upon which he touches—doesn't let itself be incorporated, appropriated, and fixed as an acquisition. If sense were acquired or, what amounts to the same thing, needed to be acquired, there would be no ethical possibility. If, however, the action of sense is the exercising of the relation with ("touching") what is nearest but cannot be appropriated as a being, then not only is there an ethics, but ethics becomes the ontology of ontology itself (as for appropriation, it is the event of being, the *Ereignis*).

"Nearness occurs essentially as language itself."[48] This essential role of language doesn't contradict the primacy of action. It's not a case of saying that the exercising of language is the only real action, relegating "practical" actions to second place. Later on we will have to make clear a few reservations regarding the role Heidegger entrusts to language (even though the potential for countering such reservations can be found in Heidegger himself). For the moment, however, we need to situate language as accurately as possible.

Language isn't a superior kind of conduct. It is the element in which conduct confirms itself as conduct of sense. On the one hand, language experiences sense as what is to be asked or questioned. It is "a questioning that experiences."[49] On the other hand, what it experiences—the sense of being, in other words, being as sense[50]—it experiences or undergoes as "the *transcendens* pure and simple."[51] Language responds to being as the *transcendens*: what it doesn't do is respond to it by assigning the *transcendens*; rather, it responds by co-responding to the transcendence of the *transcendens* and responds thus to transcendence by taking responsibility for it. This is why language itself is "the house of being, which is propriated [*ereignet*] by being and pervaded by being."[52] As a structure of language, it is less a "lodging" for a particular sense than the very *Ereignis* of sense, the event-appropriation (desire/ability) of sense. Why? Because it is properly the element of sense. And yet, it is not so much an element as a production of significations. It is so in that significations can only ever be signified on the ground of making-sense, which is not itself a signification (and which refers perhaps rather to "due silence").[53]

In truth, "language" designates much less the order of the verbal than that on the basis of which this order can take place,[54] and which is, precisely, the experience of transcendence (or, more exactly, experience as transcendence, and as its responsibility). Nevertheless, transcendence has to be understood very precisely, not as that which might transcend existence towards a pure "beyond" (and which, by the same token, would no longer pertain to language but to a different experience, a—let us say mystical—

experience of the *transcendens* as such, rather than of transcendence), but as that which structures existence itself into a "beyond," into ek-sistence.[55] The transcendence (of the sense) of being is a transcendence of and for immanence: it is nothing other than the desire/ability of making-sense, and this desire/ability *as* making-sense.

On this basis, the transcendence of being can and must be explicitly expressed as "originary ethics."[56] Sense, in fact, does not relate a particular to a transcendent signification that sublimates it outside of itself. Sense appears instead as "the demand . . . for an obligating intimation and for rules that say how man, experienced from ek-sistence towards being, ought to live in a manner befitting his destiny."[57] Such an intimation is unnecessary, since there would need to be an obligation to enforce a law, about which, moreover, we would still know nothing. It is, on the contrary, the manifestation of sense as such, as the sense of action. (If you like, we could say: sense is the law.) As regards Kant, Heidegger writes: "the respect before the law . . . is in itself a making-manifest of myself as acting self," whereas "Reason, as free, gives to itself that for which the respect is respect, the moral law."[58] (Let me take the opportunity here to emphasize once again the importance of Kant to all this. It is as though Heidegger's concern was to regain the point at which Kantian subjectivity frees itself, by itself, from its subjective foundation—from representation, from signification—and confirms itself as acting, in other words, as exposed to a sense that isn't given.)

Here, *ethics* isn't the effect of a distribution of disciplines that would distinguish the order of moral significations (values) from the order of cognitive or natural significations ("logic" or "physics").[59] In fact, "disciplines" can find their place as regimes of signification only "after" making-sense as such. Making-sense as such is prior to any such division, an "intimation" of it, just as the conduct of existence is prior to any determination of significations (from which we ought logically to deduce that all disciplines are "originarily ethical"—the cognitive, the logical, the physical, and the aesthetic just as much as the moral).

Ethos needs to be understood as "abode" (following Heraclitus's saying: *ethos anthropoi daimon*.)[60] The abode is the "there" in that it is open. As such, the abode is much more a conduct than it is a residence; more accurately, "residing" is principally a conduct, the conduct of being-the-there. To think this conduct is thus "originary ethics," since it involves thinking *ethos* as the conduct of/according to the truth of being. This sort of thinking is more fundamental than any ontology, therefore; it doesn't think "beings in their being" but "the truth of being." It was in this sense that the thinking that took place in *Being and Time* had already been described as "fundamental ontology."[61] What becomes clear now, however, is not simply that the thinking of being involves an ethics but, far more radically, that it involves itself as an ethics. "Originary ethics" is a more appropriate name for "fundamental ontology." Ethics *is* what is fundamental about fundamental ontology. Nonetheless, we cannot simply substitute one name for the other without losing sight of the following essential point: *ethos* isn't external to or superimposed upon being; it is not added to it, does not happen to it, does not give it rules that come from elsewhere. Rather, being *is*—because it is in no sense a being—what ek-sists beings, what ex-poses them to making-sense. Being is the ek-sistent conduct of Dasein. And this is also why, in preference to any term that might evoke a "moral philosophy" deduced from a "first philosophy," Heidegger retains the expression "the thinking about Being," stating that it is "neither ethics nor ontology," "neither theoretical nor practical."[62]

This thinking "has no result."[63] It gives neither norms nor values. It does not guide conduct but conducts itself toward the thinking of conduct in general[64]—not as something to be normalized or finalized, but as what constitutes dignity itself, namely, having, in one's own being, to make sense of being. Besides, if thinking as originary ethics were to provide "maxims that could be reckoned up unequivocally," it "would deny to existence nothing less than the very *possibility of acting*."[65]

What is deliberately provocative in the expression "this thinking has no result" requires careful consideration. It also amounts to saying that such a thinking is its own result, or "effect"[66]—not because the purity of its speculation leads it around in circles, but because it is only possible as a thinking (in the manner of all true thinking) insofar as it is itself a conduct, an existential action. It posits and posits itself actively, which is also to say that it obligates itself to encounter human dignity insofar as the latter is incommensurable with a fixing of signification and a filling out of sense: in other words, it is ultimately incommensurable with any "thinking" in the usual sense of the word (idea, concept, discourse, etc.). Neither a sense projected indefinitely beyond (a "philosophy of values") nor sense captured and fixed as pure autonomy (the subjectivism of free choice) can ensure such a dignity. Both, moreover, lead to bitter disappointments that are rather different from what initially seems to emerge from Heidegger's notion of thinking as having "no result." Indeed, this is shown by contemporary moral confusion, which fails to find either values or free will. Doing so, however, it shows that it has no sense of an ethics.

Dignity is possible only if it measures up to finitude, and finitude, as will now be clear, means the condition of a mode of being whose sense *makes-sense* as a ground and a truth. (Infinitude, by contrast, would be the condition of a mode of being that results in a sense being produced, acquired, and related back to itself.) Schematically speaking, therefore: ek-sistence *is* sense; it *has* no sense.

Existence, however, still has various senses (and non-senses). It can and must have them, can and must receive, choose, and invent them. Their number and scope is incommensurable with the unitary sense of dignity. *Touching* on this sense—not absorbing it as a signification, therefore, but ex-posing ourselves to it—such is the conduct toward which thinking strives. What marks it out as a conduct is the fact that it knows that it is conducting itself toward the "shattering" that consists in "shattering against the hardness of its matter."[67] This is a long way from being either a conduct of shattering or a way of "philosophizing" about shattering.[68] Rather, it is a conduct that conducts itself in such a way as to take the measure of the incommensurable interval between every "thinking" (idea, representation, etc.) and the fundamental action through which it makes itself think. It takes the measure of the absolute interval that sense is.

There's nothing mystical about all this; what is mystical, though, is thinking that immediately projects its insufficiency onto the sufficiency of a signified effusion that somehow lies beyond it. Here, however, thinking merely experiences the relation of the improper to the proper as what properly needs to be thought, despite its being precisely *not* an "object of thinking" but the gesture of conduct or, more than this, the event of being that ek-sists as the conduct of sense. What we call "thinking" is not a discursive and representational elaboration "about" this conduct, therefore; it is being-engaged in it.

Let me recall briefly just how this event of being comes to be described in *Being and Time* as a "call of conscience."[69] The call "makes" Dasein *schuldig*, guilty or in debt.[70] However, this idea of *Schuldigsein* isn't simply a matter of "'having debts' and law-breaking."[71] Rather, it is "a predicate for the 'I am.'"[72] In this sense, then, it is the "responsibility" that is incumbent upon me insofar as I am "the ground of a nullity [*Nichtigkeit*],[73] in other words, the "ground" of ek-sisting as such. In the terms used by the "Letter on 'Humanism'": I am responsible for the gift as such.

At the same time, responsibility isn't played out between an impersonal "being" and an isolated "self." There is no "impersonal being." Rather, being is, if you like, the being-person of Dasein or, a little differently, in a formulation that would be both provocative and humorous, the personal being of Dasein.[74] Hence, responsibility only ever takes place as a responsibility with and toward others.[75]

Thinking in the sense of "originary ethics" is the experience of this absolute responsibility for sense. Nevertheless, this way of "experiencing" isn't a "feeling" (a word that isn't used in the text, and that I'm only using here as a provisional recourse). This ethics is no more an aesthetics than it is a mysticism. It is not a matter of feeling the sublime sentiment of incommensurable dignity, and the action of thinking doesn't consist in savoring its mixture of pleasure and pain . . . It is a matter of exposing ourselves to the absence of concept and affect (we should think, once again, of Kant's notion of respect—but also, if we reread the texts carefully, of the sublime as *apatheia*) that constitutes the articulation of being as ek-sistence or as making-sense. The intimation of sense and/or its desire is without concept and without affect. Or rather, the original *ethos* is the ek-sistent *a priori* synthesis of concept and affect in general. And it is only thus that, rather than being the object of thinking, it is its very matter.

Opening ourselves to making-sense as such, as what is at stake in being, means at the same time opening ourselves to the possibility of evil. "Being nihilates—as being."[76] In other words, the gift, as the possibility/intimation of making-sense, also gives itself as the possibility of not receiving the gift as a gift (without which it would be neither a "gift" nor "desire" nor "intimation"—nor what is more properly the synthetic *a priori* of these three categories). It isn't a matter of denouncing human "badness" as opposed to the generosity of being.[77] This generosity itself offers the possibility of the "nothing" within the essence of being. This isn't to say that there is no difference between the two antagonistic possibilities; were that so, they could hardly be called "good" and "evil." Rather, then, it means that evil is possible as the "rage" that precipitates being into the nothingness that it also is.[78]

How can ek-sisting, precipitated thus into its nothingness, be distinguished from ek-sisting exposed to its ownmost possibility of sense? Basically, how can one nothingness be distinguished from the other? Heidegger wants us to understand that no distinguishing ("normative") proposition can have any real sense if thinking is not firmly upheld in the face of the possibility that making-sense might "nihilate" or destroy itself as such. No doubt the glaring tension in this text's refusal to attempt even the slightest determination of evil can seem a touch worrying. This would need to be addressed elsewhere. What has to be conceded is the fact that any determination of evil would lead us away from the necessity of thinking the possibility of evil as a possibility of ek-sistence. It would lead us away from the possibility of being as ek-sistence.

This is what Heidegger indicates in the passage in which he sketches out a recent history of negativity "in the essence of being"[79] (revealing "nihilation" to be indissociable from "the history of being"—or from being as history—that brings it to light in its essential character). He notes that it's with speculative dialectics that negativity appears in being, but he does so merely in order to observe that "being is thought there as will that wills itself as the will to knowledge and to love";[80] in other words, dialectics sublates evil in this knowledge and this love. In this, the most recent form of theodicy, "nihilation" remains "essentially veiled." "Being as will to power is still concealed." Hence it is as will to power that nihilation has manifested itself without dialectical resorption. We can gloss this indication by thinking of the date of the text: 1946. If Heidegger isn't more explicit, that is surely because he refuses to separate the question of Nazism from that of an essential *Weltnot*,[81] a distress or deficiency in the modern world linked to the unleashing of "technology" (which it's not enough to oppose with a moral protest). This means, at least, that the modern world—or being in its most recent "sending"—brings to light, to a harsh light, an unreserved "engagement" of ek-sisting in the complete responsibility for sense (which may mean, moreover, that the demand to which the Nazi engagement was intended to respond was ethical *and* that Nazism ultimately showed itself to be the movement of this demand over into "rage"). In this, "originary ethics" is not only the fundamental structure or conduct of thinking, it is also what is delivered at the end of and as the accomplishment of the history of "the West" or of "metaphysics." We can no longer refer to available senses; we have to take absolute responsibility for making-sense of the world. We cannot ease the "distress" by filling up the horizon with the same "values" whose inconsistency—once their metaphysical foundation had collapsed—allowed the "will to power" to unfold. What this means, however, is that the ground needs to be thought somewhat differently: as ek-sistence.

This is how original ethical conduct encounters its law, its proper *nomos*: the *nomos* of the "abode," of "upholding" according to ek-sistence.[82] It is a matter of upholding ourselves and "bearing" or "carrying" ourselves in a way that befits the injunction of being—the injunction to be-ek-sistent. Conduct, dignity, is a matter of bearing. We have to bear ourselves, bear up before the responsibility for making-sense that has unfolded unreservedly. Man has to understand himself according to this responsibility.

This bearing is above all that of language. "Thinking" action consists in "bringing to language." What has to be brought to language isn't of the order of maxims. These, as such, don't need to be brought to language; they are, at least to a certain extent, available significations. (To take up the example once again: we can express a "respect for life," yes, but that says nothing about what does or does not make sense through "life" and our "respect" for it.)

This bearing of and in language is nothing more than respect or care for the job of making-sense; the refusal, consequently, to reduce it to facile moralizations or aestheticizing seductions (whence, for example, the reason why *Being and Time* was to dismiss interpretations of "responding to the call" as "wanting to have a 'good conscience'" or as "cultivating the call voluntarily."[83] None of which rules out the fact that the "Rectoral Address" fell into both of these traps.)

Hence it is with regard to the bearing of language that the "Letter on 'Humanism'" expresses what are, properly speaking, its only maxims, the maxims of "bearing" itself: "rigor of meditation, carefulness in saying, frugality with words."[84] These three maxims propose no values. Nor could they be used simply to measure the "ethicity" of any given discourse. The careful—even fastidious—restraint that they evoke, which has a whole Kantian and Hölderlinian tradition behind it, can just as easily be turned into puritanical affectation. The ethics of "bringing to language" should not be confused with a morality, still less with a policing of styles. These three maxims are merely the maxim of the measure of language in its relation with the unmeasurable character of making-sense.

All of which explains why Heidegger takes as his example of "the inconspicuous deed of thinking" the use of the expression "bring to language itself," an expression that he has just said needs to be taken "quite literally."[85] If we think it, he says, then "we have brought something of the essence of being itself to language." This means that "bringing to language" doesn't consist in expressing through words a sense laid down in the thing that we call being (being is precisely *not* a thing). It means literally (and we probably ought to say "physically," had we the time to explain ourselves on this point) *bringing* being itself, as ek-sisting, to the advent or the event that it is: to the action of making-sense. Language doesn't signify being but makes it be. But "making being being" means opening it to the conduct of sense that it is. Language is the exercising of the principle of responsibility. Hence, saying "man" or the *humanitas* of man—provided we have "bearing"—cannot amount to expressing an acquired value. It will always mean, so to speak, letting ourselves be conducted by the experience of a question—What is man?—that is already experienced as being beyond any question to which a signification could respond. Language is action in that it is indefinitely obligated to act. "Bringing to language" doesn't mean entrusting ourselves to words; on the contrary, it means entrusting the acts of language, as all acts, to the conduct of sense, to the finitude of being, in other words, to the ek-sistence in which "man infinitely exceeds man."

If it isn't going too far, allow me three brief concluding remarks. which will extend beyond the scope of an article such as this. This isn't the place to develop them, but it's relevant to mention them, since it would demonstrate a marked failure of integrity not to indicate the perspectives from which it has here been possible to present my remarks on Heideggerian ethics (and it should be pointed out that these perspectives are in line with a whole history of post-Heideggerian elaboration, particularly in France, Italy, and the United States).

a. Unquestionably, Heideggerian ethics is a long way from stressing the "being-the-there-with-others" that is, according to *Being and Time*, co-implied in ek-sistence. That sense is or makes sense only in the sharing that finitude essentially *is*, this is what is not emphasized. And this is doubtless the reason why it will have been possible, without further ado, to treat a "people" as an individual. In order to be rigorous, the analysis would need to extend to plural singularity as the condition of ek-sistence. Such singularity isn't that of the "individual," but that of each event of being in "the same" individual and "the same" group. Moreover, the singularity of the event of being also needs to be considered insofar as it affects the totality of beings. It would also be necessary to "bring to language" the being or the ethical sense of nonhuman beings. At any rate, "bringing to language" is indissociable from a "communicating," something over which Heidegger

does not linger. This isn't the communication of a message (of a signification), but that of making-sense-in-common, something that is quite different from making common sense. It is finitude as sharing.

b. At the same time, the attention paid to language—particularly in
the form of poetry—is always, and above all in the Heidegger of the essays
on language, on the point of privileging a silent enunciation, one that
might well prove to have the structure, nature, and appearance of a pure
utterance of sense (and not of what I have been calling the "conduct of
sense") as the sole and final (no longer "original") action. Poetry—and/or
thinking—would give sense, even if silently, instead of opening onto it. At
this precise point, at the apex of the action that "brings to language," we
would need to think how the "bringing," bringing being itself, is action
properly speaking, more so than language, and how existing ex-poses itself
outside language through language itself, something that would take place,
in particular, within making-sense-in-common; in other words, through a
language that is first and foremost an *address*. We might well say: ethics
would need to be "phatic" rather than "semantic." And I would also suggest that we put it in the following way: making-sense *ex-scribes itself* rather
than being inscribed in maxims or works.

These two points amount to saying that "originary ethics" still fails
to think the responsibility for its own ex-position (to others, to the world),
an ex-position that constitutes its true logic.

c. By claiming the title "originary ethics" and by identifying it with a
"fundamental ontology" prior to every ontological and ethical partition of
philosophy, Heidegger cannot but have kept deliberately quiet about the
only major work of philosophy entitled *Ethics* that is itself an "ontology" as
well as a "logic" and an "ethics." His silence about Spinoza is well known,
but it is doubtless here that it is at its most deafening. There would be lots
to say about this, but the most summary of observations will suffice: to say
that *ethos* is the ek-sisting of existence itself might be another way of saying
that "blessedness is not the reward of virtue, but virtue itself."[86]

Translated by Duncan Large

PART FIVE

PLEASURE

The Kantian Pleasure System

In what follows I offer only a programmatic remark on the systematic place occupied by "pleasure" in the overall organization of the Kantian edifice. This takes the form of a commentary on the early sections—principally the third—of the First Introduction to the *Critique of Judgment*.[1]

This Introduction is concerned more or less entirely with the notion of "system": the system of "philosophy," of the "powers of the human mind," and of "experience." It is the system of "powers" that makes it possible to think of experience as a "system," that is, to confer on it the kind of purposive organization that is lacking in mere knowledge of objects as this is defined in the *Critique of Pure Reason*. Moreover, it will ensure a systematic correlation between "*theoretical* philosophy," which posits objects without purpose or ends, and "*practical* philosophy," which posits unconditioned purposes or ends without objects.[2] The systematic knot must then, by tying together ends in general with experience in general, secure the ends of philosophy itself, as "the *system* of rational cognition through concepts." Critique has merely established the conditions for such a system by bringing out and delimiting against each other the central concepts of "nature" and "freedom." Only "purpose" or "purposiveness" assures a connection between the two, without overstepping their strict reciprocal demarcation.

From the standpoint of the "powers of the human mind," the distinction in question is between the understanding and reason. It is here that the determination of powers and their arrangement on one side or the other of the strict boundaries of critique assumes greatest importance: the transcendental procedure demands that the powers (= faculties) be considered first as they are in themselves, that is to say, in terms of their capacities and their orders of legitimation, thus their circumscriptions, their reciprocal division, and therefore precisely the consideration of *powers*, in the plural. This plurality is what constitutes the unity of pure reason and is the condition of its systematicity.

The system of powers is thus secured, not by an immediate unification after the fashion of the *intuitus originarius* (which would not, in fact, be a "power" in the strict sense at all, but a summary expenditure of power suppressing all potentiality), but by another kind of power altogether. A third power is introduced, signifying straightaway both the possibility of connecting the other two *and* the desirability of maintaining their reciprocal demarcation by means of what we might call a supplementary demarcation: neither cognitive nor normative, the *faculty of judgment* makes up for the lack of an a priori legislation of purposiveness. It will be charged with thinking "experience *as a system in term of to empirical laws*," that is, an experience that would not only be not the experience of an object, but also be that of the "necessity of the whole" of nature in all its diversity and "considerable heterogeneity."[3] The "necessity of the whole" is nothing other than the connection between nature, which is given, and freedom, which is commanded, and this connection must present itself as purposiveness.

Here, however, we are dealing with nothing more than the "higher cognitive powers," which are themselves at the "basis of philosophy."[4] As such, they designate and circumscribe the different kinds of cognition: of the object (understanding); of freedom (reason); and of purposiveness (the faculty of reflective judgment). But these types of philosophical knowledge are not yet ways of apprehending representations. To each kind of knowledge there corresponds a state of "mind (*Gemüt*)": "cognition" *stricto sensu*, "desire," and the "feeling of pleasure and displeasure."[5] It follows that philosophical knowledge, in its systematic unity, will be "cognition" only in a sense that is very broad and above all not identical to itself. Either it is a question of ("theoretical") cognition of objects (where in cognizing one cognizes oneself as restricted to experience), or of ("practical") cognition of the will (where in cognizing one recognizes oneself as free), or else of a third kind of relation to representations, which is the "feeling of pleasure and displeasure."

Only the first two "powers" are actually called powers (*Vermögen*) here. The third is termed a "feeling," thereby conferring on it from the outset, by its very name and by the disymmetry of the appellation, a distinct tonality, which I shall term that of the "passive power." In consequence, the tripartite distinction with which Kant opens section III of the First Introduction rapidly turns into a bipartite one. On the one hand, there are representations that "are referred merely to the object and to the unity of consciousness these representations [contain]," just as there are representations considered "as cause of the actuality of the object" in accordance with that other "unity of consciousness," the will (or desire): in both, these concern the relation of the object to the subject. On the other hand, there are representations that are "referred merely to the subject," and thus to the feeling of pleasure and displeasure.[6] Here representations are not just "mine"; although they are representations of an object and exist only in relation to that object (nature or freedom), they have validity because of being mine. This is to say that they vouch for nothing but themselves, since this "mineness" refers to no substantial subject of appropriation. Such representations "themselves are bases merely for . . . preserving their own existence in the subject."[7] The feeling of pleasure is the maintenance of representation for itself, without any relation either to the object (of cognition or action) or to the subject (of cognition or action).

(The feeling of displeasure, one should note, is the refusal or rejection of this maintenance, again without consideration for cognition or action. It is undoubtedly significant that Kant should characterize feeling solely in terms of pleasure, apparently forgetting or withdrawing the symmetrical "displeasure." Here, though, I can't deal with this any further. For present purposes, suffice it to say that I shall speak sometimes of "feeling," since in Kant typically it is the *Gefühl der Lust und Unlust*, the feeling of pleasure and displeasure, which amounts to *Gefühl* in general, and sometimes of "pleasure," since Kant often restricts himself to this half of the dyad. In any case, the examination that I want to undertake will show just how delicate this apparently simple matter of designation is: What, exactly, are we talking about?)

∼

Given the setup briefly described above, we might expect feeling to remain carefully distinguished from the other two powers. Indeed, it is presented as so distinct and separate as not to merit the title "power" at all, since it "neither is nor provides any cognition whatsoever."[8] Feeling is the noncognitive mode of combining or connecting representations and at the same time the nonlegislative mode (lacking the legality given by either the understanding or reason).

In fact, Kant emphasizes, while it is relatively easy to recognize "empirically" a "connection" between cognition or will and feeling, "this link . . . is not based on any *a priori* principle."[9] That some act of cognizing or willing should please or displease me is an entirely contingent affair. Consequently, the incipient "organization" we can detect here, since it is not "based on any *a priori* principle," does not form a "system, but only an *aggregate*" of faculties.[10]

Nevertheless, Kant feels bound to add in the next sentence that "it is true that we can show an *a priori* connection between the feeling of pleasure and the other two powers." This is a matter, he explains, of the link between our *a priori* cognition of freedom with the will as the basis of this cognition: which is nothing other than the link given in the form of the categorical imperative. Therefore, "in this objective determination"— which is objective because it refers to an object of cognition and is at the same time engaged in the actualization of this object in experience—we can "find . . . something subjective as well: a feeling of pleasure."[11] But, Kant adds, this pleasure does not precede the will: it follows it, "or perhaps is nothing other than our sensation of this very ability of the will to be determined by reason." Thus we shouldn't speak of a new *a priori* principle here, though this is precisely what is required if the autonomy of the third "higher power" is to be established.

There are several things that merit our attention here. First, the exceptional "case"[12] that Kant claims to have discovered, in order immediately to challenge it, is set up in a peculiar way: with respect to the first power, he invokes an "*a priori* cognition," which is cognition not of an object, but of freedom. Now this cognition, as is well known, is a knowing (*wissen*) without perception or comprehension (*einsehen*).[13] It is not of the same order as cognition of an object, even though it is itself cognition of a fact of experience and as such *scibile*.[14] Only a certain distortion, therefore, allows Kant to claim to be speaking about the first, cognitive power here. If we *are* dealing with a power, then it is the power of a paradoxical "cognition," one lacking an object, or having an object only in the needing-to-be-an-object of its object itself (namely, nature under the law of freedom).

The first power, therefore, appears here at best in an amputated form, limited to a cognition of concepts without intuition—or else, as cognition whose intuitions have peculiar characteristics that are not those of space and time . . . In such a cognition, in any event, nothing is known (and nothing is theoretical) other than the practical determination of reason.

However, if there is something like an intuition to which some cognition corresponds, if there is something which can be grasped, perceived, or felt (*eingesehen*), then this might well be something along the lines of the feeling that Kant introduces here. But he adds that this feeling plays no role in the *a priori* constitution of the practical determination of reason; were it to do so, it would run counter to the autonomy of that determination. The "connection" between the first two powers remains at least incomplete, or as if one-sided, and quite a lot is needed if they are to be "connected" with the third. (It is worth noting that in both instances Kant uses the word *Verknüpfung*, "knotting together," although the translation uses "connection" or "link.")

We know that the feeling that cannot but follow from the moral law is respect. What Kant says here about the secondary status of feeling fits with what he says in the *Critique of Practical Reason*, in the section "On the Incentives of Pure Practical Reason."[15] He also says in that section, though, that this feeling, which belongs to "reason," is "the only one that we can cognize completely *a priori* and the necessity of which we can discern [*einsehen*]."[16] In the Introduction, however, this *einsehen* seems somewhat blurred or confused by Kant's hesitation about the nature of the feeling in question ("or perhaps [it] is nothing other than"). Moreover, respect is not mentioned explicitly, and the allusive circumlocution that could only refer to it seems unsatisfactory: because it concerns a "feeling of *pleasure*," a quality that the second *Critique* sedulously denies to respect: "*So little* is respect *a feeling of* pleasure that we give way to it only *reluctantly* with regard to a human being." Equally, however, there is "*so little displeasure* is there in it that . . . one can never get enough of contemplating the majesty of this [moral] law."[17]

Be that as it may, respect is clearly the *incentive* of pure practical reason. In the Introduction, the anonymous feeling which stands in for or supplements it is only the appreciation of or approbation for an "aptitude" and does not constitute a "special feeling." From one to the other, there is a displacement, even a discord. Respect, insofar as it is an incentive, and thus wholly distinct from pleasure and pain, produces nothing less than an "interest which we call *moral*." This interest is pure because the feeling "depends on the representation of a law only as to its form and not on account of any object of the law":[18] respect thus behaves (or structures itself) like a pleasure, that is, like the self-relating of a representation which contains in itself the grounds for its own continued existence . . .

In §37 of the *Critique of Judgment* Kant presents the same argument for depriving feeling of any determinate apriority:

> I cannot connect *a priori* a definite feeling (of pleasure or displeasure) with any representation, except in the case where an underlying *a priori* principle in reason determines the will; but in that case the pleasure (in moral feeling) is the consequence of that principle, and that is precisely why it is not at all comparable to the pleasure in taste.[19]

Though they differ in character, the two different sorts of pleasure nevertheless share the same name, which suggests, despite everything, a close natural kinship. In §12 Kant attempts an awkward variation on this argument, describing respect as "a special and peculiar modification of the feeling of pleasure and displeasure which does seem to differ somehow from both the pleasure and displeasure we get from empirical objects."[20] "Modification" implies some commonality of substance.

Now this commonality characterizes a very odd sort of apriority, adumbrated in §12. The *a priori* ruled out in the connection of pleasure with representation is that causality. That some feeling is the effect of a representation is something that "can never be cognized otherwise than *a posteriori*" (whether that feeling is "one arising from the pathological basis, agreeableness," or "one arising from the intellectual basis, the conceived good," the latter, as we know, being only the consequence of a "postulate").[21] Yet there is a pleasure which, without being the effect of a representation, is just this same representation relating to itself by means of an "internal (final) causality." This is the "state of mind of a will determined by something or other," and thus the state par excellence of the categorical imperative. This state is "in itself already a feeling of pleasure," rather than being the cause of some affection or other. Pleasure is always the delight (*jouissance*) in itself of a representation, that is, of a "state of mind" in its pure form. But this pleasure can either be "merely contemplative" or "practical." Which is to say that the representation can either be that of a "merely formal purposiveness in the play of the cognitive powers" or that of the will.

The two "*a priori* pleasures" are distinguished from one another solely by two forms or states of mind, which are themselves just two modes of self-relation: representation as an end in itself, or representation as cause of its own actuality. At this point, the two pleasures constitute a system in the strongest sense: the system of the cause and the end of reason for itself.

But it is precisely here that Kant finds it necessary to invoke once again a rigorous distinction between the two pleasures in order to stave off the possibility that one might contaminate the other or, rather and above all, that a pure will might be contaminated by a pure affection. This distinction entails that the apriority of respect be regarded as not comparable with that which it most resembles. What cannot be compared to it is this: although in respect everything takes place as with pleasure (or pain), nothing can be allowed to cause pleasure or pain. We find in respect the form or structure of pleasure, but not the taste or flavor.

~

In order to cut short an analysis that really demands almost endless refinement,[22] we could say that pleasure is certainly not connected *a priori* to the power of desire, but that it is instead—what is at once less and more—included in it *a priori* as rejected or forbidden pleasure, or as that singular pleasure, within reason, to which the *a priori* banishment of pleasure itself gives birth.

Thus Kant's complicated and awkward discussion of the possibility, which he ultimately dismisses, of an "*a priori* connection" plays a highly ambiguous role. What it takes back with one hand, it gives with another, "surreptitiously" there is something about pleasure or, if one dare say so, a "principle of pleasure," that is not entirely foreign to pure reason's power of desire. There is a trace of the third power in the second.

Equally, though, we have seen that the power of cognition is present in this connection only in a limited and ambiguous manner. At the very least, it concerns only the cognition of freedom, which is a knowing without objective content (the only cognition of this kind). And yet, in showing us this side of the first power, Kant's text itself allows us to find a hint of a pleasure of a different kind.

In section VI of the published Introduction to the *Critique of Judgment*, we are told that "we do not find that the concurrence of our perceptions with the laws governed by universal concepts (the categories) has the slightest effect upon our feeling of pleasure; nor can there ever be any such effect, because the understanding proceeds with these laws unintentionally, by the necessity of its own nature."[23] This "concurrence" with laws is a mere *Zusammentreffen*, an encounter, and not a *Zusammenhang*, or internal organization (one of the leitmotivs of the First Introduction). Furthermore, says Kant, "it is a fact that when we discover that two or more heterogeneous empirical laws of nature can be unified [*Vereinbarkeit*] under one principle that comprises them both, the discovery does give rise to a quite noticeable pleasure, frequently even admiration, even an admiration that does not cease when we have become fairly familiar with its object."[24] Thus Kant announces the motif of a supreme pleasure in purposiveness, which reappears, in the guise of "admiration," in the closing pages of the third *Critique*.[25] There, admiration, which is both the support of and supplement to the thinking of purposes, is said to have something about it "similar to a *religious* feeling" and, as such, seems to "affect the moral feeling (of gratitude and veneration toward the cause we do not know), because we judge in a way analogous to the moral way."[26]

Cognition is thus entitled to expect a specific pleasure, constrained, needless to say, by the conditions of the reflective judgment through which purposes are posited, but passing beyond the theoretical so as to effect, again in strictly analogical fashion, a kind of reinforcing of "moral feeling" and, by extension, of the pure incentive of practical reason: *as if* something in the final purpose was susceptible of being cognized in order to determine the will. This something is certainly not unknowable freedom—but neither is it simply its opposite. Rather, it must be the knowledge of freedom as a knowing delighting in itself.

But this simple representation of purposiveness and of such a pleasure under an analogical or "symbolic" condition cannot itself be represented as a delight on the part of cognition if the latter did not, as it were, contain the seeds of it from the very beginning. At least this is what Kant goes on to suggest in the Introduction:

It is true that we no longer feel any noticeable pleasure resulting from our being able to grasp nature and the unity in its division into genera and species that alone make possible the empirical concepts by means of which we cognize nature in terms of its particular laws. But this pleasure was no doubt there at one time, and it is only because even the commonest experience would be impossible without it that we have gradually come to mix it in with mere cognition and no longer take any special notice of it.[27]

There was once, there necessarily must have been, therefore, a primitive pleasure in cognition. Granted, Kant is speaking here only about cognition through "empirical concepts" and "particular laws," and not about the cognition through "universal concepts" to which he referred a few lines earlier. But the two are not easily separated. Besides, we can see just how hesitant Kant's text is: he coordinates an ability to "grasp nature," which we can assume corresponds to a general cognition characteristic of the understanding, with a "unity in its [nature's] division into genera and species," which does not stem from the understanding alone but is, on the contrary, the occasion for the critique of the power of judgment. Here mathematico-physical cognition is distinct neither from chemico-biological cognition nor from culture and taste, and the analogy links up in some manner to determination . . .

If, from the point of view of the object, the cognition produced by determinant judgments has nothing to do with the cognition that follows from reflective judgments—no more than mechanism has to do with purposiveness—the purposive unity of nature nevertheless presupposes, as its minimal condition, the unity of a nature in general, the "*a priori* unity [without which] no unity of experience, thus also no determination of the objects in it, would be possible."[28]

So the "commonest experience" to which Kant refers is not, in its generality and its principle, divisible into *a priori* and *a posteriori* experience (into "possible experience" and the empirical). Rather, it is a matter of that which, in the *a priori*, aims from the outset at the *a posteriori* as such: the givenness of the material, sensible manifold, its heterogeneity, and the problematic character of its unity *qua* purposive unity. This apriority, which is neither that of the forms of intuition nor that of the categories— nor of schematism itself—is the supplementary apriority of a feeling: of the representation of unity in general delighting in itself. Without this we wouldn't even have begun to be subjects of some experience or other. If the most general condition of the cognition of the understanding is the synopsis of intuition in conjunction with categorial synthesis,[29] it is necessary nonetheless to suppose—and this is something that the *Critique of Pure Reason* doesn't do—the existence of something like an incentive for the activity of cognition.

Of course this incentive has to be located in cognitive activity itself, specifically in the relation of cognition to itself, which is to say, in the relation to itself of representation *qua* combination, or in the relation to itself of the combination of representations. But there has to be an incentive. It isn't enough for experience to be possible; the mind has to put itself in motion in order to actualize this possibility. And that motion cannot take place without—or as—a feeling, and not just as the exposition of the principles of the possibility of experience.

Everything happens here as if the *Critique of Judgment* has, discreetly, provided the transcendental incentive, if we can call it that, for the experience whose *a priori* conditions of possibility had been established in the *Critique of Pure Reason*, including the bounds of its legitimacy. Everything happens as if, on the one hand, the critical concern with the demarcations in cognition had left the incentive and motivating force behind the act of cognizing shrouded in obscurity, but on the other hand, as if the question concerning such a motivating force—rarely posed in itself wherever theory, and not freedom, is the "*keystone* of the whole . . . system of pure reason"[30]—reappeared here once the interests of a mere critique of possible cognition had been superseded. If, therefore, there is indeed a trace of pleasure in the first of the "powers of the human mind," it is not a mere residue, but an indication that reason is impelled or driven toward a delight beyond cognition: a delight in itself.

Given this, we might well be surprised to see that Kant, by asserting that the understanding experiences no "feeling of pleasure" when it "proceeds . . . unintentionally [and] by the necessity of its own nature," seems unaware that this procedure of the understanding, precisely because it entails the simple conformity of the understanding's activity with itself, provides exactly the conditions which constitute pleasure . . . But perhaps that is exactly what he means when he speaks of a lost, forgotten, or muted pleasure.

(Again, we would need to ask whether it is possible to find, on the side of theoretical pleasure, a counterpart to what practical pleasure presented to us as a connection with theoretical representation, of which, as I remarked earlier, it appears as a first power limited to concepts without intuitions. No doubt one would find this symmetrical counterpart in the universal communicability of aesthetic pleasure:[31] this sensible and pragmatic, if not strictly speaking practical, universal is like a universal of the understanding cut off, this time, from its own legislation.)

∼

Once the active and disruptive presence of pleasure in the two powers of reason, properly so called, is recognized, we can better understand the full implications of the "transcendental definition" Kant provides, once he has set up aesthetic judgment as the relation of a representation to the feeling of pleasure and displeasure:

A definition of this feeling in general terms, *without considering the distinction as to whether it accompanies the feeling of meaning [Sinnesempfindung], or accompanies reflection, or the determination of the will,* must be transcendental. It could be formulated thus: *Pleasure* is a mental *state* in which a representation is in harmony with itself and which is the basis [*Grund*] either for merely preserving this state itself . . . or for producing the object of this representation. On the first alternative, the judgment about the given representation is an aesthetic judgment of reflection; on the second, a pathological aesthetic judgment or a practical aesthetic judgment.[32]

This tripartition of aesthetic judgment will have been abandoned in the *Critique of Judgment*, at least as far as its third term is concerned, and this proves, once again, just how difficult Kant finds it to maintain simultaneously a strict critical separation of "powers" *and* what is nothing less than reason's single and most intimate motivating force, its *Trieb* as *Triebfeder* (incentive) for its highest vocation and, ultimately, as the *Grund* of its very being as *reason.*

Pleasure, therefore, as it appears in the *Critique of Judgment,* is less a third power than the exhibition for itself of an active principle—if not the sole really active and motivating principle—at the heart of the two theoretical and practical powers. Considered in isolation, pleasure displays only the form—internal agreement, self-preservation and delight in itself—of the ultimate and intimate incentive of reason in its double guise. This form is active in theoretical reason, though it appears there only as effaced or lost through habit, just as it is active in practical reason, but appears only as curbed or sublimated in obedience.

Rather, pleasure is active *as* theoretical reason and *as* practical reason, but this activity itself requires that pleasure be denied or forgotten: in sum, it requires that pleasure be repressed in two different but parallel ways. This repression of pleasure is necessary so long as the main concern of critique is to ensure that reason does not delight immediately in itself, in metaphysical *Schwämerei* and in the claim to know intuitively the Good and the Kingdom of Ends. This double repression is the condition that makes possible and necessary the exhibition of pure pleasure as the principle of a third faculty or power, which is charged not just with maintaining the critical separation between the other two *but also*, if one can say so, with generating reason's sole incentive, under the auspices of a pleasure that is irresistibly both one and many, self-identical in its foreignness to itself.

If the concept of repression runs the risk of bringing in something too distant or anachronistic here, and uselessly raises the question of what it is that exercises repression, we might speak of something being given up or relinquished: Kantian reason relinquishes or is deprived of delight in itself—but it does so or is so precisely in order to make clear that its vocation lies in the act of enjoyment or delight that Spinoza terms "beatitude" and "joy" and that shows up here as division in and of itself.

Hence pleasure organizes the system and is at the heart of it. Or, more exactly, the heart of the system, what articulates it and puts it into play, what gives it the internal consistency and purposiveness that makes up genuine systematicity, is the feeling of pleasure and displeasure.[33] This is to say that, if "pleasure" is always the value of the highest vocation, its deep structure is that of self-relating, and this self-relating, insofar as it is not given (but rather, in a way, sets itself in motion for itself), displays in a fundamental way the ambivalence of the permanent possibility of discord or disagreement. To take pleasure or displeasure in itself: Kantian reason falls prey to this anxiety. This is why its whole predicament is summed up in the famous formulation at the end of the *Critique of Practical Reason*: "*the starry heavens above me and the moral law within me*" are the twin objects and sources of an "ever new and increasing admiration" which, at one and the same time, "annihilates, as it were, my importance as an *animal creature*, which must give back to the planet . . . the matter from which it came" *and* "infinitely raises my worth as an intelligence by my personality, in which the moral law reveals to me a life independent of all animality."[34]

This anxiety can appear narcissistic, and undoubtedly it is: though not in the sense either of a vain indulgence or an auto-eroticism. It is narcissistic in the sense that such identification is necessary, and to the extent that the absence of this identification (that of an *intuitus originarius*) *grounds* Kantian reason so dramatically in a double divestiture—a forgetting and a forbidding—of delight in itself, its principle, and its purpose.

Translated by Jonathan Derbyshire

11

The Sublime Offering

The sublime is in fashion.[1] All fashions, in spite of or thanks to their futility, are means to the presentation of something other than fashion: they are also of the order of necessity or destiny. For destinies, indeed, fashions are perhaps only a particularly secret and discreet way of offering themselves. What then offers itself or what is offered in this recent fashion of the sublime? I will attempt to answer: the offering itself, as the destiny of art.

But the fashion of the sublime has the supplementary privilege of being extremely old. It is at least as old as Boileau's translation of Longinus and the distinction Boileau drew between "the sublime style" and the sublime taken in the absolute sense. From that point on, what had once been, under the names of *hypsos* or *sublimitas,* a category of rhetoric[2]—the discourse that specialized in subjects of great elevation—become a concern, a demand, an adoration, or a torment, more or less avowed but always present, for aesthetics and philosophy, for philosophy *of* aesthetics and philosophy *in* the aesthetic, for the thought of art and for art as thought. In this sense, the sublime forms a fashion that has persisted uninterruptedly into our own time from the beginnings of modernity, a fashion at once continuous and discontinuous, monotonous and spasmodic. The "sublime" has not always taken this name, but it has always been present. It has always been a fashion because it has always concerned a break within or from aesthetics (whether "aesthetics" designates taste or theory). And this break has been willed, intended, evoked, or demanded more than it has been truly revealed or demonstrated: it has been a kind of defiance with which aesthetics provokes itself—"enough beauty already, we must be sublime!" But at the same time, it has not been a matter of mere fashion, as I said, but necessity itself.

The motif of the sublime (the name and category of which are perhaps not even up to the standards of what they indicate, being too used up, already or still too aesthetic, too ethical, too virtuous, too elevated, in short, too sublime, and I will return to this below)—the motif of the sublime, then, announces the necessity of what happens to art in or as its modern destiny. Art itself is doubtless that which is happening par excellence to us (to us others, the Occidentals), that which is offering us our destiny or deranging our history. But in the sublime, art itself is deranged, offered to yet another destiny; it has its own destiny in a certain sense outside of itself. The sublime is tied in an essential way to the *end* of art in all its senses: that for which art is there, its destination or *telos*, and the cessation, overcoming, or suspension of art.

There is no contemporary thought of art and its end which does not, in one manner or another, pay tribute to the thought of the sublime, whether or not it explicitly refers to this thought. One could research and retrace the genealogies, filiations, and transmissions, from Walter Benjamin—whose role is certainly decisive—to ourselves. But necessity is always deeper than genealogies, beginning with the necessity that related Benjamin himself to Kant, or with the necessity that related Kant, and all of the others with him, to the destiny or task of art in thought.[3]

I will not explore this history or network. I will content myself with placing here, by way of opening, several fragments that ought to speak for themselves:

For the sake of the unity which the veil and that which is veiled comprise in it, the Idea can be essentially valid only where the duality of nakedness and veiling does not yet obtain: in art and in the appearances of mere nature. On the other hand, the more distinctly this duality expresses itself, in order finally in man to reach its greatest force, the more this becomes clear: in veil-less nakedness the essentially beautiful has withdrawn and in the naked body of the human being a Being beyond all beauty is attained—the sublime, and a work beyond all images [*Gebilden*]—the work of the creator. (Benjamin[4])

In the work, truth is at work and therefore not merely something true. . . . The appearance arranged in the work is the beautiful. Beauty is a mode of being and of presence of truth qua unveiling. (Heidegger[5])

The Kantian theory of the sublime describes . . . an art which shudders within itself: it suspends itself in the name of the content of truth deprived of appearance, but without, qua art, renouncing its character as appearance. (Adorno[6])

Just as prose is not separated from poetry by any threshold, art expressive of anguish is not truly separated from that expressive of joy . . . it is no longer a matter of dilettantism: sovereign art accedes to the extremity of the possible. (Bataille[7])

It would still be necessary to investigate whether this placing-in-question of art, which the most illustrious part of the art of the past thirty years represents, does not presuppose the sliding, the displacement of a force at work in [*puissance au travail dans*] the secrecy of works and refusing to step into the light of day. (Blanchot[8])

What is at stake in the sublime is a suspension of art, a placing in question of art within art itself as work or as task. In the name of the sublime, or under the pressure of something that often (but not exclusively) has carried this name, art is interrogated or provoked in view of something other than art. More precisely, it is a matter of a double suspense or a double placement in question. On the one hand, it is aesthetics as a regional philosophical discipline that is refused in the thought of art seized by the sublime. Kant is the first to do justice to the aesthetic at the heart of what one can call a "first philosophy": but he is also, and for this very reason, the first to suppress aesthetics as a part or domain of philosophy. As is well known, there is no Kantian aesthetics. And there is not, after Kant, any thought of art (or of the beautiful) that does not refuse aesthetics and interrogate in art something other than art: let us say, truth, or experience, the experience of truth or the experience of thought. On the other hand, it is art that suspends itself and shudders, as Adorno says, art that trembles on the border of art, giving itself as its task something other than art, something other than the world of the fine arts or than beautiful works of art: something "sublime."

It is as if "aesthetics" as object, as well as the aesthetic object, had dissolved upon the touch of philosophy (and it makes no difference whether they have offered themselves to philosophy or whether philosophy has attempted to conquer them by violence), to leave room for something else (nothing less, in Kant, than the sublime destination of reason itself: freedom). But it is also as if, at the same time, the capture and flight of these objects had required philosophy to think of both art and itself otherwise. In the suspension of art, the task of thought is in question.

But it is in question in such a manner that it does not take over the relay where art leaves off, where art would be both suppressed and con-

served in the "true" presentation of truth. Such a thought of the relay, or
of the sublation [*relève, Aufhebung*] of art by philosophy forms the most
visible part of Hegel's thought of the end of art. But the essential point is
precisely that the claim of the sublime forms the exact reverse of the sublation of art.[9]

The thought of the end of art as its sublation and, consequently, as its
completion or achievement—which suppresses art as art and consecrates it
as philosophy, which suppresses philosophy as discourse and conserves it as
art, as the pure art of pure thought—such thought reverses the sublime.
This does not mean that there are two symmetrically opposed ways of
thinking art. It means rather that there is one type of thought that reab-
sorbs art and another that thinks it in its destination. The latter is the
thought of the sublime. The former thought, that of Hegel—philosophy as
such—does not in fact think art as destiny or as destination but rather the
reverse, the *end* of art, its goal, reason, and accomplishment. It puts an end
to what it thinks: it thus does not think it at all, but only its end. It puts an
end to art by preserving art in and as philosophy. It puts an end to art in
the presentation of truth. To be sure, such thought views art as having
heretofore comprised this presentation—as a representation and perhaps as
presentation in general, always sensible, always aesthetic—but it views art
as no longer adequate to this task of representative presentation now that
truth has become capable of presenting itself on its own. Thus the end of
art is attained, and art is properly *sublated* as presentation, in the presentation of the true. It is suppressed as art and preserved as pure presentation.

What is the case then with art *as* art? What remains of it and where?
Art as such—as all that is designated as "art" in Hegel or elsewhere and,
for example, as figuration or expression, as literature or painting, as form
or beauty, as work or value—art as such can remain nowhere but in the
element of representation, the end of which was presentation itself. The
art that remains there (if such an "art" exists, or if it still merits this name),
the art that conceives itself as representation or as expression is in fact a
finite art—finished, dead. But the thought that finished it off suppressed
itself as the thought of art. For it never thought that which it brought to
completion.

It never thought what it brought to completion because art, in truth,
was already no longer dwelling in the element of (re)presentation. Perhaps
art never served to (re)present except in the philosophical representation of
art. Art was elsewhere: Hegel (at least a certain Hegel) wasn't aware of it,

but as for Kant, he had begun to recognize that what was at stake in art was not the representation of the truth, but—to put it briefly—*the presentation of freedom*. It was this recognition that was engaged in and by the thought of the sublime. Not only was art not completed by philosophy in this thought, but art began to tremble there, suspended over itself, unachieved, perhaps unachievable, on the border of philosophy—which art thus made shudder or interrupt itself in its turn.

For Kant, the beautiful and the sublime have in common that they have to do with presentation and only with presentation.[10] In both nothing plays itself out but the play of presentation itself, without any represented *object*. (There ought therefore to be a concept, or an experience, of presentation that would not be submitted to the general logic of (re)presentation, that is, of the presentation by a subject and for a subject: basically, the entire question is there). On the occasion of an object of the senses, the imagination—which is the faculty of presentation—plays at finding a form in accord with its free play. It presents (to itself) this: that there is a free accord between the sensible (which is essentially multiple or manifold) and a unity (which is not a concept, but rather free indeterminate unity). The imagination thus presents the image, or rather that there is (such a thing as) "image" (*Bild*). The image here is not the representative image, and it is not the object. It is not the placing-in-form of something else but form forming itself, for itself, without object: fundamentally, art, according to Kant, represents nothing in either the beautiful or the sublime. The "imagination" does not signify the subject who makes an image of something but rather the image imaging itself, not as a figure of something else but as form forming itself; unity happening upon manifoldness, coming out of a manifoldness, in the manifold of sensibility, simply as unity without object and without subject—and thus without end. It is on the basis of this general situation of free aesthetic presentation that one must attempt to appreciate the respective stakes of the beautiful and the sublime.

Kant calls the free *Bild* that precedes all images, all representations, and all figurations (one is tempted to say the nonfigurative *Bild*) a *schema* in the first *Critique*. He says in the third *Critique* that aesthetic judgment is nothing other than the reflexive play of the imagination when it "schematizes without concepts": that is, when the world that forms itself, that manifests itself, is not a universe of objects but merely a schema (*skema*, "form," or "figure"), merely a *Bild* that makes a "world" on its own, because it forms itself, because it designs itself. The *schema* is the figure—but the imagination that figures without concepts figures nothing: the schematism of aesthetic judgment is intransitive. It is merely the figure that figures itself. It is not a world nor the world that takes on figure, but the figure that makes world. It is perhaps indissociable from the fake, the fiction, and the dream of a Narcissus: but all of that comes only after the fact. In order that there should be these figures and this scene of representations, there must first be the throw, the surging and beating, of a design, a form, which *figures itself* in giving itself figure, in conferring upon itself a free unity. It confers this unity upon itself, or it receives this unity—for at first it does not have any unity at its disposal. Such is the essential characteristic of imagination, of *Einbildung* operating without a concept: imagination is unity that precedes itself, anticipates itself, and manifests itself, free figure prior to any further determination.

From this starting point—that is, barely having entered into the first modern philosophical assignation of the aesthetic—one can *finish* very quickly if one likes. By pursuing the logic of this initial constellation of the aesthetic schematism, one can very quickly arrive at the end of art. Indeed, in a sense one must pursue it if only in order to discover that it can function only by ignoring the sublime, which nothing I have said thus far has distinguished as such.

In the first *Critique* the schematism was said to be a "technique hidden in the depths of the soul." Does the secret of this technique unveil itself in the aesthetic schematism, which presents essentially the pure form of the schematism? It is tempting to think so. The schematism would then be aesthetic. The technique of the schema would be an art. After all, it is the same word, *ars* or *die Kunst*. Reason would be an artist, the world of objects a work—and art would be the first or supreme technique, the creative or self-creative technique, the technique of the unity of subject and object, unity positing itself in the work. One can believe this and proceed to draw the consequences.

One will very quickly obtain two versions of a thereby completed thought of the schematism: either the version of an originary and infinite art, a poetry never ceasing to give itself form in giving form to the world as to thought—and this is the romantic version—or else the version of a technique of originary judgment, which divides judgment in order to relate it to itself as unity and so to give it its absolute figure—and this is the Hegelian version. Either aesthetics sublates philosophy or the converse. In both cases, the schematism is understood (its secret revealed) and accomplished: art or technique—and doubtless, according to the play of complicitous exchange between the two versions, art *and* technique, technique of art and art of technique—the schema is the originary figure of *figuration itself.* That which figures (or that which presents, for here, figuring is presenting), the faculty of figuration or of presentation has itself already a figure, and has already presented itself. It is reason as artist or technician, which comes down to the same thing: *Deus artifex.*

Thus, the imagination that schematizes without a concept would schematize itself of itself in aesthetic judgment. And this is certainly, in one sense, what it does: it presents itself as unity and it presents its unity to itself, presenting nothing other than itself, presenting the faculty of presentation in its free play, that is, again, presenting the one presenting, or *representing,* absolutely. Here, the presenting one—the subject—is the presented. In the beautiful and in the sublime—which are neither things nor qualities of objects but judgments, and more precisely, aesthetic judgments, i.e., the proper judgments of sensibility when it is determined neither by concepts nor by empirical sensation (which constitutes the agreeable, not the beautiful)—the unity of spirit, the spirit as unity, and the accord of the faculties operated in the imagination or, more precisely, *as* imagination presents itself to itself.

It is not so much that art comes to find its reason or reasons here but rather that Reason takes possession of art in order to make of it the technique of its self-presentation. This self-presentation is thus the presentation of the very technique of reason, of a technique conceived as the primary or ultimate nature of reason, in accordance with which reason produces, operates, figures, and presents itself on its own. The schematism is on this account the anticipation of the unity of presentation (or of that which presents) in presentation itself (or in the presented), an anticipation which doubtless constitutes the only possible technique (the only *Handgriff,* "sleight of hand," as the first *Critique* puts it) by means of which a presentation, in this strict philosophic sense, could ever take place. How would I trace any figure at all, if I did not anticipate its unity, or more precisely, if I did not anticipate myself, the one who presents this figure, as its unity? There is a kind of fore-sight or providence at the heart of reason. The schema is reason which fore-sees and prefigures itself. It is thus of the nature of the schematism, this artistic *coup de main* of reason, to be "hidden in the depths of the soul": the prefiguration escapes in its anticipation. And it is even basically the hidden, secret character of the schematism that unveils it for what it is: the technique, already dissimulated behind all visible figures, of figurative or presentational anticipation.

In this "schematism without concepts," in this "free legality" or in this "sketch" of the world[11] for the free subject, the cosmetic is the anticipation of the cosmic. The beautiful is not here a quality, intrinsic or extrinsic, subjective or objective, it is more than a quality. Indeed, it constitutes the status and the very being of the subject which forms itself and which presents itself in order to be able to (re)present for itself a world of phenomena. The aesthetic is itself the anticipation of knowledge, art is the anticipation of technical reason, and taste is the schema of experience—the schema or the pleasure, for precisely here *the two are confounded.* Did not Kant write that a primitive pleasure must have presided over the very first knowledge, "a remarkable pleasure, without which the most common experience would not have been possible"?[12] There is a pure, painless pleasure, then, at the philosophical origin of knowledge and world domination. (That there is no admixture of pain in this pleasure implies that the sublime is not yet involved, a point to which I will return below.) This pleasure consists in the satisfaction provided by unity in general, by (re)discovering (re)union of the manifold, the heterogeneous, under a principle or law. Anticipation arises out of or resides within this enjoyment [*jouissance*] of unity which is necessary to reason. Without unity, the manifold is nothing but chaos and vertiginous danger. United with its unity—a unity which one must therefore have anticipated in order to be able to rediscover and (re)present it, and a unity thus technically and artistically produced— the manifold becomes enjoyment: at once pleasure and appropriation.

Enjoyment, according to Kant, belongs to the *agreeable,* which must be carefully distinguished from the beautiful. The agreeable is attached to an interest, whereas the beautiful is not. The beautiful is not linked to any interest, for in aesthetic judgment I do not depend at all on the existence of the object, and what is important is merely "what I discover in myself" on the occasion of this object.[13]

But does not self-enjoyment arise out of a supreme and secret interest of reason? The disinterestedness of the judgment of beauty, caught in the logic of the *ratio artifex,* is a profound interestedness: one has an interest in the being-anticipated of unity, in the (pre)formation of the figure, in the avoidance of chaos.

Here, the category of the beautiful begins to reveal itself in its extreme fragility. The beautiful and the agreeable already have in common that they "please immediately," in distinction to the good, on the one hand, and the sublime, on the other. If one must also establish a rapport between them in terms of interest—interest in the object in the case of the agreeable and interest in oneself in the case of the beautiful (and are these two things really so different?)—then one will have to say that the beautiful too involves enjoyment, the enjoyment of anticipation and self-presentation. The beautiful in Kant, and perhaps all simple *beauty* since Kant, arises from the enjoyment of the subject, and indeed constitutes the subject as enjoying itself, its unity and its free legality, as that artist-reason which insures itself against the chaos of sensible experience and clandestinely re-appropriates for itself—thanks to its "hidden art"—the satisfactions that it had lost with God. Unless—even more brutally—it was the subject-artist (the subject of art, philosophy, and technique) who ravished God of His enjoyment.

When it presents itself in philosophy, or rather when it anticipates itself in philosophy (anticipating, in Kant's time, the essentially technical and artificial character of modern reason), aesthetics is suppressed twice in a single instant: once in the end of art and once in the enjoyment of imaginative reason. The two are the same, as one can clearly see: art meets its end, for it consists in the enjoyment in which it achieves itself. Kant is not in this the other of Hegel: in both, what is at stake in the aesthetic is presentation. The presentation of truth rests on the truth of presentation, which is the enjoyment of prefigured unity. The Hegelian spirit does not enjoy itself in any other way: the Kantian imagination is what it enjoys. Or again, the Hegelian spirit is itself the *final* self-appropriating enjoyment of the Kantian imagination. And philosophy gets off on art, makes of art and the beautiful its own enjoyment, suppresses them as simple pleasures, one could say, and preserves them as the pure self-enjoyment of Reason. The *Aufhebung* of art in philosophy has the structure of enjoyment—and in this infinite structure, art in its turn enjoys itself: it can become, as philosophic art, as art or technique of philosophical presentation (for example, dialectical, scientific, or poetic presentation), the orgiastic self-enjoyment of Spirit itself.

Once upon a time, the beautiful was "the splendor of the true": by a singular perversion, which it is difficult to consider without unease, the splendor of the true has become the self-enjoyment of reason.

This is perhaps the philosophic fate of the aesthetic as well as the aesthetic fate of philosophy. Art and beauty: presentations of the true, which uses them for its own enjoyment, anticipates itself in them, and finishes them off.

But far from finishing, we have hardly begun by proceeding thus. We have not even begun to deal with the sublime, and art, in Kant, does not offer itself to analysis before one has passed by way of the analysis of the sublime, which in several respects feeds into the examination of art, in particular by way of the decisive motif of genius. (This is not the place to dwell on it, but let me at least mention here that one can only thoroughly comprehend the Kantian theory of the arts, regardless of Kant's intentions, if one understands its dependence upon the theory of the sublime. This dependence is manifested, for example, by the ordering of his apparently poorly justified table of contents, which places the theory of art within the "Analytic of the Sublime," whereas the latter was supposed to be "a mere appendix" to the "Analytic of Aesthetic Judgments.")

One can gain access to the sublime by passing argumentatively through the insufficiencies of the beautiful. We have just seen beauty thicken suddenly, if I dare put it this way, into the pleasure or satisfaction of reason. This signifies nothing other than that the beautiful is an unstable category, insufficiently contained or retained in the order that was to be properly its own (the pure presentation of presentation). The beautiful is perhaps not quite as autonomous as it appears and as Kant would like. Taken literally as the pure pleasure of pure presentation, the beautiful reveals itself to be responsive to the interest of reason, which is all the more interested because it is hidden: it satisfies itself with and is satisfied by its power to present and to present itself. It admires itself on the occasion of its objects, and it tends, according to what is for Kant the law of all pleasure, to preserve its current condition, to preserve the enjoyment of its proper *Bild* and *Ein-bildung*. Doubtless the beautiful, rigorously considered, *is* not in this state of enjoyment, but it is always about to slide into it, to become confused with it: and this ever imminent sliding is not accidental but belongs to the very structure of the beautiful. (In the same manner, one can apply to the judgment of taste the rule applied to moral judgment: one can never say for certain that an action has been accomplished by pure morality; likewise, one can never say that a judgment of taste is a pure judgment of beauty: it is always possible that some interest—empirical or not—has intruded itself. Even more radically or rigorously, it is possible that there is no such thing as a pure judgment of taste and that its disinterest is always interested in the profound self-enjoyment of the imagination.)

However, the same instability, the same constitutive lability that makes the beautiful slide into the agreeable can also carry it off into the sublime. Indeed, the beautiful is perhaps only an intermediate, ungraspable formation, impossible to fix except as a limit, a border, a place of equivocation (but perhaps also of exchange) between the agreeable and the sublime, that is, between enjoyment and joy [*la jouissance et la joie*], to which I will return below.

If a transport of the beautiful into the sublime is indeed the counterpart or reversal of its sliding into the agreeable—and this is what we shall verify—and if in the agreeable the beautiful ultimately loses its quality of beauty (for in enjoyment, in the beautiful as satisfied or satisfying, the beautiful is finished—and art along with it), then one must expect the beautiful truly to attain its "proper" quality only in another sort of departure from itself—into the sublime. That is, the beautiful becomes the beautiful only beyond itself, or else it slides into the space this side of itself. By itself, it has no position. Either it achieves itself—in satisfaction, or philosophy—or it suspends itself, unachieved, in the sublime (and in art, or at least in art that has not been sublated by philosophy).

The sublime forms neither a second wing of aesthetics nor another kind of aesthetic. After all, it is rather unaesthetic and unartistic for an aesthetic. And in the final analysis, it would seem more like an ethics, if one holds to the declared intentions of Kant. But Kant does not seem to see quite what is at stake when he introduces the sublime. He treats the sublime as a mere "appendix" to the analysis of aesthetic judgment,[14] but in reality, the sublime represents in the *Critique* nothing less than that without which the beautiful could not be the beautiful or without which the beautiful could be nothing but the beautiful (which paradoxically comes down to the same thing). Far from being a subordinate kind of aesthetic, the sublime constitutes a decisive moment in the thought of the beautiful and of art as such. It does not merely add itself to the beautiful but transforms or transfigures the beautiful. Consequently—and this is what I am attempting to show—the sublime does not constitute in the general field of (re)presentation just one more instance or problematic: it transforms or redirects the entire motif of presentation. (And this transformation continues to be at work in our own day.)

There is nothing new about the idea that the sublime represents that without which beauty itself would *not* be beautiful, or would be *merely* beautiful, that is, enjoyment and preservation of the *Bild*. It dates from the modern (re)naissance of the sublime. Boileau spoke of "this *je-ne-sais-quoi* which charms us and without which beauty itself would have neither grace nor beauty." Beauty without beauty is beauty which is merely beautiful, that is, merely pleasing (and not "charming"). Fénelon writes: "The beautiful which is only beautiful, that is, brilliant, is only half-beautiful." In a sense, all of modern aesthetics, that is, all "aesthetics," has its origin and raison d'être in the impossibility of attributing beauty merely to beauty and in the consequent skidding or overflowing of the beautiful beyond itself. What is mere beauty? Mere beauty, or beauty alone and isolated for itself, is form in its pure self-adequation, in its pure accord with the imagination, the faculty of presentation (or formation). Mere beauty, without interest, concept, or idea, is the simple accord—which is by itself a pleasure—of the thing presented with the presentation. At least, this is what modern beauty has been or attempted to be: a presentation that is successful and without remainder in accord with itself. (At bottom, this is subjectivity qua beauty.) In short, it is a matter of the schema in the pure state of a schematism without concepts, considered in its free accord with itself, where freedom is confused with the simple necessity that form should be adequate to its proper form, should present just the form that it is, or should be just the form that it presents. The beautiful is the figure that figures itself in accord with itself, the strict accord of its contour with its design.

Form or contour is limitation, which is the concern of the beautiful: the *unlimited*, to the contrary, is the concern of the sublime.

The unlimited maintains doubtless the closest, the most intimate relations with the infinite. The concept of the infinite (or its different possible concepts) gives us in a sense the internal structure of the unlimited. But the infinite does not exhaust the being of the unlimited, it does not offer the true moment of the unlimited. If the analysis of the sublime ought to begin, as it does in Kant, with the unlimited, and if it ought to transport into itself and replay the analysis of beauty (and thus of limitation), it must above all not proceed simply as the analysis of a particular kind of presentation, the presentation of the infinite. Nearly imperceptible at the outset, this frequently committed error can considerably distort the final results of the analysis. In the sublime, it is not a matter of the presentation or nonpresentation of the infinite, placed beside the presentation of the finite and construed in accordance with an analogous model. Rather, it is a matter—and this is something completely different—of the movement of the unlimited, or more exactly, of "the unlimitation" (*die Unbegrenztheit*) *that takes place on the border of the limit, and thus on the border of presentation.*

The unlimited as such is that which sets itself off on the border of the limit, that which detaches itself and subtracts itself from limitation (and hence from beauty) by an unlimitation that is coextensive with the external border of limitation. In one sense, *nothing* sets itself off thus. But if it is permissible to speak of the "unlimited" as of "something" that sets itself off "somewhere," it is because in the judgment or the feeling of the sublime we are offered a seizure, an apprehension of this unlimitation that comes to raise itself up like a figure against a ground, although strictly speaking, it is always simply the limit that raises a figure up against a nondelimited ground. In the sublime, it is a question of the figure of the ground, of the figure that the ground cuts, but precisely insofar as the ground cannot constitute a figure and yet remains a "raising that razes" [*un "enlèvement"*], an unlimiting outline, along the limited figure.

The unlimited begins on the external border of the limit: and it does nothing but begin, never to finish. In addition, its infinity is neither that of a simple potential progression to infinity nor that of a simple actual infinity (or of "infinity collected into a whole," as Kant puts it, and he in fact uses both of these figures or concepts of the infinite). Rather, *it is the infinity of a beginning* (and this is much more than the contrary of a completion, much more than the inversion of a presentation). It is not simply the infinite sprawl of a pure absence of figure. Rather, the unlimited engenders and engages itself in the very tracing of the limit: it retraces and carries off, so to speak, "unto the ground" what this tracing cuts on the edge of the figure as its contour. It retraces "unto the ground" the operation of *Ein-bildung*: but this does not constitute a replication, even a negative replication, of this operation. It does not constitute an infinite figure or image but the movement of a cutting, delineation, and seizure. The sublime will always invoke—that is, if it is anything at all and if it can constitute an aesthetics—an aesthetics of movement as opposed to an aesthetics of the static or the state. But this movement is neither an animation nor an agitation, as opposed to an immobility. (One could doubtless easily be misled, but it is not a version of the ordinary—if not Nietzschean—doctrine of the couple Dionysos/Apollo.) It is perhaps not a movement in any of the available senses of this word. It is the unlimited beginning of the delimitation of a form and, consequently, of the state of a form and of the form of a state. The unlimited gets carried away with delimiting. It does not consist by itself in a delimitation, even if negative, for the latter would still be, precisely, a delimitation, and the unlimited would end up having its proper form—say, the form of an infinite.

But the infinite, Kant declares, cannot be thought "as completely given." This does not mean that Kant, contrary to what I indicated above, has in mind exclusively a potential infinity, the bad infinity, as Hegel would say, of a progression without end. It means, once again, that in the unlimitation involved in the feeling of the sublime it is not exactly a matter of the infinite. The infinite would be merely the "numerical concept," to speak like Kant, of the unlimited, the "presentation" of which is at stake in the sublime. One would have to say that the unlimited is not the *number* but the *gesture* of the infinite.[15] That is, the gesture by which all (finite) form gets carried away into the absence of form. It is the gesture of formation, of figuration itself (of *Ein-bildung*), but only insofar as the formless too stands out—without itself taking on any form—along the form that traces itself, joins itself to itself, and presents itself.

Because unlimitation is not the number but the gesture, or if one prefers, the motion, of the infinite, there can be no presentation of the unlimited. The expressions that Kant does not cease to attempt throughout the paragraphs dedicated to the sublime, those of "negative presentation," or "indirect presentation," as well as all the "so to speaks" and the "in a certain sense" strewn throughout the text, indicate merely his difficulty with the contradiction of a presentation *without* presentation. A presentation, even if it is negative or indirect, is always a presentation, and to this extent it is always in the final analysis direct and positive. But the deep logic of Kant's text is not a logic of presentation and does not pursue the thread of these clumsy expressions. It is not a matter of indirect presentation by means of some analogy or symbol—it is hence not a matter of figuring the nonfigurable[16]—and it is not a matter of negative presentation in the sense of the designation of a pure absence or of a pure lack or in any sense of the positivity of a "nothingness." To this (double) extent, one could say that the logic of the sublime is not to be confused with either a logic of fiction or a logic of desire, that is, again, with either a logic of representation (something in the place of something else) or a logic of absence (of the thing that is lacking in its place). Fiction and desire, at least in these classical functions, perhaps always frame and determine aesthetics as such, all aesthetics. And the aesthetics of mere beauty, of the pure self-adequation of presentation, with its incessant sliding into the enjoyment of the self, indeed, arises out of fiction and desire.

But it is precisely no longer a matter of the adequation of presentation. It is also not a matter of its inadequation. Nor is it a matter of pure presentation, whether this presentation be that of adequation or of inadequation, nor is it even a matter of the presentation of the fact that there is such a thing as the nonpresentable.[17] In the sublime—or perhaps more precisely at a certain extreme point to which the sublime leads us—it is no longer a matter of (re)presentation in general.

It is a matter of something else, which takes place, happens, or occurs *in* presentation itself and in sum *through* it but which is not presentation: this motion through which, incessantly, the unlimited raises and razes itself, unlimits itself, along the limit that delimits and presents itself. This motion would trace in a certain way the *external* border of the limit. But this external border is precisely not an outline: it is not a second outline homologous to the internal border and stuck to it. In one sense, it is the same as the (re)presentational outline. In another sense, and simultaneously, it is an unlimitation, a dissipation of the border on the border itself—an unbordering or overbordering, or overboarding, an "effusion" (*Ergießung*), Kant says. What takes place in this going overboard of the border, what happens in this effusion? As I have indicated above, I call it the offering, but we need time to get there.

In the sublime, then, presentation itself is at stake: neither something to be presented or represented nor something that is nonpresentable (nor the nonpresentability of the thing in general), nor even the fact that it [*ça*] presents itself to a subject and through a subject (representation), but the fact *that* it presents itself and *as* it presents itself: it presents itself in unlimitation, it presents itself always *at the limit*.

This limit, in Kantian terms, is that of the imagination. For there is an absolute limit to the imagination, a maximum of *Bild* and *Bildung*. We receive an analogical indication of this maximum in the greatness of certain objects both natural and artificial, for example, in oceans or pyramids. But these objective grandeurs, these very great figures, are precisely nothing but analogical occasions for thinking the sublime. In the sublime, it is not a matter of great figures but of absolute greatness. Absolute greatness is not greater than the greatest greatness: it designates rather that there is, absolutely, greatness. It is a matter of *magnitudo*, Kant says, and not of *quantitas*. *Quantitas* can be measured, whereas *magnitudo* presides over the possibility of measure in general: it is the fact in itself of greatness, the fact that, in order for there to be forms of figures which are more or less large, there must be, on the edge of all form or figure, greatness as *such*. Greatness is not, in this sense, a quantity, but a quality, or more precisely, it is quantity *qua* quality. It is in this way that for Kant the beautiful concerns quality, the sublime quantity. The beautiful resides in form as such, in the form of form, if one can put it this way, or in the figure that it makes. The sublime resides in the tracing-out, the setting-off and seizure of form, independently of the figure this form delimits, and hence in its quantity taken absolutely, as *magnitudo*. The beautiful is the proper of such and such an image, the pleasure of its (re)presentation. The sublime is: *that* there is an image, hence a limit, along whose edge unlimitation makes itself felt.

Thus, the beautiful and the sublime, if they are not identical—and indeed, quite the contrary—take place *on the same site*, and in a certain sense the one upon the other, the one along the edge of the other, and perhaps—I will come back to this—the one through the other. The beautiful and the sublime *are* presentation but in such a manner that the beautiful is the presented *in its presentation*, whereas the sublime is the presentation *in its movement*—which is the absolute re-moval of the unlimited along the edge of any limit. The sublime is not "greater than" the beautiful, it is not more elevated [*élevé*], but in turn, it is, if I dare put it this way, more removed [*enlevé*], in the sense that it is itself the unlimited removal of the beautiful.

What gets removed and carried away is all form as such. In the manifestation of a world or in the composition of a work, form carries itself away or removes itself, that is, at once traces itself and unborders itself, limits itself and unlimits itself (which is nothing other than the most strict logic of the limit). All form as such, all figure is small with regard to the unlimitedness against which it sets itself off and which carries it away. "That is sublime," writes Kant, "in comparison with which all the rest is small." The sublime is hence not a greatness that would be "less small" and would still take place along, even if at the summit of, a scale of comparison: for in this case, certain parts of the rest would not be "small," but simply less great. The sublime is incomparable, it is of a greatness with relation to which all the others are "small," that is, are not of the same order whatsoever, and are therefore no longer properly comparable.

The sublime *magnitudo* resides—or rather befalls and surprises—at the limit, and in the ravishment and removal of the limit. Sublime greatness is: *that there is* such a thing as measurable, presentable greatness, such a thing as limitation, hence such a thing as form and figure. A limit raises itself or is raised, a contour traces itself, and thus a multiplicity, a dispersed manifold comes to be presented as a unity. Unity comes to it from its limit—say, through its internal border, but *that* there is this unity, absolutely, or again that this outline should make up a *whole*, comes—to put it still in the same manner—from the external border, from the unlimited raising and razing of the limit. The sublime concerns the totality (the general concept of which is the concept of unified multiplicity). The totality of a form, of a presentation, is neither its completeness nor the exhaustive summation of its parts. Rather, this totality is what takes place where the form has no parts, and consequently (re)presents nothing, but presents itself. The sublime takes place, Kant says, in a "representation of the unlimited to which is added nonetheless the thought of its totality" (and this is why, as he specifies, the sublime can be found in a formless object as well as in a form). A presentation takes place only if *all* the rest, *all* the unlimitedness from which it detaches itself, sets itself off along its border—and at once, in its own way, presents itself or rather sets itself off and upsets itself all along the presentation.

The sublime totality is not at all the totality of the infinite conceived as something other than finite and beautiful forms (and which by virtue of this otherness would give way to a second, special aesthetics which would be that of the sublime), nor is it the totality of an infinite that would be the summation of all forms (and would make of the aesthetics of the sublime a "superior" or "total"[18] aesthetics). The sublime totality is rather the totality of the unlimited, insofar as the unlimited is beyond (or this side of) all form and all sum, insofar as the unlimited is, in general, on the far side of the limit, that is, *beyond the maximum.*

The sublime totality is beyond the maximum, which is to say that it is *beyond everything.* Everything is small in the face of the sublime, all form, all figure is small, but also, each form, each figure is or can be the *maximum.* The *maximum* (or *magnitudo,* which is its external border) is there whenever the imagination has (re)presented the thing to itself, big or small. The imagination can do no more: it is defined by the *Bildung* of the *Bild.*

However, the imagination can do more—or at least, if it is no longer at this point properly a "power" (*Kraft*), it receives more—there where it can do no more. And it is there that the sublime is decided: the imagination can still feel its limit, its powerlessness, its incommensurability with relation to the totality of the unlimited. This totality is not an object, it is nothing (re)presented, neither positively nor negatively, but corresponds to this: that presentation takes place. It is not presentation itself—neither the exhibition of what is presented nor the presence of what presents—but rather it is *that presentation takes place*. This is the formless form or the form of the formless, the setting-off of the limit's external border from the limit itself, the motion of the unlimited.

This totality is not, in fact, exactly the unity of the manifold: the unlimited offers properly neither a manifold nor the number of a unity. But what Kant calls "the Idea of a whole" is the *union* through which the unity of a whole is possible in general. The sublime is concerned with union, as the beautiful is concerned with unity. But union is the work of the imagination (as unity is its product): it unites concept and intuition, sensibility and understanding, the manifold and the identical. In the sublime, the imagination no longer has to do with its products but with its operation— and thus with its limit.

For there are two ways of conceiving of union. There is the Hegelian, dialectical way, which considers union as a process of reunion, as a purposiveness or finality of unification, and as its result, which is supposed to be a unity. Thus, for example, the truth of the union of the sexes for Hegel is to be found in the unity of the child. The Kantian concept of union is different. Thus, in the *Anthropology* the union of the sexes remains an abyss for reason, just as the schematizing union remains an "art" that has forever escaped our grasp. This means that Kant takes into account union *as such*, precisely in its difference from unity, precisely insofar as it is not or does not constitute by itself a unity (neither an object nor a subject). Union is more than the sum of the parts and less than their unity: like *magnitudo*, it escapes all calculation. As "Idea of the whole," union is neither the one nor the many: it is beyond everything, it is the "totality" on the far or near side of the formal unity of the whole, elsewhere, nonlocalizable, but nonetheless it takes place. Or more precisely, it is the *taking place* of all or the whole in general (thus, it is the contrary of a totalization or of a completion and instead a completing or dawning). That this should take place, that it should present itself, that it should take on form and figure, this "that" is union, is the totality beyond the whole—in relation to which all presentation is small and all greatness remains a little *maximum* where the imagination reaches its limit.

Because it reaches this limit, it exceeds this limit. It overflows itself, in reaching the overflowing of the unlimited, where unity gets carried away into union. The sublime is the self-overflowing of the imagination. Not that the imagination imagines beyond its *maximum* (and still less that it imagines *itself*: we have to do here with exactly the reverse of its self-presentation). It imagines no longer and there is no longer anything to imagine, there is no *Bild* beyond *Einbildung*—and no negative *Bild* either, nor the *Bild* of the absence of the *Bild*. The faculty of presentation (i.e., the imagination) presents nothing beyond the limit, for presentation is delimitation itself. However, it gains access to something, reaches or touches upon something (or it is reached or touched by something): union, precisely, the "Idea" of the union of the unlimited, which borders upon and unborders the limit.

What operates this union? The imagination itself. At the limit, it gains access to itself as in its speculative self-presentation. But here, the reverse is the case: that "part" of itself that it touches is its limit, or it touches itself as limit. "The imagination," Kant writes, "attains to its maximum, and in the effort to go beyond this limit it sinks back into itself, and in so doing is displaced into a moving satisfaction."[19] (The question arises immediately, since there is satisfaction or enjoyment here, why is this not a mere repetition of self-presentation? Nothing is pure here, nothing made up of simple oppositions, everything happens as the reversal of itself, and the sublime transport is the exact reverse of the dialectical sublation.)

At the limit, there is no longer either figure or figuration or form. Nor is there the ground as something to which one could proceed or in which one could exceed oneself, as in the Hegelian infinite, that is, as in a nonfigurable instance which, infinite in its way, would not cease to cut a figure. (Such is, in general, it seems to me, the concept with which one ends up as soon as one names something like "the nonfigurable" or "the nonpresentable": one (re)presents its nonpresentability, and one has thus aligned it, however negatively, with the order of presentable things.) At the limit, one does not *pass* on. But it is there that *everything* comes to pass, it is there that the totality of the unlimited plays itself out, as *that which throws into mutual relief the two borders, external and internal, of all figures,* adjoining them and separating them, *delimiting and unlimiting the limit thus in a single gesture.*

It is at once an infinitely subtle, infinitely complex operation, and the most simple movement in the world, the strict beating of the line against itself in the motion of its outline. Two borders in one, union "itself," nothing less is required by all figures, as every painter, writer, and dancer knows. It is presentation itself, but no longer presentation as the operation of a (re)presenter producing or exhibiting a (re)presented. It is presentation *itself* at the point where it can no longer be said to be "itself," at the point where one can no longer say *the* presentation, and where it is consequently no longer a question of saying either that it presents itself or that it is nonpresentable. Presentation "itself" is the instantaneous division of and by the limit, between figure and elimination, the one against the other, the one upon the other, the one at the other, coupled and uncoupled in a single movement, in the same incision, the same beating.

What comes to pass here, at the limit—and which never gets definitively past the limit—is union, imagination, presentation. It is neither the production of the homogeneous (which is in principle the ordinary task of the schema) nor the simple and free accord of self-recognition in which beauty consists, for it is this side of or beyond the accord of beauty. But it is also not the union of heterogeneous elements, which would be already too romantic and too dialectical for the strict limit in question here. The union with which one has to do in the sublime does not consist in coupling absolute greatness with finite limits: for *there is nothing beyond the limit*, nothing either presentable or nonpresentable. It is indeed this affirmation, "there is nothing beyond the limit," that properly and absolutely distinguishes the thought of the sublime (and art) from dialectical thought (and the end of art as its completion). Union does not take place between an outside and an inside in order to engender the unity of a limit where unity would present itself (according to this logic, the limit itself becomes infinite, and the only art is that which traces the Hegelian "circle of circles.") But there is only the limit, united with unlimitation insofar as the latter sets itself off, sets itself up, and upsets itself incessantly on its border, and consequently insofar as the limit, unity, divides itself infinitely in its own presentation.

For dialectical thought, the contour of a design, the frame of a picture, the trace of writing point beyond themselves to the teleological absolute of a (positive or negative) total presentation. For the thought of the sublime, the contour, the frame, and the trace point to nothing but themselves—and even this is saying too much: they do not point at all, but present (themselves), and their presentation presents its own interruption,

the contour, frame, or trace. The union from which the presented or figured unity arises presents itself as this interruption, as this suspension of
imagination (or figuration) in which the limit traces and effaces itself. The
whole here—the totality to which every presentation, every work, cannot
but lay claim—is nowhere but in this suspension itself. In truth, the whole,
on the limit, divides itself just as much as it unites itself, and the whole is
nothing but that: the sublime totality does not respond, despite certain appearances, to the supreme schema of a "total presentation," even in the
sense of a negative presentation or a presentation of the impossibility of
presentation (for that always presupposes a complement, an object of presentation, and the entire logic of re-presentation: here there is nothing to
present but merely that it [*ça*] presents itself.) The sublime totality does
not respond to a schema of the Whole, but rather, if one can put it this
way, to the whole of the schematism: that is, to the incessant beating with
which the trace of the *skema* affects itself, the carrying away of the figure
against which the carrying away of unlimitedness does not cease to do bat-
tle, this tiny, infinite pulsation, this tiny, infinite, rhythmic burst that produces itself continuously in the trace of the least contour and through
which the limit itself presents itself, and on the limit, the *magnitudo*, the
absolute of greatness *in which* all greatness (or quantity)—is traced, in
which all imagination both imagines and—on the same limit, in the same
beating—fails to imagine. That which indefinitely trembles at the border
of the sketch, the suspended whiteness of the page or the canvas: the experience of the sublime demands no more than this.

In sum, from the beautiful to the sublime one more step is taken in
the "hidden art" of the schematism: in beauty the schema is the unity of
the presentation; in the sublime, the schema is the pulsation of the unity.
That is, at once its absolute value (*magnitudo*) and its absolute distension,
union that takes place in and as suspension. In beauty, it is a matter of accord; in the sublime, it is a matter of the syncopated rhythm of the trace of
the accord, spasmodic vanishing of the limit all along itself, into unlimitedness, that is, into nothing. The sublime schematism of the totality is
made up of a syncopation at the heart of the schematism itself: simultaneous reunion and distension of the limit of presentation—or more exactly,
and more inexorably: reunion and distension, positing and vanishing *of* simultaneity (and thus of presentation) itself. Instantaneous flight and presence of the instantaneous, grouping and strewn division of a present. (I
will not insist further on this here, but it is doubtless in terms of time that

one ought finally to interpret the aesthetics of the sublime. This presupposes perhaps the thought of a time of the limit, of a time of the fainting of the figure, which would be the proper time of art?)

That the imagination—that is, presentation in the active sense—attains the limit, that it faints and vanishes there, "sinks back into itself," and thus comes to present itself, in the foundering of a syncopation or rather as this syncopation "itself," this exposes the imagination to its destiny. The "proper destiny of the subject" is definitively the "absolute greatness" of the sublime. What the imagination, in failing, avows to be unimaginable, is its proper greatness. The imagination is thus destined for the beyond of the image. This beyond is not a primordial (or ultimate) presence (or absence) which images would represent or of which images would present the fact that it is not (re)presentable. Rather, the beyond of the image, which is not "beyond," but on the limit, is in the *Bildung* of the *Bild* itself, and thus at or on the edge of the *Bild*, the outline of the figure, the tracing, the separating-uniting incision, the beating of the schema: the syncopation, which is in truth the other name of the schema, its sublime name, if there be such things as sublime names.

The imagination (or the subject) is destined for, sent toward, dedicated and addressed to this syncopation. That is, presentation is dedicated, addressed to the presentation of *presentation* itself: this is the general destiny of aesthetics, of reason in aesthetics, as I said at the outset. But in the sublime, it turns out that this destiny implies an unbordering or a going overboard of the beautiful, for the presentation of presentation itself, far from being the imagination of the imagination and the schema of the schema, far from being the figuration of the self-figuration of the subject, takes place in and as syncopation, and thus does not take *place*, does not have at its disposal the unified space of a figure, but rather is given in the schematic spacing and throbbing of the trace of figures, and thus only comes to pass in the syncopated time of the passage of the limit to the limit.

However, syncopated imagination is still imagination. It is still the faculty of presentation, and like the beautiful, the sublime is still tied "to mere presentation." (In this sense, it is not beyond the beautiful: it is merely the beautiful's unbordering, on the border itself, not going beyond the border—and this is also why, as I will consider further below, the entire affair of the sublime occurs on the edges of works of "fine art," on their borders, frames, or contours: on the border of art, but not beyond art.)

How, then, does the imagination (re)present the limit, or rather—for this is perhaps the same question—how does it present itself at the limit?

The mode of presentation of a limit in general cannot be the image properly speaking. The image properly speaking presupposes the limit which presents it or within which it presents itself. But the singular mode of the presentation of a limit is that this limit must be reached, must come to be *touched*. This is, in fact, the sense of the word *sublimitas*: what stays just below the limit, what touches the limit (limit being conceived, in terms of height, as absolute height). Sublime imagination touches the limit, and this touch lets it feel "its own powerlessness." If presentation takes place above all in the realm of the sensible—to present is to render sensible—sublime imagination is always involved in presentation insofar as this imagination is sensible. But here sensibility no longer comprises the perception of a figure but rather the arrival at the limit. More precisely, sensibility is here to be situated in the imagination's *sentiment* of itself when it touches its limit. The imagination feels itself passing to the limit. It feels itself, and it has the feeling of the sublime in its "effort" (*Bestrebung*), impulse, or tension, which makes itself felt as such at the moment when the limit is touched, in the suspension of the impulse, the broken tension, the fainting or fading of a syncopation.

The sublime is a feeling, and yet, more than a feeling in the banal sense, it is the emotion of the subject at the limit. The subject of the sublime, if there is one, is a subject who is moved. In the thought of the sublime, it is a question of the emotion of the subject, of that emotion which neither the philosophy of subjectivity and beauty nor the aesthetics of fiction and desire is capable of thinking through, for they think necessarily and solely within the horizon of the enjoyment of the subject (and of the subject as enjoyment). And enjoyment qua satisfaction of an appropriate presentation cuts emotion short.

Thus it is a question here of this emotion without which, to be sure, there would be no beauty, artwork, or thought—but which the concepts of beauty, the work, and philosophy, by themselves and in principle, cannot touch. The problem is not that they are too "cold" (they can be quite lively and warm) but that they (and their system—beauty/work/philosophy) are constructed according to the logic I have designated above as the logic of the self-enjoyment of Reason, the logic of the self-presentation of imagination. It is the aesthetic logic of philosophy and the philosophical logic of aesthetics. The feeling of the sublime, in its emotion, makes this logic vacillate, because it substitutes for this logic what forms, again, its exact re-

verse, or rather (which comes down to the same thing) a sort of logical exasperation, a passage to the limit: touching presentation on its limit, or
rather, being touched, attained by it. This emotion does not consist in the
sweetly proprietary pathos of what one can call "aesthetic emotion." To this
extent, it would be better to say that the feeling of the sublime is hardly an
emotion at all but rather the mere motion of presentation—at the limit
and syncopated. This (e)motion is without complacency and without satisfaction: it is not a pleasure without being at the same time a pain, which
constitutes the affective characteristic of the Kantian sublime. But its ambivalence does not make it any less sensible, does not render it less effectively or less precisely sensible: *it is the sensibility of the fading of the sensible.*

Kant characterizes this sensibility in terms of striving and transport
[*élan*]. Striving, transport, and tension make themselves felt (and perhaps
this is their general logic or "pathetics") insofar as they are suspended, at
the limit (there is no striving or tension except at the limit), in the instant
and the beating of their suspension.[20] It is a matter, Kant writes, of the
"feeling of an arrest of the vital forces" (*Hemmung*, "inhibition," "im-
pinging upon," or "blockage"). Suspended life, breath cut off—the beating heart.

It is here that sublime presentation properly takes place. It takes
place in effort and feeling: "Reason . . . as faculty of the independence of
the absolute totality . . . sustains the effort, admittedly sterile, of the spirit
to harmonize the representation of the senses with Totality. This effort and
the feeling that the Idea is inaccessible to imagination constitute in and of
themselves a presentation of the subjective purposiveness of our spirit in
the use of the imagination concerning its super-sensible destiny."[21]

"Striving," *Bestreben*, is not to be understood here in the sense of a
project, an envisioned undertaking that one could evaluate either in terms
of its intention or in terms of its result. This striving cannot be conceived
in terms of either a logic of desire and potentiality or a logic of the transi-
tion to action and the work or a logic of the will and energy (even if all of
that is doubtless also present and is not to be neglected if one wishes to
provide an account of Kant's thought, which is not my intention here).
Rather, striving is to be understood on its own terms, insofar as it obeys in
itself only a logic (as well as a "pathetics" and an ethics) of the limit. Striving or transport is by definition a matter of the limit. It consists in a relation to the limit: a continuous effort is the continuous displacement of a
limit. The effort ceases where the limit cedes its place. Striving and exer-

tion transport the limit into themselves: it becomes their structure. In striving as such—and not in its success or failure—it is less a question of a tendency toward something, of the direction or project of a struggling subject, than of the tension of the limit itself. What tends, and what tends here toward or in the extreme, is the limit. The schema of the image, of any image—or the schema of totality, the schematism of total union—is extended toward and tensed in the extreme: it is the limit at the limit of its (ex)tension, the tracing—which is no longer quantifiable or hence traceable—of *magnitudo*. Stretched to the limit, the limit (the contour of the figure) is stretched to the breaking point, as one says, and it in fact does break, dividing itself in the instant between two borders, the border of the figure and its unlimited unbordering. Sublime presentation is the feeling of this striving at the instant of rupture, the imagination still for an instant sensible to itself although no longer itself, in extreme tension and distension ("overflowing" or "abyss").

(Or again, the striving is a striving to reach and touch the limit. The limit is the striving itself and the touching. Touching is the limit of itself: the limit of images and words, contact—and with this, paradoxically, the impossibility of *touching* inscribed in touching, since touching is the limit. Thus, touching is striving, because it is not a state of affairs but a limit. It is not one sensory state among others, it is neither as active nor as passive as the others. If all of the senses sense themselves sensing, as Aristotle would have it [who, moreover, established already that there can be no true contact, either in the water or in the air], touching more than the other senses takes place only in touching itself. But more than the others also, it thus touches its limit, itself as limit: it does not attain itself, for one touches only in general [at] the limit. Touching does not touch itself, at least not as seeing sees itself.)

The sublime presentation is a presentation because it gives itself to be sensed. But this sentiment, this feeling is singular. As a sentiment of the limit, it is the sentiment of an insensibility, a nonsensible sentiment (*apatheia, phlegma in significatu bono*, Kant says), a syncopation of sentiment. But it is absolute sentiment as well, not determined as pleasure or as pain but touching the one through the other, touched by the one in the other. The alliance of pleasure with pain ought not to be understood in terms of ease and unease, of comfort and discomfort combined in one subject by a perverse contradiction. For this singular ambivalence has to do first of all with the fact that the subject vanished into it. It is also not the case that the subject gains pleasure by means of pain (as Kant tends to put it); it does not pay the price of the one in order to have the other: rather, the pain here is the pleasure, that is, once again, the limit touched, life suspended, the beating heart.

If feeling properly so called is always subjective, if it is indeed the core of subjectivity in a primordial "feeling oneself" of which all the great philosophies of the subject could provide evidence, including the most "intellectualist" among them, then the feeling of the sublime sets itself off—or affects itself—precisely as the reversal of both feeling and subjectivity. The sublime affection, Kant affirms, goes as far as the suspension of affection, the pathos of apathy. This feeling is not a feeling-oneself, and in this sense, it is not a feeling at all. One could say that it is what remains of feeling at the limit, when feeling no longer feels itself, or when there is no longer anything to feel. Of the beating heart, one can say with equal justification either that it feels only its beating or that it no longer feels anything at all.

On the border of the syncopation, feeling, for a moment, still feels, without any longer being able to relate (itself) to its feeling. It loses feeling: it feels its loss, but this feeling no longer belongs to it: although this feeling is quite singularly its own, this feeling is nonetheless also taken up in the loss of which it is the feeling. This is no longer to feel but to be exposed.

Or in other words, one would have to construct a double analytic of feeling: one analytic of the feeling of appropriation, and another analytic of the feeling of exposition: one of a feeling through or by oneself and another of a feeling through or by the other. Can one feel through the other, through the outside, even though feeling seems to depend on the self as its means and even though precisely this dependence conditions aesthetic judgment? This is what the feeling of the sublime forces us to think.[22] The subjectivity of feeling and of the judgment of taste are converted here into the singularity of a feeling and a judgment that remain, to be sure, singular, but where the singular as such is first of all exposed to the unlimited totality of an "outside" rather than related to its proper intimacy. Or in other words, it is the intimacy of the "to feel" and the "to feel oneself" that produces itself here, paradoxically, as exposition to what is beyond the self, passage to the (in)sensible or (un)feeling limit of the self.

Can one still say that the totality is presented in this instant? If it were properly presented, it would be in or to that instance of presentification (or [re]presentation) which is the subjectivity of feeling. But the un-limitedness that affects the exposed feeling of the sublime cannot be presented to it, that is, this unlimitedness cannot become present in and for a subject. In its syncopation, the imagination presents itself, presents itself as unlimited, beyond (its) figure, but this means that it is affected by (its) nonpresentation. When Kant characterizes feeling, in the striving for the limit, as "a representation," one must consider this concept in the absence of the values of presence and the present. One must learn—and this is perhaps the secret of the sublime as well as the secret of the schematism—that presentation does indeed take place but that it does not *present* anything. Pure presentation (presentation of presentation itself) or presentation of the totality presents nothing at all. One could no doubt say, in a certain vocabulary, that it presents nothing or *the* nothing. In another vocabulary, one could say that it presents the nonpresentable. Kant himself writes that the genius (who represents *a parte subjecti* the instance of the sublime in art) "expresses and communicates the unnamable." The without-name is named, the inexpressible is communicated: *all is presented—at the limit.* But in the end, and precisely at this limit itself, where all is achieved and where all begins, it will be necessary to deny presentation its name.

It will be necessary to say that the totality—or the union of the un-limited and the unlimitedness of union, or, again, presentation itself, its faculty, act, and subject—is *offered* to the feeling of the sublime or is *offered*, in the sublime, to feeling. The offering retains of the "present" implied by presentation only the gesture of presenting. The offering offers, carries, and places before (etymologically, of-fering is not very different from ob-ject), but it does not install in presence. What is offered remains at a limit, suspended on the border of a reception, an acceptance—which cannot in its turn have any form other than that of an offering. To the offered totality, the imagination is offered—that is, also "sacrificed" (*aufgeopfert*), as Kant writes.[23] The sacrificed imagination is the imagination offered to its limit.

The offering is the sublime presentation: it withdraws or suspends the values and powers of the present. What takes place is neither a coming-into-presence nor a gift. It is rather the one or the other, or the one and the other, but as abandoned, given up. The offering is the giving up of the gift and of the present. Offering is not giving—it is suspending or giving up the gift in the face of a freedom that can take it or leave it.

What is offered is offered up—addressed, destined, abandoned—to the possibility of a presentation to come, but it is left to this coming and does not impose or determine it. "In sublime contemplation," Kant writes, "the spirit abandons itself, without paying attention to the form of things, to the imagination and to reason, which only enlarges the imagination." The abandon is the abandon to total extension, unlimited, and thus at the limit. What comes to pass at the limit is the offering.

The offering takes place between presentation and representation, between the thing and the subject, elsewhere. This is not a *place*, you will say. Indeed, it is the offering—it is being offered to the offering.

The offering does not offer the Whole. It does not offer the present totality of the unlimited. Nor, despite certain pompous accents audible in Kant's text (and in every text dedicated to the sublime, in the word *sublime* itself), does it offer the sovereign satisfaction of a spirit capable of the infinite. For if such a capacity, at the limit, is supposed to be attained, it consists in nothing but an offering, or in being-offered. In fact, it is not a matter here of the Whole or the imagination of the Whole. It is a matter of its Idea and of the destiny of reason. The Idea of the Whole is not a supreme image, nor is it a grandiose form—nor deformity—beyond all images, any more than the destiny of reason consists in a triumphant Ideal. The Idea of the whole means rather (finally, neither "Idea" nor "Whole") the possibility of engaging a totality, the possibility of involving oneself in the union of a totality, the possibility of beginning, along the edge of the unlimited, the outline of a figure. If it is a matter of the whole, then as "the fundamentally open" of which Deleuze speaks with respect to the sublime.[24] The opening is offered to the possibility of gesture which "totalizes" figures, or traces. This possibility of a beginning is freedom. Freedom is the sublime idea *kat'exocēn*. This means neither that freedom is the content or the object of the judgment of the sublime nor that it is freedom that makes itself felt in the feeling of the sublime. In all likelihood, that would make no sense whatsoever, for freedom is not a content, if indeed it is any thing at all. Instead, one must understand this: that the sublime offering is the act—or the motion or emotion—of freedom. The sublime offering is the act of freedom in the double sense that freedom is both what offers and what is offered—just as the word *offering* designates now the gesture, now the present offered.

In the sublime, the imagination qua free play of presentation comes into contact with its limit—which is freedom. Or, more exactly, freedom itself is a limit, because its Idea not only cannot be an image but also cannot—in spite of Kant's vocabulary—be an Idea (which is always something like a hyperimage, a nonpresentable image). It must be an offering.[25]

The sublime does not escape to a space beyond the limit. It remains at the limit and takes place there. This means, further, that it does not leave aesthetics in order to penetrate ethics. At the limit of the sublime, there is neither aesthetics nor ethics. There is a thought of the offering which defies this distinction.

The aesthetics of the beautiful transports itself into the sublime whenever it does not slide into mere enjoyment. The beautiful by itself is nothing—the mere self-accord of presentation. The spirit can enjoy this accord, or it can carry itself to the limit of this accord. The unlimited border of the limit is the offering. The offering offers something. I said above that it offers freedom. But freedom is also what does the offering here. Something, a sensible thing, is offered in the offering of freedom. It is in this sensible thing, on the edge of this sensible thing that the limit makes itself felt. This sensible thing is the beautiful, the figure presented by schematism without concepts. The condition of the schematism is nothing other than freedom itself. Kant declares this explicitly when he writes: "the imagination itself is, in accordance with the principles of the schematism of the faculty of judgment (consequently, to the extent that it is subordinate to freedom), the instrument of reason and its Ideas."[26] Thus, freedom offers the schematism, or, again, freedom schematizes and offers itself in this very gesture, in its "hidden art."

The sublime offering takes place neither in a hidden world withdrawn from our own nor in a world of "Ideas" nor in any world of a "nonpresentable" something or other. The sublime offering is the limit of presentation, and it takes place on and all along this limit, along the contour of form. The thing offered can be a thing of nature, and this is ordinarily, according to Kant, the occasion of the feeling of the sublime. But since this thing, as a thing of freedom, is not merely offered but also offers itself, offers freedom—in the striving of the imagination and in the feeling of this striving—then this thing will be instead a thing of art (moreover, nature itself is always grasped here as a work of art, a work of supreme freedom). Kant places poetry above all the other arts, describing it as follows: "it enlarges the soul by giving freedom to the imagination and by offering[27] within the limits of a given concept, among the limitless diversity of forms which might accord with it, that form which links the presentation of this concept with a plenitude of thoughts, to which no expression of language is perfectly adequate, and which in so doing elevates itself aesthetically to the level of the Ideas."

There is thus in art more than one occasion for experiencing sublimity. There is—in poetry at least[28]—an *elevation* (that is, a sublime motion: Kant uses the verb *erheben* here) to the "Ideas," which, even though it is an elevation, remains aesthetic, that is, sensible. Would one have to conclude from this that there could be another form or mode of sublime presentation in art, that of moral feeling, which would be distinct from the first mode? But in truth, it is in art and as art that the sublime offering happens. There is no opposition between an aesthetics of form and an ethical meta-aesthetics of the formless. The aesthetic always concerns form; the totality always concerns the formless. The sublime is their mutual offering. It is neither simply the formation or formalization of the formless nor the infinitization of form (which are both philosophical procedures). It is how the limit offers itself to the border of the unlimited, or how the limit makes itself felt: exactly on the cutting edge of the figure the work of art cuts.

It would not be difficult to demonstrate—and I dispense with doing so here—the systematic engenderment or derivation of art, in Kant, on the basis of both the beautiful and the sublime. Only in this way can one understand both the order of Kant's table of contents in the third *Critique* and the doctrine of genius, as well as the doctrine of the beautiful as "symbol" of the ethically good.

Beginning with Kant, the sublime will constitute the most proper, decisive moment in the thought of art. The sublime will comprise the heart of the thought of the arts, the beautiful merely its rule. This means not only that, as I have said, mere beauty can always slide into the agreeable (and, for example, into the "sublime style") but perhaps, above all, that there is no "pure" sublime purely distinguished from the beautiful. The sublime is that through which the beautiful *touches* us and not that through which it pleases us. It is joy and not enjoyment [*la joie, non la jouissance*]: the two words are originally the same word. The same word, the same limit affected by the beating of joy and enjoyment. To be touched is sublime because it is to be exposed and to be offered. To experience joy is to be exposed in enjoyment, to be offered there. The sublime is in the contact of the work, not in its form. This contact is beyond the work, at its limit, in a sense beyond art: but without art, it would not take place. The sublime is—that art should be [*soit*] exposed and offered.

Since the epoch of Kant—of Diderot, Kant, and Hölderlin—art has been destined for the sublime: it has been destined to touch us, in touching upon our destiny or destination. It is only in this sense that one must comprehend, in the end, *the end of art.*

What art is at stake here? In a sense, one has no choice, neither between particular arts nor between artistic tonalities and registers. Poetry is exemplary—but which poetry? Quite indirectly, Kant has given us an example. When he cites "the most sublime passage of the Book of the Law of the Jews," that which articulates the prohibition of images, the sublime, in fact, is present twice. It is present first in the content of the divine commandment, in the distancing of representation. But a more attentive reading shows that the sublime is present also, and perhaps more essentially, in the "form" of the biblical text. For this passage is quoted in the middle of what properly constitutes the search for the genre or aesthetics of "sublime presentation." This presentation must attempt neither to "agitate" nor to "excite" the imagination but ought always to be concerned with the "domination of reason over sensibility." And this presupposes a "withdrawn or separated presentation" (*abgezogen, abgesondert*), which will be called a bit further on "pure, merely negative." This presentation is the commandment, the law that commands the abstention from images.[29] The commandment, as such, is itself a form, a presentation, a style.

And so sublime poetry would have the style of the commandment? Rather, the commandment, the categorical imperative, is sublime because it commands nothing other than freedom. And if that comprises a style, it cannot be the muscular style of the commandment. It is what Kant calls simplicity: "Simplicity (purposiveness without art) is so to speak the style of nature in the sublime, as of morality which is a second nature."

It is not the commandment that is simple but rather simplicity that commands. The art of which Kant speaks—or of which, at the limit, he does not manage to speak, while speaking of the Bible, poetry, and forms of union in the fine arts—is the art of which the "simplicity" (or the "withdrawal" or the "separation") commands by itself, that is, addresses or exposes to freedom, with the simplicity of the offering: the offering as law of style.

"Purposiveness without art" (without artifice) is the art (the style) of purposiveness without purpose, that is, of the purposiveness of humanity in its free destination: humans are not devoted to the servility of representation but destined to the freedom of presentation and to the presentation of freedom—to their offering, which is a withdrawn or separate presentation (freedom is offered to them, they offer it, they are offered by it). This style is the style of a commandment or proscription because it is the style of a literature that proscribes for itself to be "literature," that withdraws from literary prestige and pleasure (which Kant compares to the massages of the "voluptuous orientals"): the effort by means of which it withdraws is itself a sublime offering. In short, the offering of literature itself, or the offering of all art—in all possible senses of the expression.

But "style" is doubtless here already one concept too many, like "poetry," "literature," and perhaps even "art" itself. They are certainly inappropriate and superfluous here if they remain caught up in a logic of lack and its substitute, presence and its representation (as this logic still governs, at least in part, the Kantian doctrine of art as a "symbol"). For nothing is lacking in the offering. Nothing is lacking, everything is offered: *the whole* is offered (opened), the totality of freedom. But to receive the offering, or to offer oneself to it (to joy), presupposes precisely the freedom of a gesture—of reception and offering. This gesture traces a limit. It is not the contour of a figure of freedom. But it is a contour, an outline, because it arises in freedom, which is the freedom to begin, to incise, here or there, an outline, an inscription, not merely arbitrarily, but still in a chancy, daring, playful, abandoned manner.

Abandoned but nonetheless regulated: the syncopation does not take place independently of all syntax, but rather imposes one, or better, it is one itself. In its pulsation—which assembles—in its suspension—which establishes and extends a rhythm—, the syncopation offers its syntax, its sublime grammar, on the edge of the language (or the drawing, or the song). Consequently, this trace is still or again art, this inscription still or again style, poetry: for the gesture of freedom is each time a *singular* manner of abandoning oneself (there is no such thing as general freedom, no such thing as general sublimity). This is not style "in the accoustico-decorative sense of the term" (Borges), but it is also not the pure absence of style of which the philosopher[30] dreams (philosophy as such and without offering, as opposed to or rather differentiated from thought): it is style, and the thought of a "withdrawn, separated presentation." It is not *a* style—there is no sublime style, and there is no simple style—but constitutes a trace, puts the limit into play, touches without delay all extremities—and it is perhaps this that art obeys.

In the final analysis, there is perhaps no sublime art and no sublime work, but the sublime takes place wherever works touch. If they touch, there are sensible pleasure and pain—all pleasure is physical, Kant repeats with Epicurus. There is enjoyment, and there is joy in enjoyment. The sublime is not what would take its distance from enjoyment. Enjoyment is mere enjoyment when it does nothing but please: in the beautiful. But there is the place (or the time) where (or when) enjoyment does not merely please, is not simply pleasure (if there is ever such a thing as simple pleasure): in the sublime, enjoyment touches, moves, that is, also commands. It is not commanded (an obligation to enjoy is absurd, Kant writes, and Lacan remembered this), but commands one to pass beyond it, beyond pathos, into ethos, if you like, but without ceasing to enjoy: touching or emotion qua law—and the law is necessarily a-pathetic. Here, "sovereign art," as Bataille writes, "accedes to the extremity of the possible." This art is indissociably "art expressive of anguish" and "that expressive of joy." The one and the other in an enjoyment, in a dispropriated enjoyment—that is, in tragic joy, or in this animated joy of the "vivacity of the affects" of which Kant speaks (§54) and which extends to the point of laughter and gaiety— they too being syncopated, at the limit of (re)presentation, at the limit of the "body" and the "spirit," at the limit of art itself .

. . . at the limit of art: which does not mean "beyond" art. There is nonetheless a beyond, as art is always an art of the limit. But at the limit of art there is the gesture of the offering: the gesture that offers art and the gesture through which art itself reaches, touches upon, and interferes with its limit.

As offering, it may be that the sublime surpasses the sublime—passes it by or withdraws from it. To the extent that the sublime still combines pathos and ethos, art and nature, it continues to designate these concepts, and this is why, as such, it belongs still to a space and problematic of (re)presentation. It is for this reason that the word "sublime" always risks burdening art either with pathos or morality (too much presentation or too much representation). But the offering no longer even arises out of an alliance of pathos and ethos. It comes to pass elsewhere: offering occurs in a simplicity anterior to the distinction between pathos and ethos. Kant speaks of "the simplicity which does not yet know how to dissimulate"; he calls it "naïveté," and the laughter or rather the smile in the face of this naïveté (which one must not confuse, he insists, with the rustic simplicity of the one who doesn't know how to live) possesses something of the sublime. However, "to represent naïveté in a poetic character is certainly a possible and beautiful art, but a rare one."

Would he characterize this extremely rare art as being henceforth a *telos* of art? There is in the offering something of the "naïve" in Kant's sense. There is sometimes, in today's art, something of the offering understood in this way. Let us say: something of a childhood (doubtless nothing new about this but a more strongly marked accent). This childlike art no longer inhabits the heights or the depths as did the sublime but simply touches the limit, without any disarticulating excess, without "sublime" exaltation, but also without puerility or silliness. It is a powerful but delicate vibration, difficult, continuous, acute, offered upon the surfaces of canvasses, screens, music, dance, and writing. Mondrian spoke, apropos of jazz and "neo-plasticism," of "the joy and the seriousness which are simultaneously lacking in the bloodless culture of form." In what offers art today to its future, there is a certain kind of serenity (Mondrian's word). It is neither reconciliation nor immobility nor peaceful beauty, but it is not sublime (self-)laceration either, assuming the sublime is supposed to involve (self-)laceration. The offering renounces (self-)laceration, excessive tension, and sublime spasms and syncopations. But it does not renounce infinite tension and distance, striving and respect, and the always renewed suspension that gives art its rhythm like a sacred inauguration and interruption. It simply lets them be offered to us.

> My painting, I know what it is beneath its
> appearances, its violence, its perpetual play of
> force; it is a fragile thing in the sense of the
> good, the sublime, it is fragile like love.
> —Nicolas de Staël

Translated by Jeffrey Libbrett

12

Shattered Love

Thinking: of Love

I love you more than all that has been thought and can be thought. I give my soul to you.
—Henriette Vogel to Heinrich von Kleist

I

The thinking of love, so ancient, so abundant and diverse in its forms and in its modulations, asks for an extreme reticence as soon as it is solicited. It is a question of modesty, perhaps, but it is also a question of exhaustion: Has not everything been said on the subject of love? Every excess and every exactitude? Has not the impossibility of speaking about love been as violently recognized as has been the experience of love itself as the true source of the possibility of speaking in general? We know the words of love to be inexhaustible, but as to speaking *about* love, could we perhaps be exhausted?

It might well be appropriate that a discourse on love—supposing that it still has something to say—be at the same time a communication of love, a letter, a missive, since love sends itself as much as it enunciates itself. But the words of love, as is well known, sparsely, miserably repeat their one declaration, which is always the same, always already suspected of lacking love because it declares it. Or else this declaration always carries the promise of revealing itself as the unique incarnation, the unique and certain, if derisory manifestation of the love that it declares. The discourse might well have nothing more to say or to describe than this communal indigence, these dispersed and tarnished flashes of an all-too-familiar love.

This is why, at our slightest attempt to solicit the thinking of love, we are invited to an extreme reticence. (Should this thinking be solicited? I will not discuss this. As it happens, it is. As it happens, indeed, this solicitation regularly returns, throughout our history, to formulate its demands. One asks what has become of love, but one does not forget to return to it after a certain period. When, for example, as is the case today, love is no longer the dominant theme of poetry, when it seems to be essentially relegated to dime-store novels instead, it is then that we inquire and question ourselves about love, about the possibility of thinking love. As though this possibility were always, recurringly indispensable to the possibility of thinking in general—that is to say, to the possibility of the life of a community, of a time and a space of humanity—something that would not be the case for other objects, such as God, for example, or history, or literature, or even philosophy.)

This reticence of thinking that beckons to us does not imply that it would be indiscreet to deflower love. Love deflowers and is itself deflowered by its very essence, and its unrestrained and brazen exploitation in all the genres of speech or of art is perhaps an integral part of this essence—a part at once secret and boisterous, miserable and sumptuous. But this reticence might signify that all, of love, is possible and necessary, that all the loves possible are in fact the possibilities of love, its voices or its characteristics, which are impossible to confuse and yet ineluctably entangled: charity and pleasure, emotion and pornography, the neighbor and the infant, the love of lovers and the love of God, fraternal love and the love of art, the kiss, passion, friendship. . . . To think love would thus demand a boundless generosity toward all these possibilities, and it is this generosity that would command reticence: the generosity not to choose between loves, not to privilege, not to hierarchize, not to exclude. Because love is not their substance or their common concept, is not something one can extricate and contemplate at a distance. Love in its singularity, when it is grasped absolutely, is itself perhaps nothing but the indefinite abundance of all possible loves, and an abandonment to their dissemination, indeed to the disorder of these explosions. The thinking of love should learn to yield to this abandon: to receive the prodigality, the collisions, and the contradictions of love, without submitting them to an order that they essentially defy.

But this generous reticence would be no different from the exercise of thought itself. Thinking rejects abstraction and conceptualization as these are recognized by understanding. Thinking does not produce the operators of a knowledge; it undergoes an experience, and lets the experience inscribe itself. Thought therefore essentially takes place in the reticence that lets the singular moments of this experience offer and arrange themselves. The thinking of love—if it is necessary to solicit it, or if it is necessary that it be proposed anew, as a theme to be discussed or as a question to be posed— does not therefore lay claim to a particular register of thinking: it invites us to thinking as such. Love does not call for a certain kind of thinking, or for a thinking of love, but for thinking in essence and in its totality. And this is because thinking, most properly speaking, is love. It is the love for that which reaches experience; that is to say, for that aspect of being that gives itself to be welcomed. In the movement across discourse, proof, and concept, nothing but this love is at stake for thought. Without this love, the exercise of the intellect or of reason would be utterly worthless.

This intimate connivance between love and thinking is present in our origins: the word "philosophy" betrays it. Whatever its legendary inventor might have meant by it, "philosophy," in spite of everything—and perhaps in spite of all philosophies—means this: love of thinking, since thinking is love. (Love of love, love of the self, in consequence? Perhaps, but we will have to return to this.)

We cannot, however, dispense with asking what we must understand by this. To say that "thinking is love" does not mean that love can be understood as a response to the question of thinking—and certainly not in the manner of a sentimental response, in the direction of a unifying, effusive, or orgiastic doctrine of thinking. Even though the paradox might appear simple, it is necessary to say that "thinking is love" is a difficult, severe thought that promises rigor rather than effusion. Faced with this thought about thinking, we can do nothing but begin the quest for an ignored essence of thinking for which we lack any evident access. It might well be that nothing that has been designated, celebrated, or meditated under the name of "love" is appropriate for this determination: "Thinking is love." It might also be that everything is appropriate, that all loves are at stake in thinking and as thinking.

In fact, to say "thinking is love" (*la pensée est amour*) is different from saying "thinking is Love," (*la pensée est l'amour*)[1] or "Thinking is a certain species of love." Neither genre nor species, perhaps not any genre or perhaps all species. However this may be, "love" thus employed would be, so to speak, existential rather than categorial, or again it would name the act of thinking as much as or more than it would its nature. (The model for this phrase is obviously the ancient "God is love," which entailed the same formal implications.) We know nothing more about what this means. We only know, by a sort of obscure certainty or premonition, that it is necessary or that it will one day be necessary to attest this phrase: *Thinking is love.* But philosophy has never explicitly attested this.

One single time, however, the first philosopher expressly authenticated an identity of love and of philosophy. Plato's *Symposium* does not represent a particular treatise that this author set aside for love at the heart of his work, as others would do later (and often by relating to this same Plato: Ficino, among others, or Leon the Hebrew, as though Plato were the unique or at least necessary philosophical reference, *de amore*, always present, beyond the epoch of treatises, in Hegel or in Nietzsche—"philosophy in the manner of Plato is an erotic duel"—in Freud or in Lacan). But the *Symposium* signifies first that for Plato the exposition of philosophy, as such, is not possible without the presentation of philosophic love. The commentary on the text gives innumerable confirmations of this, from the portrait of Eros to the role of Socrates and to the figure—who appeared here once and for all on the philosophical scene—of Diotima.

Although the *Symposium* speaks of love, it also does more than that; it opens thought to love as to its own essence. This is why this dialogue is more than any other the dialogue of Plato's generosity: here he invites orators or thinkers and offers them a speech tempered altogether differently from the speech of the interlocutors of Socrates. The scene itself, the gaiety or the joy that traverses it, attests to a consideration that is unique in Plato (to such a degree, at least)—consideration for others, as well as for the object of discourse. All the different kinds of loves are welcomed in the *Symposium*; there is discussion, but there is no exclusion. And the love that is finally exhibited as true love, philosophical Eros, does not only present itself with the mastery of a triumphant doctrine; it also appears in a state of deprivation and weakness, which allows the experience of the limit, where thought takes place, to be recognized. In the *Symposium*, Plato broaches the limits, and all his thinking displays a reticence or reserve not always present elsewhere: it broaches its own limit, that is to say, its source; it effaces itself before the love (or in the love?) that it recognizes as its truth. Thus it thinks its own birth and its own effacement, but it thinks in such a way that it restores to love, to the limit, its very task and destination. Philosophy is not occupied with gathering and interpreting the experiences of love here. Instead, in the final analysis, it is love that receives and deploys the experience of thinking.

But this has only taken place once, at the inauguration of philosophy, and even that time it did not really take place, since it did not reach its ends. For all its generosity, the *Symposium* also exercises a mastery over love. At any rate, we cannot fail to read or to deduce here, in the order and the choices of philosophical knowledge, a truth regarding love, one that assigns its experience and hierarchizes its moments by substituting the impatience and *conatus* of desire for its joyous abandon. Thus in Plato, thinking will have said and will have failed to say that it is love—or to explain what this means.

There is not one philosophy that has escaped this double constraint. In each, love occupies a place that is at once evident and dissimulated (as, in Descartes, between the theory of union and that of admiration), or embarrassed and decisive (as, in Kant, in the theory of sublime reason), or essential and subordinate (as, in Hegel, in the theory of the State). At the cost of these contradictions and evasions, love consistently finds the place that it cannot not have, but it only finds it at this cost. What we would have to understand is why this place is essential for it, and why it is essential to pay this price.

II

Philosophy never arrives at this thinking—that "thinking is love"— even though it is inscribed at the head of its program, or as the general epigraph to all its treatises. One might say: it reaches toward it; it does not reach it. But this does not mean that it does not have any thinking of love. Quite the contrary. Since the *Symposium*—or, if you prefer, since before Plato, in Heraclitus or Empedocles, in Pythagoras or Parmenides—the general schema of a philosophy of love is at work, and it has not ceased to operate even now, determining philosophy as it understands and construes itself, as well as love as we understand it and as we make it.

If it were necessary to take the risk of grasping this schema in a formula, one might try this: love is the extreme movement, beyond the self, of a being reaching completion. The first meaning of this formula (and it deliberately has several meanings) would be that philosophy always thinks love as an accomplishment, arriving at a final and definitive completion.

The second meaning would be that philosophy thinks love as an access rather than an end: the end is the completion of being (even though this might also be conceived as "love," which would thus designate its own result). The third meaning would be that philosophy thinks the being in love[2] as incomplete and led by love toward a completion. The fourth meaning, that this completion surpasses what it completes, and consequently fulfills it only by depriving it of itself—which comes down to suppressing its tension: thus, love suppresses itself (inasmuch as it reaches its end). The fifth meaning would be that philosophy thinks the suppression of self in love, and the correlative suppression of the self of love, as its ultimate truth and as its ultimate effectivity: thus, love infinitely restitutes itself beyond itself (in the final analysis, death and transfiguration—and this is not by chance the title of a musical work, since music accomplishes the philosophical erotic). The sixth meaning would be that this "beyond the self" in which, in a very general manner, love has taken place is necessarily the place of the other, or of an alterity without which neither love nor completion would be possible. But the seventh meaning would nevertheless be that this "beyond" is the place of the same, where love fulfills itself, the place of the same in the other, if love consists, in Hegel's terms, of "having in an other the moment of one's subsistence."

According to this schema, the nature of love is shown to be double and contradictory, even though it also contains the infinite resolution of its own contradiction. This nature is thus neither simple nor contradictory: it is the contradiction of contradiction and of noncontradiction. It operates in an identical manner between all the terms in play: the access and the end, the incomplete being and the completed being, the self and the beyond of the self, the one and the other, the identical and the different. The contradiction of the contradiction and of the noncontradiction organizes love infinitely and in each of its meanings. It is this that definitively confers on love the universality and the totality to which, according to philosophy, it is destined by right—and that have crystallized in the figure of Christian love, where the love of God and the love of men form the poles of a new contradiction and of its resolution, since each of them is carried out by the other and in the other.

Of course, this kind of philosophical thinking is not confined only to philosophical discourse or to its theological avatar. It is easy to see that it structures all occidental experience and expression of love (it is not certain that the "Occident," here, might not include both Islam and Buddhism):

its poetics, its drama, its pathos, its mystique, from the Grand Rhetoricians to Baudelaire, from the troubadours to Wagner or Strauss, from Saint John of the Cross to Strindberg, and moving through Racine or Kleist, Marivaux or Maturin, Monteverdi or Freud. For all of them, love is double, conflictual, or ambivalent: necessary and impossible, sweet and bitter, free and chained, spiritual and sensual, enlivening and mortal, lucid and blind, altruistic and egoistic. For all, these oppositional couples constitute the very structure and life of love, while at the same time, love carries out the resolution of these very oppositions, or surpasses them. Or more often, it simultaneously surpasses them and maintains them: in the realization of love, the subject of love is dead and alive, free and imprisoned, restored to the self and outside of the self. One sentence by René Char best epitomizes this thinking and its entire tradition: "The poem is the fulfilled love of desire remaining desire."[3] This sentence, in effect, does not only speak the truth of the poem, according to Char; it speaks the truth of love. More precisely, it intends to speak the truth of the poem by grace of the truth of love, thus confirming, moreover, that love holds the highest truth for us: the contradiction (desire) opposed to the noncontradiction (love) and reconciled with it ("remaining desire").

But this thinking that so profoundly and so continually innervates so much of our thought received its name and its concept in philosophy: it is the thinking of the dialectic. One might say that love is the living hypothesis of a dialectic, which formulates the law of its process by way of a return. This law is not only the formal rule of the resolution of a contradiction that remains a contradiction: it gives, under this rule, the law and the logic of being in general. By being thought according to the dialectic and as the essence of the dialectic, love is assigned to the heart of the very movement of being. And it is not surprising that these two ideas have coexisted or have even intermixed: that "God is love" and that God is the Supreme Being. Love is not only subject to the ontological dialectic, it does not only form one case of its ontic application. If one may say so—and one may, rightly, in the most accurate or proper manner—love is the heart of this dialectic. The idea of love is in the dialectic, and the idea of the dialectic is in love. Hegel transcribing Christian theology into the ontology of the statement "The Absolute wishes to be close to us" says nothing other: The Absolute loves us—and the Absolute dialectizes itself. Love is at the heart of being.

Again it is necessary that being have a heart, or still more rigorously, that being be a heart. "The heart of being" means nothing but the being of being, that by virtue of which it is being. To suppose that "the being of being," or "the essence of being," is an expression endowed with meaning, it would be necessary to suppose that the essence of being is something like a heart—that is to say: that which alone is capable of love. Now this is precisely what has never been attested by philosophy.

Perhaps being, in its essence, is affected by the dialectic that annihilates its simple position in order to reveal this contradiction in the becoming of reality (or of reason, of the Idea, of history)—and in this sense one might say that being *beats*, that it essentially is in the beating, indeed, in the e-motion of its own heart: being-nothingness-becoming, as an infinite pulsation. And yet, this heart of being is not a heart, and it does not beat from the throbbing of love. Philosophy never says this, and above all, never explains its implications, as close as it might come to thinking it. It is not that love is excluded from fundamental ontology; on the contrary, everything summons it thither, as we have just shown. Thus, one must rather say that love is missing from the very place where it is prescribed. Or better still, love is missing from the very place where this dialectical law operates—the law that we have had to recognize as the law of love. And there is nothing dialectical about this loss or this "lack": it is not a contradiction, it is not made to be sublated or resorbed. Love remains absent from the heart of being.

That love is missing from philosophical ontology does not mean that the dialectical law of being is inappropriate for love. In one sense, nothing is false in what we have just demonstrated regarding this law and the nature of love. Nothing is false, but love is missing, because the heart of being, which has shown itself to be commanded by the dialectic, is not a heart. That which has the power of the dialectic is not a heart, but a subject. Perhaps one could find a heart in the subject. But this heart (if there is one) designates the place where the dialectical power is suspended (or perhaps shattered). The heart does not sublate contradictions, since in a general sense, it does not live under the regime of contradiction—contrary to what poetry (or perhaps only its philosophical reading?) might allow us to believe. The heart lives—that is to say, it beats—under the regime of exposition.

If the dialectic is the process of that which must appropriate its own becoming in order to be, exposition, on the other hand, is the condition of that whose essence or destination consists in being presented: given over, offered to the outside, to others, and even to the self. The two regimes do not exclude one another (they do not form a contradiction), but they are not of the same order. The being that has *become* through a dialectical process is perhaps destined to be exposed (one could show that this is what happens, despite everything, at the end of *The Phenomenology of Spirit*)—but the dialectic knows nothing of this, it believes it has absorbed the entire destination in the becoming-proper. The *exposed* being is perhaps also the subject of a dialectical process, but what is exposed, what makes it exposed, is that it is not completed by this process, and it "incompletes itself" to the outside; it is presented, offered to something that is not it nor its proper becoming.

The heart exposes, and it is exposed. It loves, it is loved, it does not love, it is not loved. Affirmation and negation are present here as in the dialectic. But in its modes of affirmation and negation, the heart does not operate by reporting its own judgment to itself (if it is a judgment). It does not say "*I love*," which is the reflection or the speculation of an ego (and which engages love neither more nor less than the *cogito*), but it says "I love you," a declaration where "I" is posed only by being exposed to "you." That is to say that the heart is not a subject, even if it is the heart of a subject. The subject is one who reports to himself, as his own, his judgments and their contradiction, in order to constitute therefrom his proper being: for example, that he is (Descartes), that he is not his immediate being (Spinoza), that he becomes what he is by traversing the other (Hegel). This resembles love; in any case it calls to and even demands love—and yet this is not love. The subject poses its own contradiction in order to report it to itself and to "maintain it in itself," as Hegel says. Thus it surmounts it or infinitely sublates it. By principle, the moment of exposition is evaded, even though it dimly emerges. This is the moment when it is not a matter of posing or of opposing and then of resorbing the same and the other. It is when the affirmation "I love you" is given over to that which is neither contradictory nor noncontradictory with it: the risk that the other does not love me, or the risk that I do not keep the promise of my love.

The being of philosophy is the subject. The heart of the subject is again a subject: it is the infinite rapport to the self. That this rapport demands, in turn, an infinite migration through the other, even the gift of the self, does not in any way hinder the structure of the subject from thence deriving all its consistency. Philosophy will not fail to retort: what is at stake is nothing but a dialectic of the heart and the subject, of love and the conscience or the reason. From Pascal to Hegel and beyond, this dialectic is well attested. But the response of philosophy is not admissible. There is no dialectic of the heart and the reason, not because they would be irreconcilable (the question of their rapport, if it be a question, cannot be posed in these terms; the perhaps pseudo-Pascal of the *Discourse on the Passions of Love* writes, "They have inappropriately removed the name of reason from love, and they have opposed them without a sound foundation, since love and reason is but the same thing"), but because the heart is not able to enter into a dialectic: it cannot be posed, disposed, and sublated in a superior moment. The heart does not return to itself beyond itself, and this is not, as Hegel would have wished, "the spirit which is attendant to the power of the heart." Or again, there is no sublimation of the heart, nor of love. Love is what it is, identical and plural, in all its registers or in all its explosions, and it does not sublimate itself, even when it is "sublime." It is always the beating of an exposed heart.

This argument carries a corollary: because it is a stranger to the dialectic, the heart does not maintain itself in opposition to the subject, any more than love does to reason. But they are one in the other, and one to the other, in a manner that is neither a mode of contradiction nor of identity nor of propriety. This mode might declare itself thus: The heart exposes the subject. It does not deny it, it does not surpass it, it is not sublated or sublimated in it; the heart exposes the subject to everything that is not its dialectic and its mastery as a subject. Thus, the heart can beat at the heart of the subject, it can even beat in a movement similar to that of the dialectic, but it does not confuse itself with that.

This is why love is always missed by philosophy, which nevertheless does not cease to designate and assign it. Perhaps it cannot help but be missed: one would not know how to seize or catch up with that which exposes. If thinking is love, that would mean (insofar as thinking is confused with philosophy) that thinking misses its own essence—that it misses by essence its own essence. In philosophy (and in mysticism, in poetics, etc.) thinking would thus have said all that it could and all that it should have said about love—by missing it and by missing itself. Loving, and loving love, it will have lost love. It is thence that Saint Augustine's *amare amabam* draws its exemplary force of confession.

This does not at all mean that in all this tradition thinking has never occurred, or that love has never occurred, or that thinking about love has never occurred. On the contrary. But this does mean that love itself, in that it is missed by thinking, and by the love of thinking, gives itself again to thinking. This is to say that in thinking, it calls forth once again this love that it is. Something revealed and re-veiled with the *Symposium*, like a missed rendezvous, calls again for its repetition.

The Heart: Broken

Love is a series of scars. "No heart is as whole as a broken heart," said the celebrated Rabbi Nahman of Bratzlav.
—Elie Wiesel, *The Fifth Son*

I

One would want to be able to engage this repetition, at least in part, outside of the Occident, that is to say, apart from love as we have come to know it from our history and from our thinking. That which is not the Occident is, in fact, no stranger to any of the figures or forms we know as love (sexuality, erotism, tenderness, passion, friendship, fraternity, or even fidelity, abandon, union, desire, jealousy, or what we represent as the emotion of love, as the adoration or supplication of love, or the gift of the self, or deliverance by love, etc.). But in all these figures (which their occidental denominations here risk falsifying, and which, moreover, are perhaps not figures, but rather so many distinct essences—or so many flashes) what is at issue, outside of the Occident, is not *love* absolutely. Only the Occident designates within love—absolutely and in every sense, or in the absolute of all its conjoined meanings, which obstinately make up one sole meaning, one sole essence—an ordering (or disordering) principle of the totality of being and of beings, of nature, of the city, of knowledge, and of God. Only the Occident raises with this one name, "love," such a claim to universality. That this claim is continually disappointed or ridiculed, that it is continually found guilty of delirium, of contradiction or of bad faith, only confirms its imperious, demanding, insistent, or insidious character. When we name love, we name something—and without a doubt, the only thing of this kind—that diffuses itself through all things, that comes closer and closer to totality, because this thing is the principle or the movement of proximity and of the neighbor, because it is the evidence and the certainty of recognition, and at the same time the power of fulfillment. Diverse as the realities are that are designated by *amor fati*, by the love of

God, by the love of Tristan, by love in the afternoon, love on the ground, love in flight, or by the sacred love of the fatherland, the meaning remains the same, unchangeable and infinite: it is always the furthest movement of a completion.

If we take love within the Occident, and the Occident in turn within love, how then can we hope to repeat the rendezvous that seems to have been missed once and for all, since it is the very nature of this love—unique and universal, plenary, fulfilling—that caused the rendezvous to be missed?

If such an undertaking will always be in vain, it is nonetheless certain that love is not to be found elsewhere. Elsewhere (if such an "elsewhere" exists, but this is not the question here), one will find, by definition, only pleasure or desire, vows, sacrifice, or ecstasy, but "love" will not be found. We will not be able to redirect love to the edges of the Occident, if such edges exist, in order to abandon it to voluptuous rituals, innocent games, or heroic communions, as certain ethnological or archaeological fictions would like to do. For there we would instantly lose what makes "love," its unique nomination, and the intimate communication it establishes between caress and devotion, between charity and nuptials (we would, in fact, lose the very meaning of these words, of all love's words). Nothing leads us more surely back to ourselves (to the Occident, to philosophy, to the dialectic, to literature) than love.

That is why one would want to separate oneself from love, free oneself from it. Instead of this law of the completion of being, one would want to deal only with a moment of contact between beings, a light, cutting, and delicious moment of contact, at once eternal and fleeting. In its philosophical assignation, love seems to skirt this touch of the heart that would not complete anything, that would go nowhere, graceful and casual, the joy of the soul and the pleasure of the skin, simple luminous flashes of love freed from itself. That is Don Juan's wish, it is his fervor, it is even his success: but we can think Don Juan only condemned, unless we represent his impunity as a diabolical or perverse challenge to the very law of love. Thus there is no innocent or joyous Don Juan. Mozart's, it is true, continues up until the end merrily thwarting the condemnation. And, yet, perhaps in spite of himself, Mozart let him be condemned. But even in hell, the figure of Don Juan testifies with remarkable force and insistence that this style of love as heart's touch obstinately haunts the thinking of love as law of fulfillment.

(Actually, when we represent modes of existence and thinking foreign to the law of love, we supplement this law, in our representations, by something else: it is a sacred order, a social tie, or a natural attraction that plays, in the final analysis, the role of love and that gives tenderness, erotism, and fraternity their independence. This means that we think love in the guise of a substitute or a transfiguration of these things that our imaginary figures as realities that we would have possessed, then lost: religion, community, the immediate emotion of the other and of the divine. But this substitute is not satisfied with coming to the place of what would have been lost—or, in the most Christian version, it is not satisfied with transfiguring it. Love conceals a fundamental ambivalence in which it at the same time challenges that which it must replace: we represent love as hostile or as foreign to the city and to religion—so that while affirming that they are founded within love or virtually fulfilled in it, they multiply with respect to love the procedures of control or of conciliation. But for itself, in its living essence, love is reputed to be rebellious, fugitive, errant, unassignable, and inassimilable. Thus love is at once the promise of completion—but a promise always disappearing—and the threat of decomposition, always imminent. An entire modern eroticism and an entire modern spirituality, those of romantic love, of savage love, of transgressive love, are determined according to this dialectic.)

Love is thus not here, and it is not elsewhere. One can neither attain it nor free oneself from it, and this is at bottom exactly what it is: the excess or the lack of this completion, which is represented as the truth of love. In other words, and as it has been extensively said, extensively represented, and extensively theorized for some two centuries: the impossible.

II

We will thus have to engage the repetition differently. We will have to stop thinking in terms of possibility and impossibility. We will have to maintain that love is always present and never recognized in anything that we name "love." We will have to admit that the rendezvous, our rendezvous with love, takes place not once, but an indefinite number of times and that it is never "love" that is at the rendezvous, or unique and universal love (*Catholic* love), or nomadic and multiple loves, but another presence or another movement of love. Or rather, another love presence or another love movement that we in fact touch or that touches us, but that is not the "love" we were expecting. (Classical figure of romantic comedy or drama: it is another who is at the rendezvous, but it is love itself that is revealed thereby—and betrayed. *Così fan tutte.*) Another love presence or another love movement: that is what the repetition should let emerge. This would not at all imply the invention of another "love" or of a beyond love. It would imply letting love once again open up its paths within thought, letting it once again call thought toward it, thought exposed to missing love as well as to being touched by it, exposed to being betrayed, as well as to taking account of its miserable means of loving.

We will set out again from the given that is perhaps the simplest and that is offered right in the middle of the tradition. In this tradition, love is defined above all as *that which is not self-love.* Any other determination—ontological, erotic, political—is excluded from the start and could only be recaptured, if that is necessary, starting from there.

(It was within the spirituality of the mystic tradition that this formulation of love came to be privileged. As an example, some lines from Fénelon:

The ownership condemned with such rigor by the mystics, and often called impurity, is only the search for one's own solace and one's own interest in the *jouissance* of the gifts of God, at the expense of the jealousy of the pure love that wants everything for God and nothing for the creature. The angel's sin was a sin of ownership; *stetit in se,* as Saint Augustine says. Ownership, of course, is nothing but self-love or pride, which is the love of one's own excellence insofar as it is one's own, and which, instead of coming back completely and uniquely to God, still to a small extent brings the gifts of God back to the self so that it can take pleasure in them.

What is expressed in these terms and under the rubric of a relation to "God" belongs in one way or another to all modes and all forms of the thinking of love that we have been able to know. In one sense, this does not say anything other than what the philosophical schema of love already contains, and, nonetheless, it displaces its entire economy of a fulfillment *proper.* It is simply a matter of letting oneself be carried by a tiny movement, barely perceptible, which would not reconstitute the dialectical logic, but which would touch the heart of the schema, the heart of love itself.)

Love defines itself as the absolute opposite and as the destruction of self-love. Self-love is not simply the love of the self; it is, as we have just read, "the love of one's own excellence *insofar as it is one's own.*" One can love oneself with a real love, and it might even be that one must do so (however, it is not certain that these words, "the self," "oneself," can let us discover, without being themselves put into play, precisely *who* is at issue in this love of "self": that is a question that we will have to take up again later). But self-love, understood according to the signification the spiritual authors gave to it, and not as a term in psychology almost synonymous with sensitivity, is the love (which, from this moment on, is no longer one) of possession. It is the love of the self as property.

Property is an ontological determination. It does not designate the object possessed, but the subject in the object. "Matter, for itself, is not proper to itself" (Hegel), it can therefore become my possession. But in this possession, it is I myself, as subject, who find myself realized, it is my subjectivity (*me* as will, need, desire, consciousness—of *me*), and in this respect possession properly becomes property. Which is to say that property is the objectivized presence of subjectivity, its realization in the outside world, and thus "the first existence of freedom" (Hegel). Property is the attestation and the assurance of the self in the actuality of the world. The self presents itself there outside itself, but in this presentation it is itself that it posits. Self-love is the desire and the affirmation of this autoposition: outside itself, in objectivity and in exteriority, the subject has the moment of its authenticity and the truth of its fulfillment.

Thus self-love indeed has the structure of love: here also, it is a matter of "having in another the moment of one's subsistence." In one sense, the formulas of love and of property respond to each other infinitely in the philosophical economy, each one giving to the other its stability or its movement.

If love is the gift of the self, it would thus also be, dialectically, the appropriation of the self. Self-love would therefore be at the heart of love, it would be its heart, the heart of love, and this implacably reconstituted economy—the dialectical economy of fulfillment, the capitalist economy of an absolute surplus value of the self—would proscribe love from the heart of love itself. The tradition knows well this absence of love from love itself. La Rochefoucauld, in this respect, sums it all up, or there is Nietzsche's formula "a refined parasitism," and so on until Levinas, for example, who writes, "To love is also to love oneself within love and thus to return to the self." Actually, the problem has been posed since the Aristotelian discussion of *philautia*, of the love of oneself, and it has traversed and troubled all Christian thought since Saint Augustine. (The question that dominated all the debates of the Middle Ages about love was the question of knowing "if man, by nature, is capable of loving God more than himself.") One could even explain by way of this absence the missed rendezvous between philosophy and love: if the latter always frustrates love or diverts it to self-love, if love finally lies to itself and lacks itself, how could one fail to forever lack it? And how could one not substitute for it sometimes its dismembered parts (the sexual organ, sentiment . . .), sometimes its sublimations (friendship, charity . . .)?

III

But this knowledge is too slight. Love frustrates the simple opposition between economy and noneconomy. Love is precisely—when it is, when it is the act of a singular being, of a body, of a heart, of a thinking— that which brings an end to the dichotomy between the love in which I lose myself without reserve and the love in which I recuperate myself, to the opposition between gift and property.

Of course, philosophy and theology have always surmounted and dialecticized this opposition: God's love for himself in his son brings itself about as a love for man on the part of this same Son, given, abandoned, and retaken in glory, with all of creation redeemed and brought into relation, through the love thus received, with its creator. But the separation is thus surmounted only because it is annulled in its principle: God gives only what he possesses infinitely (in a sense, he thus gives nothing), and reciprocally, he possesses only what he gives. (He is the proprietor par excellence; he appears to himself in the totality of objectivity—and that is what the idea of the "creation," in this respect, signifies. And if our time still had to be one of such a research, it is in an entirely different direction that we would have to look for the mystery of the "god of love.")

Love brings an end to the opposition between gift and property without surmounting and without sublating it: if I return to myself within love, I do not return to myself *from* love (the dialectic, on the contrary, feeds on the equivocation). *I* do not return from it, and consequently, something of *I* is definitively lost or dissociated in its act of loving. That is undoubtedly why *I* return (at least if the image of a return is appropriate here), but *I* return broken: I come back to myself, or I come out of it, broken. The "return" does not annul the break; it neither repairs it nor sublates it, for the return in fact takes place only across the break itself, keeping it open. Love re-presents *I* to itself broken (and this is not a representation). It presents this to it: he, this subject, was touched, broken into, in his subjectivity, and he *is* from then on, for the time of love, opened by this slice, broken or fractured, even if only slightly. He *is*, which is to say that the break or the wound is not an accident, and neither is it a property that the subject could relate to himself. For the break is a break in his self-possession as subject; it is, essentially, an interruption of the process of relating oneself to oneself outside of oneself. From then on, *I* is *constituted broken*. As soon as there is love, the slightest act of love, the slightest spark, there is this ontological fissure that cuts across and that disconnects the elements of the subject-proper—the fibers of its heart. One hour of love is enough, one kiss alone, provided that it is out of love—and can there, in truth, be any other kind? Can one do it without love, without being broken into, even if only slightly?

The love break simply means this: that I can no longer, whatever presence to myself I may maintain or that sustains me, pro-pose myself to myself (nor im-pose myself on another) without remains, without something of me *remaining*, outside of me. This signifies that the immanence of the subject (to which the dialectic always returns to fulfill itself, including in what we call "intersubjectivity" or even "communication" or "communion") is opened up, broken into—and this is what is called, in all rigor, a transcendence. Love is the act of a transcendence (of a transport, of a transgression, of a transparency, also: immanence is no longer opaque). But this transcendence is not the one that passes into—and through—an exteriority or an alterity in order to reflect itself in it and to reconstitute in it the interior and the identical (God, the certainty of the *cogito*, the evidence of a property). It does not pass through the outside, because it comes from it. (Transcendence is always thought as a self-surpassing: but here it is not at all a "surpassing," and even less "self-"; transcendence is the disimplication of the immanence that can come to it only from the outside.) Love does not stop, as long as love lasts, coming from the outside. It does not remain outside; it *is* this outside itself, the other, each time singular, a blade thrust in me, and that I do not rejoin, because it disjoins me (it does not wound, properly speaking: it is something else, foreign to a certain dramatics of love).

The movement of the transcendence of love does not go from the singular being toward the other, toward the outside. It is not the singular being that puts itself outside itself: it is the other, and in the other it is not the subject's identity that operates this movement or this touch. But in the other it is this movement that makes it other and which is always other than "itself" in its identity; that is what transcends "in me." This transcendence thus fulfills nothing: it cuts, it breaks, and it exposes so that there is no domain or instance of being where love would fulfill itself.

This does not mean that this transcendence accomplishes only what we would call—for example, in the theory of the sublime—a "negative presentation." (Love, certainly, has the most intimate relations with the sublime and with this extreme mode of presentation that I have attempted to designate elsewhere as the "sublime offering" (see Chapter 11); but with the offering, it is already a question of what, in fact, exceeds the sublime itself, and within love it is perhaps a question, in the final analysis, of that which exceeds love.) When the transcendence that touches me presents the unfulfillment of love (which becomes neither substance nor subject), it at the same time offers its actual advent: love takes place, it happens, and it happens endlessly in the withdrawal of its own presentation. It is an offering, which is to say that love is always proposed, addressed, suspended in its arrival, and not presented, imposed, already having reached its end. Love arrives, it comes, or else it is not love. But it is thus that it endlessly goes elsewhere than to "me" who would receive it: its coming is only a departure for the other, its departure only the coming of the other.

What is offered by transcendence, or as transcendence, is this arrival and this departure, this incessant coming-and-going. What is offered is the offered being itself: exposed to arrival and to departure, the singular being is traversed by the alterity of the other, which does not stop or fix itself anywhere, neither in "him," nor in "me," because it is nothing other than the coming-and-going. The other comes and cuts across me, because it immediately leaves for the other: it does not return to itself, because it leaves only in order to come again. This crossing breaks the heart: this is not necessarily bloody or tragic, it is beyond an opposition between the tragic and serenity or gaiety. The break is nothing more than a touch, but the touch is not less deep than a wound.

Transcendence will thus be better named the crossing of love. What love cuts across, and what it reveals by its crossing, is what is exposed to the crossing, to its coming-and-going—and this is nothing other than finitude. Because the singular being is finite, the other cuts across it (and never does the other "penetrate" the singular being or "unite itself" with it or "commune"). Love unveils finitude. Finitude is the being of that which is infinitely inappropriable, not having the consistency of its essence either in itself or in a dialectical sublation of the self. Neither the other nor love nor I can appropriate itself nor be appropriated ("Infinity of one and of the other, in the other and in the one"—Valéry).

This is why desire is not love. Desire lacks its object—which is the subject—and lacks it while appropriating it to itself (or rather, it appropriates it to itself while lacking it). Desire—I mean that which philosophy has thought as desire: will, appetite, conatus, libido—is foreign to love because it sublates, be it negatively, the logic of fulfillment. Desire is self extending toward its end—but love does not extend, nor does it extend itself toward an end. If it is extended, it is by an upheaval of the other in me. (Along with desire, all the terms of this contemporary lexicon are foreign to love: demand, seduction, dependence, and so on, and more generally, an entire analytics—that is not only of the "psych" variety—of the amorous operation as calculation, investment, completion, retribution, and the like.)

Desire is unhappiness without end: it is the subjectivist reverse of the infinite exposition of finitude. Desire is the negative appropriation that the dialectic tries indefinitely to convert into positivity. It is infelicitous love and the exasperation of the desired happiness. But in the broken heart, desire itself is broken. This heart is no more unhappy than it is happy. It is offered, at the limit between one and the other "sentiment," or one and the other "state." And this limit corresponds to that of its finitude: the heart does not belong to itself, not even in the mode of a desire, and even less in the mode of happiness or unhappiness. To love "with all my heart" puts a totality into play—that of the crossing—to which I cannot accede. *Cor tuum nondum est totum tuum* (Baudoin du Devon). The heart of the singular being *is* that which is not totally his, but it is thus that it is *his heart*.

(Actually, the heart is not broken, in the sense that it does not exist before the break. But it is the break itself that makes the heart. The heart is not an organ, and neither is it a faculty. It is: that I is broken and traversed by the other where its presence is most intimate and its life most open. The beating of the heart—rhythm of the partition of being, syncope of the sharing of singularity—cuts across presence, life, consciousness. That is why thinking—which is nothing other than the *weighing* or testing of the limits, the ends, of presence, of life, of consciousness—thinking itself is love.)

Love does not transfigure finitude, and it does not carry out its transsubstantiation in infinity. (The transsubstantiation is infinite, without being the infinite.) Love cuts across finitude, always from the other to the other, which never returns to the same—and all loves, so humbly alike, are superbly singular. Love offers finitude in its truth; it is finitude's dazzling presentation. (This could be said in English: *glamor*, this fascination, this seducing splendor reserved today for the language of makeup and of the staging of faces. *Glamor*: love's preparations and promises.)

Or perhaps love itself is eclipsed in this outburst, at once because it does not stop coming and going, never being simply present, and because it is always put into play farther off than everything that would have to qualify it (sublime love, tender love, foolish love, implacable love, pure love, abandoned love). Nietzsche's Zarathustra says: "Great loves do not want love—they want more:"

To Joy and Concern

So I say it again and again, pleasure is shared.
—Lucretius

I

In one sense—and in a sense that will perhaps always conceal the totality of *sense*, assignable as such—love is the impossible, and it does not arrive, or it arrives only at the limit, while crossing. It is also for this reason that it is missed by philosophy and no less by poetry. They do not miss love simply because they say it and because they say that it is fulfilled, whether by a divine force or in the splendor of words. It is true that in saying "I love you," I suspend all recourse to gods as much as I put myself back in their power, and that I unseat the power of words as much as I affirm that power at its peak. But philosophy and poetry still feed themselves on these contradictions. But there is more, for in one sense, nothing happens with "I love you," neither power nor effacement. "I love you" is not a performative (neither is it a descriptive nor a prescriptive statement). This sentence names nothing and does nothing. ("Though spoken billions of times, *I-love-you* is extralexicographical; it is a figure whose definition cannot transcend the heading.")[4] It is the very sentence of indigence, immediately destined to its own lie, or to its own ignorance, and immediately abandoned to the harassment of a reality that will never authenticate it without reserve. In one sense, love does not arrive, and, on the contrary, it always arrives, so that in one way or another "the love boat has crashed against the everyday" (Mayakovsky).

But "I love you" (which is the unique utterance of love and which is, at bottom, its name: love's name is not "love," which would be a substance or a faculty, but it is this sentence, the "I love you," just as one says "the cogito")—the "I love you" is something else. It is a promise. The promise, by constitution, is an utterance that draws itself back before the law that it lets appear. The promise neither describes nor prescribes nor performs. It does nothing and thus is always vain. But it lets a law appear, the law of the given word: that this must be. "I love you" says nothing (except a limit of speech), but it allows to emerge the fact that love must arrive and that nothing, absolutely nothing, can relax, divert, or suspend the rigor of this law. The promise does not anticipate or assure the future: it is possible that one day I will no longer love you, and this possibility cannot be taken away from love—it belongs to it. It is against this possibility, but also *with* it, that the promise is made, the word given. Love is its own promised eternity, its own eternity unveiled as law.

Of course, the promise must be kept. But if it is not, that does not mean that there was no love, nor even that there was not love. Love is faithful only to itself. The promise must be kept, and nonetheless love is not the promise *plus* the keeping of the promise. It cannot be subjected in this way to verification, to justification, and to accumulation (even if there are, indisputably, illusory or deceitful loves, loves without faith and law, that are no longer of love—but these are counterfeits, and even Don Juan is not one of them). Love is the promise and its keeping, the one independent of the other. How could it be otherwise, since one never knows what must be kept? Perhaps unlike all other promises, one must keep only the promise itself: not its "contents" ("love"), but its utterance ("I love you"). That is why love's ultimate paradox, untenable and nonetheless inevitable, is that its law lets itself be represented simultaneously by figures like Tristan and Isolde, Don Juan, or Baucis and Philemon—and that these figures are neither the types of a genre nor the metaphors of a unique reality, but rather so many bursts of love, which reflect love in its entirety each time without ever imprisoning it or holding it back.

When the promise is kept, it is not the keeping, but it is still the promise that makes love. Love does not fulfill itself, it always arrives in the promise and as the promise. It is thus that it touches and that it traverses. For one does not know what one says when one says "I love you," and one does not say anything, but one knows that one says it and that it is law, absolutely: instantly, one is shared and traversed by that which does not fix it-self in any subject or in any signification. (If one more proof or account were necessary: the same holds true when one hears "I love you" said by an other whom one does not love and whose expectations will not be met. Despite everything, it cannot be that one is not traversed by something that, while not love itself, is nonetheless the way in which its promise touches us.)

II

Love arrives then in the promise. In one sense (in another sense, al-ways other, always at the limit of sense), it always arrives, as soon as it is promised, in words or in gestures. That is why, if we are exhausted or ex-asperated by the proliferating and contradictory multiplicity of representa-tions and thoughts of love—which compose in effect the enclosure and the extenuation of a history of love—this same multiplicity still offers, how-ever, another thought: love arrives in all the forms and in all the figures of love; it is projected in all its shatters.

There are no parts, moments, types, or stages of love. There is only an infinity of shatters: love is wholly complete in one sole embrace or in the history of a life, in jealous passion or in tireless devotion. It consists as much in taking as in giving, as much in requiring as in renouncing, as much in protecting as in exposing. It is in the jolt and in appeasement, in the fever and in serenity, in the exception and in the rule. It is sexual, and it is not: it cuts across the sexes with another difference (Derrida, in *Geschlecht*, initiated the analysis of this) that does not abolish them, but displaces their identities. Whatever my love is, it cuts across my identity, my sexual property, that objectification by which I am a masculine or fem-inine subject. It is Uranian Aphrodite and Pandemian Aphrodite; it is Eros, Cupid, Isis and Osiris, Diane and Acteon, Ariadne and Dionysus; it is the *princesse de Clèves* or the *enfant de Bohême*; it is Death enlaced around a naked woman; it is the letters of Hyperion, of Kierkegaard, or of Kafka.

(It is perhaps that—a hypothesis that I leave open here—in love and in hate, but according to a regime other than that of Freudian ambiva-lence, there would not be a reversal from hate to love, but in hate I would be traversed by the love of another whom I deny in his alterity. Ultimately, I would be traversed by this negation. This would be the limit of love, but still its black glimmer. Perverse acts of violence, or the cold rage to annihi-late, are not hate.)

From one burst to another, never does love resemble itself. It always makes itself recognized, but it is always unrecognizable, and moreover it is not in any one of its shatters, or it is always on the way to not being there. Its unity, or its truth as love, consists only in this proliferation, in this in-definite luxuriance of its essence—and this essence itself at once gives it-self and flees itself in the crossing of this profusion. Pure love refuses or-gasm, the seducer laughs at adoration—blind to the fact that they each pass through the other, even though neither stops in the other. Plato had encountered the nature of Eros; son of Poros and of Penia, of resources and indigence, love multiplies itself to infinity, offering nothing other than its poverty of substance and of property.

But love is not "polymorphous," and it does not take on a series of disguises. It does not withhold its identity behind its shatters: it *is* itself the eruption of their multiplicity, it is itself their multiplication in one single act of love, it is the trembling of emotion in a brothel, and the distress of a desire within fraternity. Love does not simply cut across, it cuts itself across itself, it arrives and arrives at itself as that by which nothing arrives, except that there is "arriving," arrival and departure: of the other, always of the other, so much *other* that it is never *made*, or done (one makes love, be-cause it is never *made*) and so much other that it is never *my* love (if I say to the other "my love," it is of the other, precisely, that I speak, and noth-ing is "mine").

There is no master figure, there is no major representation of love, nor is there any common assumption of its scattered and inextricable shat-ters. That is why "love" is saturated, exhausted with philosophy and poetry (and threatened with falling into sexology, marriage counseling, newsstand novels, and moral edification all at once, as soon as it no longer supports its major figures, sealed in the destiny of occidental love), if we miss what love itself misses: that it comes *across* and never simply *comes* to its place or to term, that it comes across itself and overtakes itself, being the finite touch of the infinite crossing of the other.

III

What thus arrives in the crossing, crosswise, is not an accident of be-ing, nor an episode of existence. It is an ontological determination of that existent that Heidegger names *Dasein*—which is to say, the being in which Being is put into play. The putting into play of Being in Dasein and as Da-sein is indissociable from the following: that the world of Dasein is right away a world "that I share with others," or a "world-with." Because Heidegger, at the final frontier of philosophy, is the first to have assigned the being-with in Being itself, we must consider him for a moment.

The "world" that is here in question is not an exteriority of objects, nor an environment or neighborhood. It designates the mode of the putting into play of Being: through Dasein, Being is being-in-the-world (thrown, abandoned, offered, and set free: that is what "in the world" means). If the world is *Mitwelt*, shared world, Being insofar as it is "in the world" is constitutively being-with, and being-according-to-the-sharing. The originary sharing of the world is the sharing of Being, and the Being of the Dasein is nothing other than the Being of this sharing. (One could transpose this approximately into a more classical language as follows: that which confers Being, on whatever it may be, is that which puts in the world; but the world is a "with"; Being consists thus in being delivered to the "with.") Dasein is what it is in being originarily *with* others. And if concern most properly creates the Being of Dasein ("concern," that is to say the structure and the thrust of the existent that is offered-to, ahead of itself), concern for the other is its constitutive determination. Heidegger names it *Fürsorge*, "concern for" the other, whose analysis shows that it is, in its "advancing" (as opposed to its domineering) form, the movement of touching the other in his own concern, of restoring him to this concern or of liberating him for it, instead of exempting him from it. The concern for the other sends the other—in sending me to him—ahead of him, outside of him, once more into the world. The shared world as the world of concern for-the-other is a world of the crossing of singular beings by this sharing itself that constitutes them, that makes them be, by addressing them one to the other, which is to say one by the other beyond the one and the other.

I am certainly betraying in part the Heideggerian description. Concern or preoccupation for things—and not for others—that are in the world (*Besorgen*) plays a role in Heidegger parallel to the *Fürsorge*, and although the latter is in effect a fundamental ontological determination, it does not exactly accede to the privileged position I have just given it. The analytic of the being-with remains a moment, which is not returned to thematically, in a general analytic where Dasein appears first of all and most frequently as in some way isolated, even though Heidegger himself emphasizes that there is solitude "only *in* and *for* a being-with." Moreover, love is never named and consequently never furnishes, as such, an ontologico-existential character (although the description of *Fürsorge* greatly resembles a certain classical description of the most demanding, most noble, and most spiritual love).

I will not undertake here the dense and meticulous explication that Heidegger's text would demand. I will be content to propose dryly this double hypothesis: in approaching more closely than we ever have the *altered* (crossed by the other) constitution of Being in its singularity, Heidegger (1) determined the essence of the Dasein outside of subjectivity (and a fortiori outside of inter-subjectivity) in a being-exposed or in a being-offered to others, of which philosophy (since Plato? despite Plato?) has always been, despite everything, the denial, and (2) kept (despite himself?) the assignation of this Dasein in the apparent form of a distinct individuality, as much opposed as exposed to other individualities and thus irremediably kept in a sphere of autonomic, if not subjective, allure. In accordance with these two gestures, Heidegger was prevented from summoning love to the ontological register. On the one hand, he could, in effect, only collide with the metaphysical-dialectical thinking of love, which had redirected *Mitsein* into the space of subjectivity. On the other hand, love insofar as it is traversed by Being exceeds the very movement of *Fürsorge*, which "surpasses and liberates the other": this movement is still thought *starting* from an "I" or from an "identity" that goes toward the other, and it is not thought as what cuts across and alters I going to the other while the other comes to it.

It is not at all by chance that Heidegger is silent about love (at least his references to Scheler, his critique of the theory of empathy, and at least one allusion made to love demonstrate that this silence was deliberate—if it were not already obvious that it is deliberate with respect to the entire philosophical tradition). Love forms the limit of a thinking that carries itself to the limit of philosophy. Until thinking extricates itself, it will not be able to reach love. But what this thinking, at its limit, lets emerge could be this: that one never *reaches* love, even though love is always happening to us. Or rather, love is always offered to us. Or yet again, we are always, in our Being—and in us Being is—exposed to love.

(*Note*: I will be even less explicit with Levinas than with Heidegger. Every philosophical inquiry on love today carries an obvious debt to Levinas, as well as points of proximity, such as are easily detected here. For Levinas cleared the path toward what one can call, in the language of *Totality and Infinity*, a metaphysics of love, to the point that this metaphysics commands, at bottom, his entire oeuvre. For this very reason, a discussion of Levinas would have to be an enterprise distinct from this essay. I should, however, indicate what its principle would be. As a citation above recalled, love remains *equivocal* for Levinas, reducing itself to egotism. Its transcendence lifts the equivocation only by transcending itself into fecundity, filiation, and fraternity. If I, for my part, do not thematize such notions here, it is because another work would be necessary to attempt to extract them from the oriented sequence that, in Levinas, in a rather classical manner, hierarchizes them and prescribes them to a teleology. This teleology proceeds from the first given of his thought, "the epiphany of the face": love is the movement stressed by this epiphany, a movement that transcends it in order to reach, beyond the face, beyond vision and the "you," the "hidden—never hidden enough—absolutely ungraspable."[5] From this "vertigo that no signification any longer clarifies" (that of the Eros), the fraternity of children, lifting its equivocation, can emerge, the fraternity of children in which, again, the epiphany of the face is produced. Love thus retains at least certain traits of a dialectical moment. It retains them, it seems to me, due to the motif of the face. The latter signifies the primordial relation as the expression of another and as signification. Because this signification is given at the beginning, it must disappear within love and be recaptured in its surpassing. I can, on the contrary, grasp the relation with the face only as second and as constituted. Levinas opposes it, and pre-poses it, "to the unveiling of Being in general," a Heideggerian theme in which he sees "the absolute indetermination of the *there is*—of an existing without existents—incessant negation, infinite limitation," "anarchic." I can be in solidarity with Levinas's distaste for certain accents, shall we say, of dereliction in Heidegger's discourse. But in the *es gibt* ("it gives [itself]") of Being, one can see everything except "generality." *There is* the "each time," an-archic in fact (or even archi-archic, as Derrida might say?), of an existing, singular occurrence. *There is no* existing without existents, and *there is no* "existing" by itself, no concept—it does not *give itself*—but there is always being, precise and hard, the theft of the generality. Being is at stake there, it is in shatters, offered dazzling, multiplied, shrill and singular, hard and cut across: its being is there. Being-with is constitutive of this stake—and that is what Levinas, before anyone, understood. But being-with takes place only according to the occurrence of being, or its posing into shatters. And the crossing—the coming-and-going, the comings-and-goings of love—is constitutive of the occurrence. This takes place before the face and signification. Or rather, this takes place on another level: *at the heart* of being.)

IV

We are exposed by concern—not that which "we" "hold" for the other, but by this concern, this solicitude, this consideration, and this renunciation for the other that cuts across us and does not come back to us, that comes and goes incessantly, as the being-other of the other inscribed in being itself: at the *heart* of being, or as the *promise* of being.

This concern exposes us to joying.[6] To joy is no more impossible, as Lacan wanted it, than possible, as the sexologist would want it. To joy is not an eventuality that one might expect, that one might exclude, or that one might provoke. To joy is not a fulfillment, and it is not even an event. Nonetheless, it happens, it arrives—and it arrives as it departs, it arrives in departing and it departs in the arrival, in the same beat of the heart. To joy is the crossing of the other. The other cuts across me, I cut across it. Each one is the other for the other—but also for the self. In this sense, one joys in the other for the self: to be passed to the other. This is the syncope of identity in singularity. A syncope: the step marked, in a suspense, from the other to me, neither confusion nor fading, clarity itself, the beating of the heart, the cadence and the cut of another heart within it.

Everything has been said of joying, as of love, but this word resists. It is the verb of love, and this verb speaks the act of joy (the *joi* of courtly love). Something resists, through these two words (that are only one), the overwhelming exhaustiveness of discourses on love. It is not so much a result, or "discharge," as Freud says and as it is said vulgarly, as an acute insistence, the very formation of a shatter (one might say, like Deleuze, "a hardening that is one with love"). It is not something unspeakable, because it is spoken, the joy is named, but it is something with which discourses (narratives and poems) can never be even. They have never said it enough, having always discoursed it too much, declared it too much.

Joy is the trembling of a deliverance beyond all freedom: it is to be cut across, undone, it is to be joyed as much as to joy: "Love is joy accompanied by the idea of an exterior cause," writes Spinoza, and he specifies that with this joy it is not a matter of desire, for "this definition explains with enough clarity the essence of love. Regarding that of the authors who define love as *the will of he who loves to join himself to the loved object*, it does not express the essence of love, but its property." But we have to push "the idea of an exterior cause" to this: to be joyed—to face the extremity of being, which is to say at once its completion and its limit, beyond desire or short of it. This is joy, and this also reflects on the essence of chagrin and of pain. For joy is not appeasement, but a serenity without rest. To joy is not to be satisfied—it is to be filled, overflowed. It is to be cut across without even being able to hold onto what "to joy" makes happen. To joy cannot contain *itself.* Joy is not even to contain joy itself, nor the pain that consequently accompanies it. The joy of joying does not come back to anyone, neither to me nor to you, for in each it opens the other. In the one and the other, and in the one by the other, joy offers being itself, it makes being felt, shared. Joy knows concern, and is known by it. Joy makes felt, *and* it lets go the very essence of the sharing that is being. (Although it means diverting the sentence from its proper context, I will cite Michel Henry: "Far from coming after the arrival of being and marveling before it, joy is consubstantial with it, founds it and constitutes it.")

This puts one beside oneself, this irritates and exasperates, and the language for saying it is exasperated. (It would be better to let another speak, and in a language that would remain, somewhat, on the side:[7]

Laura the basilisk made entirely of asbestos, walking to the fiery stake with a mouth full of gum. Hunkydory is the word on her lips. The heavy fluted lips on the sea shell, Laura's lips, the lips of lost Uranian love. All floating shadowward through the slanting fog. Last murmuring dregs of shell-like lips slipping off the Labrador coast, oozing eastward with the mud tides, easing starward in the iodine drift. . . . I kept it up like a Juggernaut. Moloch fucking a piece of bombazine. Organza Friganza. The bolero in straight jabs. . . . We embraced one another silently and then we slid into a long fuck. [Henry Miller])

But this is shared too much within the other. It is not that identity, in joying, simply loses itself. It is there at its peak. There is in fact too much identity—and joying opens the enigma of that which, in the syncope of the subject, in the crossing of the other, affirms an absolute *self.* To joy poses without reserve the question of the singular being, which we are no doubt barely on the way to broaching. It is the question *of that which remains "self" when nothing returns to the self:* the very question of love, if love is always proffered ("*I* love you") and if joy, coming from the other, coming and going, is, however, always mine.

It is the question of a presence: to joy is an extremity of presence, *self* exposed, presence *of self* joying outside itself, in a presence that no present absorbs and that does not (re)present, but that offers itself endlessly.

To try to enter into the question, one could say at least this: *self* that joys joys of its presence in *the presence of the other.* He, she, is only the presence of the reception of the other presence—and the latter cuts across. The presence that cuts across is a burst. To joy, joy itself, is to receive the burst of a singular being: its more than manifest presence, its seeming beyond all appearance—*ekphanestaton*, Plato said. But it is *by oneself* also that he, she who joys is bedazzled. It is in himself thus that he is delighted. But he does not belong to himself, and he does not come back to himself: he is shared, like the joy he shares.

What appears in this light, at once excessive and impeccable, what is offered like a belly, like a kissed mouth, is the singular being insofar as it is this "self" that is neither a subject nor an individual nor a communal being, but *that*—she or he—which cuts across, that which arrives and departs. The singular being affirms even better its absolute singularity, which it offers only in passing, which it brings about immediately in the crossing. What is offered through the singular being—through you or me, across this relation that is only cut across—is the singularity of being, which is to say this: that being itself, "being" taken absolutely, is absolutely singular (thus it would be that which remains "self" when nothing comes back to the self).

This constitution is buried at the heart of being, but it emerges in outbursts of joy. One could say: being joys. One would thus define an ontological necessity of love. But love is neither unique nor necessary. It comes, it is offered; it is not established as a structure of being or as its principle, and even less as its subjectivity. One would thus define a necessity without a law, or a law without necessity, thus: the heart of being within love, and love in surplus of being. One could say, at the limit, the fundamental ontology *and* the caprices of love. The correlation would neither be causal nor expressive nor essential nor existential nor of any other known genre. Perhaps it would no longer be necessary to speak of correlation. But there is this brilliant, shattering constitution of being. "Love" does not define it, but it names it, and obliges us to think it.

Postscriptum

—You wrote: "It might well be appropriate that a discourse on love be at the same time a communication of love, a letter, a missive, since love sends itself as much as it enunciates itself." But you didn't send this text to anyone. And you know very well that that doesn't mean that you sent it to everyone. One can't love everyone.

—But a letter, a missive, once published, is no longer a missive. It is a citation or a mimicking of one. About how many poets do the biographers or the critics tell us that their poems are far from the reality of their loves?

—And don't you think that "I love you," by itself, is already a citation? Listen to Valéry: "To say to anyone *I love you* is to recite a lesson. It was never invented!" Recitation for citation, you might have risked that. You might have risked playing at losing the distance of discourse.

—I didn't want to. I was afraid, if I played that game, that it would be even more discourse, and not necessarily more love.

—And nonetheless, aren't you ever touched by a poem, by a letter, by a dialogue of love? And do you really believe that your love—if you have one, how could one know?—owes nothing to these public dispatches?

—I know. I know my debt, and I know that I don't pay returns. But you also read that I would want to be exempt from love, to be even with it. The splinters that cut across me, coming from another, from you perhaps, or coming from me, that is still something other than "love," other than this burden of the word and its declaration. It is lighter, more relaxed; it is not subject to the grandiloquence of love.

—There is then no excess, no infinite transport in this raving: it must be only *this other*? Only him, her, to whom you send your love, and if not there is no love? But each time, and even if you switched every day, and even if you love several at a time, love is addressed to one alone, singularly and infinitely: does not your lightness forget that?

—No, I haven't forgotten that. But this infinity is minute, and the words of love are too big for it. Or rather, they are really too small. . . . I don't know anymore. I should perhaps give them all to you, send them all to you, all imprinted, as one touches everywhere the minute infinity of skin, with impatience, with this boundless disorder that never finds an order or a measure, except by being always shaken, always broken, rushed to multiply itself, a nervousness of fingers on masses, on flanks, and in secret folds—with nothing more that is secret, in the end. . . . I should have sent everything, a thousand pages of love and not one word on it, to you alone. All the words of love from everyone. . . . It would have flown into pieces, barely thrown toward you, as it always flies into pieces as soon as it is sent.

—Yes, it's made for that.

Translated by Lisa Garbus and Simona Sawhney

PART SIX

WORLD

In Praise of the Melee
For Sarajevo, March 1993

"Sarajevo" has become the name for a complete system of reduction to identity. It is no longer a sign beside a road or in a history; it is no longer a place to visit, to conduct business or a liaison; nor is it the uncertain space of fortuitous encounter or of distracted meandering. It is a dimensionless point on a diagram of sovereignty, an orthonormal index on a balistico-political computer, an immobilized target in a gun sight; and it is the very cipher of exact aim, the pure pinpoint of an essence. Somewhere out there, a pure Subject declares that it is the People, the Law, the State, the Identity in the name of which "Sarajevo" must be purely and simply identified as a target.

Sarajevo: no longer even a name, but a sign hung over our eyes in such a way that there would no longer be a Sarajevo landscape or journey to Sarajevo, merely a pure and naked identity. Nothing else should come into consideration; nor should we—other cosmopolitan Europeans—get mixed up in it.

~

A city doesn't need to be identified by anything other than a name, which marks a locus, the locus of a melee, of crossing and halt, of entanglement and commerce, competition, release, circulation, scattering of lights. The name of a city, like that of a country, like that of a people, and like that of a person, should never be the name of any one person; it should always be the name of no one who could actually be presented in person, as it were, or as his or her own person. The "proper name" has no meaning or, rather, the meaning that it has is little more than the sketch of a description, indefinite in principle and in fact. An inchoate and stochastic sense, a melee of syllables swarming over the border of a semantic identity that is gently, obstinately deferred. From the moment that a proper name arraigns a presence in person, a sovereign Subject, this sovereignty is threatened, hemmed in, under siege. In order to live in Sarajevo, there was no need to identify it. From this point on, however, those who die in Sarajevo will die of the death of Sarajevo itself; they will die of the militarily imposed possibility of identifying this name with some substance or some presence that measures up to the "nation" or the "state," some bodily symbol erected precisely in order to body forth and to symbolize what was only a place and a passage. Those who are exiles from Sarajevo have been exiled from this place, expunged by that body. They have been exiled from the mix, from the melee that made Sarajevo what it was, but that, as such, *made* nothing, engendered no ego. The "proper" name should always dissolve the ego: the latter opens sense, a pure source of sense, while the former points to a melee, gives rise to a melody: *Sarajevo*.

~

I was asked to write something "in praise of mixture." What I'd like to do is to write praise that is itself "mixed." Not in the literal sense of writing something that is partly praise and partly blame, only to end up with a null account of loss and gain, nor in the sense of singing faint praise, evoking, an odd concept, a sort of extreme lukewarmth. Instead, it is a matter (as everyone knows; it's there for all to see, if only we knew how to look for it and to accept what is at stake), against wind and tide—and we know how many of those there can be—simply a matter, of conceding nothing, neither concerning identity *nor* concerning what mixes with it or mixes it up *fons et origo*. What we need, then, is praise mixed with reserve, with the reserve used when we do not want—that's the last thing we want!—our praise to betray its object by having identified it all too well.

In truth, the most fitting and most beautiful praise of mixture would be not to have to praise it, since it's scarcely possible to discern or identify this notion. It presupposes isolated pure substances and then the operation of their mixture. It's a notion that belongs in the laboratory. But would it ever occur to a painter to praise the blending of colors? He or she has nothing to do with the specter of pure colors; the painter has no choice but to concern him- or herself with the infinite derivation and melee of their nuances.

Now, because it was always possible that someone was going to coin the detestable slogan "ethnic cleansing," this demands some sort of response. Not a response in the form of a symmetrical counter-slogan, however. This is why I'm seeking, above all, to avoid conferring too much identity on mixture itself. To make sure of this, we're going to need to shift accent and genre; we're going to need to move from mixture to melee.

~

To do justice to identities—without giving in to their delusion, to the presumption that they are, substantially, identities ("subjects" in this sense): this is the job in hand. It's both immense and very simple: to remake culture, no less, to remake thought so that it is not crude, rubbish, like any thinking of purity; to remix lineages, paths, and skins, but also to describe their heterogeneous trajectories, their networks, which are at once crossed *and* distinct. In no way, though, is this to believe "man" to be simple, homogeneous, or present. Nor woman. Nor the Croat, nor the Serb, nor the Bosnian. To know (but what sort of knowledge is this?) that, from now on, the subject of knowledge can only be someone, like everyone, of *mixed blood.*

Mixing is a delicate operation, fragile, subtle, and volatile; today, this delicacy is usually coarsened, obscured. There does exist—and I'm not the first to point this out—a version of praise for mixture that derives from the more acceptable forms of "political correctness," that is, from the normative petrification of the most well-founded exigencies. This kind of praise can celebrate, if need be, multiculturalism, hybridization, generalized exchange and sharing, or a transcendental variegation.

But we know, or we feel we know, that things are not quite so simple, that turbulence, mixtures, errancies, or confusions aren't enough *in themselves.* Or rather, and first of all, we know that they do not lend themselves to being thought as such. And that's the whole question.[1]

But there also remains—and, sadly, this is something with which we're even more familiar—a discourse that simplifies in order to fuel its rage, to inflate the value of distinction, identity, propriety, purity, a discourse that employs the word "cosmopolitan," for example, with evident contempt and even disgust (sometimes clearly tinged with anti-Semitism) for what it denotes.

Finally, and as is only fitting, there are those who step back from the conflict between these two forms of "correctness" and who recite an endless catechism of unity within diversity, of complementarity, and of well-tempered differences. This well-intentioned discourse, though often welcome amidst the cries of moral and political urgency, remains on the level of intention and exhortation. It doesn't address the very things that are at stake.

∼

Let's be clear on this from the start: the simplistic praise of mixture may well have lead to mistakes, but the simplistic praise of purity has upheld and upholds crimes. In this respect, we don't need to sustain any sense of symmetry, of equilibrium. There's no happy medium here. There's nothing to discuss. Even the most meager discussion, the least second thought about any racism or about any "purification" whatsoever, already participates in the crime. Moreover, the crime here is always double, both moral and intellectual. Every racism is stupid, obtuse, fearful. (I always feel a certain reticence when faced with long discourses and big colloquia on the subject of racism: it seems to me that we bestow too much honor on this trash. And this is why I am bothered by the idea of a "praise of mixture": it is as if mixture as such were a "value" or an "authenticity" yet to be revealed, whereas it is, in fact, obvious or, rather, on closer inspection, proves not even to exist—if it is indeed the case that there has never been anything "pure" that one could or should "mix" with some other "purity.")

We're not talking about maintaining some happy medium between these opposed theses. These theses only exist insofar as there is some simplification and denaturation of what's at stake.

∼

By definition, a mixture is not a simple substance to which we could assign a specific place or nature, that we could claim as such, and that we could consequently praise without hesitation. By definition, identity is not an absolute distinction, cut off from everything and therefore distinct from nothing: it is always the other of an other identity. "He's different. Just like everybody else."[2] Difference as such is indiscernible. Mixture and identity cannot pin one another down. They have both always already happened, are both always already past or both always still to come. And they are common, shared by everyone, between everyone, as much as they are shared by one another.

~

Precisely because mixture is put into the mix (mixed up in the melee), it isn't a substance. Nor can we replace the nonsubstantiality of its content with the supposed consistency of the container: such is the difficulty with ideologies of the melting pot, which suppose the "pot" to contain, in every sense of the word, with all the virtues of its own identity, the enigmas of mixture along with its disruptive forces.

Hybridization [*métissage*] isn't "some*thing*," and, if the hybrid—this hybrid [*métis*] that each of us in one way or another is—is some*one*, this isn't due to an essence of hybridization (a contradictory notion), but is so insofar as the hybrid gives a punctuation, a singular configuration, to the without-essence of hybridization. To essentialize mixture is already to have dissolved it, to have melted it into something other than itself. Hence, we shouldn't claim to be speaking about mixture as such, least of all in order to be hymning its praise.

Mixture, as such, can take two forms: that of a fusion, an accomplished osmosis, or that of an achieved disorder. Alchemy or entropy, two phantasmatic extremities—which can only join up or be identified with one another in an apocalypse or a black hole. And yet mixture is neither the one nor the other; nor is it a happy medium between the two. It is something other, or, rather, it "is" otherwise, totally otherwise.

~

Rather than mixture, therefore, we would be better off speaking of *melee*: of an action rather than a substance. To begin with, there are at least two kinds of melee—indeed, there is perhaps never any such thing as a melee "pure and simple." There is the melee of combat, and the melee of love. The melee of Ares, the melee of Aphrodite. Neither is never identified with the other. There is neither entropy nor alchemy. A joust that couldn't happen without desire and without jealous assault, without appeal to the other as an always other other.

(The melee of Ares isn't war in the modern sense of the term, however, something that is usually a long way removed from a melee, moving as it has toward extermination even before any hand-to-hand combat, something that aims to crush or to suppress the opponent rather than take him or her out of the fight, something that has no room for combat, no "combat zone," but instead spreads out indiscriminately, killing, raping, irradiating, gassing, and infecting "civil" space as a whole. Today, war is pure mixture without limits, and not a melee. And we could make the same point with respect to the melee of Aphrodite, about the orgy or the porn movie.)

Mixture, therefore, *is* not. It happens, it emerges. There is melee, crossing, weaving, exchange, sharing; and these are neither a single thing nor the same thing. To begin with, mixture is an "it happens" rather than an "it is": displacements, hazards, migrations, clinamens, encounters, chances, and risks. So there is no *one*, nothing unitary: in a melee, there is countervalence and encounter, there's resemblance and distancing, contact and contraction, concentration and dissemination, identification and alteration.

Mixture is not simply "rich" with the diversity that it mixes. Insofar as it is *itself* nothing, it ceaselessly escapes this diversity, as well. There is a rather foolish quantitative discourse—a basically capitalizing or profiteering discourse—of "mutual enrichment." But what is at stake here is neither wealth nor poverty. Cultures—or what are called cultures—don't add up. They encounter one another, mix with one another, alter one another, reconfigure one another. All cultures cultivate one another: they clear one another's ground, irrigate or drain one another, plough one another, or graft themselves onto one another.

To begin with, every culture is a configuration, a melee from the offset. The first culture was a melee of races or species, *erectus, faber, sapiens.* The West, so proud of the "Greek miracle" of its foundation, should constantly ponder the ethnic and cultural diversity, the movement of peoples, the transferences and transformations of practices, the deviations of language and morals, that configured "the Hellenes," made them what they were. Let us reread the history of this melee:

The beginning of the second millennium B.C. sees a phenomenon of extraordinary novelty: a cosmopolitan culture emerges in which we can recognize the input of diverse civilizations built next to or in the middle of the sea. The civilizations were either those internal to empires—Egypt, Mesopotamia, the Asia Minor of the Hittites—or those scattered upon the seas and sustained by cities—the Syrian-Lebanese coast, Crete, and later Mycenae. From that point on, however, they all communicate between one another. All of them, even Egypt, ordinarily so closed in on itself, turn toward the outside with a passionate curiosity. It is the era of voyages, of the exchange of gifts, of diplomatic correspondences, and of princesses sent to be spouses to foreign kings as a token of these new "international" relations. The era when all the peoples of the Near East and the Agaean—Cretans, Mycenaeans, Palestinians, Nubians, Canannites—begin to show up in their native costumes on the frescos in Egyptian tombs.[3]

Every culture is in itself "multicultural," not only because there is a prior acculturation or because there is no pure and simple provenance, but more importantly because the gesture of culture is itself a gesture of melee: of confrontation, transformation, deviation, development, recomposition, combination, cobbling together.

~

It's not that there's no "identity." A culture is single and unique (always assuming that we're still happy with the word "culture," which seems to have identified in advance what is at stake in it. And yet this word identifies precisely nothing. It is a way of short-circuiting all the difficulties that crowd in when we try to say "people," "nation," "civilization," "spirit," "personality," etc.). A "culture" denotes a certain "unity," a "one." And we cannot neglect the fact and the principle of this "one," still less deny it, in the name of an essentialization of "mixture."

And yet, to the extent that this "one" is clearly distinct and thus distinguished, it is still not its own pure and proper foundation. Avoiding confusion between distinction and foundation is undoubtedly the whole problem; it is this confusion and this distinction that are, philosophically, ethically, and politically at stake in the discourse that surrounds "identity" or "subjects" of all types. As such, the absolute distinction of Descartes's *ego existo* ought not to be confused with the foundation that Descartes links to it, in the purity of a *res cogitans*, In the same way, for example, "French" identity doesn't need to found itself in Vercingetorix or Joan of Arc in order to exist . . .

The unity and unicity of a culture are one and the same by way of a mixture or of a melee. It is a melee that, within any given "culture," brings out a style or a tone; equally, however, it brings out the various voices or vocal ranges that are needed in order for this tone to be interpreted. There is a French culture. But this culture has many voices and is nowhere present "in person," as it were—except for those who confuse it with the Gallic cock, or with Dupont-la-Joie. The voice of Voltaire isn't the same as that of Proust, nor is Proust's voice the same as that of Pasteur, Pasteur's not the same Rita Mitsouko's. Equally, it's perhaps not as though such voices are ever *purely and simply* French: what is and is not French in Stendhal, in Hugo, in Picasso, in Levinas, in Godard, in Johnny Hallyday, in Kat'Onoma, in Chamoiseau, in Dib? Again, this doesn't mean that there's no "French identity": it means that an identity of this type is never simply identical in the way that a pencil is identically the same today as it was yesterday (supposing, at least, that this example isn't always going to be materially imprecise . . .). The identity of the pencil leaves this precise pencil much less identifiable as "this one here" (which is, up to a certain point, any pencil whatsoever) than the identity of a culture leaves that particular culture, or the identity of a person leaves that particular person. In order to illustrate the difference, we might term the second identity an *ipseity*, a "being-self-same."

An ipseity is not the pure inertia of the same remaining entirely the same set at no distance from itself: that's how we imagine the being of a stone or of God . . . An ipseity can be identified or makes its identity known. In order for that to occur, there needs to be a network of exchanges, recognitions, relays from one ipseity to another, from difference to difference. An ipseity takes on matter through and for the other, provided that there is an other or that there are others from which, with its singular touch, it takes and to which it gives a certain identifiable tone— that is, a tone which is unidentifiable, inimitable, unattributable to *an* identity. "Ipseity" would name what precisely it is about an identity that it is always and necessarily impossible to identify.

As a matter of fact, a pure identity would not only be inert, empty, colorless, and flavorless (words which describe many of those who uphold pure identities): it would be an absurdity. A pure identity annuls itself, cannot identify itself. It is solely identical to an itself that is identical to itself, and that thus goes around in a circle and never attains existence.

Was there, for example, anyone pure enough to be worthy of the name "Aryan"? We know how this question could lead a real Nazi, a Nazi who identified absolutely with his cause or with his thing, to sterilization or even to suicide.

Purity is a crystalline abyss in which the identical, the proper, or the authentic collapses into itself, null, taking the other with itself so as to convert it into the abyss. The absolute and vertiginous law of the proper is that it purely and simply alienates itself in appropriating its own purity. Another form of mixture: mixing-in-itself, auto-mixture, autism, autoeroticism.

∼

A language is always a melee of languages, something halfway between the total confusion of Babel and the immediate transparency of a glossolalia. A style is always an intersection of tones, borrowings, intervals, and forced correspondences, to which it lends a trope. Undoubtedly, every style seems to tend toward an ultimate, sovereign trope, which would be the trope of an absolutely proper language, an absolute idiolect. But an absolute idiolect or idiom would no longer be a language at all; it would no longer be able to mix it up with other languages in order to be the language that it is; *it could no longer be translated so as to be the untranslatable that it is*. A pure idiolect would be idiotic, wholly deprived of relations and so of identity. A pure culture, a pure propriety would be idiotic.

∼

What is a community? It is neither a macro-organism nor a big family (always assuming we know what an organism or what a family actually are . . .). The *common*, having-in-common or being-in-common excludes from itself any interior unity, any subsistence and presence in itself or by itself. To be with, to be together, and even to be "united" is precisely not to be "one." Of communities that are at one with themselves, there are only dead ones. These are not to be found in the cemetery, moreover, a place of dispersed space, of distinction; no, they lie in the ashes of ovens or under the soil of mass graves.

So, too, has the systematic rape of Bosnian women unfurled in exemplary fashion all the figures of the delusional affirmation of a community "one" with itself: rape in order to engender "bastards," deemed unacceptable, excluded *a priori* from the presupposed unity; rape in order to force the abortion of these bastards; rape, then, in order to kill and destroy the very possibility of the bastard; rape so that this repeated act will draw its victims into the fantastic unity of their "community"; rape in order to make manifest in every possible way that there *should be no relations* between communities. A null act, a negation of sex itself, a negation of relation, a negation of the child, of the woman; an act of pure affirmation on the part of the rapist, in whom a "pure identity" (a "racialized" identity) is unable to offer anything better than a vile imitation of what it negates: relation and being-together. (In general, what undoubtedly remains exemplary about rape is that it operates through a relation of which it is also the negation. It pursues relation, pursues melee.)

What we have in common is always also what distinguishes us and differentiates us. What I have in common with a Frenchman is that I am *not* the same Frenchman as he is, the fact that our "Frenchness" is nowhere to be found, in no essence, no completed figure. In saying this, it's not a matter of the nothingness of a figure, but a matter of an outline that's always in the process of being traced, a fiction that's always in the process of being invented, a melee of traits. It is not that identity is "always on the way," projected onto the horizon as a guiding star, as a value or as a regulative idea. Even as an infinite projection, identity is not going to arrive, is not going to identify itself. Why? Because the melee is *already there.*

I am already there when my mother and my father get mixed up with one another. It is I who mixes them together. I am their melee. Yet I do not engender myself.

What is a people? Yes, there are ethnic traits. It's rare for us to take a Sicilian for a Norwegian (even though the Normans were also mixed up in Sicily . . .). But could we confuse a Sicilian "of the people" with an upper class Sicilian? Perhaps we'd have more chance in Chicago, say, of confusing a Sicilian "of the people" with a Pole of the same "people," an aristocrat from Palermo with a *grand-bourgeois* from Lyons. As a result of no longer wanting to know anything about classes, we end up disavowing the most everyday realities. Granted, a class is no longer conceivable as an identity, and it's (perhaps) because classes were configured as identities rather than as conditions that certain totalitarianisms were possible. But it's precisely not a matter of pitting one identity against another. It's a matter of practicing singularities, of practicing what only gives or exposes itself in the plural: *singuli*, "one by one," is a word that only exists in the plural. Ipseity only exists singularly distributed: it is "itself," so to speak, the originary distribution, dissemination, sharing of what—*Ipse* itself—is never present anywhere as such, "in person."[4] *Ipse* "is" its own dispersion.

It is nothing—it's everything, even—but we still have to think this totality of dispersion, this whole. We still have to think a melee.

Mixture as such does not exist, any more than purity as such. There is neither pure mixture nor intact purity. Not only is there no such thing, but this lack is itself the law of the "there is": there would be nothing if there was anything pure and intact. Nothing "pure" exists that does not touch otherness, not because we can't help rubbing shoulders with others, as if this were simply an accidental condition, but because only touch exposes us to these limits on which identities or ipseities can sort things out [*se démêler*] between themselves or can extricate themselves from one another, from the midst of all the others. There is neither the simply mixed nor the simply identical; what there is is the always-incessant mix-up of one with the other.

The melee is not accidental; it's originary. It is not contingent; it's necessary. It is not; it always happens.

Melee of Ares and melee of Aphrodite, melee of these melees: blows and embraces, assaults and truces, rivalry and desire, supplication and defiance, dialogue and dispute, fear and pity, and laughter as well. And melee of Hermes, melee of messages and conduits, bifurcations, substitutions, competition between codes, configurations of spaces, borders made to cross, so that crossing becomes sharing, because there's identity only when shared, divided, mixed, distinguished, cut off, common, substitutable, unsubstitutable, withdrawn, exposed.

Why is the "passport photo," the photo most oriented toward identity, the most colorless of all photos? Why is it always the worst likeness? Equally, why are ten passport photos of the same person always so different from one another? When does someone resemble him- or herself? When the photos show what it is about him or her that is more than identifiable, more than the "face," the "image," the "traits," or the "portrait" insofar as they are functions of the diacritical marks of an "identity" ("black hair, blue eyes, pug-nosed, etc."), and when these give rise to an interminable melee, peoples, parents, kinds of work, pains, pleasures, refusals, oblivions, wrong paths, expectations, dreams, stories, and all that shakes and rattles at the gates of the image. Nothing imaginary, nothing but the real: the real is the real of the melee. A true passport photo, a true "photo of identity," would be an indefinite melee of photos and graphics that would resemble nothing and beneath which the proper name would be inscribed as a caption.

～

This caption would have to be read, decoded, and narrated—but it wouldn't be a myth: that is precisely to say, it wouldn't confer an identity upon the *ipse* or upon someone for whom it would be the *legendum est*, the "this is to be read." What is to be read is what has been written. Myth isn't written: it's projected and proffered, pure flourish or upsurge, without trace, without history. Not only does myth identify, but, above all, it identifies itself: it is the infinite presupposition of its identity and of its authenticity. If I say "Ares," "Aphrodite," "Hermes," or "France" in a mythic mode, I may have already said in these names more than all that can be said about them—and we can never say anything legitimate about them that would not have been authenticated in them in advance. Only the voice of France can utter what is French. Myth is sense that is its own subject, the proper name as the idiosemy of an idiolect.

But what is written and what is there to be read is something that doesn't precede its own tracing; it is the melee of the traces of a sense that gets lost as it seeks itself and invents itself. Only today I read that Sarajevo is a city made up of at least three cities, both successive and simultaneous. I read that Bosna-Saray is mixed together with Milijacka and with Ilidza.

Translated by Steven Miller

14

Responding to Existence

For what are we responsible? For the possible effects of the space probe that passes outside the solar system; for the fragile constitution of Bosnia-Herzegovina; for the juridical problems posed by the Internet; for the transformation of the objects of African rituals into art curios; for the spread of AIDS; for the return of scurvy; for the invention of marine agriculture; for television programs; for public support of poetry; for poetry with or without support; for the memory and the explanation of all genocides; for the history of the West, now spread to the entire world, at least in Deleuze's sense when he says that "we are not responsible for the victims but responsible before them."[1] Ultimately, we are responsible for everything that could possibly be said to concern action or morals, nature or history; we are responsible—so we tell ourselves, and so, in any case, thinkers and writers tell us—for being, for God, for the law, for death, for birth, for our own existence, for beings as a whole. But which we? We, each one of us, insofar as we know where the individual begins and ends (and it is surely from the standpoint of responsibility that things are least determinable); but also we, all of us, insofar as we know what it is to be-together (and here again responsibility makes choice into a problem). Knowing this, and the problems or aporias that follow from it, is our responsibility. As for knowing or thinking what is meant by a responsibility limited by nothing in space or time, limited neither by imputing subjects nor by fields of application, this is, again and above all, our responsibility, a responsibility, moreover, that faces no one but ourselves.

This isn't a caricature. If it initially seems like one, that is because it is hard for us to focus on a situation from which we can't take a distance and that, from every side, represents the self-consciousness of our times. Once there's nothing—no power, no index of *sense* or *nonsense*—that could be said to be in charge of a destiny (taken here in the broadest sense of the term: story, lot, providence, destination, etc.), once there is no authority that could measure responsibility for us, divide it into circumscribed parts and define its scope, then there is nothing that could be sheltered from a responsibility that slowly becomes identical to existence itself. Or, perhaps a little more accurately: if the word *destiny* still makes sense, however we choose to understand this (as tragedy or progress, salvation or catastrophe, liberation or errancy, *moira, anankē*, vocation, *envoi*), it will always be as *responsibility*. A measureless responsibility is only the measure of a destiny that defies all the dimensions of destiny itself.

At such an extreme, does the word "responsibility" still mean anything? Of course, a measureless responsibility is quite prepared to dissolve all actual responsibility by deferring it from one subject to the next ad infinitum and by drowning obligation in an absolute and ungraspable equation of freedom and necessity. A double ideology of general responsibility thus emerges: on the one hand, the responsibility of progressively greater collective authorities: organizations, States, markets, networks, systems; on the other, the progressively more open responsibility of the individual, who is required to take charge of his or her own life, his or her own work, leisure, environment, relations, and, since one thing leads to the next, the entire interdependence of systems themselves. On the one hand, it calls for connections without either interruption or end; on the other, it calls for effective solidarities between subjects who are themselves supposed to be absolute persons of reason and right. Ultimately, these two sides cover each other and dissolve into one another. The responsible subject escapes and is still at large.

In this regard, there can be no doubt that the moral, juridical, and political task is always going to be that of determining—in legislation, in evaluation, in the instruction of cases—what it is that will allow us prudently to determine (in the old and strongest sense of the word "prudence," which, in fact, paves the way for the sense of the word "responsibility") the measure of an imputable responsibility. And yet, like a mounting responsibility whose charge is neither given nor programmed, this means that the "reasonable" and the "acceptable" can be only mediocre and even labile means. If we were able to distinguish between essences, we might say that, in a world of guilt, relation to the law is fixed and given, whereas in a world of responsibility, the subject's engagement precedes and exceeds the law. (Between them, we might situate the Christian world of sin, in which it is the sinner who is first accused rather than the crime itself.) This is also why the exercise of responsibility can be rewarded and honored as well as punished according to its outcome; in the same way, I can make myself responsible for something for which no other authority can charge me.

Without there being any legislator to give us an *a priori* measure, if it falls thus to us to take responsibility for measuring responsibilities and for discerning responsible persons as well as their obligations and engagements, then our self-consciousness of our times wouldn't grasp in vain at a disturbing excess of responsibility that can equally lead toward the anguish of irresponsible gaiety. We call *responsible* any being capable of promising: thus Nietzsche, who was doubtless the first to speak of a total responsibility, of a humanity boundlessly responsible to itself and to the world.[2] Humanity becomes thus the promise of itself. And this, perhaps, is modern history and its worlding: not simply being *given*, any more than being simply promised or given over by someone to someone else, but being a promise of the self such that the "self" ends up being confused with this promise and is bound thus to answer the anticipation of an infinite law—"to stand security for one's own future," Nietzsche says.[3] Surely this is our truth; strange, provocative, incisive, like all truth.

Now, it's not by chance that Nietzsche calls the subject of this responsibility "the philosopher." He writes: "The philosopher as *we* understand him, we free spirits—, as the man of the most comprehensive responsibility who bears the burden of the over-all development of mankind."[4] We can read this phrase in one of two ways. We can understand it as basically "totalitarian" and thus suppose that the "philosopher" is a distinct—individual or collective—figure, the messenger of a vision of humanity upon which he undertakes to model humanity. But we can also read it as saying that what is named or, rather, denoted here by "the philosopher" isn't a figure living out a fantasy but is defined only by this measureless responsibility that is itself the responsibility of man insofar as he is determined *not* as man but, as Nietzsche says immediately afterward, as the "as yet undetermined animal."[5] "Philosophy" means, therefore, neither knowledge nor belief, but responsibility for what is neither knowledge nor revelation, for what is not available, for what does not even have concept or signification.

In this way, Nietszsche's phrases punctuate what must surely be seen as one of the most powerful traditions of modern philosophy, if not its tradition par excellence or its first virtue: it places at the apex or end of thought the act of commitment to an unconditional demand, a demand that doesn't come to it from outside itself or from outside thinking thought as the thinking of humanity in the double sense of the genitive. In fact, this was already present in the sense that Kant gave to the notion of freedom and, with it, to a responsibility in which the subject—the "intelligible person"—is confronted in itself as if by a "holy being" and sees "all our duties" as divine commands.[6] These very duties, however, are properly without end; they are the duty to treat humanity—defined not by any *given* rationality or any nature but as the being of ends alone—as an end in itself. Kant's conception of humanity, to which we are all heirs, lies in being responsible for oneself as an infinite end.

Were there more space we could show how this thought is deployed and modulated in Hegel (for whom Reason is nothing given and consists only in engaging and deciding for itself), in Schopenhauer, in Kierkegaard, in Marx, in Husserl (who, in his marginal notes to *Being and Time*, addresses the possibility of what he calls the philosophy of "absolute responsibility"),[7] in Bruno Bauch or Nicolaï Hartmann, in Heidegger (for whom ontological being-in-debt is founded upon the ontic model of responsibility).[8] (Allow me to break off at this point in order to point out that there would be plenty to say about the importance of the general and generalized thinking about responsibility that took place in the twenties and thirties, just after the Great War, and about the way in which this thinking engages in an intimate and complex discussion around the motifs of destiny, history, or fatality—a discussion to which Valéry's reflections, for example, are a reliable witness). Finally, and as we know only too well, responsibility has had a continuous hold right up to our own time, whether in Sartre (let me cite just one remark that is perhaps emblematic in this regard: "to make ourselves responsible for the world as if it were our own creation"),[9] Blanchot, Adorno, Bloch, Levinas, Hans Jonas, or Derrida.

The common thread that ties together such disparate names is itself woven into two separate strands: first, there is the prevalent motif of responsibility, of being or existence ultimately defined by responsibility; second, there is the motif that philosophy or thinking is itself both responsibility and "absolute" responsibility. We need to focus on the interweaving of these two motifs in order to refine the observations opened up by Nietzsche. Not only has responsibility become a principle theme in modernity and, moreover, an ontological theme at that; not only has it become a theme of quite staggering range (in Jonas: responsibility for the entirety of history, for nature and culture, for God himself); more than all this, philosophy, which thinks this limitless responsibility, has come to see itself as the exercise of a sort of archi-responsibility. In other words, thinking isn't initially or only given in the form, the tone, or the style of knowledge or in a particular "conception of the world," but has been shown to be an engagement and a promise (a "prophecy" in Bloch's sense of the term). As a result, thinking has changed its tone, its style of writing; it ensures that what is at stake in and for it isn't just a representation or an interpretation but *itself*. In linguistic terms: this thinking is already the performative of the responsibility that it wants to think.

One response to this is to say that this was always philosophy's pretense and that, in fact, philosophy wouldn't know how to do without it. But once philosophy declares and "performs" or demonstrates itself to be responsible and absolutely responsible, it commits itself to sense and thus to a sense that is still to come, to sense's future, rather than merely describing or delivering sense as if it were already in place. Philosophy in *this* sense exposes rather than proposes; more accurately, its propositions (its meaning or its truth) are indissociable from the exposition through which it commits itself, promises itself, and risks itself.

This doesn't mean, then, that thinking is simply responsible. Rather, it is a thinking for which responsibility constitutes both the content *and* the act (or, drawing, tongue in cheek, on a more Husserlian vocabulary: *noema and noesis*). This thinking can only think in terms of responsible engagement: far from thinking denoting a disengagement from latent meaning, it denotes an opening onto a possible sense, a sense that isn't given but promised or guaranteed as something that is to come—"to come" not in the sense of something that will "definitely be there tomorrow" but, on the contrary, in the sense of something risked in the manner of the unknown and unforeseeable character of what is still to come. In short, the only thing that is assured is the risk; but the language of certainties is of little use here, and doesn't mean that the risk is covered over. It means that it is open.

Once again, however: what this thought commits to and takes re-

sponsibility for is responsibility itself, the content of a "responsibility principle." Redoubling, *mise en abyme,* or infinite regress, perhaps, but it is to
this that thinking commits itself; essentially, it is a matter of being responsible, of being absolutely responsible, of a responsibility without limits, of
a responsibility that is nothing less than being itself, a responsibility for beings as a whole or for God (Jonas) or one for the other (Levinas), for the
infinite or the absolute, for truth, for its eternity and the present of its
manifestation.

The question arises once more: For what is there responsibility?—a
question that is now sharpened or disturbed by the insistent, obsessive testimony that philosophy bears, a testimony that is necessary regardless of
whether we disqualify it as ideology, as the illusion of the temporary substitution of a real failure and a deception of action, or approach it head on
in order to understand it.

~

In what does absolute responsibility consist, therefore—whether as a
responsibility *to* responsibility itself or as a responsibility *for* responsibility?
In what does pure responsibility consist, responsibility that is responsible
for nothing definite and that is faced with itself alone, but faced with itself
as if it were faced with every other and as if it were faced in another direction entirely, facing a subject of responsibility defined only by an *analogon*
of holiness, for whom, still according to Kant, this analogical character is
precisely what removes all positivity, all determination? Yes, it is described
in terms of holiness, but this holiness is without paradise or beatitude,
without glory, without grace, without virtue.

What we have to do, therefore, is think this responsibility as nothing
other than the responsibility of sense. But sense is still, is always, what responds to a responsibility. By this I mean that while we are absolutely responsible for sense, while sense (or truth; in this instance I'd be prepared to
run them together) is that for which we are responsible, sense isn't just one
more thing for which we can be responsible (like the management of a job,
the solidity of a wall, health, happiness, or someone's life). Sense is not in
itself independent of the responsibility of sense. It only gives itself to a being that is in a position to answer for it. Every act of language, every exchange of signs, consists in the anticipation of sense, the promise or guarantee that what ought to come from the other alone and be or make sense

only in, for, and by him will actually reach the other—as well as the other in me. As such, it's not that I grant sense because I already possess it. It's not that I draw on a secure reserve of sense that I simply then transmit. Rather, I promise, I anticipate a sense that is not yet there and will, in fact, never be there as something completed and presentable, a sense that is always in and according to the other, making sense only by being exposed to the other, to the risk of not making sense, to the always certain risk of changing the sense of the other and so of always being other, always being altered, always being outside, being by itself, as sense, a being-infinitely-for-of-the-other.

Without this infinity, there is no sense; as such, it is nothing less than an unreserved responsibility for this infinity. Absolute responsibility came to us with the absolute infinity of grounds and ends, with the moral law and the starry sky, with the death of God and the birth of the world, that is to say, with existence submitted to our absolute responsibility. Nothing else counts, nothing else is seriously at stake, above all not those values, virtues, and supplements of the soul that some have made a profession of spouting and that have no sense outside the absolute break with all received horizons.

What continually precedes itself in another or—and the two are much the same—the aspect of the other that continually precedes itself in me and hence in all others, assuming that nothing holds this proliferation back and fixes it, is sense: a sense that has neither direction nor signification, which takes every possible means [*voies*] of exchange, and plays with all the references [*renvois*] of the sign. What makes sense is always beyond sense, in truth: a future, an encounter, a work, an event; and once the future has become present, once the encounter has taken place, the work realized, the event faded, then sense—their own sense—moves along again, passing beyond and elsewhere. When we're given a reason to live, always supposing that this happens, when such a reason is given, deposited and available (whether it takes the form of the life of a child or of a just society), it still has to have another reason beyond it, beyond even life or justice, one that is not present—this is the moment of dying, which is yet another way in which sense is punctuated by the truth of its referral to the other and of its absence of certainty. Sense is only guaranteed by its own movement of expansion or flight—or, if you prefer, its own imminent contagion or its own transcendent excess.

Sense, then, has the same structure as responsibility: it is engagement, oath. *Spondere* is to engage by a ritualized oath.[10] To one's *sponsio*, the other's *re-sponsio* responds. The response is first of all a re-engagement—an engagement in return for what engaged us or what engaged itself for us: the world, existence, others. It is a guaranteed exchange without any guarantee of making sense. It is a mutual pledge to truthfulness without which neither speech nor expression [*regard*] would be possible. So, when one answers *for*, one also responds *to*—to a call, to an invitation, to a question or to a defiance of sense. And when one responds *to*, one answers *for*—for the sense that is promised or guaranteed. If I'm asked the time, I guarantee that I will give the right time. If I'm asked about love or justice, I guarantee the unassureable infinity of these words. What we usually call a "response" is a solution; here, though, it is a matter of the referral or the return [*renvoi*] of the promise or the engagement. Sense is the engagement between several beings, and truth always, inevitably, lies in this between or in this with.

This is our responsibility: it isn't a task assigned to us, but an assignment that constitutes our being. We exist *as* this responsibility; that is, to use Heidegger's term, we *ek-sist*, we are exposed to one another and together to world, to the world that is nothing other than this exposition itself. Existence is responsibility for existence. To which we should immediately add: we can substitute the difficult word "democracy," but the logic is the same.

This responsibility is as empty as it is absolute. This emptiness is its truth: the opening of sense. This emptiness is everything, therefore, everything except nothingness in the sense that nihilism understands it. Nihilism affirms that there is no sense, that the heavens of sense are empty. *In a sense*, absolute responsibility says the same thing: that there is no given (present, available, configured, attested, deposited, assured) sense, that sense can never be given. It says that existence is engaged in this absence of the given in order to give sense every chance—indeed, perhaps sense is made up of nothing but chances.

∼

There is a measureless responsibility because there is, on the one hand, an unlimited interdependence of humans, of things, of nature and history, of information and decision, and, on the other hand, an imputing subject who is nothing other than each and every one of us together, and in each and every one of us an indefinite number of instances, degrees, stages, and connections. We might well go along with Derrida, therefore, in saying that "consciousness of a *limited responsibility* is a '*good conscience*'" and that "good conscience" is the negation of conscience.[11] The responsibility of the "intelligible person" has boiled down to the responsibility of the world. The world is responsible for itself. Better still: the world—or the totality of sense's references—*is* this responsibility and nothing else. The world is constituted thus by a promise-of-self, by an anticipation of its being and its world-truth. Here, however, anticipation does not mean forecasting or predicting a future. Yes, it involves foresight, but it assures no providence. It signals that the world precedes itself, passes beyond itself, transcends or transgresses itself in a sense-of-the-world that is its truth. This movement beyond the self toward the other, this excess of the other in the self, is both sense and responsibility. Each in the other and each for the other: this is what we call thinking.

Thinking, though, not in the sense of a reserved exercise or a philosophical discipline, but in the sense of the responsible *praxis* of sense. Thinking in the sense of its becoming the oath of truth, the engagement, the pledge and the putting into play of the response to what never ceases to call, to "interpellate," as they say today, calling the subject of sense that everyone is. Indeed, each one of us is this subject to such an extent that each one of us is it infinitely, absolutely, well beyond or before all egoism, all individual personality or community.

Hence, too, existence realizes that it is responsible "to the point of irresponsibility," as Blanchot was to say of Bataille, or as Adorno similarly said of art.[12] It knows that what it responds to is, in the end, the absence of response, and thus a total freedom and dispersion of responses. We have to be able to engage ourselves to the point of play and gaiety, of promising intoxication or of no longer promising anything.

We are responsible for sense, since sense is not the response of a signification that would saturate the announcement, the sending or the gift of sense, thereby bringing our responsibility to an end. This is why Ernst Tugendhat, for example, can define responsibility in community by calling into question what it is that defines the idea of the "good life" as an "appropriation (of this idea) on the model of the question of truth'" or on the model according to which "the perspective of the good is offered to us in the knowledge of nonknowledge."[13]

What's more, we can be fairly certain that no final signification—

God or Humanity, Knowledge or Justice, Power or Happiness—ever genuinely had as its function the abolition of the infinity of sense and the absoluteness of (ir)responsibility. What confronts us today is precisely the formal knowledge—the knowledge of nonknowledge, even—of the fact that every supreme signification always signifies, beyond itself, the responsibility for an ultimate irresponsibility of sense. In the last instance, we are accountants of the measureless, and this requires that we be able to bear and to settle, precisely and prudently, the absence of every given response and the eternal return of this silence in response. Existing requires nothing less of us.

This is the most rigorous and most severe of demands. It is the very place of rigor, logic, ethics, poetics, the place of responsibility that thought is: to resist being seized by a captation of sense, to resist identifying it, assigning it, or embodying it, figuring it or reifying it by turning it into doctrine or intellectual traffic. But to do so while ceaselessly and endlessly taking up the engagement, reengaging it beyond any possible certainty, to take the disproportionate risk, and to make of it our ownmost measure. Equally, and for the same reasons, to abdicate the serious pose and the pedantic precautions of those who would give lessons about responsibility.

Existence and democracy—if these words didn't have to denote the dull horizon of acquired certainties—democratic existence is neither a given, nor a matter of regime, nor an armature of rights. It is an equal and necessary sharing of thought as the absolute responsibility of sense.

And yet—as I hope I have made clear—it's not enough simply to name sense and then leave it to its indetermination, as if it were some sort of magic word. And this, even less than the word, which should serve me again today, is already visibly abandoned to usury or to inflation. "Sense," it should again be said, is not an available or constructable entity, any more than it is the more or less illusory fulfillment of its pure intention. Sense is what makes one return to the other and what therefore makes it so that there is one *with* the other. This is why it is always of the order of response: not the response to the question, which closes research or relieves the demand, but the response to the address. One always addresses the truth in me—and I always return the address to the truth in the other. It is often said that philosophy only poses questions. I would say that today it has to think only of the response: not a response-solution or a response-verdict, but a co-respondence. In such co-respondence—which defines our co-responsibility—there must be something that does not close the exchange but, on the contrary, institutes and relaunches it. There must be voices, timbres, and singular modes. These voices are in themselves, in their co-respondance, the creation of sense. Democratic responsibility is responsibility for such a creation. But immediately and from the outset, this means that democracy itself is not something given, an available sense. It is responsible precisely for what is not given: the *demos*, the people, the ones with the others.

Translated by Sara Guyer

Changing of the World

During the sixth decade of the twentieth century—the twentieth of these centuries counted up in the computer of a culture that they will soon overflow—a form of civilization, and thus a figure of existence, began to show the marks, the fissures, the inclinations of its disappearance, and so also the marks, fissures, inclinations of its metamorphosis into another configuration.

Not a "crisis," then, as was said for decades and as is sometimes still said today (decades later, while the displacement continues on its way, interminable and always barely perceptible, like all transformations that one day show that they have divided history into large, heterogeneous blocks). A crisis appears to a *continuum* that it affects and that it perhaps deforms or reforms, all the while keeping it as its point of reference. On the other hand, the metamorphosis (the rupture) of figures of existence takes place in a discontinuity of histories and in the incommensurability of their worlds, for which there is no point of reference. But the breach is at once so slow and proliferates so widely that it is only perceptible from afar, once it has been completed.

In fact, today, since the "sixties," we have been engaged in an analogous passage from one "age" to another. The twofold difference between these ages lies in the fact that, on the one hand, there is no Christianity (no eschatological resource) and, on the other, we now know that the course of history is continually broken up by the mortality of civilizations. No more than our distant ancestors, however, do we have the benefit of a vantage point from which we could see the fault opening beneath our feet, the shifts that are under way, or what it is that either makes the leap or is engulfed by it as it widens. Regardless of whether it's a matter of someone who has lived an entire lifetime or a matter of the generations that hand down memories, no aspect of the upheaval can be given a form or the reasons for it be provided.

Yet we are talking about major ruptures that affect everyone, every generation, and all their images, languages, ways of life. From one moment to the next, this opens in us, allowing us to see this vast drift [*dérive*] of the world. From one moment to the next, we find ourselves sensibly and physically outside ourselves, outside the blind slipping away of our little stretch of time. We see the night that borders our time, and we touch on some aspect of it—not the future, but the coming of something or someone: the coming of something that is already of us and of the world, but that has to come from somewhere else, displaced elsewhere into an unimaginable elsewhere.

Perhaps it is an ability to touch, in the darkness, this coming elsewhere, this breaching of time, of space, and of all orientation, that will have defined a character trait specific to modernity. Modernity knows itself to be exposed (this is both a threat *and* a desire) to what is not itself and is not there, but is nonetheless very close or continually approaching.

Exposed: turned toward, yes, but without thereby having either a specific course or a guide, perhaps without even an awaiting, but in a situation that verges on exceeding both waiting and nostalgia. Finally, despite everything, an inclination to be and to practice this riven (gaping? open? offered?) present. Neither comic nor tragic, this inclination could better be thought as an active abandonment, an engagement fixed on the impossible, that is, on the infinite possibility (the impossibility of saturating a signifying order) that lies at the heart of what has been thought under the name "finitude," a thought that has followed various paths between the stitches or folds of the "sixties."

(Of course, the division between decades doesn't have the same analytic relevance as the division between single years or centuries. It "fixes ideas," as it were, at a point at which nothing is fixed. But this kind of periodization, abusive as it is and overused as it has become—doubtless having become so since the "sixties" themselves, a term that, we should note, is an American one—indicates a stake and a concern, that of getting some hold on a passage or a rupture whose event, while sensible, gives a poor account of itself when marked as an evidential point: "1968," for example.)

~

So what, then, is at stake in this new and barely discernible present? It is a matter of the retreat of accomplishment, its model, its horizon, its normativity. It is a matter of thinking otherwise, elsewhere, from a different side; not in opposition to accomplishment, though, not in terms of a dissatisfaction and a lack, but in terms of a displacement as regards the opposition between what is lacking and what is accomplished.

Accomplishment has started to retreat from its values of completeness, of fulfillment and satisfied identification. The subject of accomplishment—although it would probably be more accurate to say the subject of practice, of carrying out or effectuation—is no longer the subject (of history, of knowledge, of humanity) that accomplishes itself in a return to itself. This subject has begun to shift, eroding its return-to-itself (its propriety, its authenticity, its purity) with a strangeness that is far closer to it than any being-self or any being-to-itself. The age-old saying "become what you are" has changed: "be what you are becoming," and be so to the very infinity of your possibilities, without any final consecration.

Hegemonic enterprises (the clash of powers) have turned into totalizing operations (absorption and exhaustion under a schema). One after another, these operations have killed off in their horror every destinal figure, every final representation: those of peoples, of a people, of *the* people, of humanity, even. The kingdom of ends has ended by been worn down. But it was only during the sixties that we could actually begin to discern the first traits of another space and the beginnings of another, unprecedented, sovereignty.

In fact, it was the so-called world wars—along with the as yet uninterrupted chain of postcolonial wars that followed in their wake—that opened up the possibility of the market becoming truly global; suddenly it seemed as though there was no more man, no more history, no more world spirit. True, capital, released from the old forms that had shackled it, has developed a terrifying autonomy and autotelism. At the same time, however, it reaches an extreme point where it is no longer opposed to or justified by anything; such is the double bind that slowly, quietly, gets tighter and tighter as we still profess our belief, here in socialism, there in humanism . . .

The market consumes itself. It becomes like the pure machine of the pure subject: the return to self of the most abstract identity, of a general equivalence that amounts to nothing but its own equivalence (to the averred nothingness of values). One way or another, the market will soon have no choice but to find a way out of this stranglehold or else go into convulsions.

The years of the "sixties" didn't see all this, but they did have some inkling of the progressive, insidious erosion of the checks on and justifications of capital. A fault in history opens up and widens, therefore: a suspension of sense.

Sense was assured by the distinction between different equivalencies (commercial, technological, democratic) and absolute value (humanity, dignity, community), itself articulated as the active relation between the progression of a history and its culmination in an end (knowledge, justice, nature). But this distinction has given way to a general circulation, a simple distinction between places or moments; this no longer seems to make sense, providing instead a combination or exchange of roles. Imperceptibly the category of "some day" has lost its appeal. The present appears devoid of either tradition or future; it has become an unheard-of enigma.

~

A general malaise, a paralysis, if you like, has taken hold of discourse. In a very short space of time, the same texts and the same theses that once inspired hope that the world might be made anew, discourses of resistance and renaissance always bound up, more or less openly, with the demand for revolution (itself understood as accomplishment), have shown their irrelevance. In this context, we would need to write the history of discourses on "alienation" and the difficulties into which they fell; more generally, though, what has been shown to be false is every thinking of propriety, the proper, the pure, the originary, or the authentic, whether these be individual or collective, whether they concern "sense," "nature," or "history." There are those who feel that these discourses did indeed make it through the war, but it was the war that cut into them, punctured them, put them beyond use.

It is not that the "war" (and everything that the word might denote in this context) was simply a ruinous crisis. The war, which was actually something very different from a war (this, at least, is one sense of the epithet "world" war), was already a kind of response to an upheaval from out of the very heart of things, from out of the accomplishment—or the exhaustion—of a certain form of existence. It took twenty years for that upheaval to start becoming visible.

For the moment, though, none of this is available to us, except as a sort of profound discomfort. Somewhere, discourse shattered, but it's hard to say exactly where. And it's not as if we have another discourse to fall back on. For a long time yet we will have to extend ourselves in the search for discourses that might supplement the one we have, relay it, start it over. And while this is going on, the nature of the rift is only going to become more evident. We have no other discourse; all we know is that something has been interrupted, broken down at the heart of discourses that, once cherished, have now become untenable (philosophies of history, moral philosophies, and even philosophies, literatures, and poetries as a whole). We have no other discourse because it is undoubtedly—we're just beginning to sense this—the general function of discourse itself that's at stake here: sense's distinction is coming to an end. It is as if all possible sense had been produced and, ultimately, "sense" itself turned out to be a crazed machine and the demand for it a senseless one.

Speech has been severed from speech, and speech now cuts short what it says. Language has begun to speak through and about the interruption of discourse. It's not a matter of a silence, however, since silence, along with its potential for mysticism or wisdom, has remained upstream from the interruption. Rather, it is a matter of another regime of speech, another concern, another way of working speech. Speech becomes difficult and withheld; it can no longer trust in the accomplishment of sense. It learns another confidence, one that it sets within its trajectory, its tracing, another way of being delivered over.

If language has become, in recent years, an object of an interest that is powerful and polymorphous (perverse, say those who refuse to understand), this is because it needs now to be received naked, the prestige of sense stripped away, and put back to work, to invention. There needs to be a meticulous decomposition of the effects and articulations of language; bit by bit, other voices need to be heard, addressed differently and with different rhythms. No longer a differential of sense but a differential of voice, therefore: something about song renders discourse asunder (breath, modulation, rhythmic transport of words, throat noise). At the same time, however, something strangles song.

~

By the same token, things emerge in a new light, in a region of presence that signification can no longer reach. All questions regarding presence (or the world) are transformed and begin to slip outside the remit of questioning (what is it? who is it? whence? why?) and to attain a new kind of assertion (given, withheld, withdrawn, touched). Such questions slip outside the remit of intention and interpretation, entering into another truth, flagrant, evanescent, pointed, suspended. This truth is no longer the truth of objects of knowledge—these take up precise places, ever better planned and articulated, in constant circulation—but the fantastic effect of Science suppresses itself. Knowledge shows itself to be endless, since it's no longer itself an end, an exponential development of proliferating technologies.

There is an unprecedented load of the real: things, matters, supports, skins, grains, and fibers. Art is displaced, therefore; it stops seeking out new forms and instead transforms itself and, imperceptibly, transports itself outside its site. Its horizon is no longer that of transfiguration, therefore, but of a patient practice this side of figures, flush against surfaces, bodies, clays, pulps, beats, or rhythms, in the very place where objects become strange, where the world is emptied, decomposed, or recomposed through and through.

It is no longer a matter of the composition of forms but a matter of touching on grounds, ploughing them, scratching them, pinching them, piercing them, moving thus to the far side of accomplishment, into beginnings, nascent states, alongside unfettered energies and unleashed tensions, the breaks and tremors of origins.

$\sim$

What is happening is that the immense coexistence of things and people, of beings (in short, the world), has begun to pull away from the representation of a destiny (from an arrangement, an Idea, a kingdom of ends), has started to matter in and of itself, to refer to and to network with itself; in short, it has started to comprise a co-existence. The sense of the world no longer lies outside of it; in it, it is its proximity and its strangeness, each one infinite.

This is why, in 1968, the politics of destination—of the model, of project or accomplishment, and might that not also be politics as a whole (or the politics of the "theologico-political"), if it's true that we have no other conception of it—first came to an end. The generalized "democracy" that has gone hand in hand with the generalization of the market is not another political figure; it's the retreat of the political.[1]

Whence the composite and contradictory character of a conjunction that mixes a crisis of democratic or market growth and a properly unprecedented retreat of schemas, discourses, ideals. "May '68" was neither a revolt, nor a reform, nor a revolution, although it borrowed from—or had something about—all three, yet in that respect was nothing new. The novelty came from the fact that each one of the three neutralized the others and that nothing really came of it. What actually took place (and went mostly unnoticed) was the retreat of various modes of political organization and signification. Whence, at the very moment of the events themselves, an entirely different notion of being-together. That is what was properly unprecedented and blinding. That was what made "1968" an event.

"Retreat" doesn't mean "abolition." On the contrary, it means to retrace, to pick up the traces by way of an effacement of signs and directions. The retreat retires behind forms, cuts into the grounds, the dark exterior and the palimpsest of rebeginnings.

The co-existence of the world (not "in" the world, since the world isn't a container but the extension of co-existence itself), devoid of any given composition, system, synthesis, or final assumption, is what has to be traced.

The culture that's coming to an end is one that thought the coherence of the world, its congruence, or its conformity with an order, a plan, a principle, or an end (immanent, transcendent, both immanent *and* transcendent). The culture in the offing has the job of co-existence, a co-existence that's bound neither to conformity nor to accomplishing itself. It consists in co-presence alone. And co-presence doesn't just refer to itself; it refers to everyone and to no one, the circulation of a sense that nothing either retains or saturates, a circulation found in the movement between places and beings, between all places and all beings, the infinite circulation of a sense that will end up having its entire sense in this *with*.

Granted, sense has never before welled up here and now rather than further away and later on, at a remove. Humanity has never taken place so exactly, so properly, any more than, say, the world, "nature," and "history," given within their strict measure: without epic or apocalypse, without assumption, without transfiguration, without exhalation. Yet a sense (a truth) as sober and as dense as the being-together of all the pieces of the world, whose proximity, whose community, it provides.

~

Over thirty years later, it would be possible for us to believe that nothing actually took place except collapse and engorgement: a world slumped in upon itself, saturated with physical, economic, and spiritual devastations. A humanity that knows only that it has destroyed itself—that it has its own nonbeing and the end of the world on its hands; such is the whole of its knowledge. A century and a millennium that know that they have failed to reach their goal.

What is the "historical mission" of capital of which Marx spoke, a mission that we have ended up forgetting all about simply in order to think another mission entirely, that of another Subject of history? It seems to me that this mission can only be that of paving the way to a knowledge of a hallucinated self: the knowledge of a self that has to ruin itself in order to be itself, of a richness that can only produce its own equivalence and hence its own annihilation (and, ultimately, its strict absence of any value whatsoever).

Now this knowledge isn't false. All the same, it's merely the knowledge of what's coming to an end and so fails to measure up to what never stops coming, what is neither end nor inauguration but the peculiar simultaneity of all things, unsettling, brutal, tense, and, despite everything, distributing each one of our places, alongside one another, in its cracked, gaping, open, offered present.

Finally, though, there is a sense of joy at the fact that there's neither an accomplished destiny nor one that needs to be accomplished, no solar or nocturnal substance with which it would need to be incorporated; instead, there are numerous bodies alongside one another, numerous points between which sense is spaced, shared, and scattered. A brief, almost dry moment of joy, without ecstasy or glory but as hard and alive as a flash of existence. An uncertain joy, then: almost the laughter of the insane.

Translated by Steven Miller

CODA

Res ipsa et ultima

"Is there something?" is a question that answers itself or renders itself redundant, if you like, since someone raises the question and this someone is something. In fact, before being—if it manages to be—this enigmatic or problematic *one* of someone, some*one* is something. *Quidam, res quaedam.*

In any case, this "before" doesn't denote the anteriority of a bedrock or a foundation. It is the belated anteriority of a "one" turning back on itself in order to be the one that it is, to be, in fact, the one that it is supposed to be, since *one*, as such, could never be found if it did not find itself, if it did not unify and thus relate to itself.

The thing that is someone before being someone would be this self-relation. But this relation isn't given, isn't achieved or effected, since it's only in the exercise of this relation and in its being acted out that there can, by chance, be any *one*. The only thing there could be, therefore, is the acting out of a relation and not the presence of a thing: a "subject" that is not "substance" but still underlies the *itself* which, in turn, considers the things around it. The whole of philosophy from Descartes to Husserl, with the notable exceptions of Nietzsche and Spinoza (who are not philosophers of the thing, but of force), has concerned itself with these things, often tormenting itself over them, which form the backbone of the contemporary exhaustion of the modern age.

A thing that thinks—*res cogitans*—is nothing other than a thing that relates itself to itself. A thing whose character as a thing, whose thinghood or whose thingness, as Beckett said, or whose reality (which, in Latin, is the same thing) consists in nothing other than such a relation, and not in a presence or in an existence, a being-there [*un être-là*]. "Thought" is nothing more and nothing less than everything that takes places in the mode of this relation, everything that shares its reality: feeling, wanting, imagining, conceiving, and so forth.

Res extensa, on the other hand, the extended thing, is what doesn't take place along the lines of this or, for that matter, any other relation, since all relation is ultimately a relation to and of the self: relation in general supposes that one relates, to the self or to the other. *Extensa* doesn't designate the quality of breadth, of surface magnitude: what is extended is what is precisely not "one" and what is "one" is precisely what is not extended, the *point*, say, which is what occurs at no point in space. Extension is not relation but exposure: the whole point about extension is that it is only ever exposed, put forth, turned outward without there being an inside, nowhere turned back in upon itself and hence devoid of "self."

Res cogitans, res extensa: everything hinges on the grammatical opposition of these two participle-epithets. The first is active, the second passive. One type of thing thinks (by itself, which is tautological), the other is extended by some other thing, or force, but not by itself. It has not *extended* itself. The thing that thinks can only think itself, no matter what it thinks, while the extended thing cannot extend itself: the extension is precisely what has exceeded the "self" in advance.

In relation or *exposed* are the two possible modalities of the thing in general. *In relation* supposes a subject that bears, that brings and that relates, because it can bear or present (to an apprehension, a perception, an intention) only if it has first related the thing to itself, only if it has appropriated it, only if it has grasped it and retained it, rendered it presentable. *Exposed* exclusively supposes being turned in all directions toward an exterior that is not, in turn, formed of other faces turned inward, without these faces relating in any way to the world, neither to each other or to themselves.

~

It remains to be seen what these two things have in common, at least in their denomination as *res*, as thing, which can itself be qualified thus: on the one side, as pure inside or as the infinite to-itself of relation

and, on the other, as pure exterior or as the infinite outside-itself of exposure [*l'exposition*].

(On the one side . . . on the other: but are there two sides to the
thing? Granted, it's hard to imagine a thing without sides, but is the inside
a side? It is latent, not lateral. And can the latent be lateral to the rest of lat-
erality? Is my soul the other side of my body, but still a side, still an exposed face? Or is all this just an assembly of sides, each one opposed and
exposed to the other from every direction [*sens*], lateral and patent as well
as latent? Nothing more than folded, enfolded, and unfolded sides or nothing but one immense side spread out, turned back, over, around, away, *lata
res ipsa latus*: it's this paradoxical physics and its accompanying geometry
than needs to be addressed here.)

This double qualification of the *res*—whether it be the effect of a
split, of a proliferation, of an outgrowth, or of a graft—gave birth to the
problem of the *res*, the problem of *reality*, a problem that will undoubtedly
have been the central problem of our own time (now, along with the problematic itself, moving toward exhaustion).

(Of course, and here as elsewhere, our own time has merely crystallized and sharpened the issues that have always bedeviled the West: sensi-
ble/intelligible, matter/spirit, outside/inside, improper/proper, thing/
sense, thing/event, other/self, impenetrable/impalpable, apparent/truthful,
worldly/divine, image/real, and so forth. Western history is the entire history of the problematic of the real. There is nothing very surprising in its
completing itself in the same way that it began, with the exacerbation of
the feeling that things themselves are disappearing and simulacra taking
over: this feeling, so typical of the old world, actually testifies to the ever
greater hold of the real that renews itself from start to finish.)

Now, how is it that the thing can lend itself to each of these modalities?

The problem can be resolved by resolving the name. Stop saying
"thing" and say instead *cogitans/extensum*, relational/exposed. Stop speaking of the real, except in order to speak its loss: old nihilism. Or, and this
is virtually the same thing, situate the authentic real in "spirit" and, on the
side of things, see only "thingification" or "reification," ideas that reputedly
mire the subject in its alienation.

Even the old nihilist himself, however, will soon have to realize that
passing in silence over the *res*—that is, the most general *res*, of which the
two *res* would be modes, the most general of *res* that would also be the
most real, the real itself, the real ground of the real as well as its capital [*son*

fonds], its realizing (if not wholly reifying) resource—does nothing but provoke unrest, insurrection, even, over the question of the real, the question of the *thing* or of *things*.

In fact, it's not hard to see that there can be no "relation" without "exposure," nor, consequently, one thing without the other: how could a self not turn toward a particular face, an outside, of this same self so as to relate to itself and thus to take place? How could a *self* be *its* thing without also being its *thing*? How could it be its *own* thing [*sa* propre *chose*] without also being *properly* a thing [proprement *chose*]? How, in short, does it realize itself?

Conversely: how could what is exposed *not* be exposed *to* this outside toward which it is directed but that is equally itself—endlessly the same outside, each one of its sides folded over and again? And how, then, could it not ultimately relate to itself? How could this "self" not end up resolving itself in this, its own reduction?

Still: how could the face that the self *exposes* in order to be a self *not* be its own outside, an outside that is nonetheless and necessarily improper to it, an other that is more fundamental to the self than the self itself, an other, then, that isn't the presupposition of the self but, more accurately, the presupposition of this very presupposition: the nonself, the surface putted with shadows devoid of all relation, the death's head pondered and handled by Hamlet or by the subject of the *Vanities*, the bony thing, hard and glistening, that disdainfully looks my way [*qui me regarde de nul regard*], a look with no regard for any presence that might face it but that dives into me as if into nothingness, relating to me in order to withdraw all relation and to expose me to my self-less self, which, in turn—a turn that is no longer my turn but the turn at which I have no more turns—is itself a glistening bone full of holes, dirt packed tight into the sockets.

~

Equally, however, the death's head runs the risk of distracting us from what it manifests (and it has done so throughout modern times). The way in which it is pondered and handled is equivocal, and this ambiguous fascination stems from the way in which the skull combines horror at our own disappearance (the end of all relation) with a maintaining of what disappears (the figure engaged in relation, its look and its rictus).

In this way it is still its own image that the self wants to bring before itself from and as the outside. It finds itself starting out again; it still relates to what exposes it and to which it is exposed: the subject, then, does not end up dialectizing its death, making death its thing after all.

But death is devoid of either figure or subject. It doesn't await me at the end like another me who would still be me turning back toward myself from the abyss. Rather, death is "here" from the moment that I am "here," at once and immediately my flesh and bones, the extension of what exposes *me*, the *res extensa* that opposes the *res cogitans* only to the extent that it exposes it, exposes it to itself.

It's time to put death in its place: in things, in the general connection and exposure of things, and so in the world, rather than in the hideous outside of a disfigured Subject (disfigured by the very hope of its transfiguration). Neither from within nor from without does death concern a *self*: this is its violent paradox, the paradox of being simultaneously so intimate and yet so improper, the paradox of having *already* liquidated the very intimacy that it was supposed to effect. Equally, though, it ought to denote the "death of God": the end of death as punishment, as annihilation and/or redemption and resurrection. Death becomes the absolute exposure that crosses all relation and all relations (to the self, to the other). Yet this doesn't mean that the thought of death becomes any more bearable. What it does mean, though, is that we have no relation to it, whether dialectical, tragic, mystical, whatever. Death isn't something, but the exposure of all things and—thereby—the condition of possibility for all relation (without it, everything would remain wrapped up in itself, heaped, massed, sunken, senseless).

There can only be relation (the return, the appropriation of a subject to itself or between subjects, it amounts to much the same thing) if we start with an absolute distancing, without which there would be no possibility of proximity, of identity or strangeness, of subjectivity or thinghood. First and foremost, however, this distancing distends relation to the point of exposition: scarcely am I born before I am outside myself at an infinite distance, outside simply turned out, exposed to the rest of the world, to all things. And the same goes for everything, each one exposing universal exposition differently.

Every thing outside all the others, every thing according to the stretching that spaces them and without which there would be just one indistinct thing gathered into the point at which it would annul itself, a thing unthinged, a de-realized *res*, a perfect, syncopated subject turned back in on itself without its having ever reached itself, an extinct, noiseless trinket, a *one* annihilated without its being dead: every thing, then, touching every part of every other thing, touching me in the same way, piece by piece, here and there, always, from time to time, exposing the infinity of our relations.

Things: the first stone that's thrown, a sheet of paper, galaxies, the wind, my television screen, a quark, my big toe, a trapped nerve, prostheses, organs planted or grafted beneath my skin, placed or exposed inside, all things exposing themselves and exposing us, between them and between us, between them and us, together and singularly.

~

They do so in two ways:

1. On the one hand, they border me, touch me—from a distance or from any distance, it's still a touch and all senses are senses of touch, including common sense and the sense of understanding or reason—they set me up within the multiple spaces of their spacings and according to the modes of contact particular to their respective faces, their grains, their textures (rough, shiny, prickly, harsh, supple, tight, loose, vaporous, sticky . . .); equally, they lead me to touch in turn, in an infinite number of ways, in infinite directions, with infinite gestures, in infinite senses.

Everything that touches thus—brushing up against, penetrating, distancing, knocking into, absorbing, presenting, kicking itself, hiding away, simply leaning against—all that makes up the world. The world is nothing other than the touch of all things and wherever nothing is touching, wherever contact is severed, there is nothing; this is the absolute exposure of the world turned toward an outside that never takes place, an outside that immediately turns back to the point at which the world is exposed to the universal touch of itself alone, to the point at which its "self" is concealed, to the point that makes up its entire sense.

For that same reason the sense of the world is no different from its polymorphous spacing (attraction, repulsion, curvatures of space-time, expansion, retraction, the initial or final explosion), which itself has no other sense than the cosmic contact of all things, no other sense than this sensing-of-itself that cannot be gathered as a whole.

There is no *self* of the world, no universal subject through which this touch could touch itself.

2. On the other hand, things expose the self, refuse to allow it to come to rest in itself and instead drag it and stretch it outside itself without ever leaving it to itself. "Self" is the universal relation of sense that runs through everything, from atom to man, from chlorophyll to plasma, from stone to iron and from grain to flesh, the relation that endlessly relates *itself* without ever relating anything more than what is exposed to what is exposed: the interiority of an infinite exterior.

∽

The thing is what the *res cogitans* and the *res extensa* have in common: it is their mutual, inextricable intrication. The early Descartes was well aware of this when he attributed a quite different reality to the union of the two things, from an evidence as powerful as that of the *ego* (*cogito*), but from an evidence that is entirely ordinary and immanent to the course of things, from an evidence present on the very surface of the most everyday experience of existence; an evidence that is given without thinking. There's nothing to prove; there's nothing but the test of the real [*il n'y a pas à prouver, il n'y a qu'à éprouver le réel*].

The first and last real, the ground of the real and the ground of the *res* in all its modes, *ultima res*, is the identity and difference of relation and exposure: more accurately, it is this identity *in* its difference and this difference *in* its identity (and here, *in* obviously means *outside*). The two are the same, the same *thing*—insofar as they turn things toward one another; but they differ absolutely—have *nothing* in common—since relation refers to an inside and exposure to an outside. They never encounter one another; rather, they pass through one another. The fact that one moves in the other, and vice versa, doesn't change anything; they are oblivious to one another and exclude one another as they change roles.

All of which means, then, that the "inside" and the "outside" of the world, the self and the outside-the-self, subject and thing, are strangely, paradoxically even, the same: the same real that stems from nothing and no one, that comes from nowhere and goes nowhere, that rests on no ground and goes uninterpreted, that exists by the mere fact of existing, by a perfect necessity that equates to an equally perfect contingency or to the unprecedented freedom of a being that is merely the chance and the risk of an ontological surprise.

∽

The thing itself, *res ipsa et ultima*, is not a particular thing. It is nothing.

More precisely, it is the *sameness of nothing*: the nothing relates to itself, yes, but, being precisely nothing, it is simply and immediately exposed as something, and therein lies the reason of the world—its *ultima ratio*—and its true *creatio ex nihilo*: the fact that there is something as an outcome of nothing.

By the same logic, however, the fact that there is something never appears as such: there is no such thing as "the" thing "in itself" or for itself. The thing doesn't stem from itself nor do things stem from the thing, from its essence, its origin or its substrate. Even if there is *some* thing, anything whatsoever, indeterminate and indifferent, then there is still nothing, since the indeterminate and the undifferentiated do not exist. (They do not exist, do not emerge from the pure nothingness that pure being in itself is.) "There is something" can only mean one thing: yes, there is something, no matter what it is, but every time that there is, this *what* is determined, singular, different, and hence there are already more than one of them.

If there is something, then there are some things, lots of them, whether they be shells or eyebrows, clouds or hammers: several, many, different in number as well as quality. The profusions of nature and the profusions of technology contribute to the same sort of abundance, an abundance that isn't an end.

Foam, erase, tooth, canvas, synapse, liquid crystal, tentacle, scale, plank, spume, fingernail, hail, neutron, lymph . . . and so ever indefinitely on. The time of modernity is followed by the time of things.

Translated by Steven Miller

Notes

NOTE: This essay appeared in French as "Une Pensée finie," in Jean-Luc Nancy, *Une Pensée finie* (Paris: Galilée, 1990), 9–53.

1. Friedrich Nietzsche, *Die fröhliche Wissenschaft*, in *Kritische Studienausgabe*, ed. Giorgio Colli and Mazzino Montinari (Berlin: Walter de Gruyter, 1988), 3: §357. Henceforth cited as KSA, followed by volume and page number. Translated by Josefine Nauckhoff as *The Gay Science* (Cambridge: Cambridge University Press, 2001).

2. Martin Heidegger, "Davoser Disputation zwischen Ernst Cassirer und Martin Heidegger," in *Kant und das Problem der Metaphysik, Gesamtausgabe* 3 (Frankfurt a. M.: Vittorio Klostermann, 1992), 295–96; translated by Richard Taft as *Kant and the Problem of Metaphysics* (Bloomington: Indiana University Press, 1990), 185. Henceforth cited as KPM, followed by page numbers of the German and English versions.

3. I should like to reproduce here some lines previously published in *Lettre internationale* 24 (spring 1990), in response to the events of that year in Europe. They were originally entitled "To be continued"—and I continue them here.

> No one is taken in. This is not just a crisis, or even an end of "ideologies." It is a generalized debacle of sense. "Sense" must be understood in all its senses: the sense [direction] of history, the sense [feeling] of community, the sense [direction] of peoples and nations, the sense [meaning] of existence, the sense of any transcendence or immanence whatsoever. And that's not all: it is not just the contents of sense, the meanings—all our meanings—that are now invalidated. Rather, a strange black hole is growing at the very site of the formation, birth, or donation of sense. It is as if, in the dissolution of this originary power of making or receiving sense whose many figures make up, along the way to ourselves, the history of the modern Subject (the subject of philosophy, of politics, of history, of practice, of faith, of communication, of art), a world, or worlds, or pieces of worlds, were emerg-

ing, with no one there to receive, perceive, or conceive them as a "world." The "West" can no longer receive the collapsing "East."

"Consciousness is always consciousness of something," being first of all "consciousness of self": that was our thinking in shorthand form, but now appear things that proliferate without being the objects of any consciousness, as there appear wandering "selves" with no conscious relation to themselves. "Every action aims toward the shared dwelling-place of a kingdom of freedom": such were our maxims, in shorthand form. But now each word of the formula bears the burden of an irreparable disaster.

No one is taken in. In the event, the best witnesses are those who seize grossly upon the situation to bring out their intellectual merchandise, which really is nothing but merchandise, with an expiration date long past: "liberalism," "humanism," "dialogue," "investing in people," "open socialism," "democracy" are words that even their users pronounce only with prudence, in a minor key, anxious not to lose the last pale vestiges of sense that cling to them. To be sure, the enthusiasm of those who were able to swing a pickax at the Berlin Wall is understandable and broadly shared. And likewise for those who threw out Marcos, and now Ceaucescu, and those who marched in the streets of Pretoria. But everyone also, without saying so out loud, understands and shares the discretion that follows such moments. Discretion is advised, or else no one admits the right, or the power, of being indiscreet.

Being indiscreet would mean only one thing: raising the problem of sense, or, if it is better to use a more classical, more sharply etched language, the problem of aims—of ends, of finality in general. Finality is the one topic on which the "beautiful souls" of neo-liberalism, neo-democracy, neo-aestheticism or neo-ethics are most discreet. To be sure, they speak endlessly in terms of "goals" (of "horizons," of "futures"), since such is the ordinary and obligatory diet of our thinking (and a sort of shorthand for it). But everyone is careful to avoid saying this: that all our finalities are intrinsically related to patterns of transcendence or immanence of sense that now, discreetly, go unmentioned.

Capitulation or avoidance are the responses to this fact: that the question of ends is henceforth completely in play, exhibited unreservedly before us, and not only, nor even primarily, in the form of the question "Which ends?" but as the question of the very *idea* of an "end." A fair share of contemporary intelligence is stubbornly dedicated to this deceptive maneuver.

Not that the question has failed to be raised. The exact history of thirty years of thinking has yet to be written. But the neo-liberal, neo-socialist consensus obstinately turns away from the task . . . (to be continued).

4. KPM 236 / 161. The immediate context of this phrase doesn't do it justice. Heidegger seems here to remain caught in a relativistic conception of "finite thinking," which would remain simply one "possibility" among many, unable to claim

any knowledge of finitude's "truth in itself." This requires clarification, at the very least. We don't know finitude "in itself." However, this isn't the effect of perspectivism but because there is no finitude "in itself." It is with this that we need to concern ourselves, and not the rhetoric of the modesty of thinking within which Heidegger remains trapped.

5. Nietzsche, Husserl, Derrida's reading of Husserl, Marion's reading of Husserl, Heidegger, and Deleuze are all presupposed here. This goes without saying, but it's best to say it anyway.

6. Hegel, in the *Aesthetics* (of course), had already admired the double sense of *Sinn*.

7. See "Elliptical Sense," below.

8. Martin Heidegger, *Sein und Zeit* (Tübingen: Max Niemeyer, 1993), §31. I note in passing that, although this book defines the principle of a "deconstruction" of *sense*, as the sense *of being*, Heidegger still remains within a double regime, and a classical one at that, of the presentation of sense: on the one hand, as "understanding"; on the other, as "sensing" or "state-of-mind" (*Befindlichkeit*). He repeats that the two are indissociable, but the two remain two, and Heidegger doesn't explicitly question this duality.

9. See Max Loreau, *La Genèse du phénomène* (Paris: Minuit, 1989), 301: "There is no being that is distinct from the sense of being."

10. Martin Heidegger, *Beiträge zur Philosophie, Gesamtausgabe* 65 (Frankfurt a. M.: Vittorio Klostermann, 1989), 268–69.

11. Heidegger evokes the possibility of this in "What is Philosophy?" In this sense, the difference between being and beings could not even be assigned as "difference." Being which *is* (transitively) beings only differs from the latter insofar as this very difference differs from a difference between "being" (intransitive) and beings. This last difference (which is most often taken to be the sense of the "ontico-ontological difference") differs, therefore, from itself: being does not occur as being. This is what Jacques Derrida has sought to bring out with the neither-word-nor-concept "differance." As he writes: "Finite difference is infinite" (*La Voix et le phénomène* [Paris: Presses Universitaires de France, 1967], xxx; translated by David Allison as *Speech and Phenomena* [Evanston: Northwestern University Press, 1973]). "This sentence, I fear, is meaningless," he once said. Perhaps, but it does make sense.

12. If we use the translation "for death," we introduce a finality that is wholly foreign to the text. Alternatively, the "for," the *zum*, better translated as *toward* or *to*, has to be reinterpreted. In any case, death needs to be thought here independently of all sacrificial logic, a task that would also require a critique and a deconstruction of this motif in Heidegger himself. See "The Unsacrificeable," below.

13. KPM 225–6 / 154. What follows takes the whole of §41 as its point of departure. [Each of the citations in what follows come from § 41.—Trans.]

14. And if, as a consequence, *existence* ("ek-sistence") ought not to be extended, albeit in modal form, but understood more broadly as simply human. This is a dif-

ficult question—one I have already broached in *L'Expérience de la liberté* (Paris: Galilée, 1988); translated by Bridget McDonald as *The Experience of Freedom* (Stanford: Stanford University Press, 1993)—and one that Heidegger himself didn't foresee. It is basically the question of the *existence of the world*. Not simply as the question What is the sense of (human) existence? but also, if the world is inseparable from it, if it isn't the contingent context of an existentiality but the very site of it, Why is there the world, in its totality? Not simply Why is there something? in general, but also Why is there what there is, all of what there is, and *nothing* but what there is? And so, too, Why the proliferating difference among beings, men, animals, vegetables, minerals, galaxies, and meteorites? In this regard, it must be said that it is difficult to reduce "the stone in the stone" to a "pure" immanence; "immanence," in other words, is also and in a way "to itself." The stone isn't an essence (otherwise how could its hardness *feel* hard?), an essence for the understanding alone. (On the stone, see Spinoza, *Ethics* 2, proposition 13, scholium). But in order to understand, or to touch, the minute, heavy, *almost inexistent* modality of stone's existence, we must doubtless turn to literature. In John Updike's *The Witches of Eastwick* (Harmondsworth, Middlesex: Penguin, 1985), 199, we read this, for example: "How magnificent and abysmal pebbles are! They lie all around us billions of years old, not only rounded smooth by centuries of the sea's tumbling but by their very matter churned and remixed by the rising of mountains and their chronic erosion, not once but often in the vast receding cone of aeons." Here, the existence of stones (reduced, I grant, to lying all around and to the churning of their matter) *isn't* their relation to a subjectivity; rather, it's precisely the opposite: in writing, a subjectivity reaches out to touch, as if with its fingertips, that without which there would be nothing to write, which remains outside, which is the world, and which, though, it's true, only presents itself as "existing" in this same gesture of writing. "There is" doesn't belong to the order of having. On being addressed in terms of having, see Alain Badiou's remarks on Gilles Deleuze's *Pli, Annuaire philosophique* (Paris: Seuil, 1989), 170. The verb "to have" slips from appropriation to being through the instantaneous diffraction, dislocation, and dissemination of the "having" of "being": it has no essence, all there is is being in a "there" that neither pre-exists it nor is external to it. All it "has" is the "there" of being, the "there" of every "there is." "There" doesn't exactly take up either having or being, just as it's not exactly spatial or temporal. (See my "Le Cœur des choses," in *Une Pensée finie* [Paris: Galilée, 1990], 197–224; translated by Brian Holmes and Rodney Trumble as "The Heart of Things," in Jean-Luc Nancy, *The Birth to Presence* [Stanford: Stanford University Press, 1993], 167–88.) Let us say: it takes up the event. The question, though, is: *Whence* the event of the world? Where does the world-event, in the singular dissemination of its events (which it doesn't have, but which it is, being only that), come from? From the stone? From the eruption of being that comprises being, from the eruption of being that *is* being. In these conditions, *there are only* events (essences and facts are for the understanding), and every event has the structure of the world-event. Or rather, all events are substitutable, and all are singularities. Not indifferent, but substitutable, *as singularities*, as the *absolute*, each time, of a singular. And how could there be sense if an event did not communicate (with) all events? But how could sense not be *finite* if this communication itself did not take place as a transmission of having (of qualities, of properties), but only as this universal substitutability of the "world-event"? The latter comes therefore from this—which is to say, it comes from nowhere and no one; neither from atoms nor from God. Equally, though, neither atoms (with the *clinamen*) nor God (the creator, not the supreme being, if they can be distinguished) have doubtless ever truly been thought otherwise than as the eventuality of the world without an assignable or unifiable origin. "Atom" or "God" have been the infinitizing goals of the thought of finite sense. The provenance of the world lies neither in a thoughtfulness, nor in providence. The world comes *from* its event. It *exists* therefore *right through*— even though existence is not homogeneous in itself, of man, of the stone, or of the fish. There is only sense in touching that. But in touching that, there is only finite sense.

15. Here, we would need to go back to the whole argument of *The Experience of Freedom*, the displacement of the concept of freedom as the self-legislation of an infinite Subject into that of the exposition of a finite being.

16. See my "Posséder la vérite dans une âme et un corps," in *Une Pensée finie*, 325–51; translated by Rodney Trumble as "To Possess Truth in One Soul and One Body," in *The Birth to Presence*, 284–306. As for Marx, and for those who find themselves astonished to see a thinking of finitude attributed to him, let me say that for Marx this is connected with his constant and decisive appeal to the "real," in particular to its materiality, to the ineffectiveness of all generality, and even to the contingent character of nature and history. That man remains, for Marx, generic man doesn't stop the beginning of the decomposition of the essence of man, in history *and* in freedom.

17. Here, though, I'm not really thinking about Rimbaud, but about Nietzsche and Bataille.

18. In speaking of *access*, I am, of course, thinking about Bataille—and about a different reference from the preceding one. Whatever else may need to be said, it's with Bataille that this demand emerges in all its nakedness.

19. See my "L'Histoire finie," in Jean-Luc Nancy, *La Communauté désoeuvrée* (Paris: Bourgois, 1990), 237–78; first published in English as "Finite History," in *The States of "Theory": History, Art, and Critical Discourse*, ed. David Carroll (New York: Columbia University Press, 1990), 149–72; reprinted in *The Birth to Presence*, 143–66.

20. See "The *Kategorein* of Excess," below.—Ed.

21. See *The Experience of Freedom*, chap. 12.—Ed.

22. And so, too, without going down the path of sacrifice. Misfortune and sickness can call, in different ways, on sacrifice: *we* no longer can. See "The Unsacrificeable," below.

23. Rereading Spinoza, therefore. But also Plato. The "Good," situated *epekeina tēs ousias*, "beyond being or beyond essence," isn't the good of a moral norm. Rather, it is reason and the end of all things: the beginning of every thought of the end.

24. Here one might refer to Jean-François Lyotard's analyses of the time that capital "does not leave untouched" (in *L'Inhuman: Causeries sur le temps* [Paris: Galilée, 1989], translated by Geoffrey Bennington and Rachel Bowlby as *The Inhuman: Reflections on Time* [Stanford: Stanford University Press, 1991]) and those of André Gorz in his several publications on the reduction of the workday. For the replacement of generic "man" by "singularities," see Etienne Balibar, *La Proposition de l'égaliberté* (Conférences du Perroquet, 1989).

25. Laziness and cowardice, once again. For a survey of the state of the problem, see Pascal Dumontier, *Les Situationnistes et mai 68* (Paris: Gérard Lebovici, 1990). He speaks advisedly of a "concerted silence around the topic of May '68" (13).

26. A critique carried on and then diverted or turned back by Baudrillard, who embodies, in a sense, the limits of a critique of "simulation," itself still a tributary of representation.

27. This is the sole question raised by the "end of art"—and so, too, by the birth of something else, for which the name "art" is perhaps no longer suited. I've dealt with this in "Portrait de l'art en jeune fille," in *Le Poids d'une pensée* (Grenoble: Presses Universitaires de Grenoble, 1991).

28. I'm borrowing the word "mimesis" from Philippe Lacoue-Labarthe, attempting to sum up the movement of his thinking of this concept. Moreover, I would like, and it would be useful, to demonstrate the convergence, albeit distant, of this thinking with Gilles Deleuze's thoughts about an "image" that owes nothing to representation.

29. From which it follows that the Greek *phusis*, with its complex relation to *technē*, a relation that renders the two indistinguishable, isn't "nature" in this sense. This is one of Heidegger's central theses, although he was unable to draw out its full consequences and instead allowed *phusis* to assume once again the guise of a kind of original immanence. The reactive part of his thinking about "technology" is entirely of a piece with this (although it's perhaps worth adding that Heidegger wasn't confronted by the kinds of technology we know today). On the ambiguity of Heidegger's theses about technology, see Avital Ronell, *The Telephone Book* (Lincoln: University of Nebraska Press, 1989).

30. Here we can most clearly see the error in Heidegger's conflation of the camps with the "agricultural food industry" in a single, blanket condemnation of "technology."

31. "Un-worked" (*dès-œuvrée*) in Blanchot's sense, needless to say, and thus in a necessary relation with an "unworked community." Beyond this, there would also be a good deal to say about such an un-working in the *sciences*, that is, in what should less and less be confused with the metaphysical aim of Science, with a capital "S," as the completion of sense, something that it's increasingly hard to distinguish from technologies.

32. Contrary, of course, to what Hegel sought not to do, and not without a struggle. See my "Le Rire, la présence," in *Une Pensée finie*, 297–324; translated by Emily McVarish as "Laughter, Presence," in *The Birth to Presence*, 368–92.

CHAPTER 2

NOTE: This text was written for the conference "Sartre and Bataille," organized by Jacqueline Risset, held in Rome in the autumn of 1996. It was published in book form in French in Jean-Luc Nancy, *La Pensée derobée* (Paris: Galilée, 1999).

1. Jean-Paul Sartre, *Cahiers pour une morale* (Paris: Gallimard, 1983), 499; translated by David Pellauer as *Notebooks for an Ethics* (Chicago: University of Chicago Press, 1992), 483.

2. Sartre, *Vérité et existence* (Paris: Gallimard, 1989), 66–67.

3. Georges Bataille, *Sur Nietzsche*, in *Oeuvres complètes* (Paris: Gallimard, 1973), 6: 197. All references to Bataille are to this edition, henceforth cited as OC, followed by volume and page number.

4. OC 12: 459.

5. OC 6: 260.

6. OC 6: 312.

7. OC 6: 318.

8. See Heidegger, *Beiträge zur Philosophie (vom Ereignis)*, in *Gesamtausgabe* 65 (Frankfurt a. M.: Vittorio Klostermann, 1989).

9. OC 12: 287; see also OC 12: 316, where Bataille speaks of "laying bare the flip side of thinking."

10. OC 12: 394.

11. OC 12: 316.

12. For Sartre, see, in particular, *Vérité et existence*.

13. Sartre, *Critique de la raison dialectique* (Paris: Gallimard, 1960), 107; translated by Hazel E. Barnes as *The Problem of Method* (London: Alfred Knopf, 1963), 174. The phrase "not-knowing" also crops up in the posthumous *Vérité et existence* and *Notebooks for an Ethics*.

CHAPTER 3

NOTE: This essay appeared in French in Jean-Luc Nancy, *Une Pensée finie* (Paris: Galilée, 1990), 65–106.

1. Diogenes Laertius, *Lives and Opinions of Eminent Philosophers*, trans. R. D. Hicks, Loeb Classical Library (London: Heinemann, 1942), 1: 24–25.

2. Georges Bataille, "La Limite de l'utile," in *Oeuvres complètes* (Paris: Gallimard, 1972), 7: 280. All references to Bataille are to this edition, henceforth cited as OC, followed by volume and page number.

3. G. W. F. Hegel, *Hegel's Philosophy of Mind*, trans. W. Wallace and A. V. Miller (Oxford: Oxford University Press, 1971) §392.

4. Marcel Détienne and Jean-Pierre Vernant, *La Cuisine du sacrifice en pays grec* (Paris: Gallimard, 1979), 34 (text by Détienne) and 134 (text by J.-L. Durand); translated by Paula Wissing as *The Cuisine of Sacrifice among the Greeks* (Chicago: University of Chicago Press, 1989), 20, 88. Furthermore, both authors insist upon the role of "globalized Christianity" (Détienne) in the "arbitrary" construction of the ethno-anthropo-logical notion of sacrifice. They're certainly not wrong to do so, providing that we don't forget that "Christianity" (if not the faith of Christians) is what it is only within the double philosophical dialectization from which it evolves and to which it submits. In addition, we shouldn't forget that it is philosophy that, by elaborating the idea of sacrifice, seals off access to what I shall call here, for want of a better term, "early sacrifice." When anthropological inquiry comes up against a diversity of sacrificial forms that is impossible to unify, it is perhaps subject, in turn, in inverted fashion, to this enclosure. And yet it is hard not to think that there is a real unity to this early sacrifice, albeit one to which we have no real means of access.

5. Georges Gusdorf, *L'Expérience humaine du sacrifice* (Paris: Presses Universitaires de France, 1948), viii.

6. OC 11: 484.

7. OC 7: 264.

8. OC 7: 538.

9. Plato, *Phaedo*, 114c.

10. Ibid., 117c.

11. Paul's Epistle to the Philippians, 2: 6–8.

12. Augustine, *The City of God*, cited in E. Mersch, *Le Corps mystique du Christ* (Paris: Desclée, 1951), 2: 114. The reference supplied at this point is imprecise.

13. Friedrich Nietzsche, *Werke*, ed. Karl Schlechta (Munich: Hanser, 1956), 3: 803. The citation in question is from the *Nachlass*, the unpublished writings.

14. Paul's Epistle to the Hebrews, 10: 11–14.

15. Cited in Mersch, *Le Corps mystique du Christ*, 2: 6ff.

16. Hegel, *Hegel's Philosophy of Mind*, §546.

17. Plato, *Laws*, 909d et sec.

18. OC 7: 253.

19. Plato, *Phaedo*, 118.

20. Ibid., 91b–c.

21. Pascal, *Pensées* (Paris: Gallimard-Pléiade, 1978), §268, 569; translated by A. Krailsheimer as *Pensées* (Harmondsworth, Middlesex: Penguin, 1966), §268, 109.

22. Hegel, *Lectures on the Philosophy of Religion*, ed. P. C. Hodgson, trans. R. F. Brown, P. C. Hodgson, and J. M. Steward (Berkeley: University of California Press, 1984), 1: 354 n. 178.

23. G. W. F. Hegel, *Phenomenology of Spirit*, trans. A. V. Miller (Oxford: Oxford University Press, 1977), §779. The context of the remark concerns Christ.

24. OC 7: 255.

25. Friedrich Nietzsche, *Morgenröte*, in *Kritische Studienausgabe*, ed. Giorgio Colli and Mazzino Montinari (Berlin: Walter de Gruyter, 1988), vol. 3, bk. 2, § 146; translated by R. J. Hollingdale as *Daybreak* (Cambridge: Cambridge University Press, 1982), 146..

26. Nietzsche, *Ecce Homo*, KSA 6; translated by R. J. Hollingdale as *Ecce Homo* (Harmondsworth, Middlesex: Penguin, 1989), 129–30.

27. Karl Marx, "Critique of Hegel's Doctrine of Right," in *Early Writings*, trans. and ed. Lucio Colletti (Harmondsworth, Middlesex: Penguin, 1974), 104.

28. See Thomas Aquinas, *Summa theologiae*, IIIa, qu. 22 2 c, then IIa–IIae, qu. 85 3 ad 2.

29. Cited in Gusdorf, *L'Expérience humaine du sacrifice*, 45.

30. See *Les Carnets de Lucien Lévy-Bruhl* (Paris: Presses Universitaires de France, 1949). Generally speaking, the relation between *mimesis* and sacrifice requires an examination that I cannot undertake here. If *mimesis* is an appropriation of the other through the alteration or suppression of the proper, wouldn't it have a structure equivalent to that of sacrifice? (See, e.g., "être personne—ou tout le monde" ("to be no one—or everyone"), in Philippe Lacoue-Labarthe's analysis of Diderot's *Paradox*, "Diderot: Paradox et *mimesis*," in *Typographies II: L'Imitation des modernes* (Paris: Galilée, 1986), 35; translated as "Diderot: Paradox and Mimesis," in Lacoue-Labarthe, *Typography: Mimesis, Philosophy, Politics*, ed. Christopher Fynsk (Cambridge: Harvard University Press, 1989), 259. As regards the links between sacrifice and mimesis, see also, e.g., Jacques Derrida, "La Pharmacie de Platon," in *La Dissémination* (Paris: Seuil, 1972), 152–53; translated by Barbara Johnson as "Plato's Pharmacy," in *Dissemination* (Chicago: University of Chicago Press, 1979). Should we look for a priority in this equivalence? Should we found sacrifice on mimesis, found it, for example, on an anthropology of mimetic violence and rivalry (along the lines proposed by Girard) that turns sacrifice into a symbolization after the fact and that appeals to a "revelation" in order to suspend its violence? (In which case, and however subtle the analyses may be, the so-called positive characteristic of such an anthropological "knowledge" would admittedly be as foreign to me as that other kind of "positivity" associated with the motif of "revelation.") Conversely, why shouldn't we grasp mimesis on the basis of a *methexis*, a communication or contagion that, outside the West, has perhaps never had the meaning of a communion, which we have tended to give it? What escapes us, and what "Western sacrifice" at once misses and sublates, is an essential *discontinuity* of *methexis*, an in-communication of every community. (See, e.g., Bataille on contagion, OC 7: 369–71.)

31. See Philippe Lacoue-Labarthe, *Typographies*, 42: "Is mimesis sublatable?" The question is perhaps no different from the following: Is *methexis* communal? It is perhaps in the theologico-philosophical construction of the doctrine of Christian double hypostasis, insofar as this is also the very site of sacrifice and of

all possible communion, that such questions would find their most telling documentation.

32. OC 11: 55.

33. Heidegger, *Holzwege, Gesamtausgabe* 5 (Frankfurt a. M.: Vittorio Klostermann, 1987), 50; "The Origin of the Work of Art," in *Basic Writings*, ed. David Farrell Krell (London: Routledge, 1993), 187. The theme of sacrifice returns many times in Heidegger. A critical analysis of this theme would require a separate study. Arnold Hartmann and Alexander Garcia-Düttmann will one day provide it.

34. Immanuel Kant, *Kritik der Urteilskraft*, in *Gesammelte Schriften,* ed. Königlich Preußischen Akademie der Wissenschaften (Berlin: Walter de Gruyter, 1902–), 5: 271, 252.

35. Novalis, *Heinrich von Ofterdingen*, in *Schriften*, ed. P. Kluckhohn and R. Samuel (Stuttgart: W. Kohlhamner, 1960), 1: 337.

36. OC 5: 156. See also, e.g., the remarks of *L'Erotisme* (Paris: Minuit, 1957), 98: "In actual fact, literature is situated in succession to religion . . . Sacrifice is a novel, it is a tale, illustrated in a gory fashion," etc. There's no need to underline the fact that questions of sacrifice and of myth have to be closely linked.

37. OC 11: 485.

38. Ibid.

39. Ibid.

40. F. W. J. Schelling, *Sämmtliche Werke*, ed. K. F. A. Schelling (Stuttgart: Cotta, 1865–61) 453.

41. OC 11: 485.

42. Ibid.

43. OC 11: 486.

44. OC 11: 103.

45. OC 8: 300.

46. OC 11: 262–67. [Subsequent quotes in the text are from this article.—Trans.] For want of space, I am leaving to one side the "Sartre" article on the Jews and the camps (OC 11: 226–28). The conclusions of these articles would converge: Bataille, without saying so directly, tends to view the Jews as the victims of a sacrificial immolation of "reason." For another example, see OC 7: 376–79. See also Jacques Lacan, *Séminaire XI* (Paris: Seuil, 1977), 247, and Philippe Lacoue-Labarthe, *La Fiction du politique* (Paris: Bourgous, 1989); translated by Chris Turner as *Heidegger, Art, Politics* (Oxford: Blackwell, 1991), who respectively affirm and deny the sacrificial character of the camps, and Jacques Derrida, who, in the midst of commenting on sacrifice as orality and on philosophies that "do not sacrifice sacrifice," appears to affirm such a character; see Derrida, *Shibboleth* (Paris: Galilée, 1986), 83–85.

47. OC 7: 376–79. It is worth pointing out that a comparable discussion has taken place on the subject of the sacrificial character of revolutionary regicide; see Myriam Revault d'Allones, *D'une mort à l'autre* (Paris: Seuil, 1989), 59. There are obviously considerable differences between such discussions. I merely want to sug-

gest that, under the rule of Western sacrifice, sacrifice started to decay a long time ago.

48. Adolf Hitler, *Mein Kampf* (Munich, 1936), 326.

49. Ibid., 329.

50. Ibid., 330.

51. Himmler's speech of October 4, 1943, cited in Raul Hilberg, *The Destruction of the European Jews* (London: Holmes & Meier, 1985), 3: 1009–10.

52. OC II: 101.

53. Hermann Broch, *The Death of Virgil*, trans. J. Starr Untermeyer (Harmondsworth, Middlesex: Penguin, 2000), 172.

54. On technology, *technē*, art, and the work in Nazism and/or in Heidegger's thinking, see Lacoue-Labarthe, *Heidegger, Art, Politics.*

55. See, in particular, Martin Heidegger, "Die Kehre," in *Vorträge und Aufsätze* (Pfullingen: Gunter Neske, 1954), 37–47; translated by William Lovitt as "The Turning," in Heidegger, *The Question Concerning Technology* (New York: Harper & Row, 1977), 36–49.

56. I agree with Jean-François Lyotard on this point; see Lyotard, *Heidegger et les "juifs"* (Paris: Galilée, 1988), 140; translated by Andreas Michael and Mark Roberts as *Heidegger and "the jews"* (Minneapolis: University of Minnesota Press, 1990). For me, though, his argument as a whole calls for this reservation at least: Heidegger's intended gesture here doesn't simply invalidate the thought of *Ereignis*, to which Lyotard himself, paradoxically, becomes intensely attached.

57. Lacan, *Le Séminaire XI*, 247. Here, Lacan explicitly derives this definition from the existence of the camps.

58. Martin Heidegger, *Sein und Zeit* (Tübingen: Max Niemeyer, 1992), 42.

59. See Martin Heidegger, "Zeit und Sein," in *Zur Sache des Denkens* (Tübingen: Max Niemeyer, 1969); translated by Joan Stambaugh as "Time and Being," in Heidegger, *On Time and Being* (San Francisco: Harper & Row, 1984).

60. See *The Experience of Freedom*. The theme of sacrifice was already touched upon in this book, just as it was invoked in my "Soleil cou coupé," in *Le Démon des anges* (Barcelona: Departament de Cultura, 1989).

61. Rereading these pages while editing them for their French publication as a book (August 1, 1990), I want to add the following: yesterday, between four hundred and six hundred people were massacred in a church in Monrovia, where they were taking refuge from the fighting and executions of the civil war that is tearing Liberia apart. Among them, there were many women, children, and infants. The newspaper explains that eviscerated bodies of two young children were thrown onto the altar. I'm not passing judgment on this war, or even on this particular episode. I'm insufficiently informed to do so. I simply want to note the crushing weight of this configuration of signs: in Africa, upon a Christian altar, a parody of sacrifice—yet less than a parody, more a slaughter unsupported by any sacrifice.

CHAPTER 4

NOTE: This text appeared in French in *Cahiers Intersignes*, nos. 4–5 (Paris, autumn 1992): 237–49.

NOTE: While writing these pages, I'd forgotten that one of the texts included by Blanchot in *The Infinite Conversation* carries the same title: "L'Indestructible." This was no doubt both an unconscious memory and a dialogue.

1. In English in the text.—Trans.

2. Franco Marinetti, *Selected Writings*, trans. R. W. Flint and Arthur A. Coppotelli (New York: Farrar, Strauss and Giroux, 1972), 42.

3. Hallâj al-Husayn Ibn Mansur, *Dîwân*. I am citing here from the translation by L. Massignon printed in the *Cahiers du Sud* (1955), 104. I admit that I've altered the text somewhat, aggravating Hallâj's heresy still further by erasing the "Him" to whom the text is actually addressed.

CHAPTER 5

NOTE: This text merits a place in this collection on account of its themes, particularly the theme of *sense*. Nevertheless, it has a special status, for two reasons. First, it was written for inclusion in a festschrift for Jacques Derrida and so belongs to a genre that is not really appropriate here. In recognition of this, I have removed the preamble, which was devoted entirely to this "address." [The preamble is included in an earlier translation of this text by Peter Connor, in *Derrida: A Critical Reader*, ed. David Wood (Oxford: Blackwell, 1992), 36–51.—Trans.] Second, the original circumstances in which the piece was composed—a symposium at the Collegium Phenomenologicum directed by Rodolphe Gasché in 1987—dictated that I speak about a particular text by Derrida. I chose "Ellipsis," the concluding essay of *L'Ecriture et la différance* (Paris: Seuil, 1967), 429–36; translated by Alan Bass as "Ellipsis," in Derrida, *Writing and Difference* (Chicago: University of Chicago Press, 1978), 295–300. This implies a reading of that text throughout this essay. The essay in French can be found in Jean-Luc Nancy, *Une Pensée finie* (Paris: Galilée, 1990), 269–96.

1. See, too, the opening pages of Nancy's *Le Poids d'une pensée* (Grenoble: Presses Universitaires de Grenoble, 1991)—Ed.

2. Jacques Derrida, *De la grammatologie* (Paris: Minuit, 1967), 18; translated by Gayatri Chakravorty Spivak as *Of Grammatology* (Baltimore: The Johns Hopkins University Press, 1976), 23.

3. See Jacques Derrida, *Marges de la philosophie* (Paris: Minuit, 1972); translated by Alan Bass as *Margins of Philosophy* (Chicago: University of Chicago Press, 1982), 330.

CHAPTER 6

NOTE: This essay originally appeared in Jean-Luc Nancy, *La Pensée derobée* (Paris: Galilée, 1999).

1. Everything that follows speaks, according to the rules of the game, of Derrida, from Derrida, or alongside him or his *œuvre*. I will keep textual references to a minimum; there would either have been too many or too few, and my concern here isn't a philological one. I'm searching for the extremity at which a thought begins or exhausts itself, at which its subject is stripped bare.

2. The expression appears in Jacques Derrida, *L'Ecriture et la différence* (Paris: Seuil, 1967), 364; translated by Alan Bass as *Writing and Difference* (Chicago: University of Chicago Press, 1978), 247. On the intestine, the brain, and the tympanum, see *Marges de la philosophie* (Paris: Minuit, 1972), i–iv; translated by Alan Bass as *Margins of Philosophy* (Chicago: University of Chicago Press, 1982), x–xv.

3. See "Circonfession," in Geoffrey Bennington and Jacques Derrida, *Jacques Derrida* (Paris: Seuil, 1991), 275; translated by Geoffrey Bennington as "Circumfession," in Bennington and Derrida, *Jacques Derrida* (Chicago: University of Chicago Press, 1993), 298: "the question of me, with respect to which all other questions appear derived."

4. It would be pointless to try to provide references. There are hundreds of them, unevenly distributed across texts and perhaps even across periods. Moreover, the two uses of "such," the "normal" and the "retro," often occur almost side by side. See, e.g., *Parages* (Paris: Galilée, 1986), 14.

5. Derrida, *Glas*, 7—as for the rest, I must pass it by, I forget it. But everybody knows what it concerns.

6. It is worth noting that although here Nancy credits Derrida with having raised the specter of "haunting," the term was actually part of Nancy's vocabulary long before it was adopted by Derrida. See "The *Kategorein* of Excess," below.—Ed.

7. These last two terms are employed and discussed by Philippe Lacoue-Labarthe in *Le Sujet de la philosophie* (Paris: Aubier-Flammarion, 1979), 221ff. His theme finds certain echoes here.

8. *Glas* (Paris: Galilée, 1974), 79–80; translated by John P. Leavey, Jr., as *Glas* (Lincoln: University of Nebraska Press, 1990), 67–68.

9. See a bit further on in *Glas*: "everything is always attached *from behind* [de dos], written, described from behind [*par derrière*] . . . Absolutely behind, the *Derrière* that will never have been seen face on, the *Déjà* preceded by nothing" (97 / 84).

10. *La Carte postale: De Socrate à Freud et au-delà* (Paris: Flammarion, 1980), 86; translated by Alan Bass as *The Post Card: From Socrates to Freud and Beyond* (Chicago: University of Chicago Press, 1987), 78: the *da counting for nothing with regard to* the *do* or *the dos*, "as if behind the curtains," still.

11. Martin Heidegger, *Sein und Zeit* (Tübingen: Max Neimeyer, 1993), 132.

12. See also "My signature . . . cut off before the *da*" (Jacques Derrida, *La Vérité*

en peinture [Paris: Flammarion, 1978], 181; translated by Geoffrey Bennington and Ian McLeod as *The Truth in Painting* [Chicago: University of Chicago Press, 1987], 158).

13. "And philosophy is perhaps the reassurance given against the anguish of being mad at the point of greatest proximity to madness" (Derrida, *Writing and Difference*, 92 / 59).

14. I can't attempt to locate all occurrences; I'll rest content with a hasty overview, ocular and erratic, which does, after all, constitute a test of pertinence. It might be informative to take the time to screen through the whole corpus, which would not leave less intact the game of a calculus that is proper or absent-minded, unconscious, or surconscious, of Jacques Derrida around his texts and their behinds.

15. Derrida, *The Post Card*, 44, 171 / 38, 158. One might add a caption in small caps without punctuation: "PLATO BEHIND FREUD" (422).

16. Jacques Derrida, "En cet moment même dans cet ouvrage me voici," in Derrida, *Psyché: Inventions de l'autre* (Paris: Galilée, 1987), 161; translated by Ruben Berezdivin as "At This Very Moment in This Work Here I Am," in *Re-Reading Levinas*, ed. Robert Bernasconi and Simon Critchley (Bloomington: Indiana University Press, 1991), 13.

17. An allusion to Max Stirner, *Der Einzige und sein Eigentum* (Leipzig, O. Wigard, 1882); translated by Steven T. Byington as *The Ego and His Own: The Case of the Individual against Authority* (London: A. C. Fifield, 1913)—Trans.

18. Jacques Derrida, "Moi—la psychanalyse," *Psyche*, 154; translated by Richard Klein as "Me—Psychoanalysis: An Introduction to the Translation of 'The Shell and the Kernel,' by Nicolas Abraham," *diacritics* (March 1979), 10.

19. See Derrida, "Donner la mort," in *L'Ethique du don*, ed. Jean-Michel Rabaté and Michael Wetzel (Paris: Métailié, 1992), 59ff.

20. See Derrida, *Psyché*, 626–38.

21. *The Post Card*, 125 / 114.

CHAPTER 7

NOTE: This essay appeared in French in Jean-Luc Nancy, *L'Impératif catégorique* (Paris: Flammarion, 1983), 7–32.

1. Sylvia Plath, "Channel Crossing," in *The Collected Poems* (London: Faber and Faber, 1981), 27.

2. The essay form allows me to examine this topic only in broad terms here. I hope to develop it further in a forthcoming work, *L'Expérience de la liberté* (Paris: Galilée, 1988); translated by Bridget McDonald as *The Experience of Freedom* (Stanford: Stanford University Press, 1993). [This footnote was written by Nancy in 1983, some five years before to the publication of the book to which he refers.—Ed.]

3. Here I am developing one aspect of the program of Kant analysis begun tentatively in *Logodaedalus I: Le Discours de la syncope* (Paris: Galilée, 1976).

4. Immanuel Kant, *Die Metaphysik der Sitten, in Gesammelte Schriften,* ed. Königlich Preußischen Akademie der Wissenschaften (Berlin: Walter de Gruyter, 1902–) 6: 316, §49. [Except in the case of the Nachlass, cited by fragment number, and the *Critique of Pure Reason,* where we follow the standard A and B pagination, all references to Kant are to this edition, henceforth cited as Ak, followed by volume and page number.—Trans.]

5. *Religion within the Limits of Mere Reason,* Ak 6: 41–42.

6. Ibid., Ak 6: 35.

7. See my "L'Etre abandonné," in *L'Impératif catégorique* (Paris: Flammarion, 1983), 141–53; translated by Brian Holmes as "Abandoned Being," in Jean-Luc Nancy, *The Birth to Presence* (Stanford: Stanford University Press, 1992), 36–47.

8. Except in the case of right itself, in the case of the production of legality or of the "jurisprudence" without experience that inaugurates right; see "*Lapsus judicii,*" below.

9. Elias Canetti, *Masse und Macht* (Frankfurt am Main, 1980), 335; translated by Carol Steward as *Crowds and Power* (London: Gollancz, 1962), 303.

10. By this we want to understand the particular nature of the "utterance." I have addressed this in two texts: "La Vérité impérative," in *L'Impératif catégorique,* 89–112, and "La Voix libre de l'homme," in *L'Impératif catégorique,* 115–37; translated by Richard Stamp as "The Free Voice of Man," in *Retreating the Political,* ed. Simon Sparks (London: Routledge, 1996), 32–51. If the order takes place in language, the imperative perhaps lies beyond it, even when it is uttered and even in its very utterance and discursiveness. "Imperativity" and the address as such don't happen without language, but they do arise from it. Or they arise from saying as what is not said—from a tone and a gesture.

11. Immanuel Kant, *Opus posthumum,* Ak 22: 118. Whether there is still love without duty or whether there is no law in love are questions that, for the moment, are entirely separate.

12. Kant, *Nachlass,* 8105, 1799.

13. Kant, *Opus posthumum,* Ak 22: 55.

14. Here I am borrowing a term used by Jean-François Lyotard in his analysis of the prescriptive in "Logique de Levinas," in *Textes pour Emmanuel Levinas* (Paris: Place, 1980), 113–69. I won't go into the convergences and divergences between my own path and the one taken by Lyotard. Doubtless we would both need to pursue them further.

15. *Critique of Practical Reason,* Ak 5: 31.

16. It goes without saying that, quite apart from this similarity of position, the imperative doesn't have the nature of either space or time. What it does do, however, is maintain a quite complex relationship with them. This will have to be examined later.

17. Kant, *Critique of Pure Reason,* A 19; B 33.

18. In the French text of this essay, Nancy refers to his essays collected under the title *L'Impératif catégorique*, but the comment might serve as a summation of the essays gathered here under the heading "Judging."—Ed.

19. Kant, *Religion*, Ak 6: 46.

20. Ibid., 45.

21. Emmanuel Levinas, *Totalité et infini* (The Hague: Martinus Nijhoff, 1961), 173; translated by Alphonso Lingis as *Totality and Infinity* (Pittsburgh: Duquesne University Press, 1969), 199.

22. At this point, Nietzsche, despite himself, confirms what Kant has to say. See my "Notre probité," in *L'Impératif catégorique*, 63–86; translated by Peter Conner as "'Our Probity!' On Truth in the Moral Sense in Nietzsche," in *Looking after Nietzsche*, ed. Laurence A. Rickels (Albany: State University of New York Press, 1990), 67–88.

23. In a manner that is no doubt analogous, Lacan, in "Kant avec Sade," *Ecrits* (Paris: Seuil, 1966), 765–90, attempts to understand the law as the law that constitutes the subject, not as the subject of a will to pleasure, but as the instrument of the pleasure of the other. The problem is that this reversal still maintains the "other" in the position of a subject of pleasure. Now, pleasure is without a subject—the least that we can say—such being, perhaps, the law as well as what lays down the law as the incommensurable injunction.

24. "The voice is recognized as coming from the other to the extent that we cannot respond to it, not to the measure of what, of the other, comes from the other. The very structure of the law dictates or obliges its transgression" (Jacques Derrida, in the debate that followed the presentation of "La Voix libre de l'homme," reproduced in *Les Fins de l'homme*, ed. Philippe Lacoue-Labarthe and Jean-Luc Nancy [Paris: Galilée, 1981], 183; Philippe Lacoue-Labarthe and Jean-Luc Nancy, *Retreating the Political*, ed. Simon Sparks [London: Routledge, 1997], 53). To this, we would need to attach the motif of the "madness of the law," brought to light by Derrida in "La Loi du genre," in *Parages* (Paris: Galilée, 1986), 249–87; translated by Avital Ronell as "The Law of Genre," *Critical Inquiry* 7, no. 1 (1980): 55–81.

25. Here, we are not so very far from the problematic of "sovereignty" in Bataille. I have begun to address this issue in "The Unsacrificeable," above.

26. Kant, *Opus posthumum*, Ak 22: 55.

27. Kant, "What Real Progress Has Metaphysics Made in Germany . . . ?" Ak 20: 294.

28. Kant, *Religion*, Ak 6: 49.

29. See Jean-Louis Bruch, *La Philosophie religieuse de Kant* (Paris: Aubier, 1968), 269.

30. At some point, we will need to examine the relation with the aesthetic that this motif involves (that is, with the articulation of the sublime over beauty), a relation in which the nonsubjective status of singularity is also at stake.

31. Kant, *Opus posthumum*, Ak 22: 122.

32. Apropos tragedy, let me draw attention to the connection with Philippe Lacoue-Labarthe's analysis of its Hölderlinian treatment in "La Césure du spéculatif," in *Typographies II: L'Imitation des modernes:* (Paris: Galilée, 1986); translated by Robert Eisenhauer as "The Caesura of the Spectacle," in *Typographies: Mimesis, Philosophy, Politics*, ed. Christopher Fynsk (Cambridge: Harvard University Press, 1989), 208–35. This connection is essential. As is the one to my own analysis of Hölderlin and Kant in "La Joie d'Hypérion," *Les Etudes philosophiques* 2 (1983): 177–94; translated by Christine Laennec and Michael Syrotinski as "Hyperion's Joy," in Jean-Luc Nancy, *The Birth to Presence* (Stanford: Stanford University Press, 1993), 58–81.

33. The Kantian notion of end does not denote the completion of a program. It is inaugural and without end. "So far as the concept of end is concerned, it is always something that we have to bring about, and the concept of an ultimate end needs to be seen as produced a priori by reason" (Ak 20: 294; "What Real Progress?" 123).

34. Pierre Lachièze-Rey, *L'Idéalisme kantien* (Paris: Vrin, 1950), 197.

35. Kant, *Metaphysics of Morals*, Ak 6: 222. It will be necessary to examine elsewhere the relation between this address of the law and the "call" which, for Heidegger, constitutes conscience (*Gewissen*), insofar as this call "comes from me and yet from beyond me and over me"; Heidegger, *Sein und Zeit* (Tübingen: Max Niemeyer, 1993), 275; translated by John MacQuarrie and Edward Robinson as *Being and Time* (New York: Harper & Row, 1962), 320. Certain important consequences follow from this, as I indicate in "The Free Voice of Man," consequences that complicate the analysis of the "sublime voice."

CHAPTER 8

NOTE: This essay appeared in French in Jean-Luc Nancy, *L'Impératif catégorique* (Paris: Flammarion, 1983), 33–60.

1. G. W. F. Hegel, *Phänomenologie des Geistes*, in *Werke*, ed. E. Moldenhauer and K. M. Michel (Frankfurt a. M.: Suhrkamp, 1970), 3: 356–57; translated by A. V. Miller as *Phenomenology of Spirit* (Oxford: Oxford University Press, 1977), 291–93. [Although Nancy makes due reference to Hippolyte's celebrated translation of 1939, he elides two distinct clauses in Hegel's text, reading "the loss of its essence" for "the loss of its reality [*Realität*]" and "its complete inessentiality [*Unwesentlichkeit*]" (*Werke*, 3: 357).—Trans.]

2. Chicanneau, a character from Racine, is a proverbial figure for litigiousness.—Trans.

3. This is where a long engagement with Heidegger—with the thinking that most rigorously determines the Hellenism of philosophy as such—would no doubt lead. Heidegger, in his climb toward the Greek language of philosophy, needs to point out a number of displacements introduced by Latin translation. Let

me suggest, then, that any study of these displacements would need to avoid giving them the simple form of a generalization or a deviation—a slippage, even—and instead recognize within the Latin "translation," regardless of the way in which it transmits or relays the Greek, the character of an *accident*, of a collision that redistributes entirely differently the whole semantic and conceptual apparatus over which it also "passes." Were we to do so, we could dispense with the whole motif of the accidental constitution of the *essence* of modern metaphysics. (There's no way of countering this through the empirical fact that, right up until the end of the empire, what was called "philosophy" usually spoke in Greek. Either it wasn't philosophy that was speaking, or Greece was already philosophically Latin.)

4. Georges Dumézil, *Idées romaines* (Paris: Gallimard, 1969), 41. We could hardly do better than cite Dumézil's indispensable analysis. Except perhaps to add a question about "juice" (as in the juice of a fruit, etc.), to which, as a homonym of *jus*, some philologues have lent an etymological synonymy (through the senses of "binding" and "mixing") with the *jus* of right. Something that might well support the Hegelian thesis of right as dissolution.

5. This is the problem of *origin*—which, it should probably be said, doesn't really belong to right or, if it does, does not do so at the point at which right refers to philosophy the question of its own origin (as at the start of a treatise on right, for example), but only at the point, with which we are concerned here, at which it *becomes* philosophy. *At this point* something happens to the metaphysical question of origin. For the moment, allow me simply to say that if the authority of the judge (his *imperium*) is itself a case, one whose right would need to be articulated, this case isn't an exceptional one (precisely not, in fact). Right prevents any law of exception, any *privilegium*; see, e.g., Jacques Ellul, "Sur l'artificialité du droit et la droit d'exception," *Archives de philosophie du droit* 10 (1965). The status of *judex* can be conferred, by right, on anyone whatsoever, a status whose investiture cannot be sheltered from the law. In this, the judge is already profoundly different from the philosopher as well as from the poet, both of whom Plato terms *natures*.

6. Spinoza, *Tractatus de intellectus emendatione,* §36: "De recta methodo cognoscendi" ("On the Improvement of the Understanding").

7. Right says; it doesn't execute. It never "produces" anything other than itself—or other than the fiction of its identity in the permanent mobility of its jurisprudence.

8. The totalitarianism of the modern State comes from Rome only through a major shift of nature and not of degree; namely, the unlimiting of a procedure whose strictly Latin figure is (by right . . .) that of an incessant and multiple fixing of limits (juridical, cultural, ethnic, linguistic, etc.). Rome tried—within the walls of its *limes*—to constitute the juridical unity of an internal network of limits, of boundaries and differences. Ultimately [*à la limite*] . . . we would have to say that right sanctions or signs for the differential divisions, whereas the State, having transformed procedure into (organic, historical) process, absorbs them.

9. See Duguip, *Traité de droit constitutionnel* (Paris, 1923), vol. 2, §28; and, for

a discussion of the notion of "subjective right," M. Villey, "L'Idée du droit subjectif et les systèmes juridiques romains," *Revue d'histoire du droit françaises et étranger,* 1946–47.

10. Here, the subject needs to be understood according to the metaphysical determination through which it is constructed, from the *hypokeimenon* to the *substance* of the Cartesian subject. This would be different (the problem here is one of translation . . .) were we to give back to the *subjectum* the Latin values of being-subordinate, being-subjected, being-substituted, or being-supposed.

11. Hegel, *Enzyklopädie der philosophischen Wissenschaften,* in *Werke,* vol. 7, §168; translated by William Wallace as *Hegel's Logic* (Oxford: Oxford University Press, 1975).

12. This is how the *Peri psychēs* characterizes *nous theōrētikos* (vol. 3, 5, 430 a 15).

13. It is from here that we would need to date yet another division that cuts immediately into the very unity of judgment: in Kant, the division between *judicium* and *nasus,* between what will later be called "judgment" and *esprit* in the specifically "French" sense of the word, a sense captured in English "wit," Spanish *gusto,* and, later on, German *Witz,* is already at work. *Esprit* constantly eats away at the rationality—itself already merely analogical—of judgment. Over the course of the eighteenth century, this leads inexorably toward the question of the "aesthetic" in the double sense of the term: aesthetics as the "science of sensibility" (*cognitio inferior*) and as the "science of the fine arts" (the science of taste). Under its double form, aesthetics formulates what is perhaps the ultimate question of right: *the right of what is by right without right.* This is what Kant calls the claim to universality of the judgment of taste, a motif that would have to be linked up with that of the *critica,* which appeared long before its dialectical understanding as the science (or art) of texts, of their establishment and evaluation: a discipline without any absolute criteria and always dependent on some "personal" judgment. This is *also* Kant's way of giving this critique a philosophical status. On the history of *Witz,* see "Menstruum universale," *Alea* 1 (1981); translated by Paula Moddel as "Menstruum universale," *Sub-Stance* 21 (1978); reprinted in Jean-Luc Nancy, *The Birth to Presence,* trans. Brian Holmes and others (Stanford: Stanford University Press, 1993), 248–65.

14. Immanuel Kant, *Kritik der reinen Vernunft,* ed. Jens Timmermann (Berlin: Felix Meiner, 1999), A ix-x. All references to the *Critique* are to this text, henceforth cited as KrV with standard A and B pagination.

15. KrV A xi.

16. KrV A xi.

17. Without ever turning it back into the despotism of the State: this is the most constant and most remarkable—doubtless most audacious and hence most problematic—trait of Kant's thinking (including, or even *first and foremost,* its status as a thinking of the political). Hadrian, in this story, is played by Hegel, of course.

18. What tribunal could be established without reference to a pre-existing law,

apart from a tribunal of exception? Here, I have not been able to dwell on the *law* itself. Yet if it is possible to suggest that the *lex* is never the strict equivalent of a *logos*, then we can't avoid saying that, in one way or another, every judicial institution operates in the last instance according to a rule of exception and thus according to the form that right excludes. The troubling ambiguity of right would stem from its having, in principle, withdrawn from the State and, at the same time, opened the very possibility of the tribunal of exception. In many ways, Kant's enterprise also represents, by virtue of its audacity, metaphysics' own tribunal of exception. Similar ambiguities will doubtless begin to unravel only once it has become possible for us to think *how logos constitutes our own law of exception.*

19. Do we need to point out that Kant's discourse, like every metaphysical discourse, stems from the primitive appropriation of its reason *alone*—and by the primitive warding off of any accident that might affect it? What we need to hold onto here is that, *despite all this*, an accident does happen—and happens in that primitive operation itself.

20. Heidegger, whose reading of Kant is clearly decisive here, stands in marked contrast. See, in particular, the debate with Cassirer; Martin Heidegger, "Davoser Disputation zwischen Ernst Cassirer und Martin Heidegger," in Heidegger, *Kant und das Problem der Metaphysik, Gesamtausgabe* 3 (Frankfurt a. M.: Vittorio Klostermann, 1991), 274–96; translated by Richard Taft as "Davos Disputation between Ernst Cassirer and Martin Heidegger," in Heidegger, *Kant and the Problem of Metaphysics* (Bloomington: Indiana University Press, 1990), 171–85.

21. Scientific "law" presents itself, so to speak, as the opposite of or as opposed to juridical law. Whereas the latter articulates an "area of action or claim," the former—which doesn't simply disobey the structure of articulation but also excludes it to the point where its utterances are held to be valid only insofar as they are independent of the one who utters them—establishes what *is* (regardless of the status of this "being") within a given area, the area engendered by the subject (of) science. As a philosophical, ethical, or political question, the question of the "right of science" is always badly put insofar as it ignores the profound heterogeneity that exists between the two orders. Science either has all rights, or it has none.

22. KrV B xiii.

23. KrV A 712; B 740.

24. KrV B xii.

25. As well as "on paper . . . but . . . completely *a priori*" (KrV A 713; B 741). Another essay would need to be devoted to a general analysis of schematization.

26. KrV A 33; B 50.

27. KrV A 132; B 171.

28. KrV A 134; B 173.

29. KrV A 134; B 173.

30. KrV A 135; B 174.

31. KrV A 135; B 174.

32. Despite certain variations in the Kantian vocabulary (see A. de Coninck,

L'Analytique transcendantale de Kant [Louvain, 1955], 1: 128 ff.), one notes that the *a priori* forms of sensibility are supplied, not by *deduction*, but by *exposition*.

33. KrV A 126.

34. See Luc Ferry et al., eds., *Rejouer le politique* (Paris: Gallilée, 1981), 95.

35. Jean-Luc Nancy, "The Free Voice of Man," in Philippe Lacoue-Labarthe and Jean-Luc Nancy, eds., *Retreating the Political*, ed. Simon Sparks.

CHAPTER 9

NOTE: This translation, first published in *Studies in Practical Philosophy* 1, no. 1 (1999), is based on an article first published in heavily abridged form in *Dictionnaire des Philosophes*, ed. Noella Baraquin and Jacqueline Laffitte (Paris: Armand Colin, 1997), 645–51. I would like to thank Keith Ansell Pearson and the Centre for Research in Philosophy and Literature at the University of Warwick for originally commissioning this translation, and Simon Sparks for his invaluable help in discussing aspects of the translation itself.—Trans.

1. Besides, the editors of the dictionary for which this article was first written have already settled the matter by commissioning it.

2. See Martin Heidegger, "Brief über den 'Humanismus,'" *Wegmarken, Gesamtausgabe* 9 (Frankfurt a. M.: Vittorio Klostermann, 1992), 313; translated by Frank A. Capuzzi in collaboration with J. Glenn Gray, in Martin Heidegger, *Basic Writings*, ed. David Farrell Krell (London: Routledge, 1993), 213; henceforth cited as BW.

3. BW 217.

4. Martin Heidegger, *Sein und Zeit* (Tübingen: Max Niemeyer, 1993). Henceforth cited as SZ.

5. Except for two instances of *authenticité*, Nancy uses *propre* ("proper, own, authentic") and its derivations for Heidegger's use of terms based on the root *eigen* (especially *eigentlich* and *Eigentlichkeit*). The special case of *Ereignis* is addressed in the text.—Trans.

6. BW 220.

7. SZ 152.

8. BW 220.

9. BW 218.

10. BW 217.

11. BW 220.

12. BW 218.

13. BW 225.

14. See BW 225ff.

15. See *Kant und das Problem der Metaphysik, Gesamtausgabe* 3 (Frankfurt a. M.: Vittorio Klostermann, 1991), 207 and §§38–41. Henceforth cited as KPM.

16. BW 26.

17. KPM §41.
18. See BW 229.
19. SZ 56, 135.
20. SZ 44, 136, etc.; see BW 236.
21. SZ 134.
22. See the celebrated remarks on Heraclitus (BW 256–57).
23. See BW 248–49.
24. KPM §30.
25. BW 228.
26. BW 229.
27. See SZ 134.
28. BW 230.
29. BW 229.
30. BW 229.
31. . See SZ 170.
32. SZ 123.
33. See SZ 124.
34. See KPM §30.
35. BW 233.
36. BW 251.
37. BW 234.
38. Ibid.
39. Ibid.
40. BW 238.
41. Ibid.
42. BW 234.
43. BW 235.
44. Ibid.
45. Ibid.
46. Ibid.
47. BW 236.
48. Ibid.
49. BW 246.
50. BW 240.
51. Ibid.
52. BW 236 ff.
53. BW 246.
54. BW 236.
55. See BW 252: "'the world' is, in a certain sense, precisely 'the beyond' within existence and for it."
56. BW 258.
57. BW 255.
58. KPM § 30.

59. See BW 255ff.
60. BW 256.
61. BW 258.
62. BW 259.
63. BW 259, 262.
64. See BW 260.
65. SZ 294.
66. BW 259.
67. BW 246.
68. Ibid.
69. See SZ §§56–57.
70. SZ 281. [As Heidegger points out (SZ 281–83), the words *schuldig* and *Schuld* have many different connotations, running from guilt and responsibility all the way to indebtedness. This needs to be borne in mind in the following lines.—Ed.]
71. SZ 283.
72. SZ 281.
73. SZ 283.
74. See the complex relation to the term "person" (SZ §10).
75. See SZ 288.
76. BW 261.
77. BW 260.
78. Ibid.
79. BW 261.
80. Ibid.
81. BW 265.
82. BW 260.
83. SZ 288.
84. BW 265.
85. BW 263, 262.
86. Spinoza, *Ethics*, 5 prop. 42.

CHAPTER 10

NOTE: This essay originally appeared in Jean-Luc Nancy, *La Pensée derobée* (Paris: Galilée, 1999).

1. Immanuel Kant, *Erste Fassung der Einleitung in die Kritik der Urteilskraft*, in *Gesammelte Schriften*, ed. Königlich Preußischen Akademie der Wissenschaften (Berlin: Walter de Gruyter, 1902–), 20: 195–251. [Except for the *Critique of Pure Reason*, where I follow the standard A and B pagination, all references to Kant are to this edition, henceforth cited as Ak, followed by volume and page number. Quotes from the third *Critique* are taken from Immanuel Kant, *Critique of Judg-*

ment, trans. and introd. Werner S. Pluhar (Indianapolis: Hackett, 1987). Quotes from the first *Critique* are taken from Immanuel Kant, *Critique of Pure Reason,* trans. Norman Kemp Smith (New York: St. Martin's, 1965); those of the second *Critique* are from Immanuel Kant, *Critique of Practical Reason,* trans. and ed. Mary Gregor (Cambridge: Cambridge University Press, 1997). The page number of the English translation follows that of the Akademie edition; the translation has occasionally been modified in order to correspond more closely to the French translation that Nancy quotes.—Trans.]

2. Ak 20: 195 / 385.

3. Ak 20: 203 / 392.

4. Ak 20: 201 / 390.

5. Ak 20: 205–6 / 394.

6. Ak 20: 206 / 395.

7. Ibid.

8. Ibid.

9. Ibid.

10. Ibid.

11. Ak 20: 206–7 / 395.

12. On the question of the "case" in general in Kant (even though the word "case [*Fall*]" does not figure explicitly in the German text), see the work in progress of Simon Zavadil, a fragment of which appears as "L'Evénement de la contingence, ou les limites du principe de raison," *Les Cahiers Philosophiques de Strasbourg* 5 (1997), 211–32. [See also "*Lapsus judicii,*" above.—Ed.]

13. See the preface to the *Critique of Practical Reason,* Ak 5: 4–14 / 3–11.

14. On matters of fact (*scibilia*), see §91 of the *Critique of Judgment.* This section calls for a detailed commentary, which I cannot provide here.

15. *Critique of Practical Reason,* Ak 5: 71–89 / 62–75.

16. Ak 5: 73 / 64.

17. Ak 5: 77 / 66–67.

18. Ak 5: 80 / 68.

19. *Critique of Judgment,* Ak 5: 289 / 154.

20. Ak 5: 222 / 67.

21. Ibid.

22. We would need to move from the passages on pleasure in the Introduction and certain other sections of the *Critique of Judgment* to the *Metaphysics of Morals* and the *Anthropology* (§64f).

23. *Critique of Judgment,* Ak 5: 187 / 26–27.

24. Ibid.

25. See, in particular, the "General Comment on Teleology."

26. Ak 5: 482n. / 377n. This is the only footnote in the "General Comment."

27. Ak 5: 187 / 27.

28. *Critique of Pure Reason,*A216, B263 / 237.

29. See the first-edition Transcendental Deduction, second section.

30. *Critique of Practical Reason*, Ak 5: 3 / 3.

31. See, in particular, §§60 and 83 of the *Critique of Judgment*, where we read: "the fine arts *and the sciences* . . . involve a universally communicable pleasure as well as elegance and refinement, and through these they make man, not indeed morally better for society, but still civilized for it" (Ak 5: 433 / 321; my emphasis).

32. Ak 20: 230 / 419–20.

33. See, of course, the Architectonic.

34. *Critique of Practical Reason*, Ak V: 162 / 133–34.

CHAPTER II

NOTE: This essay has been reprinted from "The Sublime Offering," by Jean-Luc Nancy, in *Of the Sublime: Presence in Question,* ed. Jeffrey S. Librett, by permission of the State University of New York Press. © 1993 State University of New York. All rights reserved. This book originally appeared in French as Jean-François Courtine et al, *Du sublime* (Paris: Belin, 1988); the essay was reprinted in *Jean-Luc Nancy, Une Pensée finie* (Paris: Galilée, 1990), 147–96.

1. The sublime is in fashion in Paris and among the theoreticians, who often refer to it in recent years (Marin, Derrida, Lyotard, Deleuze, Deguy), as well as in Los Angeles and among the artists: for example, one of the them entitled a recent exposition and performance "The Sublime" (Michael Kelley, April 1984). One finds further evidence of this fashion in Berlin (Hamacher), Rome, and Tokyo. (Not to speak of the use of the word "sublime" in the most current everyday speech.) As for the texts, they are numerous and dispersed. Let it suffice to indicate their authors here, my indebtedness to whose works it would be impossible to convey adequately. But I do not intend to add to theirs one more interpretation of the sublime. I attempt rather to come to terms with what it is that they share and that the epoch shares in this fashion: that offers us all up to a thought of the sublime.

2. This perhaps excessively concise formula adopts the general perspective of Samuel Monk's classic study *The Sublime: A Study of Critical Theories in Eighteenth-Century England* (Ann Arbor: University of Michigan Press, 1960), which has been reconsidered with respect to France by Théodore A. Litman in *Le Sublime en France* (Paris: A. G. Nizet, 1971) from both a historical and an aesthetic-conceptual perspective. My contribution is neither historical nor aesthetic.

3. I must not omit to mention at least once the name of Nietzsche, who thought, in one sense or several, something of the sublime, even if he hardly thematized it as such.

4. Walter Benjamin, *Gesammelte Schriften* (Frankfurt a. M.: Suhrkamp, 1980), I, I: 196.

5. Martin Heidegger, "Der Ursprung des Kunstwerkes," *Holzwege* (Frankfurt a. M.: Vittorio Klostermann, 1980), 42; translated by Albert Hofstadter as "The

Origin of the Work of Art," in Heidegger, *Poetry, Language, Thought* (New York: Harper & Row, 1971), 56.

6. Theodor W. Adorno, *Ästhetische Theorie* (Frankfurt a. M.: Suhrkamp, 1973), 292; translated by C. Lenhart as *Aesthetic Theory*, ed. Gretel Adorno and Rolf Tiedemann (London: Routledge and Kegan Paul, 1984), 280.

7. Georges Bataille, *Oeuvres*, vol. 7 (Paris: Gallimard, 1970).

8. Maurice Blanchot, "La Littérature et le droit à la mort," in *La Part du feu* (Paris: Gallimard, 1949), 294; translated by Lydia Davis as "Literature and the Right to Death," in *The Gaze of Orpheus,* ed. P. Adams Sitney, with a preface by Geoffrey Hartman (Barrytown, N.Y.: Station Hill, 1981), 22.

9. This means at once that these two modes of thought are opposed to each other and that the thought of the sublime doubtless infiltrates and secretly disquiets the thought of the end of art. But I will not attempt to show this here. In turn, where Hegel explicitly speaks of the sublime, he does not bring anything of the thought of the sublime to bear (see Paul de Man, "Hegel on the Sublime," in *Displacement: Derrida and After*, ed. Mark Krupnick [Bloomington: Indiana University Press, 1983], 139–53).

10. See *Critique de la faculté de juger*, trans. A. Philonenko (Paris: Vrin, 1986, §§ 23–29, 84, 114; *Critique of Judgment*, trans. J. H. Bernard (New York: Hafner, 1951), 82–120, for most of the allusions to Kant's text which follow. The reference here is to §23, 84 / 82.

11. The word can be found, e.g., in the *Critique of Judgment*, §22, 80 / 78.

12. CJ, §6, 34 / 24.

13. CJ, §2, 50 / 39.

14. CJ, §23, 86 / 85.

15. CJ, §27, 98 / 98. "In the aesthetic evaluation of grandeur, the concept of number ought to be kept at a distance or transformed."

16. In this sense, all that in Kant still derives from a classic theory of analogy and the symbol does not belong to the deep logic of which I am speaking here.

17. The latter formula is Lyotard's; see *Le Différend* (Paris: Minuit, 1983), 118–19; translated by Georges Van Den Abbeele as *The Differend: Phrases in Dispute* (Minneapolis: University of Minnesota Press, 1988), 77–78. The former formula is Derrida's, from "Le Parergon," in *La Vérité en peinture* (Paris: Flammarion, 1978); translated by Geoffrey Bennington and Ian McLeod as *The Truth in Painting* (Chicago: University of Chicago Press, 1987), 131–32. They are certainly not wrong, and they comment rigorously, together or the one against the other, upon the text of Kant. I do not attempt to discuss them here, preferring to take a different course—along the edge of presentation, but at a distance, and because presentation itself distances itself from itself. The political function of the sublime in Lyotard would call for a different discussion, which I shall undertake elsewhere.

18. Kant does not fail to indicate an aesthetic direction combining the two motifs: a sublime genre distinct from all others, and the determination of this genre as a kind of total work of art. He in fact evokes the possibility of a "presentation of

the sublime" in the fine arts in terms of the "combination of the fine arts in one single product," and he then indicates three forms: *verse tragedy*, the *didactic poem*, and the *oratorio*. There would, of course, be much to say about this. I shall content myself here with noting that it is not quite the same thing as Wagner's *Gesamtkunstwerk*. More particularly, Kant's three forms seem to turn around *poetry* as the mode of presentation of destiny, thought, and prayer, respectively, and it does not seem to be a matter of a "total" presentation.

19. CJ §26, 174; 91.

20. One ought to analyze the relations between Kant's *Bestrebung* and Freud's *Vorlust*, that is, this "preliminary pleasure," whose paradox consists in its tension and which occupies an important place in Freud's theory of the beautiful and of art.

21. CJ, §29, 105 / 128. I prefer, on this point, the first edition.

22. Hegel provides a kind of figure of this feeling by way of the other in his discussion of the infant in the womb of its mother. See Jean-Luc Nancy, "Identité et tremblement," in *Hypnoses* (Paris: Galilée, 1984), 13–47; translated by Brian Holmes as "Identity and Trembling," in Jean-Luc Nancy, *The Birth to Presence*, trans. Brian Holmes and others (Stanford: Stanford University Press, 1993, 9–35).

23. I am choosing to ignore here the *economy* of sacrifice, which is quite visible in Kant's text, where the imagination acquires "an extension and power greater than that which it has lost." I do not pretend that the offering is simply "pure loss." But at the heart of the economy (of presence, art, thought), it [*ça*] offers it-self *also*, *there is* also offering, neither lost nor gained.

24. Gilles Deleuze, *Cinéma*, vol. 1, *L'Image-mouvement* (Paris: Minuit, 1983), 69; translated by Hugh Tomlinson and Barbara Habberjam as *Cinema*, vol. I, *The Movement-Image* (Minneapolis: University of Minnesota Press, 1986), 46.

25. I suspend here an analysis I pursue in *L'Expérience de la liberté* (Paris: Galilée, 1988); translated by Bridget McDonald as *The Experience of Freedom* (Stanford: Stanford University Press, 1993).

26. CJ, §29, 106 / 109–10.

27. *Darbieten* or *Darbietung* ("offering") would be the word to substitute on the register of the sublime for *Darstellung* ("presentation"). But it is in each case a matter of the *dar*, of a sensible "here" or "here it is."

28. See note 18, above.

29. It is remarkable that another Biblical commandment—the *Fiat lux* of Genesis—had been already a privileged example of the sublime for Longinus and for his classical commentators. From the one example to the other as from the one commandment to the other, one can appreciate the continuity and the rupture.

30. See Jean-Luc Nancy, *Le Discours de la syncope: I. Logodaedalus* (Paris: Flammarion, 1976).

CHAPTER 12

NOTE: The title of the original French text is "L'Amour éclats." The word *éclat* should be read in all its outbursts. The word can mean, and appears here as: shatter, piece, splinter, glimmer, flash, spark, burst, outburst, explosion, brilliance, dazzle, and splendor.—Trans.

The English translation of this essay originally appeared as "Shattered Love," in Jean-Luc Nancy, *The Inoperative Community* (Minneapolis: University of Minnesota Press, 1991), 83–109. The French text can be found in Jean-Luc Nancy, *Une Pensée finie* (Paris: Galilée, 1990), 225–68.

1. The distinction that Nancy makes here is very easy to render in French, where abstract nouns may or may not be preceded by the definite article, depending upon the context. Hence, Nancy is able to distinguish between "la pensée est amour" and "la pensée est l'amour." In the first instance, love qualifies or describes thinking; in the second, it is offered more as a definition of thinking: thinking is love; it is identical with love.—Trans.

2. The French text reads, "l'être dans l'amour," but it is important to remember that the English expression "being in love" does not translate literally into idiomatic French. That might, then, be one of the meanings invoked here, but it is not necessarily the sole or dominant one.—Trans.

3. René Char, *Hypnos Waking*, trans. Jackson Mathews (New York: Random House, 1956), 59.

4. Roland Barthes, *A Lover's Discourse: Fragments*, trans. Richard Howard (New York: Farrar, Strauss and Giroux, 1978), 148.

5. See Emmanuel Levinas, *Totality and Infinity*, trans. Alphonso Lingis (Pittsburgh: Duquesne University Press, 1969), 50ff.

6. There is no adequate translation for the French verb *jouir*. Translated as "to enjoy," *jouir* loses its sexual connotation; translated as "to come," it loses its relation to "joy." Following a suggestion by Nancy, I have created a new verb to translate *jouir*: "to joy."—Trans.

7. The citation is in English in the original.—Trans.

CHAPTER 13

NOTE: This essay originally appeared in *Transeuropéennes*, no. 1 (autumn 1993): 8–18.

1. Schematically, and rather arbitrarily, I want to indicate three points of reference or three possible directions within the immense space, crossed today from every possible angle, of this question:

(1) The program marked out by the title of Etienne Balibar and Immanuel Wallerstein, *Race, Nation, Class: Ambiguous Identities* (London: Verso, 1992).

(2) The terms and the motifs of "intermixing," "relation," and "creolization" as deployed by Edouard Glissant in *Poétique de la relation* (Paris: Gallimard, 1990); translated by Betsy Wing as *Poetics of Relation* (Ann Arbor: University of Michigan

Press, 1993), and, along with Glissant, all the other "creoles" of art and literature, for whom Salman Rushdie could also be considered an emblem.

(3) The vision of a "universal" hybridization or mixed race presented in Michel Serres's *Le Tiers-Instruit* (Paris: Bourin, 1991), a vision that poses many of the problems elicited by Bruno Tackels in "Où est le métis?" *Correspondances* 4, "Le(s) Métissage(s)," UFR des Arts (Strasbourg: Presses Universitaires de Strasbourg, 1993).

2. Bernardo Bertolucci, *The Last Tango in Paris*.

3. Fernand Braudel, *La Méditerranée* (Paris: Flammarion, 1985), 134.

4. See, but with a different value placed on the "ipse," Gérard Granel, "Ipse Dasein?" in *La Phénoménologie aux confins* (Mauvezin: T. E. R., 1992).

CHAPTER 14

NOTE: This essay originally appeared in Jean-Luc Nancy, *La Pensée derobée* (Paris: Galilée, 1999).

1. Gilles Deleuze and Félix Guattari, *Qu'est-ce que la philosophie?* (Paris: Minuit, 1991), 103; translated by Graham Burchell and Hugh Tomlinson as *What Is Philosophy?* (London: Verso, 1994), 108.

2. See Friedrich Nietzsche, *Zur Genealogie der Moral*, in *Kritische Studienausgabe*, ed. Giorgio Colli and Mazzino Montinari (Berlin: Walter de Gruyter, 1988) 5: 293–94. Henceforth cited as KSA, followed by volume and page number, then the page number of the English translation. Translated by Walter Kaufman as *On the Genealogy of Morals* (New York: Vintage, 1967), 59–60. See also KSA 5: 79–81; translated by Walter Kaufman as *Beyond Good and Evil* (New York: Vintage, 1992), 74–76.

3. KSA 5: 292 / *Genealogy*, 58.

4. KSA 5: 79 / *Beyond Good and Evil*, 72.

5. KSA 5: 81 / *Beyond Good and Evil*, 74.

6. Immanuel Kant, *Die Metaphysik der Sitten*, in *Gesammelte Schriften*, ed. Königlich Preußischen Akademie der Wissenschaften (Berlin: Walter de Gruyter, 1902–) 6: 439–40.

7. See Edmund Husserl, *Psychological and Transcendental Phenomenology and the Confrontation with Heidegger (1927–1931)*, trans. and ed. Thomas Sheehan and Richard E. Palmer (Dordrecht: Kluwer, 1997), 492.

8. Martin Heidegger, *Sein und Zeit* (Tübingen: Max Niemeyer, 1992), §58.

9. Jean-Paul Sartre, *Vérité et existence* (Paris: Gallimard, 1989), 63; translated by Adrian van den Hoven as *Truth and Existence* (Chicago: University of Chicago Press, 1992), 30.

10. Emile Benveniste, *Vocabulaire des institutions indo-européennes* (Paris: Minuit, 1969), 2: 165.

11. Jacques Derrida, *Du droit à la philosophie* (Paris: Gallimard, 1990), 108;

translated by Jan Plug as Jacques Derrida, *Who's Afraid of Philosophy? Right to Philosophy I* (Stanford: Stanford University Press, 2002), 66.

12. See Maurice Blanchot, *L'Amitié* (Paris: Gallimard, 1989), 326; translated by Elizabeth Rottenberg as *Friendship* (Stanford: Stanford University Press, 1997), 289, 326. See, too, Theodor W. Adorno, *Aesthetic Theory,* trans. Robert Hullot-Kentor (Minneapolis: University of Minnesota Press, 1997), 39.

13. Ernst Tugendhat, *Self-consciousness and Self-determination*, trans. Paul Stern (Cambridge: The MIT Press, 1986), 297–98.

CHAPTER 15

NOTE: This essay originally appeared in Jean-Luc Nancy, *La Pensée derobée* (Paris: Galilée, 1999).

1. On this phrase, see the introductory remarks to two collections edited by Philippe Lacoue-Labarthe and Jean-Luc Nancy: *Le Retrait du politique* (Paris: Galilée, 1983) and *Rejouer le politique* (Paris: Galilée, 1981); translated and edited by Simon Sparks as *Retreating the Political* (London: Routledge, 1996).—Ed.

Cultural Memory | *in the Present*

Niklas Luhmann, *Theories of Distinction: Redescribing the Descriptions of Modernity*, ed. and introd. William Rasch

Johannes Fabian, *Anthropology with an Attitude: Critical Essays*

Michel Henry, *I Am the Truth: Toward a Philosophy of Christianity*

Gil Anidjar, *"Our Place in Al-Andalus": Kabbalah, Philosophy, Literature in Arab-Jewish Letters*

Hélène Cixous and Jacques Derrida, *Veils*

F. R. Ankersmit, *Historical Representation*

F. R. Ankersmit, *Political Representation*

Elissa Marder, *Dead Time: Temporal Disorders in the Wake of Modernity (Baudelaire and Flaubert)*

Reinhart Koselleck, *The Practice of Conceptual History: Timing History, Spacing Concepts*

Niklas Luhmann, *The Reality of the Mass Media*

Hubert Damisch, *A Childhood Memory by Piero della Francesca*

Hubert Damisch, *A Theory of /Cloud/: Toward a History of Painting*

Jean-Luc Nancy, *The Speculative Remark (One of Hegel's Bons Mots)*

Jean-François Lyotard, *Soundproof Room: Malraux's Anti-Aesthetics*

Jan Patočka, *Plato and Europe*

Hubert Damisch, *Skyline: The Narcissistic City*

Isabel Hoving, *In Praise of New Travelers: Reading Caribbean Migrant Women Writers*

Richard Rand, ed., *Futures: Of Derrida*

William Rasch, *Niklas Luhmann's Modernity: The Paradox of System Differentiation*

Jacques Derrida and Anne Dufourmantelle, *Of Hospitality*

Jean-François Lyotard, *The Confession of Augustine*

Kaja Silverman, *World Spectators*

Samuel Weber, *Institution and Interpretation: Expanded Edition*

Jeffrey S. Librett, *The Rhetoric of Cultural Dialogue: Jews and Germans in the Epoch of Emancipation*

Ulrich Baer, *Remnants of Song: Trauma and the Experience of Modernity in Charles Baudelaire and Paul Celan*

Samuel C. Wheeler III, *Deconstruction as Analytic Philosophy*

David S. Ferris, *Silent Urns: Romanticism, Hellenism, Modernity*

Rodolphe Gasché, *Of Minimal Things: Studies on the Notion of Relation*

Sarah Winter, *Freud and the Institution of Psychoanalytic Knowledge*

Samuel Weber, *The Legend of Freud: Expanded Edition*

Aris Fioretos, ed., *The Solid Letter: Readings of Friedrich Hölderlin*

J. Hillis Miller / Manuel Asensi, *Black Holes / J. Hillis Miller; or, Boustrophedonic Reading*

Miryam Sas, *Fault Lines: Cultural Memory and Japanese Surrealism*

Peter Schwenger, *Fantasm and Fiction: On Textual Envisioning*

Didier Maleuvre, *Museum Memories: History, Technology, Art*

Jacques Derrida, *Monolingualism of the Other; or, The Prosthesis of Origin*

Andrew Baruch Wachtel, *Making a Nation, Breaking a Nation: Literature and Cultural Politics in Yugoslavia*

Niklas Luhmann, *Love as Passion: The Codification of Intimacy*

Mieke Bal, ed., *The Practice of Cultural Analysis: Exposing Interdisciplinary Interpretation*

Jacques Derrida and Gianni Vattimo, eds., *Religion*